# Religion
# and the
# Cold War

# Religion and the Cold War

## A GLOBAL PERSPECTIVE

EDITED BY

Philip E. Muehlenbeck

Vanderbilt University Press
Nashville

© 2012 by Vanderbilt University Press
Nashville, Tennessee 37235
All rights reserved
First printing 2012

This book is printed on acid-free paper.
Manufactured in the United States of America

Library of Congress Cataloging-in-Publication Data on file
LC control number 2011038282
LC classification number D842.R45 2012
Dewey class number 909.82'5—dc23

ISBN 978-0-8265-1852-1 (cloth)
ISBN 978-0-8265-1853-8 (paperback)
ISBN 978-0-8265-1854-5 (e-book)

# Contents

# PREFACE

In the past decade, scholarship examining the ways in which religion has influenced the foreign and domestic policies of the United States, the Vatican, and to a lesser extent Western Europe during the Cold War has flourished to the point of establishing its own subgenre.[1] Yet what is striking is the dearth of scholarship in the English language that focuses on the ways in which religion influenced the policies of other states during this period. To date, the only internationalized history of religion in the Cold War has been Dianne Kirby's edited volume *Religion and the Cold War*, published a decade ago. Yet outside of one chapter on the Soviet Union, Kirby's volume was constrained to covering Christianity in the United States and Western Europe between 1945 and 1960. This volume builds on the foundation laid by Kirby and her contributors to expand the scholarship of religion in the Cold War geographically, chronologically, and spiritually. It attempts to show that religion had an impact on the Cold War policies of countries all over the world.

While in the past, diplomatic historians largely ignored or at least underappreciated religion as an important variable in the Cold War, more recently a handful of historians have begun to overemphasize the importance of religion to the global conflict.[2] For example, William Inboden claims that "only by summoning the American people to a religious crusade could US leaders maintain domestic support for the extraordinary measures needed to fight the Cold War."[3] This is undoubtedly an exaggeration of the role religion played in the creation of the Cold War consensus. Many atheists, agnostics, and secular nonpracticing Christians were of course staunch Cold Warriors. Inboden also asserts that "religion functioned in two distinct yet related ways in the great conflict [the Cold War]: as a cause and as an instrument. As a cause, it helped determine why the United States opposed the Soviet Union in the Cold War. . . . In addition to being a cause, it was an instrument in America's Cold War effort, a factor in how the United States fought the Soviet Union."[4] Inboden's emphasis on the role of religion in causing the Cold War seems overblown in the face of the political, economic, and security concerns that weighed on both Washington and Moscow. However, Inboden's scholarship is illuminating in helping explain how the United States mobilized for its global conflict against the Soviet Union. This volume seeks to make a less ambitious claim—that religion played a significant role in determining the scope and stratagems of the global Cold War, but it was a factor in the Cold War, not the factor.

This volume is not comprehensive, of course, nor could such a collection of essays ever hope to be so. Unfortunately, several important topics—such as the religious dimensions of the Indian-Pakistani rivalry over Kashmir or the role of religion and Pope John Paul II in ending Communism in Eastern Europe—go unexamined. While certainly part of the Cold War, the Arab-Israeli dispute is also not covered here, largely because it has already been the focus of voluminous scholarship. However, by broadening the study of religion and the Cold War away from the United States, Western Europe, and the Middle East and toward the rest of the world, this volume—with its multidisciplinary approach and emphasis on multiarchival and multinational research (primary source research for this project was conducted in eighteen different countries and on every continent other than Antarctica)—aspires to serve as an inspiration for further research on how religion affected the Cold War.

I would like to thank the following individuals for offering peer review comments on one or more chapters of this volume: Philip Boobbyer, Gregg Brazinsky, Philip Catton, Nathan Citino, Ben Cowan, Craig Daigle, Darren Dochuk, Christine Fair, Sumit Ganguly, Kristen Ghodsee, Steve Gish, Robert Goeckel, Katrina Hagen, Jonathan Herzog, Seth Jacobs, Ian Jones, Tony Kemp-Welch, Timothy Lee, Zinovia Lialiouti, Matthew Masur, Eric McGlinchey, Getachew Metaferia, Eric Payseur, Andy Rotter, Tom Schwartz, Ian Talbot, Dustin Walcher, David Zietsma, and the anonymous readers for Vanderbilt University Press.

I would also like to extend a special thanks to Ismail Ginwala, Elizabeth Kostendt, and Katherine Meier-Davis, students at George Washington University who assisted me in editing these chapters with an eye to comprehension by an advanced undergraduate student. Finally, Eli Bortz, my acquisitions editor at Vanderbilt University Press, was an integral part of this project from conception to completion and went above and beyond the call of duty to make sure that this project was a success. This volume is much better because of his involvement.

## Notes

1. For representative works about the impact of religion on US foreign policy in the Cold War, see David Foglesong, *The American Mission and the "Evil" Empire* (New

York: Cambridge University Press, 2007); William Inboden, *Religion and American Foreign Policy, 1945–1960: The Soul of Containment* (New York: Cambridge University Press, 2008); Jonathan Herzog, *The Spiritual-Industrial Complex: America's Religious Battle against Communism in the Early Cold War* (New York: Oxford University Press, 2011); Seth Jacobs, *America's Miracle Man in Vietnam: Ngo Dinh Diem, Religion, Race, and U.S. Intervention in Southeast Asia* (Durham, NC: Duke University Press, 2005); Thomas Jeremy Gunn, *Spiritual Weapons: The Cold War and the Forging of an American National Religion* (Westport, CT: Praeger, 2009); and Andrew Rotter, *Comrades at Odds: The United States and India, 1947–1964* (Ithaca, NY: Cornell University Press, 2000). For works on religion, the Vatican, and Europe in the Cold War, see Owen Chadwick, *The Christian Church in the Cold War* (New York: Penguin, 1993); Diane Kirby, ed., *Religion and the Cold War* (New York: Palgrave Macmillan, 2002); John Koehler, *Spies in the Vatican: The Soviet Union's Cold War against the Catholic Church* (New York: Pegasus, 2011); Peter C. Kent, *The Lonely Cold War of Pope Pius XII: The Roman Catholic Church and the Division of Europe, 1943–1950* (Montreal: McGill-Queen's Press, 2002); and Michael Phayer, *Pius XII, the Holocaust, and the Cold War* (Bloomington: Indiana University Press, 2007).

2. On the traditional neglect of religion in US diplomatic history, see Andrew Preston, "Bridging the Gap between Church and State in the History of American Foreign Relations," *Diplomatic History* 30 (November 2006): 783–812; and Andrew Preston, "Reviving Religion in the History of American Foreign Relations," in *God and Global Order: The Power of Religion in American Foreign Policy*, ed. Jonathan Chaplin and Robert Joustra (Waco, TX: Baylor University Press, 2010), 25–44.

3. Inboden, *Religion and American Foreign Policy*, 5.

4. Ibid., 2–5.

# INTRODUCTION

## *The Religious Cold War*

*Andrew Preston*

This is a book about religion in the Cold War, a subject once confined to the periphery of the historical imagination when it was noticed at all. Thankfully, neglect no longer seems to be the problem. Historians of the Cold War, and not just historians of religion in the Cold War, are acknowledging the importance of the topic more frequently and in greater numbers. International relations theory, which also neglected religion, has recently shown signs of doing the same. Scholars of many disciplines now recognize that religion was a factor throughout the Cold War, from its origins in the division of early postwar Europe to the collapse of Communist rule in Eastern Europe and the Soviet Union just over four decades later. Long mired in obscurity, the role of religion in the Cold War is now an important aspect of international history.[1]

But we would do just as well to speak not simply of "religion *and* the Cold War" or of "religion *in* the Cold War," but of "*the religious* Cold War," for matters of faith permeated the conflict, particularly certain episodes, to the extent that they often came to define the struggle between the United States and the Soviet Union and between West and East.

In fact, it was the very nature of the Cold War that allowed religion to play a greater role in international history than ever before. The previously unimaginable carnage and devastation of World War II, followed by the advent of nuclear weapons and the thermonuclear arms race, made the superpowers reluctant to fight each other directly. Though the Cold War was by no means a "long peace," the specter of nuclear war meant that the great powers would not risk a direct military confrontation with each other. Each side had to demonstrate the superiority of its system—liberal capitalist democracy or

Communist people's democracy—and the only ways to measure such a contest were through economic progress and attracting other nations to one's system. The Cold War, in other words, was a contest over legitimacy. This meant that progress in the Cold War was determined not by the occupation of territory or the movement of a front line, but by representative symbolic victories. One such measurement was the number of nations supporting each side, which invested countries on the periphery (such as Cuba, Chile, Ethiopia, and Angola) with an importance far beyond their normal geopolitical value. When neither the United States nor the Soviet Union could claim a clear victory in contested battlegrounds on the periphery, they fought each other indirectly. Thus, the absence of direct superpower engagement gave rise to proxy wars in places like Korea, Vietnam, and Afghanistan.[2]

But the nature of the Cold War also meant that politics and culture assumed an unusual and perhaps even unprecedented role in world politics. Economic growth, technological innovation, and the ability to attract allies were all measurements of legitimacy, and thus of success. But in a decolonizing and democratic age—after all, even North Korea and East Germany proudly called themselves democracies—legitimacy also rested on the power of ideas. It is no coincidence that the Cold War marked the apogee of nonmilitary forms of warfare, such as espionage and economic sanctions. This dynamic also created space for the diplomatic uses of propaganda, the media, and the arts, and for this reason historians have rightly branded the postwar conflict "the cultural Cold War."[3]

The power of ideas, then, proved central to the Cold War rivalry—and few phenomena are as powerful a source of ideas as religion. Religion was a major component of World War II, when legitimacy, and through it propaganda and the power of ideas, was also important. But religion had never before assumed the centrality it possessed during the Cold War, when direct fighting between the main antagonists was largely absent. Indeed, the presence of nuclear weapons not only made the Cold War an indirect clash between the United States and the Soviet Union, it also raised the ultimate questions of life and death, and of the very meaning of life. Not surprisingly, existentialism and disillusionment were two common responses to the nuclear revolution. Naturally, so too was religious faith.[4]

Partly as a result of the Cold War and partly as a result of other structural factors, religion experienced a revival throughout the postwar world (with the possible exceptions of the Soviet Union, the People's Republic of China, and some of their allies). In the United States, postwar religiosity soared with the surge of evangelical piety and the maturation of an interfaith "Judeo-Christian" identity that had formed in the 1930s.[5] In Latin America, the Catholic Church took an active part in supporting both conservative reactionary regimes and their leftist challengers. In the United Kingdom, Britons conflated Christianity with civilization, and saw both as under threat from atheistic Communism. In Western Europe, now seen as a bastion of secularism, Christian Democracy combined conservative politics with conservative faith (Catholic and Protestant) to provide the most robust challenge to both Communism and fascism. In Soviet-occupied Eastern Europe, Roman Catholics maintained a quiet opposition to Communism that the authorities could never entirely extinguish because it was so much a part of popular and national cultures. In the Soviet Union itself, Jews constantly campaigned for their human rights, especially the freedoms of worship and movement, which severely undermined Moscow's claims to rightful rule. In Africa, Christians, Muslims, and atheistic Marxists battled for control of the continent. In the Middle East, Zionists established the state of Israel; Muslim fundamentalists formed popular protest movements against both socialism and Zionism, and in some countries actually took power. In South Asia, nationalism combined with religion to produce instability. And in Southeast Asia, Buddhism provided the basis for independence movements that were both anti-American and anti-Communist. Overall, around the world, religion permeated the Cold War by providing its rationale for many of its contestants.

Unsurprisingly, both the United States and the Soviet Union perceived each other through a religious lens. There was a religious Cold War because its main adversaries saw it that way, and to a certain extent framed their rivalry in religious terms. In 1943, upon appointing Andrei Gromyko as his ambassador to the United States, Stalin advised Gromyko to make a habit of attending Sunday morning services in ordinary American churches. That way, he would not only improve his English, especially his knowledge of American idioms, but also come to a much better understanding of what made Americans tick.[6]

Stalin, a shrewd observer of international relations, was not wrong in attributing a large role to religion in the framing of an American worldview. The three presidents with whom he dealt, Franklin D. Roosevelt, Harry S. Truman, and Dwight D. Eisenhower, all explicitly framed US foreign policy in religious terms. "Where freedom of religion has been attacked, the attack has come from sources opposed to democracy," Roosevelt warned in his State of the Union address of January 1939. "Where democracy has been overthrown, the spirit of free worship has disappeared. And where religion and democracy have vanished, good faith and reason in international affairs have given way to strident ambition and brute force."[7] Two years later, in his 1941 State of the Union address, FDR framed America's cause around the Four Freedoms, the second of which was freedom of worship (the other three were freedom of speech and expression, freedom from want, and freedom from fear).[8] Truman constantly spoke of the Cold War as a struggle between the morality of belief and the immorality of unbelief. In 1947, he tasked his personal envoy to the Vatican, Myron C. Taylor, with the job of organizing a world summit in Washington of religious leaders, where Truman would rally the forces of faith, be they Christian, Jewish, Muslim, Hindu, Buddhist, or any other, against the forces of Communist atheism. In partnership with Secretary of State John Foster Dulles, a devout Presbyterian, Eisenhower continued Roosevelt and Truman's spiritual diplomacy. He was the first president to be baptized in the White House and the first president since the Civil War to have an ordained minister as a presidential assistant. Eisenhower argued, just as explicitly as his predecessors had argued, that the world was divided into freedom and slavery and that the presence of religion corresponded directly with the presence of freedom.[9]

Such a religion-centered view of the world provided US foreign policy makers with both a diagnosis and a cure for the ills of world politics. Following James Madison, and more recently Woodrow Wilson, Presidents Roosevelt, Truman, and Eisenhower had all argued that the spread of democracy was vital because democracies, which represented the will of naturally peace-loving people, did not instigate wars of aggression. Religion, which provided the source of individual conscience and morality, was a prerequisite to democratic freedom, because if a state allowed for the freedom of individual conscience through religion, it would be unable to stop the growth of other liberties. Wherever religion was prohibited, democracy would be prohibited, no matter what the authorities claimed; such nations were inherently aggressive because they lacked a basic common morality and reflected the ambitions and whims of a tyrant rather than the will of the people. By the same token, if authoritarian regimes respected freedom of worship, they retained the potential for eventual democratic reform. Religion therefore provided US officials with a leading indicator of countries that could pose a threat.

But religion also gave them a weapon to wage the Cold War, for faith had a unique capacity to undermine irreligious (usually Communist) dictatorial regimes. The Christian churches, wrote Carl Friedrich and Zbigniew Brzezinski in 1955, "have shown themselves to be a real bulwark against the claim to total power of the totalitarian dictatorship, perhaps more real than any others." Friedrich was a political scientist at Harvard University; Brzezinski, then a professor of political science at Columbia University, later served as Jimmy Carter's national security adviser. "Whether Protestant or Catholic," they continued, "the genuine Christian cannot accept totalitarianism. For Christianity claims the whole man and the last word with regard to man's values and man's destiny. This claim the totalitarians cannot accept."[10] This was the consensus view among US foreign policy elites. Hence the importance successive US presidents attached to the promotion of religion, from Eisenhower's offer of asylum to persecuted Catholics in Hungary (namely, József Cardinal Mindszenty), to Richard Nixon's encouragement of radical Islam in the Middle East, to Ronald Reagan's partnership with the Vatican in Europe, Muslim radicals in Afghanistan, and Jews and Pentecostals in the Soviet Union.[11]

But the religious Cold War extended far beyond the American imagination—indeed, many of the religious movements Washington encouraged ended up being hostile not only to Soviet Communism, but also to the United States. Historians now rightly speak of a "global Cold War" that transcended the narrow confines of the rivalry between Washington and Moscow, and it is interesting to note that the global Cold War mapped out almost exactly with the patterns of world religion, albeit in unpredictable ways. Just as the Cold War as a whole was not only about the United States and the Soviet Union, the religious Cold War was not merely a struggle between America's "Judeo-Christianity" and Soviet-sponsored atheism. And neither side could claim a monopoly on religious influence. In several cases, the role of religion would act independently of both Washington and Moscow. Religion was not just as a source of nationalism and independence, but also a means of escape from the Cold War itself.

The Vatican provided a prime example. On one hand, Pope Pius XII (pontiff from 1939 until 1958) and Pope John Paul II (1978–2005) were themselves staunchly opposed to the Soviet Union and steered the Vatican in a fiercely anti-Communist direction. Pius discussed the containment of Communism with Truman, and John Paul acted in concert with Reagan to delegitimize Communist rule in Eastern Europe. On the other hand, both Pius and John Paul were at times critical of US foreign policy, especially its reliance on nuclear weapons, and of American social life more generally. Pius was furious with the World War II strategy of "unconditional surrender" on which Roosevelt and his war planners insisted, and he condemned the atomic bombing of Japan. After the war, he feared that the Marshall Plan would inculcate American (and Protestant) individualism in Catholic European societies. And sometimes the Vatican forged a completely independent path that outright challenged Washington's preoccupation with containment. In three encyclicals, issued in 1961, 1963, and 1967, the Vatican excoriated the West for its preoccupation with material culture, its obsession with containment, and its neglect of the developing world's crippling poverty. The Catholic Church's reconsideration of the Cold War came in the midst of the greatest upheaval in the Catholic Church since the Reformation: the Second Vatican Council, which met in Rome from 1962 to 1965. Vatican II provided the backdrop to the 1963 encyclical *Pacem in Terris* (Peace on earth), an especially pointed appeal to both Washington and Moscow to pursue a true peace based on mutual understanding rather than unlimited competition.[12]

Shortly after, Roman Catholics in Latin America charted a similarly independent course. Their means of escape was liberation theology, a blend of progressive politics and the New Testament's gospel of love and social justice, first devised by priests and nuns in Colombia in the late 1960s. Liberation theology proved effective not only in Latin America. It was soon imported into the United States by students and faculty at liberal divinity schools and theological seminaries, and provided greater coherence to domestic American liberation movements such as Black Power and second-wave feminism. Through the 1970s and into the 1980s, principally in Central America, advocates of liberation theology used a Marxist emphasis on social justice and a commitment to nationalist independence from multinational corporations as well as US-backed right-wing regimes to assert their resistance to the Cold War. Many of the Cold War–inflected civil wars of the period, particularly in El Salvador and Nicaragua, assumed the character of religious wars, as the Catholic Church divided into factions of left and right. Anticlerical violence reached depths not seen in the region since Mexico's turmoil in the 1920s and 1930s. The violence shocked Catholics in the United States and Europe, who in turn applied enormous pressure to the Reagan administration to halt its support for right-wing anti-Communists, such as the authoritarian regime in El Salvador and the contras in Nicaragua. This was, ironically enough, the same Reagan administration that had partnered with the Vatican to fight Communism in Eastern Europe.[13]

Something similar happened in South Vietnam in the 1960s during the escalation and Americanization of the Vietnamese civil war. In 1954, the United States sponsored Ngo Dinh Diem, a Catholic, for president despite the fact that South Vietnam was overwhelmingly a nation of Buddhists. Diem's family was deeply Roman Catholic; one of his brothers, Ngo Dinh Thuc, was the archbishop of Hue. Nine years later, in May 1963, South Vietnam's Buddhist monks provoked a confrontation with the Diem regime over the flying of celebratory flags on the Buddha's birthday, which the government had expressly prohibited. The confrontation led to a Buddhist uprising that infamously featured the self-immolation of monks and the destruction of pagodas in Saigon and Hue. It also led, in November, to the overthrow and murder of Diem and his brother and confidant Ngo Dinh Nhu. In turn, the ouster of Diem and Nhu ushered in a period of political instability and deteriorating security that led directly to the Americanization of the war in July 1965. Yet the Buddhist monks were not finished. Unhappy with the unrepresentative government of President Nguyen Van Thieu, a Catholic who assumed power in 1965, they revolted again in March 1966, severely destabilizing South Vietnam even more. The monks were unique in Vietnamese politics: non-Communist, nationalist, anti-American, and genuinely popular. Neither Saigon nor Washington recognized the power of religious nationalism, despite efforts by each government to wield it, and both found the monks difficult if not impossible to control. For their ignorance and incompetence on the religious question, South Vietnamese and US officials paid a heavy price.[14]

Religion enabled another group of dissidents, Muslims, to carve out their own independence in the Cold War world. Beginning in the 1960s, Islamic fundamentalists throughout the Middle East began to assert themselves and their religion against the forces of modernity that underpinned the Cold War. Though the Islamic resurgence included different sects from different ethnicities and countries, including Sunnis in Egypt and Shiites in Iran, it was held together by a common bond of traditionalist revolt against the Cold War order. In both Egypt and Iran, Islamic activists campaigned against the high modernization projects that in many ways defined the Cold War. The Sunni Muslim Brotherhood surged in popularity as Egyptians became dissatisfied with President Gamal Abdel Nasser's modernization projects (the building of large infrastructure and development projects, such as hydroelectric dams) and secular political Ba'athism. Farther east, the Ayatollah Ruhollah Khomeini rallied Shiite Iranians against Shah Reza Pahlavi's White Revolution, a modernist development program typical of the Cold War, and his reliance on the United States. Khomeini also campaigned against the shah's repression of religion, particularly traditionalist religion, as the Iranian leadership attempted to modernize Iran for good.[15]

The emergence of traditionalism was by no means unique to the Muslim Middle East, where the rise of radical Islam paralleled the rise of Protestant fundamentalism in the United States and Hindu fundamentalism in South Asia. In all three regions, a reassertion of nationalism combined with a distrust of modernism and secularism to produce a highly charged religious atmosphere.[16] Religion's relationship to the Cold War, then, could be inward as well as outward. Just as religion had the capacity to influence the course of the Cold War at certain moments and in certain places, the Cold War also retained a capability to shape the evolution of religion in domestic societies.

The Cold War ended in the late 1980s much as it had begun, as a religious conflict within a larger geopolitical struggle. In 1983, Reagan used a speech at the annual convention of the National Association of Evangelicals to condemn the Soviet Union as an "evil empire." But Reagan's first private meeting with the Soviet ambassador to Washington, Anatoly Dobrynin, took place in the winter of 1983 because of a group of Russian Pentecostals confined in the basement of the US embassy in Moscow, where they had claimed asylum five years earlier. Reagan wanted to secure their release, which the Kremlin had thus far refused to allow. All the parties to this extraordinary meeting—Reagan, Dobrynin, Secretary of State George Shultz, and US diplomat Jack Matlock—agreed that Reagan's willingness to work productively with Dobrynin, and through him with the Soviet leadership, paved the way for the détente that ended the Cold War six years later.[17] From there, encouraged by the thaw in Soviet-US relations and by the relaxation of the Soviet Union's control of its client regimes after Mikhail Gorbachev came to power in 1985, Eastern European Catholics and Protestants, with moral support from Washington and the Vatican, led successful challenges to Communist rule and legitimacy from within, especially in Poland, East Germany, and Czechoslovakia.[18]

Of course, religion alone neither caused nor ended the Cold War. It is likely that the rivalry between the United States and the Soviet Union would have erupted, and ended, roughly along the same lines whether religion played a role or not. But these are counterfactuals. The Cold War as it actually did unfold owed a good deal to the persistence of a worldwide religious influence. Religious faith, and especially the exercise of political protest and popular mobilization by institutional religion through the world's churches, synagogues, mosques, and temples, underpinned one of the era's most significant mass movements. Religion and antireligion also provided the Cold War's contestants with their ideas, values, and motivations. And religion itself changed as the Cold War brought new pressures, especially modernization and state centralization, to bear on individuals, nations, and societies.

The chapters in this book illustrate these themes well, and of course in much greater detail. Overall, they help confirm four final generalizations about religion's role in the causes, course, and consequences of the Cold War. First, religion was neither static nor monolithic. Its relationship to the Cold War ebbed and flowed in response to international events, and in turn religion shaped the pattern of the Cold War itself. Second, it is very difficult to generalize about a single religious influence. In terms of public life, politics, and diplomacy, religion became more important to some parts of the world, such as the Middle East, and less important to others, like Western Europe. In some parts of the world, for example, China, religion was consistently a negligible factor, while in others, such as most of the Western Hemisphere except Canada, it remained consistently prominent and important. Thus when we speak of the religious Cold War, we must always bear in mind its diversity. Third, religion mattered. Any account of the Cold War that ignores religion is not necessarily wrong, but to a great extent incomplete and therefore inadequate. Finally, and perhaps most importantly, the religious influence can be measured not only as a specific tool of diplomacy but also as a determinant of popular responses to and political pressures within the Cold War. Indeed, it is this richness that helps explain why and how religion could play such an intimate role in the international history of the Cold War.

## Notes

1. On the traditional neglect of religion in US diplomatic history, see Andrew Preston, "Bridging the Gap between Church and State in the History of American Foreign Relations," *Diplomatic History* 30 (November 2006): 783–812; and Andrew Preston, "Reviving Religion in the History of American Foreign Relations," in *God and Global Order: The Power of Religion in American Foreign Policy*, ed. Jonathan Chaplin and Robert Joustra (Waco, TX: Baylor University Press, 2010), 25–44. In international history, there has been a great deal of recent work on specific case studies of religion's role in the Cold War, but overviews remain rare. For one of the few but effective exceptions, see Dianne Kirby, ed., *Religion and the Cold War* (New York: Palgrave Macmillan, 2003). Moreover, many of the most important and voluminous introductions to Cold War studies fail to examine religion as a separate category of analysis. For a recent and perhaps the most prominent example, see Melvyn P. Leffler and Odd Arne Westad, eds., *The Cambridge History of the Cold War*, 3 vols. (Cambridge: Cambridge University Press, 2010), which does not include a separate chapter on religion despite its otherwise exhaustive coverage of cultural and ideological aspects. On religion and international relations theory, see Elizabeth Shakman Hurd, *The Politics of Secularism in International Relations* (Princeton, NJ: Princeton University Press, 2008). For works examining specific aspects of religion in international relations, see Fabio Petito and Pavlos Hatzopoulos, eds., *Religion in International Relations* (New York: Palgrave Macmillan, 2003); Jonathan Fox and Shmuel Sandler, *Bringing Religion into International Relations* (New York: Palgrave Macmillan, 2004); and Scott M. Thomas, *The Global Resurgence of Religion and the Transformation of International Relations: The Struggle for the Soul of the Twenty-First Century* (New York: Palgrave Macmillan, 2005).
2. For "long peace," see John Lewis Gaddis, *The Long Peace: Inquiries into the History of the Cold War* (New York: Oxford University Press, 1987). For the Cold War on the periphery, see Odd Arne Westad, *The Global Cold War: Third World Interventions and the Making of Our Times* (Cambridge: Cambridge University Press, 2005).
3. Frances Stonor Saunders, *The Cultural Cold War: The CIA and the World of Arts and Letters* (New York: New Press, 2000).
4. On the role of religion in World War II, see, for example, Gerald L. Sittser, *A Cautious Patriotism: The American Churches and the Second World War* (Chapel Hill: University of North Carolina Press, 1997); and Steven Merritt Miner, *Stalin's Holy War: Religion, Nationalism, and Alliance Politics, 1941–1945* (Chapel Hill: University of North Carolina Press, 2003). On existentialism, particularly as it related to religion, see Doug Rossinow, *The Politics of Authenticity: Liberalism, Christianity, and the New Left in America* (New York: Columbia University Press, 1998). On disillusionment, see Jeremi Suri, *Power and Protest: Global Revolution and the Rise of Détente* (Cambridge, MA: Harvard University Press, 2003).
5. Wendy L. Wall, *Inventing the "American Way": The Politics of Consensus from the New Deal to the Civil Rights Movement* (New York: Oxford University Press, 2008).
6. William Inboden, *Religion and American Foreign Policy, 1945–1960: The Soul of Containment* (Cambridge: Cambridge University Press, 2008), 1.

7. Franklin D. Roosevelt, "Annual Message to the Congress," January 4, 1939, in *The Public Papers and Addresses of Franklin D. Roosevelt* (New York: Macmillan, 1941), 8:1.

8. Franklin D. Roosevelt, "Annual Message to the Congress," January 6, 1941, in *The Public Papers and Addresses of Franklin D. Roosevelt* (New York: Macmillan, 1941), 9:672.

9. On Truman and Taylor, and Eisenhower and Dulles, see Inboden, *Religion and American Foreign Policy*.

10. Carl J. Friedrich and Zbigniew K. Brzezinski, *Totalitarian Dictatorship and Autocracy*, 2nd ed. (New York: Praeger, 1966), 314.

11. On Eisenhower and Mindszenty, see Johanna Granville, *The First Domino: International Decision Making during the Hungarian Crisis of 1956* (College Station: Texas A&M University Press, 2004). On Nixon and Islam, see Paul Chamberlin, "A World Restored: Religion, Counterrevolution, and the Search for Order in the Middle East," *Diplomatic History* 32 (June 2008): 441–69.

12. On Vatican II, see Andrew M. Greeley, *The Catholic Revolution: New Wine, Old Wineskins, and the Second Vatican Council* (Berkeley: University of California Press, 2004).

13. On liberation theology, see Daniel H. Levine, *Religion and Politics in Latin America: The Catholic Church in Venezuela and Colombia* (Princeton, NJ: Princeton University Press, 1981), 20–53; and Scott Mainwaring and Alexander Wilde, "The Progressive Church in Latin America: An Interpretation," in *The Progressive Church in Latin America*, ed. Scott Mainwaring and Alexander Wilde (Notre Dame, IN: University of Notre Dame Press, 1989), 1–37. On its importation into the United States, see J. Philip Wogaman, *Christian Perspectives on Politics*, rev. ed. (Louisville, KY: Westminster John Knox Press, 2000), 79–101; and Patrick Allitt, *Religion in America since 1945: A History* (New York: Columbia University Press, 2003), 113–14, 127–28, 174–75.

14. Robert J. Topmiller, *The Lotus Unleashed: The Buddhist Peace Movement in South Vietnam* (Lexington: University Press of Kentucky, 2002). On Diem's Catholicism and its effect on US foreign policy, see Seth Jacobs, *America's Miracle Man in Vietnam: Ngo Dinh Diem, Religion, Race, and U.S. Intervention in Southeast Asia* (Durham, NC: Duke University Press, 2004).

15. On Egypt, see Denis J. Sullivan and Sana Abed-Kotob, *Islam in Contemporary Egypt: Civil Society vs. the State* (Boulder, CO: Lynne Rienner, 1999), 41–70. On Iran, see James A. Bill, *The Eagle and the Lion: The Tragedy of American-Iranian Relations* (New Haven, CT: Yale University Press, 1989), 148–82; and Mohsen M. Milani, *The Making of Iran's Islamic Revolution: From Monarchy to Islamic Republic*, 2nd ed. (Boulder, CO: Westview Press, 1994), 47–52.

16. David C. Rapoport, "Comparing Militant Fundamentalist Movements and Groups," in *Fundamentalisms and the State: Remaking Polities, Economies, and Militance*, ed. Martin E. Marty and R. Scott Appleby (Chicago: University of Chicago Press, 1993), 429–61.

17. See Ronald Reagan, *An American Life* (New York: Simon and Schuster, 1990), 558; Anatoly Dobrynin, *In Confidence: Moscow's Ambassador to America's Six Cold*

*War Presidents, 1962–1986* (New York: Times Books, 1995), 523–28; George P.
Shultz, *Turmoil and Triumph: My Years as Secretary of State* (New York: Scribner,
1993), 167–71; and Jack F. Matlock Jr., *Reagan and Gorbachev: How the Cold War
Ended* (New York: Random House, 2004), 55–57. For the "evil empire" speech, see
"Remarks at the Annual Convention of the National Association of Evangelicals,"
March 8, 1983, in *Public Papers of the Presidents of the United States: Ronald Reagan,
1983*, 1:362–64.

18. J. F. Brown, *Surge to Freedom: The End of Communist Rule in Eastern Europe*
(Durham, NC: Duke University Press, 1991); and Charles S. Maier, *Dissolution:
The Crisis of Communism and the End of East Germany* (Princeton, NJ: Princeton
University Press, 1997).

## Selected References

Allitt, Patrick. *Religion in America since 1945: A History.* New York: Columbia
University Press, 2003.
Chamberlin, Paul. "A World Restored: Religion, Counterrevolution, and the Search for
Order in the Middle East." *Diplomatic History* 32 (June 2008): 441–69.
Fox, Jonathan, and Shmuel Sandler. *Bringing Religion into International Relations.* New
York: Palgrave Macmillan, 2004.
Greeley, Andrew M. *The Catholic Revolution: New Wine, Old Wineskins, and the Second
Vatican Council.* Berkeley: University of California Press, 2004.
Inboden, William. *Religion and American Foreign Policy, 1945–1960: The Soul of
Containment.* Cambridge: Cambridge University Press, 2008.
Jacobs, Seth. *America's Miracle Man in Vietnam: Ngo Dinh Diem, Religion, Race, and
U.S. Intervention in Southeast Asia.* Durham, NC: Duke University Press, 2004.
Kirby, Dianne, ed. *Religion and the Cold War.* New York: Palgrave Macmillan, 2003.
Levine, Daniel H. *Religion and Politics in Latin America: The Catholic Church in
Venezuela and Colombia.* Princeton, NJ: Princeton University Press, 1981.
Mainwaring, Scott, and Alexander Wilde. "The Progressive Church in Latin America:
An Interpretation." In *The Progressive Church in Latin America*, ed. Scott
Mainwaring and Alexander Wilde, 1–37. Notre Dame, IN: University of Notre Dame
Press, 1989.
Milani, Mohsen M. *The Making of Iran's Islamic Revolution: From Monarchy to Islamic
Republic.* 2nd ed. Boulder, CO: Westview Press, 1994.
Miner Steven Merritt. *Stalin's Holy War: Religion, Nationalism, and Alliance Politics,
1941–1945.* Chapel Hill: University of North Carolina Press, 2003.
Petito, Fabio, and Pavlos Hatzopoulos, eds. *Religion in International Relations.* New
York: Palgrave Macmillan, 2003.
Preston, Andrew. "Bridging the Gap between Church and State in the History of
American Foreign Relations." *Diplomatic History* 30 (November 2006): 783–812.
———. "Reviving Religion in the History of American Foreign Relations." In *God
and Global Order: The Power of Religion in American Foreign Policy*, ed. Jonathan
Chaplin and Robert Joustra, 25–44. Waco, TX: Baylor University Press, 2010.

Rossinow, Doug. *The Politics of Authenticity: Liberalism, Christianity, and the New Left in America*. New York: Columbia University Press, 1998.

Saunders, Frances Stonor. *The Cultural Cold War: The CIA and the World of Arts and Letters*. New York: New Press, 2000.

Sittser, Gerald L. *A Cautious Patriotism: The American Churches and the Second World War*. Chapel Hill: University of North Carolina Press, 1997.

Sullivan, Denis J., and Sana Abed-Kotob. *Islam in Contemporary Egypt: Civil Society vs. the State*. Boulder, CO: Lynne Rienner, 1999.

Thomas, Scott M. *The Global Resurgence of Religion and the Transformation of International Relations: The Struggle for the Soul of the Twenty-First Century*. New York: Palgrave Macmillan, 2005.

Topmiller, Robert J. *The Lotus Unleashed: The Buddhist Peace Movement in South Vietnam*. Lexington: University Press of Kentucky, 2002.

Wogaman, J. Philip. *Christian Perspectives on Politics*. Rev. ed. Louisville, KY: Westminster John Knox Press, 2000.

# CHAPTER 1

# An Early Attempt to Rip
# the Iron Curtain

## *The Pomak Question, 1945–1947*

*Argyris Mamarelis*

According to the Churchill-Stalin "percentages agreement" of October 1944 in Moscow, Bulgaria would join the Soviet bloc, whereas Greece would become a part of the free world.[1] The cynical way in which the Balkans were to be divided between the two spheres of influence was admitted even by British prime minister Winston Churchill himself, but during the last days of World War II it was obvious that such a division was a matter of accurate observation rather than cynicism. In fact, in strategic terms, the resolution of the status of both countries was simple. For the British, Bulgaria was a lost cause. The presence of the Red Army in the country effectively ruled out any chance for British influence and aspirations there. But British expectations for Greece remained high, and Churchill personally had invested a lot of political capital in that country during the war. Conversely, the Soviets regarded Greece as a lost cause but had high ambitions for a traditional Balkan ally like Bulgaria. As far as Bulgaria and Greece were concerned, it seemed that the two great powers had achieved a tidy deal.

However, almost immediately after the end of the war, Greece commenced an international campaign to prove that the deal was not that tidy after all. The Greek government had a series of unsatisfied demands against Bulgaria and threw itself into the raging diplomatic antagonisms of the early postwar period, in which all the international players were trying desperately to maximize their strategic gains before Europe's irreversible division into two concrete camps. To achieve its diplomatic and strategic objectives, Greece used three main arguments.

The first was a moral one. For seven months, starting on October 28, 1940, the Greek army had fought with commitment against the invading Italian and German forces, delivering a considerable blow to the Axis and providing a morale boost during a depressing time for the Allies and especially Great Britain. In the aftermath of the Greek army's defeat, a ferocious occupation by German, Italian, and Bulgarian forces followed. The cost in civilian lives from either famine or violent reprisals by the occupation forces may well have exceeded three hundred thousand. During the occupation period, one of the most dynamic and massive European resistance movements developed in Greece, while the remains of the Greek army under the command of the exiled Greek government and the Allies continued the war effort in northern Africa. At the conclusion of the war, the Greek government and Greek public believed it was time for their country to be rewarded for the sacrifices it had made for the Allied cause.

The second argument was geostrategic. Greece came out of the war economically devastated and politically polarized. The country's economic infrastructure was completely destroyed and the postwar state administration was incapable of contributing to the country's recovery. Furthermore, it was obvious that the bloody conflict between Communist and republican resistance movements during the occupation had been the prelude to a full-scale civil war between the newly established government and the Greek Communist Party, KKE (Kommounistiko Komma Ellados).[2] From its deep anti-Communist prejudice and strong sense of insecurity, the Greek government was convinced that apart from the domestic enemy, national security was threatened by neighboring Communist countries. Indeed, Greece was isolated on the southern end of the Balkan Peninsula, surrounded exclusively by Communist states (Albania, Yugoslavia, Bulgaria) on its northern frontiers, and had no reliable armed forces. The Greek government was going to claim all the geostrategic and territorial requirements it deemed necessary to discourage its neighbors' aggressiveness.

The third argument had to do with race, ethnicity, and religion. The Greek government brought to the international diplomatic arena "the Pomak question," a case typical of attempts to claim foreign territory by arguing for the emancipation of a minority group.

The Pomaks are an ethnic and religious minority group native to Bulgaria, Greece, and Turkey. In Greece and Bulgaria, Pomaks, together with ethnic Turks and Roma, compose Muslim minorities. Based on the two most obvious features of their culture—language and religion—they can be defined as Bulgarian-speaking Muslims. However, the Pomak identity is probably one of the most contested ethnic identities in the Balkans, interpreted and constructed in multiple ways. The fact that the Pomaks inhabit three countries that have been traditional enemies makes it impossible to establish a single historical origin for them. Bulgaria, Greece, and Turkey have each produced versions of Pomak identity that fit their respective nationalist myths, promote their national interests, and serve their respective "one state, one nation" theories. According to the Bulgarian version, the Pomaks are Bulgarian Christians who were subjected to forced and often violent Islamization during the Ottoman conquest of the Balkans. According to the Greek theory, the Pomaks are the descendants of the indigenous ancient Thracians. Finally, Turkish historiography claims that the Pomaks descend from Turkish tribes who invaded the Balkans during the eleventh century.[3]

Pomaks residing in Greece are part of the Greek Muslim minority located in Western Thrace, a region of northeastern Greece bordering Bulgaria and Turkey and including the provinces of Xanthi, Rhodope, and Evros. According to the 1928 Greek census, the Muslim minority in Western Thrace numbered 102,844 people, of which 16,740 were Pomaks.[4] The majority of Pomaks resided in the highland villages of Xanthi and Rhodope Provinces along the Greek-Bulgarian border. Across the border, in Bulgaria, Pomaks are referred to as "Bulgarian Mohammedans" or "Bulgarian Muslims." They inhabit mainly the Rhodope Mountains in Southern Bulgaria (the provinces of Smolyan, Pazardzhik, Kardzhali, and Blagoevgrad). During 1947–1948, the Bulgarian Muslim minority was far more massive than the Greek and numbered almost 950,000 people, of whom 600,000 were ethnic Turks, 200,000 were Roma, and 150,000 were Pomaks.[5]

The Greek and Bulgarian Pomaks were culturally identical communities, albeit with limited interaction. Geography and politics contributed to that separateness. Since the beginning of the twentieth century, Greece and Bulgaria had in fact been enemy states. Their borders were well guarded and contact between the two communities was discouraged by local authorities. Most of the interaction was limited to occasional—and sometimes illegal—commercial transactions of livestock and other goods, and it is difficult to know whether there was a sense of mutuality between the two communities. What is certain, though, is that throughout the 1930s and 1940s, Pomaks on both sides of the border lived in parallel universes and dealt with their own hardships.

The results of Bulgaria's defeat in the First World War were catastrophic. The Neuilly Treaty signed in November 1919 between Bulgaria and the Entente required Bulgaria to abandon Western Thrace and cede it to the Entente and subsequently to Greece. Bulgaria lost its outlet to the Aegean Sea and was forced to pay enormous war reparations. The economy was sunk in a deep recession that had a dramatic effect on the rural Bulgarian Pomak communities. Further, Bulgarian Pomaks, along with ethnic Turks and Roma, had to deal with the discriminatory policies of the Bulgarian authorities. Although the Neuilly Treaty included specific provisions for the protection of the Muslim minority, these were occasionally breached. Access to public services was far more difficult for the Muslim community than for ethnic Bulgarians, and Pomak education rights were constrained. The rise of Kemalism in Turkey raised suspicion among the Bulgarian authorities toward the Muslim minority. According to the most optimistic perspective, the impact of Kemalism on Bulgarian Muslims was viewed as a means of solidifying the Turkish ethnic identity among Bulgarian Muslims. According to the most pessimistic one, it was viewed as a means to create a domestic Turkish fifth column to serve Turkish imperialism against Bulgaria. On May 19, 1934, a coup carried out by military organizations and the Bulgarian army established an authoritarian militaristic government under Kimon Georgiev. Under the new regime, restrictions and discrimination against the Muslim minority increased. Pomak schools were closed down, and the Bulgarian police and secret services put Pomak community leaders under close surveillance.[6]

During World War II, Bulgaria sided with the Axis powers, and Hitler's reward for Sofia's alliance was Western Thrace. As soon as Greece's occupation by German and Italian troops was complete, the Germans allowed Bulgarian forces to enter the Greek-Bulgarian frontier and annex the regions of Eastern Macedonia and Western Thrace. Throughout the war period, Bulgarian authorities launched a campaign of discrimination, oppression, and conversion against the Pomaks and the rest of the Muslim community. In several cases, the government used the pretext of the war effort to legislate and apply clearly discriminatory policies. Bulgarian Muslims received less food and provisions than Bulgarian Christians. Pomak muftis and teachers were dismissed from their duties and replaced by Muslim personnel loyal to the government. The term "Pomak" was banned and the Arab names of the Pomaks were replaced by Bulgarian ones. All these restrictions were abolished after the Communist government was established in Sofia in September 1944.[7]

On the other side, the Muslims of (Greek) Western Thrace had been separated from the Ottoman Empire since the Second Balkan War of 1913. Following a decade of war and rival occupations, their legal status had been determined by the Treaty of Lausanne (July 1923), which recognized the sovereignty of the Republic of Turkey.[8] The treaty also provided for the protection of the Greek Orthodox minority in Turkey and the Muslim minority in Greece.

It detailed the rights of both groups, and among its commitments guaranteed religious freedom and toleration; free use of minority languages; protection of their in the educational system; full equality before the law in civil and political matters; equal access to public employment, business, and the professions; and equal allocation of public funds. The Treaty of Lausanne placed the Muslims of Western Thrace within the strategic frame of Greco-Turkish relations and under the protection of the League of Nations. That was probably the reason why most of the treaty's provisions were respected by Greece, even though there was limited assimilation of the Muslim minority into higher education, state administration and decision making, and the Greek public sphere in general.

The most noticeable characteristics of the Pomaks of Western Thrace, even today, is their attachment to traditional Muslim values and their relative poverty. The Pomaks appear to have had a greater sense of their own separateness in the mid-twentieth century. Their geographical location in isolated mountain villages would have been relevant in this regard, since almost 90 percent of the total Greek Pomak community lived in the mountainous area of the Rhodopes. Economically, they were also isolated, involved overwhelmingly in subsistence agriculture, and seen as poorer by lowland ethnic Turks.[9] Kinship was probably more intense and endogamy more prevalent than they were for the Muslims of the lowlands; Pomaks enjoyed a tight-knit family structure.

During the 1941–1944 occupation of Western Thrace, the misery and brutality of Bulgarian rule was shared by the whole of the Muslim population; however, the Pomaks suffered most. The authorities sought to "Bulgarize" the Pomaks, to enforce their cultural assimilation into the Bulgarian collective identity and nationalist ideals. Given that the Pomak community spoke a Bulgarian dialect, the occupiers considered them potentially more receptive than either the Greeks or the Turks to their assimilation policy. Thus, the Pomaks became the victims of a campaign of systematic oppression and aggression, terrorized to drive them toward accepting Bulgarian citizenship. Community leaders were arrested and tortured. Pomak men and women were attacked by Bulgarian gendarmes simply because they wore the fez or the veil. Young male Pomaks were enlisted in the Bulgarian labor battalions, where they were forced to work to exhaustion building roads and bridges in Bulgaria. At the same time, the economic effects of the occupation reduced the local Pomak population to utter poverty. Although Greek Pomaks rejected the Bulgarian occupation of Western Thrace, they remained overwhelmingly passive and detached from the local national resistance movement. The local resistance organizations (Communist and republican) made practically no effort to involve the Pomak community in their struggle.

## Reconsidering the Percentages

Bulgaria's surrender to the Allies and the withdrawal of Bulgarian occupation forces from Greece did not bring an end to Bulgaria's aspirations in Western Thrace. Immediately after the end of World War II, the newly established Communist Bulgarian government launched a well-organized international campaign to align the country with the winner's camp. Its objective was to reinvent Bulgaria's role during the war and to persuade international public opinion and diplomacy that not only was the country a victim of Nazi aggression, but it had also paid a heavy price resisting it. Furthermore, Bulgaria's intent was not just to avoid the aftermath of its alignment with Hitler, but to claim a significant share of the winner's spoils. The new Bulgarian regime felt confident enough to reclaim Western Thrace.

The first step in the campaign was to reinvent the 1941–1944 occupation of Eastern Macedonia and Western Thrace. The Bulgarian occupation forces in the area were portrayed as peacekeepers whose sole objective had been to protect the local population from a much harsher German occupation. A typical example is reflected in the report prepared by the Bulgarian Political Mission in Washington, which summarized the Bulgarian arguments: "There has been much misrepresentation about the Bulgarian "occupation" of Thrace and Macedonia. The Bulgarian army units entered these areas long after they had been conquered by the Germans; they took no part in the invasion."[10] The Justice for Bulgaria Committee—one of the many organizations that propagandized Bulgaria's claims—put matters in simpler terms: "Bulgaria has always striven and will always strive for an expedient solution of the question for an actual territorial outlet to a free sea, by achieving the return of Western Thrace, so unjustly taken from her."[11]

Greece wasted no time in proclaiming its own territorial claims against Bulgaria as soon as the occupation forces were withdrawn and the new government under Georgios Papandreou was established. In his first official speech, Papandreou declared that after three successive Bulgarian invasions, Greece had the right to demand the strengthening of its strategic position all along the Greek-Bulgarian frontier.[12] Greece also staked two other significant territorial claims. The first was the Dodecanese, an island complex in the southeastern Aegean populated by a Greek community a hundred thousand strong.[13] The second was Northern Epirus, an area in the south of Albania populated by a substantial ethnic Greek minority. Papandreou did not get the chance to put forward these claims diplomatically, since in December 1944, less than a month after he took office, fierce fighting broke out between government forces and the Communist-led Greek People's Liberation Army, the main armed resistance movement during the occupation.[14]

The first organized attempt to claim these territories was put forward by the Greek government under Prime Minister Konstantinos Tsaldaris (April 1946 to January 1947). Tsaldaris's government responded angrily to the Bulgarian claims, insisting not only that Western Thrace remain under Greek sovereignty, but also that the Greek borders expand at the expense of Bulgaria. More specifically, Greece demanded the shifting of the Greco-Bulgarian border almost thirty-six miles to the north and the annexation of a long strip of Bulgarian land, stretching from Kresna to the west toward Harmanli to the east, populated by approximately three hundred thousand people, the majority of whom were Bulgarian Pomaks.[15] The official Greek objective was to double the distance between the Bulgarian borders and the shores of the Aegean so that Greece could reinforce its strategic defense against a possible Bulgarian invasion in the future.

In April 1946, the Greek ambassador in Washington submitted two written proposals to the US State Department asking for renegotiation of the Greco-Albanian and the Greco-Bulgarian borders. The Greek reasoning was that this had to be done for Greece to reinforce its defense against its northern neighbors, to ensure the safety of Greek communities settled along the Greek-Bulgarian border, and to strengthen Greece's strategic role as "the bulwark of the free world" in the Balkans and the Eastern Mediterranean. The State Department asked for the advice of the US Joint Chiefs of Staff, who concluded that the Greek demands against both Albania and Bulgaria were not feasible and could easily lead the Balkans into a new conflict. Later in April and May, during the proceedings of the Council of Foreign Affairs Ministers in Paris, Greece repeated its claims. Eventually it was agreed that Greece would be allowed to annex the Dodecanese. However, as far as the Greek claims toward Albania and Bulgaria were concerned, Greek diplomats encountered a discouraging and negative reaction from US and British officials.[16]

International diplomacy did not accede to the Greek claims against Bulgaria, and Turkey appeared to be the only country that took them seriously. The Turkish press reported regularly on developments in Western Thrace following the end of the occupation.[17] The vast majority of Turkish newspapers fiercely criticized the Bulgarian government and its opportunism and asked that Bulgaria be punished for its role in World War II. According to Turkish journalist Hasan Kumcay: "Instead of contemplating what to do to improve their position and to reduce their sentences as war criminals, Bulgarian politicians claim Western Thrace and speak as if they represent a country that made great sacrifices fighting side by side with the Allies during the war. Now that's an absurd misinterpretation!"[18] Anti-Bulgarian sentiment was so widespread in Turkey that during the last days of the Bulgarian occupation of Eastern Macedonia and Western Thrace, the Bulgarian ambassador made an official complaint to the Turkish Ministry of Foreign Affairs, arguing sarcastically that "if our presence in Thrace causes such a reaction because we have split you from your so beloved Greeks, you can calm down because in a very short while we will evacuate Greece."[19]

The last Greek diplomatic attempt to claim Bulgarian territory took place at the Paris Peace Conference, where Allied countries negotiated the details of the peace treaties with Italy, Finland, Romania, Hungary, and Bulgaria.[20] The Greek delegation, under Prime Minister Tsaldaris, demanded that Bulgaria cede the Kresna-Harmanli strip to Greece and claimed $700 million in reparations. The Greek demands were refused by the Soviet envoy, who supported the Bulgarian claims for an outlet to the Aegean. The Soviet Union had adopted a hard line against Greek territorial claims, and Ukraine made an official appeal to the UN Security Council, accusing Greece of threatening peace and security in the Balkans. The US envoy tried to convince Greek officials that their territorial claims were unattainable and emphasized that the best way to guarantee Greek security and territorial integrity would be protection by the United Nations, rather than territorial annexation. The US secretary of state, James F. Byrnes, promised the Greek envoy that he would do his utmost to increase US economic aid to Greece but made clear that he was not going to support its territorial claims against Bulgaria.[21] Since the reinforcement of Greece's strategic defense along the Greek-Bulgarian frontier had been the Greek government's main argument, Greece was forced to play its second diplomatic card against Bulgaria, the Pomak issue.

This was the second of the central points raised by the Greek government to make the Greek case against Bulgaria. Since the last months of 1944, the Greek Ministry of Foreign Affairs had come up with a plan to involve Greek and Bulgarian Pomaks in the Greek-Bulgarian dispute. The Greek strategy on this issue involved three key themes: to highlight the plight of the Pomaks under the Bulgarian occupation of Western Thrace during the war (and also during the 1870s and the 1910s, when the area was under Bulgarian administration); to draw attention to the oppressive measures of the new Bulgarian regime against the Pomaks of Bulgaria, many of whom had openly expressed their discontent; and to highlight the bonds of solidarity and ethnic identity that united the Pomak communities on either side of the border. The core argument was that the Greek border ought to extend into Northern Thrace to emancipate Bulgarian Pomaks and protect them from the oppression of the authoritarian Bulgarian state.

The plan was put into operation as soon as the local Greek governmental authorities were established in Thrace. By order of the Greek Ministry of Foreign Affairs, the governor-general of Thrace, Charalambos Rouchotas, along with the local authorities, approached Bulgarian and Greek Pomak community leaders.[22] Despite the poor resources available to the new Greek administration, the campaign to attract Pomak sympathies was well organized. A number of Bulgarian Pomak committees and associations were set up, such as the Northern Thrace association in Komotini. These associations were composed of Pomaks who had settled in Western Thrace during the Bulgarian occupation and now feared the prospect of returning to Communist Bulgaria. Their main—if not their sole—activity was the publication of memoirs that denounced Bulgarian persecution of the Pomaks and demanded the incorporation of the Bulgarian Pomak areas into Greece. For instance, the Northern Thrace association in Komotini sent a memorandum to the Allied Commission representatives in Drama and Sofia, claiming that "Northern Thrace is an integral part of Greek Thrace and is destined to be united with Greece" and appealing to the Allies "to use any means you deem appropriate in order to achieve the annexation of Western Thrace to Greece."[23]

Although it is reasonable to assume that officials of the Greek government would have been keen to lend a hand to the drafting of this memorandum, the Pomak population's distrust of the Bulgarians was indeed widespread. The conservative and anti-Communist Bulgarian Pomaks were skeptical toward the new Bulgarian government and many feared that their fate in Communist Bulgaria would be uncertain. Along with Bulgarian Pomaks, the Greek Pomak communities such as Miki also mobilized in support of Greece, and appealed as well for help from the local authorities:

> Now that order, safety, and justice—which is the main feature of the Greek administration—has been restored, we would like to express to you our gratitude and devotion to the government and the Greek state and our decision to fight for the harsh punishment of the murderous Bulgarians and for compensation of what we have suffered.
>
> We are appealing to you to take the necessary steps toward the Greek Government and the Allied Governments of England, America, and Russia for the fulfillment of our claims and for the protection and integration of all other desperate fellow Pomaks who suffer in Bulgaria.
>
> We are appealing for the establishment of an allied committee in the Bulgarian Pomak territories to investigate Bulgarian vandalism, atrocity, and pillage against the population.
>
> Finally, since winter will find our people exhausted, naked, barefoot, and sick with malaria and other epidemics, we appeal to you to order the distribution of clothes, shoes, medicine, and especially Anteprin [an antiseptic], which is running low. In addition to the food aid we have already received, we are asking for the distribution

of milk to the children, who are in terrible condition. We appealed for such aid to the prefecture of Xanthi two months ago.[24]

The Bulgarians quickly became aware of the Greek efforts to entice the Bulgarian Pomaks into their camp and launched their own offensive. In Bulgarian Pomak villages, proclamations were circulated, signed by community leaders, that denounced Greek imperialism. Pro-Greek Pomak associations argued that such memos were the outcome of harsh oppression by the Bulgarian police, who were harassing the Bulgarian Pomak communities to ensure their loyalty to Bulgaria.[25]

In the meantime, the Greek government continued to raise the Pomak issue at various international forums. In September 1946, the Greek Pomak Hamdi Hüseyin Fehmi, a former Bulgarian collaborationist and a former member of the Greek Parliament, attended the Paris Peace Conference with the Bulgarian Pomak landowner Haki Şüleyman. Together, they requested the incorporation of Bulgarian territories inhabited by Pomaks into Greece.[26] The Pomak delegation was discreetly organized by the Greek Ministry of Foreign Affairs.[27] The delegates, with the mediation of the Greek minister of foreign affairs, contacted the envoys of the United States, New Zealand, and India, and submitted their requests.[28] Separately from the Paris conference, memoranda by the Pomak associations of Xanthi and Komotini were sent to the United Nations.[29] According to the US State Department, the Greek Ministry of Foreign Affairs was planning to send a Pomak delegation (similar to the one for Paris) to New York as "guests of the Greek UN mission, in view of their knowledge of the Pomak question."[30]

Ultimately, however, both the Pomak delegation in Paris and the memorandums to the United Nations failed to accomplish their objectives. The Pomak delegates were not heard in the official proceedings of the conference; their activity was confined to its fringes. The only concrete benefits for the Greek government were favorable comments by a number of US newspapers.[31] In addition to generating limited impact in Paris, the Pomak delegation received a hostile reception back home. In a joint declaration submitted to the Greek government (and the minority press in Thrace), the Greek Muslim members of Parliament from Thrace—Osman Nuri, Faik Engin, Osman Üstüner, and Hüseyin Zeybek—condemned the activities of the delegation:

> Two individuals, Hamdi Hüseyin Fehmi and Haki Şüleyman, are
> in negotiations with Europe and America under the name "Pomak
> Committee" and discussed several minority issues. This has caused
> serious discontent among the Turkish minority. We declare that with
> the exception of the four members of Parliament from Rhodope, no

one else has the right to represent the minority. Moreover, we declare that we do not acknowledge Hamdi Hüseyin Fehmi as leader of the Muslim community of Xanthi. We declare that the minority of Thrace does not acknowledge this title and that we will take all the necessary steps to stop the activities of these individuals now and in the future.[32]

Caught between an unfavorable international climate and a rather non-receptive local audience among the Turks of Western Thrace, the Greek attempt to play "the Pomak card" during the aftermath of World War II resulted in failure. Eventually Greece secured $150 million as reparations from Bulgaria and Italy, but no border changes between Greece and Bulgaria were authorized. With the return to the prewar territorial status quo, both the Greek and the Bulgarian attempts at territorial expansion ended.

## A Mutually Assured Fiasco

Greece used the pretext of protecting an ethnic and religious minority to attempt the expansion of its borders into Bulgaria. This was a typical pattern in a region where minorities were traditionally used as strategic assets in international relations and moreover, as agents who could facilitate territorial disputes and military conflicts. Nonetheless, it was more than obvious that by the end of World War II such patterns had become obsolete. Borders were now considered nonnegotiable and there was very little room for the encouragement of ethnic and religious feuds.

The United States was committed to maintaining Greece as the cradle of the free world in the Balkans. It was willing to support the reconstruction of the country and provide substantial economic support. Washington was also willing to guarantee the country's territorial integrity against irredentist claims by Greece's northern Communist neighbors. The United States was prepared to start a diplomatic confrontation with the Soviet Union and the Eastern bloc over Greece, with the expectation of gaining an extra negotiating card from that dispute. Moreover, it was eager to support the Greek government's campaign against domestic Communism and to play a central role in the 1946–1949 Greek Civil War, which would become the first war, by proxy, of the Cold War era. However, there was a clear line for the United States. A change in the Greek-Bulgarian border would run up against the spirit of the "percentages agreement" between Stalin and Churchill. The consequences of such a development could be disastrous and pose an unnecessary complication to the demarcation of spheres of influence in postwar Europe. The United States and the Soviet Union were not willing to take such a risk. The emancipation of the Bulgarian Pomaks was obviously not a strong enough motive for opening this Pandora's box. It was not even a strong enough motive to take a peek inside it.

Surprisingly, it seems that Greece did not really intend to readjust the borders between the Eastern bloc and the free world in the Balkans either. Indeed, it is even rather doubtful whether the Greek government really intended to incorporate almost three hundred thousand Muslims into Western Thrace. Such an abrupt development would have dramatically altered the ethnic composition of Thrace and posed a significant long-term risk for Greek interests in the region. It would have redistributed power and authority within the local community and put the local Christian Orthodox population in a disadvantageous economic and political position. In fact, it would have completely reversed the ethnic balance in Western Thrace and turned the local Greek Orthodox community into a minority. As the British consul in Thessaloniki pointed out, such a massive Muslim minority next to the Greek-Turkish borders would have given Turkey the opportunity to question Greek sovereignty there.[33]

The Greek and Bulgarian Pomaks were clearly used by the Greek government in its conflict with Bulgaria in a rather opportunistic manner. The Pomak issue was an attempt to confront Bulgarian expansionism using a diplomatic maneuver that was from the very outset destined to fail. This view is reinforced by the fact that although the Pomak delegation in Paris was organized by the Greek government, the official Greek envoy did not try to secure official status for them or put their demands high on the agenda. The Greeks used the Pomak issue, in other words, as a secondary line of defense and offense in a diplomatic dogfight with Bulgaria. The choice of the controversial Hamdi Hüseyin Fehmi (a confirmed collaborator with the Bulgarian occupation forces) as the figurehead of the Pomak delegation was indicative of the opportunism of the Greek government.

Throughout the Cold War, the West lined up race, ethnicity, and religion in its ideological and strategic battle against Communism. In many cases, though, the geostrategic, political, and diplomatic disputes between the West and the East were so intense and perilous that it was easy to neglect the additional or collateral religious aspects of these conflicts. The numerous ethnic and religious groups behind the Iron Curtain in Europe were perceived as some of the weakest components of a political and military bloc that seemed otherwise solid. Some of the groups were disgruntled at being forced to live under Communism. Moreover, the abrupt division of Europe was not the ideal solution to the various ethnic and religious disputes within—as well as along the borders—of the Iron Curtain. With appropriate manipulation, the discontentment of such groups had the potential to cause serious problems to the coherence of the Eastern bloc.

The Pomak issue was such a case. It was a mix of geopolitics, religion, and ethnicity. In this mix, religion was integral to the Greek claim for Bulgarian territory. It was the factor Greece counted on to ensure the support of the Pomak communities across the border who felt vulnerable and insecure in the polarized postwar environment. Their ethnic and religious identities were far from being guaranteed, and Greece called on the Pomaks to decide whether their identity and religious freedoms would be better safeguarded in irreligious, Communist Bulgaria or the Greek Christian Orthodox democracy. The guarantee of religious freedoms for the Pomaks was a central point in the Greek diplomatic plan to win the sympathy and support of the Western allies.

However, during the very early stages of the Cold War, the primary concern for international players was the consolidation of gains won during World War II. Given that perspective, disputes over ethnic and religious minorities were not regarded as promising proxy wars that could undermine the enemy diplomatically or strategically. Instead, they were treated as threats to assets that had been acquired after exhaustive efforts both on the battlefield and at the negotiation table.

## Notes

1. This chapter is part of a collaborative two-year research project financed by a grant from the British Arts and Humanities Research Council under the title "The Enemy That Never Was: The Muslim Minority of Greece between International and Domestic Conflict, 1940–1949." Except where otherwise indicated, all translations in this chapter are mine.

2. See Bruce Kuniholm, *The Origins of the Cold War in the Near East: Great Power Conflict and Diplomacy in Iran, Turkey, and Greece* (Princeton, NJ: Princeton University Press, 1980); John Iatrides, ed., *Greece in the 1940s: A Nation in Crisis* (Hanover, NH: University Press of New England, 1981); and Lars Baerentzen, John Iatrides, and Ole Smith, eds., Μελέτες για τον Εμφύλιο Πόλεμο, 1945–1949 [Studies in the history of the Greek Civil War, 1945–1949] (Athens: Olkos, 2002).

3. On these different versions, see Mary Neuburger, *The Orient Within* (Ithaca, NY: Cornell University Press, 2004); Ali Eminov, *Turkish and Other Muslim Minorities of Bulgaria* (London: Hurst, 1997); Hugh Poulton and Suha Taji-Farouki, eds., *Muslim Identity and the Balkan State* (London: Hurst, 1997); Omer Turan, "Pomaks: Their Past and Present," *Journal of Muslim Minority Affairs* 19, no. 1 (1999): 69–83; Tsvetana Georgieva, "Pomaks, Muslim Bulgarians," *Islam and Christian-Muslim Relations* 12, no. 3 (July 2001): 303–16; and Paulos Chidiroglou, *The Greek Pomaks and Their Relations with Turkey* (Athens: Proskinio, 1991).

4. According to the same census, the overall population of Western Thrace was 303,171, of which 192,372 were Greek Orthodox, 84,669 were ethnic Turks, and 1,435 were Roma. Ministry of National Economy, General Statistical Service of Greece,

*Στατιστικά αποτελέσματα της απογραφής του πληθυσμού της Ελλάδος της 15–16 Μαΐου 1928* [Statistical results of the Greek population census of 15–16 May 1928] (Athens: Ethniko Typografeio, 1935).

5. Alexandre Popovic, *L'Islam Balkanique: Les Musulmans du sud-est europeen dans la period post-ottomane* [Balkan Islam: Muslims in southeastern Europe during the post-Ottoman period] (Berlin: Osteuropa-Institut, 1986), 96–98.

6. Some important studies on Bulgarian Pomaks are: Hugh Poulton, *The Balkans: Minorities and States in Conflict* (London: Minority Rights Publications, 1993); Asen Balikci, "Pomak Identity: National Prescriptions and Native Assumptions," *Ethnologia Balkanica* 3 (1999): 51–58; Yulian Konstantinov, "Strategies for Sustaining a Vulnerable Identity: The Case of the Bulgarian Pomaks," in *Muslim Identity and the Balkan State*, ed. Hugh Poulton and Suha Taji-Farouki (London: Hurst, 1997), 33–54; and Mary Neuburger, "Pomak Borderlands: Muslims on the Edge of Nations," *Nationalities Papers* 28, no. 1 (March 2000): 181–99.

7. Bulgarian Helsinki Committee, *The Human Rights of Muslims in Bulgaria in Law and Politics since 1878* (Sofia: Bulgarian Helsinki Committee, 2003).

8. Among the terms of the Treaty of Lausanne was the compulsory exchange of populations between Greece and Turkey. According to the agreement, all Muslims living in Greece—apart from the Muslims of Western Thrace—were to be evacuated to Turkey. Similarly, non-Muslims in Turkey were to be moved to Greece, except for the Greek Orthodox minorities of Istanbul and of the islands of Imvros and Tenedos. The move sent 354,647 Muslim refugees to Turkey and approximately 1.2 million Christians to Greece.

9. Ulf Brunnbauer, "Families and Mountains in the Balkans: Christian and Muslim Household Structures in the Rhodopes, 19th–20th Century," *History of the Family* 7 (2002): 333.

10. Bulgarian Political Mission to Washington, *The Truth about Bulgaria* (n.p.: Bulgarian Political Mission to Washington, 1946).

11. Justice for Bulgaria Committee, *Bulgaria Claims Western Thrace* (Sofia: Justice for Bulgaria Committee, 1946).

12. Konstantinos Svolopoulos, *Η Ελληνική Εξωτερική Πολιτική 1900–1945* [Greek foreign policy, 1900–1945] (Athens: Estia, 1997), 311.

13. Occupied by the Italians since 1912, the Dodecanese had been a British military protectorate since May 1945.

14. On the Greek People's Liberation Army, see Mark Mazower, *Inside Hitler's Greece: The Experience of the Occupation, 1941–44* (New Haven, CT: Yale University Press, 2001); Richard Clogg, *Greece, 1940–1949: Occupation, Resistance, Civil War* (New York: Palgrave Macmillan, 2003); and John Hondros, *Occupation and Resistance: The Greek Agony, 1941–1944* (New York: Pella, 1993).

15. Peter Thrax, *The Bulgars: Self-Styled Prussians of the Balkans* (New York: Greek Government Office of Information, 1944), 58–59; Christoforos Naltsas, *Τα ελληνοσλαυϊκά σύνορα: Αι προς βορράν εθνικαί μας διεκδικήσεις* [The Greco-Slav borders: Our national claims toward the North] (Thessaloniki: Etaireia Makidonikon Spoudon, 1946), 44–50; and Vasileios Kondis, *Η Αγγλοαμερικανική*

*πολιτική και το ελληνικό πρόβλημα: 1945-1949* [The Anglo-American policy and the Greek problem: 1945-1949] (Thessaloniki: Paratiritis, 1986), 160.

16. Kondis, *Η Αγγλοαμερικανική πολιτική*, 162–63.

17. Review of Turkish press, Archive of the Greek Ministry of Foreign Affairs (hereafter AGMFA), Athens, Greece, 1944/10.1.

18. Greek translation of Kumcay's article, AGMFA, 1946/42.3.

19. Raphael, Ankara, to Foreign Ministry, September 30, 1944, AGMFA, 1944/8.5.

20. Prior to the Paris Peace Conference, two meetings of the Council of Foreign Affairs Ministers had taken place, during which the annexation of the Dodecanese by Greece was approved.

21. Kondis, *Η Αγγλοαμερικανική πολιτική*, 189.

22. Panagiotis Papadimitriou, *Οι Πομάκοι της Ροδόπης: Από της εθνοτικές σχέσεις στους Βαλκανικούς Εθνικισμούς 1870-1990* [The Pomaks of Rhodope: From ethnic relations to Balkan nationalisms, 1870-1990] (Thessaloniki: Kyriakidis Brothers, 2003), 153.

23. Drama is a Greek city in Eastern Macedonia. Association "Northern Thrace" to the Allied Commission, November 8, 1944, AGMFA, 1944/10.1.

24. Community of Miki to the Prefecture of Xanthi, September 24, 1945, AGMFA, 1947/11.1. The file contains a number of similar memorandums.

25. General Association of the Muslims of Başmakli [Smolyan] and the surrounding region, to the Foreign Ministries of Britain, USA, Russia, and France, April 8, 1946, AGMFA, 1947/111.1.

26. *Elliniko Aima*, October 19, 1946, Vovolinis Archive, Athens.

27. Department of State, "Intelligence Research Report: A Survey on National Minorities in Foreign Countries," January 2, 1947, National Archives and Records Administration (hereafter NARA), College Park, MD, M1221/4209.

28. Ibid. According to the State Department source, the Indian delegate seemed to be in favor of the Pomak claim.

29. Memorandum from the Bulgarian Pomak refugees in Xanthi to the honorable UN Committee, February 13, 1947, and memorandum from the Bulgarian Pomaks, refugees in Komotini, to the honorable UN Committee, February 14, 1947, AGMFA, 1947/111.1.

30. Department of State, "Intelligence Research Report."

31. Kostas Tsioumis, *Οι Πομάκοι στο ελληνικό κράτος (1920-1950): Ιστορική προσέγγιση* [The Pomaks in the Greek state (1920-1950): A historical approach] (Thessaloniki: Promytheus, 1997), 87–88.

32. *Trakya*, January 20, 1947. Then, as now, the Muslim MPs, and indeed most Turks in Western Thrace, did not acknowledge the Pomaks as a distinct ethnic community within the Muslim minority. They considered the whole minority to have a uniform Turkish ethnic identity.

33. Letter from the British consul to Thessaloniki regarding the Pomaks of Thrace, September 1946, National Archives, Kew (London), United Kingdom, FO/371/58868. According to the consul: "While it is no doubt desirable that the Pomaks should be united under one government and while they would in present circumstances

doubtless prefer Greek to Bulgarian rule, it seems very doubtful whether the Greeks will assist their claim to Southern Bulgaria by putting the case for uniting Moslem Pomaks. If such a union were to be effected the possibility of the Moslem population then in Greece east of the Nestos [river] being in a majority over the Orthodox Greeks of the area, is not to be excluded. The Turks might then, assuming a different act of international circumstances, consider the possibilities of laying claim to the enlarged Western Thrace on the grounds that the population was predominantly Moslem. Reliable population figures are difficult to obtain but I will see if I can find some."

## References

**ARCHIVES**

Archive of the Greek Ministry of Foreign Affairs (Ελληνικό Υπουργείο Εξωτερικών, Διπλωματικό και Ιστορικό Αρχειο), Athens, Greece
National Archives, Kew (London), United Kingdom
National Archives and Records Administration, College Park, MD
Vovolinis Archive (Αρχειο Βοβολίνη), Athens, Greece

**PERIODICALS**

*Elliniko Aima*
*Trakya*

**PUBLISHED GOVERNMENT DOCUMENTS, REPORTS, AND SERIALS**

Bulgarian Helsinki Committee. *The Human Rights of Muslims in Bulgaria in Law and Politics since 1878.* Sofia: Bulgarian Helsinki Committee, 2003.
Bulgarian Political Mission to Washington. *The Truth about Bulgaria.* N.p.: Bulgarian Political Mission to Washington, 1946.
Justice for Bulgaria Committee. *Bulgaria Claims Western Thrace.* Sofia: Justice for Bulgaria Committee, 1946.
Thrax, Peter. *The Bulgars: Self-Styled Prussians of the Balkans.* New York: Greek Government Office of Information, 1944.

**SELECTED PUBLISHED WORKS**

Baerentzen, Lars, John Iatrides, and Ole Smith, eds. *Μελέτες για τον Εμφύλιο Πόλεμο, 1945–1949* [Studies in the history of the Greek Civil War, 1945–1949]. Athens: Olkos, 2002.
Balikci, Asen. "Pomak Identity: National Prescriptions and Native Assumptions." *Ethnologia Balkanica* 3 (1999): 51–58.
Brunnbauer, Ulf. "Families and Mountains in the Balkans: Christian and Muslim Household Structures in the Rhodopes, 19th–20th Century." *History of the Family* 7 (2002): 333.
Chidiroglou, Paulos. *The Greek Pomaks and Their Relations with Turkey.* Athens: Proskinio, 1991.

Eminov, Ali. *Turkish and Other Muslim Minorities of Bulgaria.* London: Hurst, 1997.

Georgieva, Tsvetana. "Pomaks, Muslim Bulgarians." *Islam and Christian-Muslim Relations* 12, no. 3 (July 2001): 303–16.

Hondros, John. *Occupation and Resistance: The Greek Agony, 1941–1944.* New York: Pella, 1993.

Iatrides, John, ed. *Greece in the 1940s: A Nation in Crisis.* Hanover, NH: University Press of New England, 1981.

Kondis, Vasileios. *Η Αγγλοαμερικανική πολιτική και το ελληνικό πρόβλημα: 1945–1949* [The Anglo-American policy and the Greek problem: 1945–1949]. Thessaloniki: Paratiritis, 1986.

Konstantinov, Yulian. "Strategies for Sustaining a Vulnerable Identity: The Case of the Bulgarian Pomaks." In Poulton and Taji-Farouki, 33–54.

Kuniholm, Bruce. *The Origins of the Cold War in the Near East: Great Power Conflict and Diplomacy in Iran, Turkey, and Greece.* Princeton, NJ: Princeton University Press, 1980.

Ministry of National Economy, General Statistical Service of Greece. *Στατιστικά αποτελέσματα της απογραφής του πληθυσμού της Ελλάδος της 15–16 Μαΐου 1928* [Statistical results of the Greek population census of 15–16 May 1928]. Athens: Ethniko Typografeio, 1935.

Naltsas, Christoforos. *Τα ελληνοσλαυϊκά σύνορα: Αι προς βορράν εθνικαί μας διεκδικήσεις* [The Greco-Slav borders: Our national claims toward the North]. Thessaloniki: Etaireia Makidonikon Spoudon, 1946.

Neuburger, Mary. *The Orient Within.* Ithaca, NY: Cornell University Press, 2004.

———. "Pomak Borderlands: Muslims on the Edge of Nations." *Nationalities Papers* 28, no. 1 (March 2000): 181–99.

Papadimitriou, Panagiotis. *Οι Πομάκοι της Ροδόπης: Από της εθνοτικές σχέσεις στους Βαλκανικούς Εθνικισμούς, 1870–1990* [The Pomaks of Rhodope: From ethnic relations to Balkan nationalisms, 1870–1990]. Thessaloniki: Kyriakidis Brothers, 2003.

Poulton, Hugh. *The Balkans: Minorities and States in Conflict.* London: Minority Rights Publications, 1993.

Poulton, Hugh, and Suha Taji-Farouki, eds. *Muslim Identity and the Balkan State.* London: Hurst, 1997.

Svolopoulos, Konstantinos. *Η Ελληνική Εξωτερική Πολιτική, 1900–1945* [Greek foreign policy, 1900–1945]. Athens: Estia, 1997.

Tsioumis, Kostas. *Οι Πομάκοι στο ελληνικό κράτος (1920–1950): Ιστορική προσέγγιση.* [The Pomaks in the Greek state (1920–1950): A historical approach]. Thessaloniki: Promytheus, 1997.

Turan, Omer. "Pomaks: Their Past and Present." *Journal of Muslim Minority Affairs* 19, no. 1 (1999): 69–83.

# CHAPTER 2

## The Western Allies, German Churches, and the Emerging Cold War in Germany, 1948–1952

*JonDavid K. Wyneken*

At the end of the Second World War in Europe, few could have predicted just how quickly quadripartite cooperation would deteriorate. The priorities of the superpowers shifted rapidly away from punishing Nazis and coming to terms with the catastrophe of the war and moved toward fighting a new Cold War, which divided Europe and much of the world into opposing ideological, political, and military camps. The defeated nation of Germany proved to be the literal and figurative divider between these opposing blocs. Shattered, occupied, and without sovereignty, Germans understandably believed that their fate in this burgeoning global conflict was not in their own hands and therefore cultivated authorities who could lobby the quadripartite powers on their behalf. The Allies, meanwhile, also sought out individuals and organizations that might support their objectives for the postwar occupation. Developments in the occupation of Germany influenced the broader international relations between the quadripartite Allied powers, while those relations symbiotically helped shape the occupation and the processes that characterized the developing Cold War. These factors all proved to be quite volatile, as a largely ambivalent and occasionally hostile German population caused difficulties for the Western Allies on a number of fronts, making inter-Allied cooperation even more difficult and feeding the tensions that steadily drove the wartime alliance apart and into a confrontational framework that would span several more generations.

In the three Western occupation zones, Allied authorities to varying degrees sought the support of German Catholic and Protestant leaders to help ensure wider German acceptance of occupation reforms. German church leaders, for their part, feared that Germany might be subjected to humiliations worse than those that had followed its defeat in 1918 and abhorred the presence of Communism on German soil. They therefore hoped to work closely with the Western Allies to restore German sovereignty quickly and prevent further expansion of Communist influence in Germany.

To the surprise of all sides, often-heated conflicts between ecclesiastical and Western Allied authorities emerged quickly after the end of the war. At issue were occupation policies meant to purge Nazism from public and private life and disagreements over relations with the Soviets. From 1945 to 1948, the Western Allies' policies governing denazification, the prosecution of German war criminals, and the treatment of displaced persons and other refugees from Eastern Europe (including German expellees and Jewish survivors of the Holocaust) drew the most ire from German church leaders, who considered them all to be motivated by "victor's justice" and the widespread Allied belief in the collective guilt of all Germans for Nazi crimes. German church leaders feared that these policies only strengthened the power of the Soviets and pushed more and more Germans to embrace Communism. Such conflicts taxed the few material resources the Western Allies had incorporated into their occupation departments to deal with religious affairs. Making matters worse, German church leaders made their complaints known internationally, which put increased pressure on the Western Allies to change their policies in Germany and Western Europe. Presenting a historically rare unified front against occupation policies, German Catholic and Protestant clerics quickly established themselves as among the most vociferous and high-profile critics of the occupation, a development that the Western Allies viewed as a serious risk to successful reform and reeducation in Germany.[1]

An open break between the Western Allies and the German churches indeed might have occurred—with all the deleterious effects that would have resulted from such a schism—had matters in Germany and among the quadripartite partners not changed significantly in 1948 with the promulgation of the new deutschmark in the Western zones, the resulting Soviet blockade of Berlin, and the subsequent airlift. In the years prior, the Western Allies' growing concern about the Soviets had converged with the German churches' long-standing fear of Communism. Despite all the aforementioned conflicts between them, this issue nonetheless steadily shifted the Western Allies toward assessing how they could assist the churches' political and propaganda efforts against the Soviets and East Germans. This new focus on building a new West German state around "good Germans"—in particular, the Christian Democratic Union, made up in large part by German religious leaders and parishioners—helped transform the international image of Germans from inherently aggressive, militaristic enemies into indispensable partners in the West's fight against Soviet-sponsored Communism.

Simultaneously and paradoxically, the German churches' united front against occupation policies collapsed as German Catholics—led politically by the devoutly Catholic Konrad Adenauer—threw their support behind the creation of a West German state. German Protestant leaders, concerned that a division of Germany would leave over 80 percent of their parishioners behind Soviet and East German lines, instead continued to push for a unified German state that would leave the German Protestant Church intact. As a result, the Protestants became increasingly reluctant after 1948 to antagonize the Soviets, despite their deep distaste for Communism. Thus, while German Catholic officials anchored their efforts in supporting their colleagues behind the Iron Curtain, Protestant leaders strove to maintain confessional unity and religious freedom among their parishioners in East Germany despite the division of Germany into two ideologically opposed and hostile states.[2]

Meanwhile, after 1948, the Americans and the British focused on ascertaining how they could use these new developments in the German churches to further their own anti-Communist policies in Europe. The Western Allies' keen interest in the activities and attitudes of the German churches thus increased in the wake of the Berlin Crisis. By the end of 1952, when in the aftermath of the Western Allies' rejection of the "Stalin Note" the Soviets abandoned their efforts to create a unified and neutral German state, German church leaders, West German officials, and their Western Allied supervisors had solidified a sometimes uneasy but workable relationship in which containing the Soviets overshadowed the previous battles over occupation policies.[3]

Therefore, the relations between the Western Allies and the German churches proved to be more instrumental in the course of the military occupation of Germany and in the development of the Cold War there and in Europe than has heretofore been recognized. No single study has been dedicated exclusively to exploring the diplomatic relationship specifically between the Western Allied occupation authorities and German church leaders, nor has any one study focused specifically on how the German churches influenced the broader Cold War politics of the Western Allies.[4] This chapter expands the discussion of the German churches to include their significant—and previously underappreciated—effects on the developing international politics and perceptions among the Western Allies of the emerging Cold War.

## The Roots of Protestant and Catholic Cooperation

Shortly before New Year's Eve, 1949, Evangelical bishop Theophil Wurm, recently retired as the first president of the Evangelische Kirche in Deutschland (EKD; Evangelical Church of Germany), the new national body of German Protestantism, wrote to the Anglican bishop of Chichester that "mankind looks back on a sea of blood and tears and has no guarantee that a third catastrophe will not take place which will surpass all that we have experienced so far." The only positive sign Wurm saw was a global "Christian unity . . . which was unknown to us before," noting that "all Christian churches are showing great willingness to help each other and have done a great deal of good."[5] The unity Wurm spoke of included the German Protestant and Catholic Churches' equal distaste for numerous occupation policies of the Western Allies. Catholic and Protestant leaders alike criticized them as immoral and prone to making Communism more appealing to Germans. Wurm, a staunch opponent of war crimes trials in particular, had told the Western Allies that "the Church was unalterably opposed to Communism and considered opposition to it a matter of religious duty since practically all Communists were anti-religious."[6] Otto Dibelius, the Evangelical bishop of Berlin-Brandenburg, argued that Bolshevism was "merely another form of National Socialism."[7] Dibelius also insisted that only Christianity could fill this vacuum, as "the Christian Church is rooted in German life, naturally."[8]

German Catholic leaders had expressed similar views since the end of the war. Prominent cardinals reiterated Pope Pius XII's deep concerns about the threat posed to Germany and to all of Christianity by the Soviet presence in Germany and in Eastern Europe. One Catholic official told the British that denazification had merely removed right-wing elements from German life, and hence "political power is only open to the left; . . . this will help Communism."[9] Catholic leaders cooperated with their Protestant counterparts to bring broader international attention to Soviet actions in East Germany, particularly the removal of German industry and the deportation of workers to the Soviet Union, the forced evacuations of Germans in occupied territories, and the attempts to curb religious influence through measures like limiting access to religious services and to youth education.[10]

From the outset of the occupation, the Western Allies paid close attention to the churches' concerns. A comprehensive US report on the churches noted that German religious leaders often asked, "Does America want to destroy the German nation by exacting the full toll of suffering in revenge for Nazi sins? Will the US zone simply be abandoned to Russia?"[11] The British concluded, "It is axiomatic for the Church that Russian intentions are hostile to Christianity. . . . When [German churches] look to the future they are immediately oppressed by the might and implacable enmity of Russian Nihilism: this fear overshadows all else, and colours the Church's interpretation of current events." The officials noted that they had "heard no good word for Russia from any German clergyman, and have detected no point of possible understanding."[12]

But in the early years of the occupation, the Western Allies remained much more undecided than the German churches about how much of a threat Communism posed. At the very least, any fears about Communism were mitigated by the Western Allies' desire to work effectively with the Soviets. This began to change officially with Secretary of State James F. Byrnes's "Stuttgart Speech" in September 1946. The shift was accelerated by the promulgation between 1946 and 1948 of the Truman Doctrine, the Marshall Plan, and the deutschmark, and culminated with the 1948 Berlin Crisis and the division of Germany into two opposing states in 1949. By that point, the Western Allies had reached a clear consensus among themselves about the need to support the new West German state and undercut the Soviets and East Germans in any way possible.

## The Division of Germany and Issues of Unity

For the German churches, the division of Germany posed new challenges and led each body to divergent courses, both politically and in their relations with the Western Allies. From 1948 to 1952, Catholic leaders in Germany increasingly aligned themselves with the policies of Adenauer and his political party, the Christian Democratic Union (CDU). The Vatican made clear its own views with what the British called its "decision on Communism," which labeled the Soviet Union and its ideology a threat to Christianity and world peace.[13] German Catholics came to support (with varying degrees of enthusiasm) the creation of a West German state (the Federal Republic of Germany, or FRG) and its rearmament as the best practical way to resist the expansion of Communism and prevent a new world war. This put German Catholics largely in line with the Western Allies' support of the new West German state and rearmament.

Protestant leaders, however, diverged from their Catholic counterparts by remaining noncommittal on division and rearmament because of grave concerns about the unity of their national church body and the fear that division would end any possibility of reunification. Protestant leaders wanted to keep open East-West dialogue on the topic; some of them—in particular Martin Niemöller—became open advocates of neutrality and reunification, and by extension became open critics of Adenauer and the West German state. For this reason, the Western Allies paid significant attention to Protestant affairs after 1949, particularly in Berlin, where the EKD sought to maintain some semblance of German unity by continuing to meet there with East German parishes and leaders. The Western Allies eventually became concerned with the potential threat posed to the West German state and to larger Allied objectives by Protestant opposition to division and rearmament.

However, in the EKD efforts to maintain unity, the Western Allies also saw an opportunity to use the Protestant churches for active (if clandestine) anti-Communist resistance behind the Iron Curtain. Occupation officials thus paid much more attention to Protestant affairs after 1949 than they did to Catholic activities, a fact reflected in the number of files in Allied archives dealing with the EKD from 1949 to 1952. East German and Soviet officials, for their part, sought to use for their own propaganda and policy purposes the Protestant desire to restore national and confessional unity. By the end of 1952, circumstances had changed enough to bring the EKD more into the camp of the Western Allies and West Germany on division and rearmament, although the Protestants never became enthusiastic about either. These developments caused significant rifts and confusion within the German churches as confronting the new totalitarian threat became more pressing for the churches and the Western Allies alike.

In July 1948, in the midst of the Berlin Crisis, the EKD met at Eisenach in the Soviet zone and made the EKD a permanent national entity, dual moves meant to underscore the solidarity of West German Protestants with their brethren in the East and to end the Nazi-era fragmentation of German Protestantism.[14] In October 1949, the Council of Brethren of the EKD, meeting in East Berlin, called for a comprehensive peace treaty, unification, and the eventual removal of occupation troops from German soil. The council asked German Protestants to maintain religious unity despite division. Otto Dibelius said that "Christians are especially fitted to create unity in the spirit of genuine understanding. The joint aim must be a united Germany." Another delegate considered the EKD to be the "last link between East and West in this tragic hour of fate."[15]

The Western Allies, for their part, focused on the situation in East Berlin as a way to better understand the conditions of churches in the German Democratic Republic (GDR; East Germany) and to ascertain if and how the EKD could be valuable against East Germany and the Soviet Union. But this proved difficult for several reasons. First, Soviet and East German media restrictions heavily colored reports by East Berlin papers and tightly controlled Western press access. Second, Western officials often received word from pastors in East Germany that horror stories about conditions for the churches under Communist rule were exaggerated. These same sources reported that stories of mass arrests of clergy and youth as spies were overblown or had been made not on religious but political grounds. In addition, there existed as of yet no official restrictions on preaching the gospel openly or on religious instruction.[16] But despite the lack of "official" changes in Soviet and East German religious policies, other signs existed in the summer of 1949 of increasing repression in Soviet-occupied areas. The Sozialistische Einheitspartei Deutschlands (SED; the Socialist Unity Party, the dominant and government-approved party of the East German state) took on more control of youth activities, and many of the regular "political arrests" of religious leaders appeared to be truly motivated by antireligious sentiments of the state (the Soviets did not make any real distinction between religious and political activities, despite their public claims otherwise).[17]

Over the next year, as the international situation worsened, the German churches began to worry increasingly about the safety of Germany and the threat of Communism to world peace, despite the "peace program" officially propagated by the Soviet Union and East Germany, which sought to capitalize on the widespread German desire for German reunification. Several events contributed to this. First, the detonation of an atomic bomb by the Soviet Union in August 1949 indicated to the churches and many others that any war between the Western Allies and the Soviets could now go nuclear. To many, this spelled certain doom for Germany because of its location on the front line of the Cold War. Second, in June 1950, North Korea invaded South Korea. To many around the world, including many in the German churches and in the West German government, the invasion strongly suggested a coordinated, unified, and global program to spread Communist ideology by force. Another worldwide war appeared possible, this time with a potentially nuclear component.

But the German Catholic and Protestant Churches took very different lessons from the Korean War. Adenauer and the Catholics saw it as proof that rearmament and integration with the West against Communism was indeed vital to German survival. Joseph Cardinal Frings went so far as to put Catholic support clearly behind rearmament, saying on several occasions in July 1950 that it was the duty of Catholics to support any efforts against those who threatened and attacked "divine order . . . in its most vital fundamentals." For these reasons, the church also stood against conscientious objection to military service, in direct contrast to the EKD. Meanwhile, the EKD saw in the Korean War proof of the dangers inherent in the division of a nation between Communist forces and the West. Korea only cemented the EKD's resistance to rearmament and reinforced their drive for national (and thus confessional) unity.[18]

## Martin Niemöller and Notions of a Third Way

For the EKD, therefore, the primary dilemma became how best to preserve the peace and thus preserve Germany in order to restore confessional and national unity and survival. The staunch anti-Communism of German Protestantism, most often expressed openly by Otto Dibelius, was well known by the Western Allies, the Soviets, and the East Germans.[19] The situation was made much more complicated for the EKD and the Allies after the emergence of a wing of Protestantism increasingly critical of the CDU, led by Martin Niemöller and supported by West German interior minister Gustav Heinemann. Heinemann was also the president of the synod of the EKD and serving in the West German government at Adenauer's request. This significant political connection, as well as Niemöller's well-known reputation as a Nazi resister, his longstanding prominence in the Protestant Council of Brethren (Bruderrat), and his position as the head of the postwar EKD foreign office, gave his ideas legitimacy in some circles and brought him significant international attention. It also gave the appearance at times that Niemöller spoke for the entire EKD, a falsehood that Niemöller's colleagues constantly had to refute.[20]

These matters greatly concerned the Western Allies, who for the next couple of years paid very close attention to Niemöller, sometimes at the expense of other matters involving the churches. The British worried that Heinemann's dual positions would make it impossible for him to remain loyal to Adenauer's policies, since Heinemann clearly supported Niemöller's arguments against division and rearmament.[21] They would turn out to be right, for Heinemann resigned in the fall of 1950 after Adenauer asked the Allies—without informing Heinemann, the interior minister—to station more troops in West Germany to allow for the creation of an integrated European army and to establish an internal security police force. Heinemann wanted Adenauer to pose these questions to the West German public, felt compelled by his Christian principles to do so, and threatened to resign in protest if Adenauer did not comply. Adenauer saw Heinemann's attempt as mixing religious and political ideals and thus accepted the resignation. Niemöller and his supporters seized on this affair as proof of Adenauer's reckless intentions and the need for reunification and neutrality.[22]

The Western Allies, for their part, came to the conclusion that despite all the attention, the pacifism displayed by Niemöller and his supporters was "based upon the fact that [Germans] are helpless to do anything rather than act upon ethical or religious considerations." But the Western Allies continued to follow Niemöller's activities closely because his efforts found open support from East Germany and Soviet Union, who wanted to further their "peace program." Among other things, it advocated, as Niemöller did, East-West talks, ostensibly to reduce international tensions and to reunify the German states someday.[23]

Niemöller had always been a staunch nationalist and anti-Communist. Yet he did not uncritically accept the West as the "good" to Communism's "evil." These dueling impulses had been on display since early in the military occupation. In June 1945, the US Office of Strategic Services (OSS) interviewers reported that Niemöller believed "Germany would soon come entirely under Russian influence," partly because of the US plan to reduce troop numbers in Europe, and "partly because it seemed to him the only spiritual power in Germany at present, aside from Christianity, and the most likely legatee of political discontent."[24] In 1947, the US State Department received a report issued by a group of British clergy who had visited Germany. The churchmen said that even though US policy had changed in 1946, Niemöller still refused to support "a crusade against Communism, a notion that had its strongest support in America." Instead, Niemöller was "convinced that Europe had only two alternatives: to be either the battlefield or the bridge between America and Russia. If she were the battlefield, that is the end. There will be no more Europe after that." Niemöller made clear even at this point that he believed "America could not possibly win in Europe." If war came, "the German people would be 90 per cent for Russia." Even as the appeal and the influence of Communist politics in Western Europe declined in the wake of the Marshall Plan, Niemöller continued to think that people would support democracy only until war erupted, and then they would largely support the Soviets. He was of the opinion that "conditions in the [E]astern zone had become progressively better and were in fact bearable," while in the Western zones "everything had become progressively worse."[25]

Niemöller believed that the increased toleration of Christianity in the Soviet Union since the war supported his idea that a bridge between the superpowers was possible. Niemöller believed that Stalin's embrace of the Russian Orthodox Church since the early days of the Second World War had not been strictly a political ploy but was instead indicative of the Soviet Union's acceptance of religion as a vital motivating force. Therefore, according to the churchmen, Niemöller asserted that everything about the superpowers "seemed in irreconcilable conflict, yet there was one element in common—the Christian church." Niemöller emphasized that one "should not underestimate the extent of the survival of the church in Russia. The church had been an effective influence there as well as in the West." By being such a bridge, the Christian faith could reconcile "certain elements . . . and the edge of conflict [could be] removed from essential differences" between the two superpowers.[26]

After the division of Germany, Niemöller continued to push for reunification and, after the outbreak of the Korean War, for West German neutrality in the

Cold War. He opposed West German rearmament, fearing it could only result in the destruction of Germany. He believed the Berlin blockade had been a clear warning to Germans from God. He also made the odd suggestion (an idea he held onto for quite some time) that under the auspices of the United Nations, Sweden should be given control of Germany, a task he thought would require only five thousand Swedish soldiers to accomplish.[27]

Niemöller's beliefs and statements stood in stark contrast with those of Adenauer and the CDU, in which Protestants were an important component. But Protestant concerns about the widening East-West divide ran deep. In a confessional meeting at Darmstadt in February 1950, officials agreed that division remained undesirable, but that it would be wrong to advocate a crusade against Bolshevism, since "Bolshevists stand in as great a need of God's Word as others." But they also accused Niemöller of following the ideas of his mentor, Karl Barth, by "trying to make Bolshevism look harmless," something they considered to be potentially "catastrophic."[28] The connection with Karl Barth—the author of the famous anti-Nazi Barmen Declaration of 1934—was significant because he had been the primary ideological force behind the Bekennende Kirche (the Confessing Church, which had challenged Nazi efforts to bring Protestantism under state control) movement in Nazi Germany. The Swiss theologian had long distrusted the West and Communism equally. In 1946, he claimed that Europe was "being ground between two millstones."[29] As the Americans would come to see it, to Barth, Niemöller, and their followers, "military or ideological resistance to Communism is unethical as long as so much social evil persists in the Western system. The tendency is to refuse to defend, or at any rate fight for, the free democratic ideals associated with Western civilization because freedom has not adequately insured the victory of goodness."[30]

This complicated ideological platform—in many ways an early call for a Third Way for Germans between the superpowers—made clear that Niemöller's first priority was Germany. In April 1950, Niemöller lamented that the Nazi years, defeat, and division had robbed Germans of their identity.[31] Moreover, he was convinced that the superpowers *wanted* to keep Germany divided. The West used the specter of totalitarianism to frighten Germans into supporting its cause, while the East promised unity and social order. Neither side could deliver, Niemöller argued. The choice between the two sides was thus a false one, and instead the only option for Germans was to be either "a battlefield for the warring elements of East and West" or "a bridge between them." Only by doing so through faith in Jesus Christ could Germany and humanity survive.[32]

Niemöller also believed that the division of Germany ensured Catholic dominance of the western state. He considered the Catholic Church—because of its support of Adenauer's policies—to have embraced the West and the idea of a crusade against Communism.[33] In an interview with the *New York Herald Tribune* that would become notorious, Niemöller was quoted as saying that the new West German government was "conceived in the Vatican and born in Washington," and that most Germans would prefer a unified Germany dominated by Communism over permanent division.[34] Niemöller repeated the same charges several days later to the *Wiesbadener Kurier*, lamenting that the war had made eastern Germany Polish and Catholic, while central Germany was dominated by the Russians and West Germany had become a Catholic state.[35] Konrad Adenauer and the Allied High Commissioners experienced "pained embarrassment" as a result of Niemöller's words.[36] In the uproar that followed, Niemöller claimed that he had been quoted out of context, insisting he had only wanted to point out the significant losses to Protestantism caused by the division of Germany. But he continued to argue that "there will be no lasting peace in Germany as long as the division between two opposing power groups continues." The division could not produce a "true peace," so Germans had a duty to "seek a way out of this dilemma," which to him meant a return to the original stipulations of the Potsdam Agreement (which, ironically, he had denounced in 1945) that promised a unified German state. If Germans did not openly challenge the superpowers' division of their country, they and the rest of the world faced destruction.[37]

Niemöller's outspokenness put the leadership of the EKD in a very uncomfortable position. Because of Niemöller's international prominence as an anti-Nazi and his role as the head of the EKD foreign office, censoring him or disagreeing with him openly could hurt the standing and support of the EKD abroad, while supporting him could alienate Protestants in West Germany, many of whom (particularly in Bavaria) supported division and rearmament. Otto Dibelius, the new president of the EKD, was the bishop of Berlin-Brandenburg and thus had jurisdiction over parishes in both the West and the East. Despite his fierce anti-Communism, he tried to adopt a middle course, but he stopped short of taking an official position on the division of Germany and on West German rearmament. Clearly, Dibelius feared doing so would bring reprisals against Protestants by East German authorities. Privately, though, a number of Niemöller's colleagues were worried. Wurm chimed in from retirement, saying that while he agreed with Niemöller on many political issues, he believed that Niemöller and Barth (a longtime nemesis of Wurm's) "in an almost perverse manner" dangerously underestimated the Soviet threat.[38] Publicly, though, the EKD defended Niemöller, saying his words in the *New York Herald Tribune* interview had been taken out of context.[39] Officially, the EKD maintained that taking sides on division, rearmament, and the East-West conflict would be a political act that the church had traditionally tried to avoid, but Niemöller was not asked to resign his position and ultimately the controversy did not silence his outspokenness.[40]

## EKD and Allied Responses

In part because of the ongoing issues with Niemöller, by early 1951 elements in the US High Commission felt compelled to use the situation with the churches and Communism to their advantage. A very frank memo to the State Department in early 1951 argued that the Protestant churches could be a vital source of anti-Communist agitation against East Germany, given their ability to communicate across zonal boundaries, but that these "very circumstances . . . which facilitate Church resistance to the East German regime, namely the position of the Church as a bridge between East and West Germany via which East German anti-Communist elements can be fed, also makes the churches vulnerable to pressure from the GDR." Because of the complex interplay of these issues, the United States needed to identify those in the Protestant churches "who render effective opposition to the Communist regime out of their conviction of the basic incompatibility between the Church and the Communist state."[41]

East German actions had helped bring the Americans to these conclusions.[42] The French reported in September 1950 that relations between Protestant leaders in Berlin and GDR officials had soured during the year despite efforts by ecclesiastical leaders to maintain their "neutral" stance between East and West Germany. East Germany wanted all church welfare organizations to coordinate their efforts solely through the state-run Volkssolidarität (People's Solidarity), an act that would cut off those organizations from the support they received from the West. East Germany also attempted to expropriate church-owned farms and banned imports of newsprint for the churches, further hurting the churches' ability to release publications.[43] Dibelius and other Protestant leaders protested these measures to East Germany's chairman of the council of ministers, Otto Grotewohl, who responded by denouncing Dibelius's recent visit to the United States, after which the bishop had seemed to become much more forceful in his criticisms of East Germany. Grotewohl accused Dibelius of being a lackey of the United States and spent a great deal of time discussing Dibelius's past dealings with the Nazis as proof of the bishop's fascist credentials.[44] Certainly Dibelius's concurrent attempts to broker meetings between West and East German officials did not help bolster his reputation in the halls of either German government. Dibelius offered repeatedly to mediate a "neutral" meeting between Adenauer and Grotewohl. This was motivated partly by the need to respond to the challenges posed by

Niemöller and partly by Dibelius's own desire to reduce East-West tensions and restore German national and Protestant unity.

The Americans dismissed Dibelius's proposal as "a gratuitous gesture made in the hope that it would ward off further action by the GDR against the church," labeling it typical wishful thinking among those Protestant leaders "who are still clinging to the fond hope that they can save the church behind a façade of political neutrality."[45] The Protestants did not seem either to realize or to care that their calls for unity were used by the East Germans and Soviets for propaganda against West German rearmament and the division of Germany. To the Americans, the unresolved situation with Niemöller was having very adverse effects on the ability of the Protestant churches to confront the realities of Communism in East Germany and in the Cold War more broadly.

Highlighting and exacerbating these growing tensions was the bold decision by the EKD to resuscitate for the first time since the end of the war their yearly Kirchentag, a national meeting of Protestant leaders and laity that was historically a centerpiece of the German Protestant year. Most importantly, the meeting would take place throughout all sectors of Berlin, thus literally crossing and challenging the East-West divide. This threatened to bring a number of elements of the broader East-West tension to a head, depending on the response of East Germany and the behavior of participants at the congress. Estimates were that at least a quarter of a million people would attend. Most disturbing to the Americans were the regular meetings between representatives of the Brandenburg church and representatives of East Germany to discuss their potential cooperation in putting on the Kirchentag. Supposedly Adenauer had been approached about the event and had reacted positively to the idea, as it might produce some East-West dialogue. The East Germans had even suggested including Niemöller and Heinemann in the gathering; no one in the Western Allied camp could predict what either man might say publicly if he attended. In addition, East Germany might pack the event with its own supporters and create a propaganda coup against the West German policies on division and rearmament.[46] The Kirchentag clearly presented possibilities for renewing discussions about matters with which the Protestant leaders were most concerned—restoration of German unity and thus the preservation of German Protestant unity—in the symbol of the divided capital.

The Kirchentag took place July 11–15, 1951. At its opening, GDR president Wilhelm Pieck made clear East Germany's aim for the event, calling on each attendee "as a German and as a Christian [to] stand up for preservation of peace and for the restoration of the unity of Germany."[47] But after the fact, the Americans concluded that the propaganda value of the event to East Germany had been negligible and did not seem to have resulted in any major Protestant shift over the division of Germany and West German rearmament. Yet US officials remained concerned that the EKD was playing a dangerous game with East Germany by courting the support of its leaders and naively downplaying the very real threats posed by Communism. The fact that ecclesiastical leaders at the event had stood at the opening ceremonies with Pieck and other prominent East German officials underscored these fears. The event also proved to the Western Allies that the EKD could be a rallying point for Germans' spiritual concerns.[48] The EKD, for its part, hoped that the Kirchentag proved that it could preserve neutrality and work to be the bridge between East and West that could perhaps restore German and confessional unity.[49]

Dibelius used the success of the Kirchentag to continue putting forward Protestant ideas that sometimes seemed quite similar to the "radical" ones pushed by Niemöller. In an attempt to clarify the EKD's positions and in further efforts to act personally and officially as a bridge, in October 1951 Dibelius penned an article in *Christ und Welt*, discussing the position of the EKD "between East and West." He stated that "before God there is no difference whether a German shoots a German or a Russian or a Frenchman." But Dibelius framed this in terms of German identity: "To be sure, murder is of course always murder; but since Cain slew his brother Abel, fratricide has always meant something terrible to the Christian conscience." The bishop denounced the idea of a crusade against Communism or on behalf of democracy and also rejected Martin Luther's "just war" theory. He concluded that "the Church with all means at its disposal must use its influence to prevent conflicts between nations and to settle peacefully any conflict which may arise."[50]

Yet Dibelius also singled out Communist nations for criticism, saying that the ultimate educational goal of Communism was the "liquidation of the remains of religious belief and above all the belief in God." Dibelius identified the mass arrests, secret trials, and unknown fates of many in the East, as well as the use of slave labor, to support his statements. Dibelius made clear that "no politician need fear that the Evangelical Church in Germany can throw itself into the arms of the East." In a thinly veiled swipe at Niemöller, Dibelius added that "everyone knows how the few 'progressive' pastors and their declarations are to be regarded." As a result, he said, the EKD would work to facilitate any dialogue between East and West. On the related issue of West German rearmament and conscription, the EKD would neither oppose nor endorse either. The EKD would continue to ask questions and discuss the morality of political, international, and military events but would not rule on whether or not it was more Christian to support a rearmed or a neutralized Germany.[51]

The Americans believed Dibelius had played right into the hands of

East Germany by taking "a neutral but not passive position on the East-West question." They concluded that East Germany hoped to "minimize or eradicate the idea that Communism poses a danger for the Christian, and break down animosity towards the Communist political program, particularly by exploiting the concept of Christian brotherhood and peace to promote its campaign for German unity." East Germany continued to hold great hopes that the Kirchentag would be the beginning of a path toward solutions in line with their policies. This, combined with Niemöller's protest against West German rearmament in late July, had given East Germany hope that its policies could be realized.[52]

But concern soared in January 1952 when Niemöller surprised the Western Allies by visiting Moscow at the invitation of the Russian Orthodox patriarch. The US embassy worried that the visit—obviously approved by the Kremlin—could signify the beginning of a Soviet plan "to exploit Niemöller's support for [the] world 'peace' movement."[53] Niemöller told the US press that he had made the trip to Moscow to "strengthen the cause of peace through church channels" and to plead for the release of the thousands of German POWs still held in the Soviet Union. Niemöller said his visit was "non-political" and primarily for "ecumenical purposes," descriptions that the US embassy believed needed to be "taken well salted" by Washington.[54] Despite concerns that Niemöller would make a statement supporting Soviet policies of unification and neutrality in return for the release of some German POWs, this did not materialize.[55] Niemöller claimed to have seen "extraordinarily large crowds" in the two Russian churches he visited (six to eight thousand in one church; two to three thousand in the other), something he considered to be evidence of "genuine spiritual life" in Russia.[56] Niemöller considered the revival of music, art, and religion he saw in Moscow to be clear evidence of this, as well as the significant growth of the number of churches in Moscow and the high membership of the Russian Baptist Church (which he claimed outnumbered the membership of the Communist Party).[57]

Niemöller's visit to Moscow gained a great deal of international attention. Unsurprisingly, American officials believed Niemöller's impressions of the religious situation in Soviet Russia "represented wishful thinking" and that his expectations were "naïve."[58] A furious Adenauer considered the visit a stab in the back; he would not make his own visit to Moscow for three more years.[59] EKD officials again publicly defended Niemöller's visit as a way to raise the POW question with Soviet officials. But even some of Niemöller's closest friends and greatest supporters expressed grave concerns or outright anger. The Bundestag member Dr. Robert Tillman, for example, derided Niemöller for not recognizing that the patriarch of Moscow was "nothing more than Hitler's Reichsbischof Mueller," simply a stooge of Stalin.[60] But the strongest reaction came from Bishop Hans Meiser of Munich. Meiser demanded that Dibelius strip Niemöller of his offices in the EKD. Dibelius declined, not out of support for Niemöller but in the interest of preventing an open break within the EKD. Dibelius feared that such an event would cause up to 20 percent of the EKD's membership to break with the church. Therefore, he refused to support any internal moves to reduce Niemöller's influence.[61] Throughout this high-wire act, Dibelius continued trying to mediate between his feuding colleagues, between the German states, and between the superpowers. He proposed holding all-German elections on division and rearmament, and suggested that the EKD could supervise them. To increasing numbers of EKD officials, "the very thing which Dibelius and others found objectionable in Niemöller was now being advocated by Dibelius."[62]

By this point, the Western Allies had grown weary of the effects Niemöller was having on West German stability, as well as increasingly worried about them. They considered Niemöller to be truly motivated by the fear that West German rearmament would end any possibility of German reunification and that the creation of an army would widen the divide between East and West. This could bring about "retaliatory measures" by East Germany and an "increased bolshevization" of the East, including a massive military buildup. To complicate matters, the Americans believed that Niemöller saw the permanent division of Germany as the true goal of Adenauer's policy, in which West German military units would act as "a kind of police force to strengthen Adenauer's hand." It was clear that Niemöller and his supporters harbored deep distrust of the Catholic chancellor and the ruling government.[63]

But the Americans were also convinced that the EKD would not effectively counter the vocal Niemöller minority for fear of destroying itself. The EKD would not discipline Niemöller lest it appear that the German Protestant Church had come out in support of West German rearmament. Any moves that could further put German Protestant unity at risk could only increase Catholic influence in West Germany, something that the Americans accurately concluded was never too distant from Protestant debates.[64]

## Endgames

Ultimately, decisions taken by the Soviets and the East Germans in 1952–1953 resolved many of these issues and concerns. By the end of 1952, the Soviets and East Germans had largely abandoned their so-called peace offensive, which had provided the basis for their "support" of religious freedom and for Niemöller's initiatives. This reduced the attention given to Niemöller's advocacy and, correspondingly, the Western Allies' intense focus on him. These changes in Soviet and East German policies stemmed from the creation in February 1952 of a draft treaty for the European Defense Community and NATO's support of it. The Western Allies rejected the subsequent "Stalin Note" from the Soviet leader, which proposed full Allied and Soviet disengagement from Germany in return for a unified, neutral, and disarmed German state. In November 1952, Dwight D. Eisenhower, a man few expected to be soft on Communism, was elected to the US presidency. In March 1953, Joseph Stalin died, creating a void of leadership and policy direction in the Soviet Union and, by extension, in its satellite states that would take time to fill, thus leaving broader Communist policies toward religion in limbo. In addition, East Germany faced a growing labor crisis that would eventually erupt in revolt in June 1953. Lastly, West German elections in September 1953 resulted in massive victories for the CDU and its domestic and foreign policies.

Although this series of events ended any ability of the German churches to independently affect changes in East-West relations, the Western Allies continued to believe that both church bodies could still play a role in undermining Communism in East Germany, particularly through their activities in Berlin. This was especially true because the churches were still officially national institutions and therefore retained provisions for operations in East Germany (this changed after the construction of the Berlin Wall in 1961). This presented opportunities the Western Allies hoped to exploit, and German Catholic and some Protestant officials proved willing to work together with Americans to use religion as a force against the Communist bloc.[65]

Indeed, the legitimacy of such an approach seemed to be validated by subsequent developments in Eastern Europe, which amounted to de facto recognition by the Soviets and their satellites that the continued operation of Christian churches undermined their credibility as popular, free states. This proved especially true for East Germany, which struggled to be seen as a legitimate German state in contrast to West Germany. In June 1952, the Soviets and their satellite states began a crackdown on Catholic clergy and programs, reflecting similar changes in policy toward the Protestant churches in East Germany. A US report on Soviet affairs concluded that efforts were underway in Eastern Europe to subject Catholic churches there to the state in ways similar to the Soviet consolidation of the Russian Orthodox Church. The Soviets sought to reduce Catholic influence to "impotency" by greatly limiting Catholic programs, forcing the church to support state programs for youth and education, and decreasing state funds for the churches. With the church thus reduced, "the Communist state then plans to substitute itself as the arbiter of these affairs." The broader goal was to cut off local churches from communication with the Vatican and to eventually transform them into national churches that would be "subservient to the Communist state" in which they were located. Finally, Soviet bloc nations abrogated many concordats with the Vatican and arrested prominent Catholic leaders, among them József Cardinal Mindszenty of Hungary.[66]

Meanwhile, in London, Dibelius recorded a talk for broadcast on the BBC that "was devoted to proving that Communism was a religion." Dibelius argued that Communism was "not only a political Weltanschauung; it is not only a social movement, having the goal of helping the poor in the fight against the rich, the workers against the capitalists; but Communism is a religion." The religion of Communism could be confronted only by Christianity, a religion "for which an even greater number of people are ready to live and die." Dibelius considered that the Christian faith was "much stronger than all the other spiritual forces in the world" and was powerful especially in the East, "where the German has to defend himself [for] the second time in one generation against the force of a state which looks to the Christian faith with resolute hostility." Communism for all these reasons had to be confronted, but only the Christian faith could effectively counter and defeat it. Dibelius's view that only Christianity could defeat Communism helps explain his and the broader EKD belief that Allied political, military, and propaganda efforts could not defeat Communism; they could serve to only either complicate or worsen the ideological confrontation between the "good" of Christianity and the "evil" of Communism.[67]

Dibelius's words made clear to the Western Allies that in 1952 significant turning points had developed in the relations between East Germany and the EKD, and in the EKD's place in the growing Cold War order. Although Dibelius still had not made any definitive statements on rearmament and continued to oppose permanent division, his renewed boldness in attacking Communism effectively made EKD opinions on those matters moot to Allied authorities, at least in terms pressuring either West or East Germany.[68]

By this point, the Western Allies understood well that German Protestant sentiments about Communism, the division of Germany, national unity, and West German rearmament were not uniform, nor did they coincide with Catholic or Allied views. Although all these groups shared deep fears of Communism in general and the Soviet Union and the East Germany in particular, this consensus was only on the most general of levels; significant differences existed between all these groups over how best to confront the Communist threat politically, an idea that for the churches (especially the EKD) often blended with the spiritual despite their official division of the two realms. Unlike the Catholics, the EKD gave German unity precedence over questions of West German integration into Europe, despite lip service to the contrary. The EKD continued to oppose many of Adenauer's policies, which the United States feared could lead to strains within the CDU. In the end, these fears proved justified, as various Protestants—especially Martin Niemöller—openly disagreed with Adenauer's policies for West German rearmament and integration with Western Europe.[69]

Participation by the churches in anti-Communist opposition was deemed vital to the Allies, particularly the United States. The Americans believed strongly that Christianity could help destroy Communism in Europe, an outcome they believed through at least 1956 to be possible. Therefore, the Americans argued that Berlin needed to become more of a focal point for this work; East and West German bishops could meet there and religious radio programming could be broadcast from the capital into East Germany. Clearly, the Allies harbored more than dreams of using the churches in some way to challenge Communism in East Germany: it had become a policy goal.

## Conclusion

The evidence from Western Allied archives indicates that by the end of 1952, the threat posed by Communism to Germany had divided many Catholics and Protestants politically on the international issues most pressing to Germany, namely division and West German rearmament. Although both the German Catholic Church and the German Protestant Church remained ideologically opposed to Communism, they advocated different methods for meeting the Communist threat. Both church bodies were also in a position to assist the Western Allies in undermining Communist influence in East Germany, and both agreed that it indeed had to be challenged. However, this new state of affairs did not necessarily translate into open Catholic or Protestant support for the agendas of the Western powers in the Cold War. Indeed, subsequent decades would prove quite the contrary. The churches, in particular the EKD, were instrumental in establishing the roots of Third Way politics in Germany and throughout Europe, ideas that reflected widespread discomfort with both Soviet and Western (mostly US) influences in Europe and the fear of being caught in the middle of superpower conflicts that in the worst-case scenario could spell a nuclear end to European civilization.

The difficulties posed to the churches by the emerging Cold War also challenged their historical notions about their political responsibilities, particularly after the establishment of two rival German states in 1949. Although lending political support to East Germany was never seriously contemplated by either body, the German Catholic and Protestant Churches reached very different conclusions about supporting the West German state; Protestant leaders had much more difficulty recognizing West Germany as the legitimate postwar German state mainly because it did not encompass all of Germany. The division of Germany presented the EKD with a confessional crisis and nightmare scenario: it feared that political circumstances would rob German Protestantism of any real influence in either East or West Germany while destroying what it felt was the truest expression of the Christian faith. In this context, it is understandable why the EKD tried to walk such a fine line between East and West. It is also therefore understandable why the Western Allies paid such close attention to the Protestants on these issues.

But the EKD's claims that it was not taking a political position through its actions do not hold up under retrospective scrutiny, something the Western Allies recognized increasingly throughout the early 1950s. Like their Catholic counterparts who, as they had done before, fused political ideals with religious and doctrinal ones in their support of Adenauer and the CDU, Protestant leaders did the same in *not* affiliating themselves with a side in the tense years of 1949–1952. While many saw Niemöller's occasionally bizarre antics and naive ideas about the Soviet Union as a blend of political and spiritual convictions, the rest of the EKD also engaged in politics; *any* position they took—even official "neutrality"—had political ramifications, whether they wanted to admit it or not. In addition, Protestant refusal to openly support Adenauer's policies through their representation in the CDU clearly had political dimensions.[70]

To a significantly greater degree than the Catholics, the Protestants struggled with the fact that, contrary to their beliefs otherwise, the line between the spiritual and the political was not at all clear in the aftermath of Nazism and the Second World War. The Protestants from 1949 until 1952 seemed preoccupied more with Soviet and GDR efforts to control them than with Communist political and ideological agendas for religion and democracy, more focused on national and confessional unity than on taking a stand against the hostile ideas and activities of the Communist states against Christian churches and other dissenters, and more focused on maintaining their own power as a bloc than in incorporating their political, social, and spiritual actions with other groups in a larger effort to confront Communism.

Catholic leaders, meanwhile, could reinforce their visions of themselves as true resisters of totalitarianism through their support of Adenauer and through their condemnation of actions taken by Communist states against Catholic parishes. Catholic support of rearmament and integration with the West certainly underscored the church's longtime antipathy toward Communism, as well as its desire to see a re-Christianization of Europe, but it also underscores the broad German Catholic failure to take similarly bold stances and political positions against the Nazis. This in turn illustrates just how much the Nazis' ardent anti-Communism was a significantly influential factor in minimizing Catholic political decisions vis-à-vis the Nazi regime in 1933 and in their tacit or active support for various elements of the Nazi program.

The Western Allies showed from 1949 to 1952 that their ideological and political foci in Germany had changed from hunting down and punishing Nazis and reeducating Germany to restructuring Western Europe in order to contain and resist Communist expansion. Although this agenda certainly held ideological components that continued to embrace democracy and free markets and to denounce totalitarianism, the Western Allies made the conscious decision to pursue these in regard to Communism by letting those ideals' application to the Nazi past lapse. It is also well known that the Western Allies (as well as the Soviets) and the West Germans allowed a number of former Nazis to take up legitimate positions in German society and government, further illustrating the degree to which concerns about Communism had come to trump fears of resurgent Nazism. Granted, the Western Allies used their understanding of the Nazi past to support efforts at containment of Communism, the need for international laws against war crimes, and the necessity of international organizations like the United Nations, but these were largely lessons the Western Allies applied to their own pasts, not the German past. This had important consequences later in Germany, when new generations of Germans saw plenty in the wartime and postwar activities of the German churches, the Western Allies, and the Soviets to cause them to reevaluate the nature of politics, international relations, history, and even human existence.

## Notes

1. These issues lay at the heart of the German churches' problems with the Western Allies during the occupation and High Commission periods. For more details, see JonDavid K. Wyneken, "Driving Out the Demons: German Churches, the Western Allies, and the Internationalization of the Nazi Past, 1945–1952" (PhD diss., Ohio University, 2007).

2. It should be noted here that the Soviets and East Germans also saw uses for the churches in assisting their agendas. In particular, during the same periods discussed here, the Sozialistische Einheitspartei Deutschlands (SED; Socialist Unity Party) and Soviets sought to divide the German churches by promising religious freedom, pledging their support for a unified German state, and insisting that contrary to statements by the Western Allies and some German church leaders, socialism and Christianity were not antithetical in East Germany or in the broader Eastern bloc. This approach, though, was abandoned after 1949. See Sean Brennan, "'Christianity and Socialism Are Not Opponents': The Propaganda Offensive in Berlin-Brandenburg under Soviet Occupation concerning 'Religious Freedom' under Communism," *Religion in Eastern Europe* 29, no. 1 (February 2009): 26–44.

3. This note from Stalin to the Western Allies (March 1952) proposed to reunify the two German states, make the new entity a neutral country, and guarantee it basic freedoms of speech, press, religion, and the like. The Western Allies doubted the

sincerity of the plan and officially rejected the idea when Stalin objected to their demand that this new state be able to join NATO.

4. The study that comes closest to this is Frederic Spotts, *The Churches and Politics in Germany* (Middletown, CT: Wesleyan University Press, 1973).

5. Landesbischof Wurm to Bishop of Chichester, December 30, 1949, Evangelical State Church Archives (Evangelisch Landeskirchliches Archiv; hereafter ELKA), Stuttgart, Germany, Wurm *Nachlass* (hereafter WN), BN D1, 235.

6. Quoted in Marshall Knappen, "Informal Conference on Distinction between Religious Freedom and Political Activity of Churchmen, held at Military Government Headquarters, Frankfurt," August 6, 1945, National Archives and Records Administration (hereafter NARA), College Park, MD, Record Group (RG) 84, Records of the Department of State (hereafter DOS), 737/1. Also in Clemens Volnhalls, *Die Evangelische Kirche nach dem Zusammenbruch: Berichte ausländischer Beobachter aus dem Jahre 1945* [The Protestant church after the breakdown: The reports of foreign observers in the year 1945] (Göttingen: Vandehoeck and Ruprecht, 1988), 88. On Wurm and the war crimes trials in Germany, see JonDavid K. Wyneken, "Memory as Diplomatic Leverage: Evangelical Bishop Theophil Wurm and War Crimes Trials, 1948–1952," *Kirchliche Zeitgeschichte* 19, no. 2 (2006): 368–88.

7. Quoted in Volnhalls, *Die Evangelische Kirche*, 103; also in Stewart W. Herman Jr., Berlin, August 9, 1945, NARA, RG 737/1.

8. Quoted in US Political Advisor for Germany Robert Murphy to Secretary of State, "Reports by Stewart W. Herman Jr. of the World Council of Churches," October 15, 1945, NARA, RG 84, DOS, 862.404/9-1245.

9. "Report on the Protestant Church Situation in the British Zone of Germany," May 1946, National Archives (hereafter NA), Kew (London), United Kingdom, Foreign Office Records (hereafter FO) 1050/1503.

10. "Report of the [Ecumenical] Council's Delegates to the German Church," June 1946, NA, FO 1050/1503.

11. Headquarters, US Forces European Theater, Military Intelligence Service Center, APO 757, "Report on the German Church View," February 28, 1946, NARA, RG 260, Office of Military Government–Bavaria (OMG–Bavaria), Records of the Education Division, Correspondence and Related Records of the Central Office, 1945–1946, Box 278, 24.

12. "Report on the Protestant Church Situation."

13. Religious Affairs Branch, HQ British Military Government, "Report for Political Division," September 1949, NA, FO 1050/1591.

14. Spotts, *Churches and Politics in Germany*, 237. The EKD's creation in 1945 had been provisional, pending reestablishment of all necessary offices and communications.

15. Memo, *Neue Post*, October 15, 1949, Press and Radio Information Service, Information Services Branch, British Military Government–Berlin, NA, FO 1050/1591.

16. Religious Affairs Branch, HQ British Military Government, "Report for Political Division," July 1949, NA, FO 1050/1591.

17. Ibid.

18. Spotts, *Churches and Politics in Germany*, 243–46.

19. Brennan, "Christianity and Socialism," 41.

20. "Comments on the Meeting of Rat der E.K.I.D. and of Reichsbruederrat," October 27, 1949, NA, FO 1050/1591; Religious Affairs Branch, "Report for Political Division," September 1949.

21. Religious Affairs Branch, "Report for Political Division," September 1949.

22. Spotts, *Churches and Politics in Germany*, 243–345. It should be noted that Heinemann left the CDU and formed his own political party, the All-German People's Party. When it met with failure in 1957, he joined the rival Sozialdemokratische Partei Deutschlands (SPD; Social Democratic Party). He eventually served as president of West Germany as an SPD member from 1969 to 1974. For more on the issues involving Heinemann and the CDU, see David Clay Large, *Germans to the Front: West German Rearmament in the Adenauer Era* (Chapel Hill: University of North Carolina Press, 1996), 74–81; Konrad H. Jarausch, *After Hitler: Recivilizing Germans, 1945–1995* (Oxford: Oxford University Press, 2006), 37–38.

23. Office memorandum, US Government, September 22, 1950, NARA, RG 84, DOS, 862.413/9-2250.

24. "OSS-Report: Interview with Pastor Niemöller," June 18, 1945, NARA, RG 84, DOS, 737/2; also in Volnhalls, *Die Evangelische Kirche*, 21.

25. "Report by a Delegation of British Churchmen Visiting UK Occupation Zone of Germany," n.d., forwarded from Landreth M. Harrison, first secretary of the US Embassy in London, to Secretary of State, January 29, 1947, NARA, RG 84, DOS, 862.404/1-2947.

26. Ibid. For the most recent study of the true dynamics of the Stalin-Russian Orthodox Church relationship during the Second World War, see Steven Merritt Miner, *Stalin's Holy War: Religion, Nationalism, and Alliance Politics, 1941–1945* (Chapel Hill: University of North Carolina Press, 2004).

27. "Once More Dr. Niemoeller," NA, FO 1050/1498.

28. "Meeting of 'The Council of Brethren' of the Confessing Church at Darmstadt—Niemöller's statements discussed," February 15, 1950, NA, FO 1050/1498.

29. Quoted in Spotts, *Churches and Politics in Germany*, 238.

30. High Commission for Occupied Germany (HICOG) Bonn (Office of Political Affairs) to Department of State, "The Protestant Church in Germany (German Studies No. 7), April 22, 1952," July 25, 1952, NARA, RG 84, DOS, 862.413/7-2552.

31. English translation of Martin Niemöller, "What Can the Church Do for Peace?" (first published in German in *Stimme der Gemeinde*), April 1950, NA, FO 1050/1498; see also "Pastor Niemoeller's Role," *Spectator,* May 5, 1950.

32. "Vortrag des Herrn Kirchenpräsident, D. Martin Niemöller am 20. April 1950 in der Marienkirche Berlin" and "The Plight of the Germans—Summary of Dr. Niemöller's Sermon in St. Mary's Church, Berlin on April 20, 1950," both in NA, FO 1050/1498.

33. "Meeting of 'The Council of Brethren.'"

34. Quoted in letter from Lord Bishop of Chichester to Major General S. C. M. Archibald, March 20, 1950, NA, FO 1050/1498; see also "Full Text of the Niemöller Interview with the Herald Tribune," December 20, 1949, NA, FO 1050/1498.

35. Spotts, *Churches and Politics in Germany*, 240.

36. Ibid.

37. Open letter from Kirchenpräsident Niemöller to Bundesminister des Innern Dr. Heinemann, December 22, 1949, ELKA, WN, BN D1, 225. See also "Worum ging es wirklich? Offener Brief Kirchenpräsident Martin Niemöller an Bundesminister des Innern Dr. Heinemann" [What was it really about? An open letter from church president Martin Niemöller to federal minister of the interior Dr. Heinemann], *Stimme der Gemeinde*, 1950 Heft 1, NA, FO 1050/1498; also available at ELKA, WN, BN D1, 225.

38. HICOG Frankfurt [Office of Intelligence] to Department of State, "Niemoeller and the E.K.D. Council at Spandau," November 1950, NARA, RG 84, DOS, 862.413/12-2950.

39. Information and Security Section [UK High Commission] to Rev. B. Nisbet [Religious Affairs Section], January 1, 1950, NA, FO 1050/1498.

40. US Embassy in Berlin to Secretary of State, November 20, 1950, NARA, RG 84, DOS, 862.413/11-2050.

41. HICOG, Eastern Element, Berlin 524, to Department of State, "Possibilities of Anti-Communist Resistance within the German Protestant Church," February 9, 1951, NARA, RG 84, DOS, 862.413/2-951.

42. For a synopsis of the relationship between the Protestant churches and the fledgling German Democratic Republic, see Victoria Barnett, *For the Soul of the People: Protestant Protest against Hitler* (New York: Oxford University Press, 1992), 256–71. See also Mary Fulbrook, *Anatomy of a Dictatorship: Inside the GDR, 1949–1989* (Oxford: Oxford University Press, 1995), 87–101.

43. Fulbrook, *Anatomy*, 87–101.

44. L'Ambassadeur de France, Haut Commissaire de la Republique en Allemagne to Son Excellence Monsieur Robert Schumann, Ministre des Affaires Etrangères, "Situation de l'Eglise Evangélique en Zone Orientale" [The situation of the evangelical churches in the Eastern Zone], Godesberg, September 8, 1950, Archives of the French Occupation in Germany and Austria (Archives de l'occupation française en Allemagne et Autriche; hereafter AOFAA), Colmar, France, Record Group (RG) 25/8.

45. HICOG, Eastern Element, Berlin Sector, to Department of State, "Evangelical Kirchentag, Berlin, July 11–15," 1951, NARA, RG 84, DOS, 862.413/8-2451.

46. HICOG, Eastern Element, Berlin Sector, to Department of State, February 24, 1951, "Background on Evangelical Kirchentag to Take Place East and West Berlin July 11–15, 1951," NARA, RG 84, DOS, 862.413/2-2451.

47. HICOG Berlin 137, "Address by GDR State President Wilhelm Pieck to the Evangelical Kirchentag at Berlin," August 24, 1951, NARA, RG 84, DOS, 862.413/8-2451.

48. HICOG, "Evangelical Kirchentag."

49. English translation of Otto Dibelius, "Evangelical Church between East and West" (first published in German in *Christ und Welt*), October 25, 1951, NARA, RG 84, DOS, 862.413/11-2151.

50. Ibid.

51. Ibid.
52. HICOG, "Evangelical Kirchentag."
53. US Embassy in Moscow to Secretary of State, January 4, 1952, NARA, RG 84, DOS, 862.413/1-452.
54. Ibid.
55. US Embassy in Moscow to Secretary of State, January 8, 1952, NARA, RG 84, DOS, 862.413/1-452.
56. Ibid.
57. US Embassy in Moscow to Secretary of State, January 4, 1952.
58. Ibid.
59. Spotts, *Churches and Politics in Germany*, 252.
60. US Embassy in Moscow to Secretary of State, January 4, 1952. Reichsbischof ("Reich's Bishop") Ludwig Mueller was the head of the *Deutsche Christen* (German Christian) movement, which sought to Nazify German Protestantism. He was appointed to his position by Hitler in 1933 to help bring all of German Protestantism under direct state control. These efforts failed, despite Mueller's persecution of the Confessing Church and recalcitrant clergymen. He committed suicide in 1945.
61. Ibid.
62. HICOG Frankfurt to Department of State, "Annual General Synod of the VELKD (United Lutheran Church of Germany)," May 21, 1952, NARA, RG 84, DOS, 862.413/5-2152.
63. HICOG Bonn (Office of Political Affairs) to Department of State, "The Protestant Church in Germany" (German Studies No. 7), April 22, 1952," July 25, 1952, NARA, RG 84, DOS, 413/7-2552.
64. Ibid.
65. HICOG, "Possibilities of Anti-Communist Resistance."
66. "Communist Inroads on the Roman Catholic Church in Eastern Europe," June 23, 1952, NARA, RG 59, General Records, IIA [International Information Administration], Deputy Director for Field Programs, Box 4, File: "Religion and Communism."
67. US Embassy in London to Department of State, "Radio Talk by Bishop Dibelius," January 15, 1952, NARA, RG 84, DOS, 862.413/1-1553.
68. W. A. Visser't Hooft (World Council of Churches) to Department of State, cc: Bishop of Chichester, April 12, 1953, NARA, RG 84, DOS, 862.413/4-3053.
69. Ibid.
70. Barnett, *For the Soul of the People*, 272–83.

## References

### ARCHIVES

Archives of the French Occupation in Germany and Austria (Archives de l'occupation française en Allemagne et Autriche), Colmar, France

Evangelical State Church Archive (Evangelisch Landeskirchliches Archiv), Stuttgart, Germany

Archbishopric Archives (Erzbischöfliches Archiv), Munich, Germany
National Archives, Kew (London), United Kingdom
National Archives and Records Administration, College Park, MD

## SELECTED PUBLISHED WORKS

Barnett, Victoria. *For the Soul of the People: Protestant Protest against Hitler*. New York: Oxford University Press, 1992.

Besier, Gerhard, Boyens, Armin, and Lindemann, Gerhard. *Nationaler Protestantismus und Ökumenische Bewegung: Kirchliches Handeln im Kalten Krieg (1945–1990)* [National Protestantism and the ecumenical movement: Church actions in the Cold War]. Berlin: Duncker and Humbolt, 1999.

Brennan, Sean. "'Christianity and Socialism Are Not Opponents': The Propaganda Offensive in Berlin-Brandenburg under Soviet Occupation Concerning 'Religious Freedom' under Communism." *Religion in Eastern Europe* 29, no. 1 (February 2009): 26–44.

Spotts, Frederic. *The Churches and Politics in Germany*. Middletown, CT: Wesleyan University Press, 1973.

Volnhalls, Clemens. *Die Evangelische Kirche nach dem Zusammenbruch: Berichte ausländischer Beobachter aus dem Jahre 1945* [The Protestant church after the breakdown: The reports of foreign observers in the year 1945]. Göttingen: Vandehoeck and Ruprecht, 1988.

Wyneken, JonDavid K. "Driving Out the Demons: German Churches, the Western Allies, and the Internationalization of the Nazi Past, 1945–1952 ." PhD diss., Ohio University, 2007.

———. "Memory as Diplomatic Leverage: Evangelical Bishop Theophil Wurm and War Crimes Trials, 1948–1952." *Kirchliche Zeitgeschichte* 19, no. 2 (2006): 368–88.

# CHAPTER 3

# From Sermon to Strategy

## *Religious Influence on the Formation and Implementation of US Foreign Policy in the Early Cold War*

*Jonathan P. Herzog*

In the late summer of 1953, thousands of balloons, each bearing a piece of religious literature or a Bible extract, took to the skies of Eastern Europe. Many thousands more would join them in the decade that followed. The balloons were hardly larger than those used at birthday parties, and yet they were considered weapons of war. US leaders hoped that they would land in city squares or schoolyards and fall into the hands of oppressed Eastern Europeans. Communist leaders tried to thwart the mission. They lodged complaints, made threats, and on occasion even instructed their militaries to fire on the balloons as they drifted lazily across the countryside.

The project was the idea of Billy James Hargis and Carl McIntire, two fundamentalist Protestant radio preachers. As for its merits, the US State Department was ambivalent, but newly elected president Dwight D. Eisenhower interceded and approved the plan. Bearing the imprimatur of the president and managed by the Crusade for Freedom, an organization founded three years earlier by the US military governor of Germany, the balloons became less the half-baked notion of two evangelists and more the long arm of US foreign policy.[1] Religious groups in the United States eagerly gathered sacred literature and sent it to volunteers in Europe who sorted and attached the compositions to the helium dirigibles. The pamphlets and excerpts first took flight on September 4, 1953, when Americans launched five thousand balloons across the Czechoslovakian border. "A new wind is blowing," the first wave of balloon messages proclaimed. "A new hope is stirring."[2]

How were preachers' sermons transformed into foreign policy? It seems like a historical eccentricity that in the age of mutually assured destruction a mighty nation like the United States would entertain the notion of floating Bibles. Scholars scanning most Cold War histories will not find mention of this project or others like it. After all, most history books tell us that for Americans the Cold War was a conflict between rival economic and political systems—of Minuteman missiles, publicized images of Soviet bread lines, and well-planned celebrations of personal liberty. But for US policy makers, the Cold War was also a contest between religious systems, and the balloons were both weapons of war and instruments of foreign policy. In a sense, it is understandable that a foreign policy initiative like this has been lost in most narratives of the Cold War. After all, by the middle of 1953, the French were teetering in Indochina, the CIA had helped to install a new leader for Iran, and analysts around the world were watching as the Soviets navigated the turmoil caused by Joseph Stalin's death. But even though the Bible balloon efforts seemed small by comparison, they were no less emblematic of the way that US leaders evaluated and maneuvered their way through the Cold War.

A growing coterie of historians has taken note of the religious facets of US foreign policy during this conflict. The goal of their scholarship is not to rewrite the entire history of the Cold War but rather to dust off one of its influential but forgotten dimensions. While this enterprise is still a work in progress, the influence of religion on US foreign policy has certainly come into sharper focus. In his examination of religious influence on US relations with South Asia, Andrew J. Rotter argued that "religious thinking infuses states" and, by extension, the foreign policy they craft. Seth Jacobs showed that religious considerations were instrumental in the selection of Ngo Dinh Diem as the president of South Vietnam. William Inboden demonstrated how religious concerns weighed on the consciences and the policies of prominent politicians and policy makers in the international arena. David S. Foglesong emphasized the religious prism through which Americans understood the Soviet Union. These works of scholarship are part of a wider attempt by scholars to bring together diplomatic history and religious history, two fields that have managed to largely ignore each other, as Andrew Preston has noted.[3] Thus is Hargis and McIntire's idea one of many windows onto a neglected avenue of an exhausting struggle.

In cases such as that of the Bible balloons, the question of whether religious beliefs shaped US foreign policy during the Cold War is settled. But two other questions present themselves. Why, by 1953, had US policy makers understood the battle against Communism as profoundly religious? And how did they translate this conceptualization into action? In a sense, each balloon floating on the winds of Eastern Europe symbolized two processes: conceptualization and implementation. The former pertained to the way that Americans made sense of Communism, and the latter related to the way that this particular interpretation was translated into policy. To understand the influence of religious leaders and ideas on US foreign policy in the early Cold War, both processes require some elucidation.

The simplest and most convenient answer to the first question would be to say that US leaders have always had a penchant for such religious conceptualizations during wartime. From this perspective, the Cold War would be no different in consideration and execution from preceding conflicts. It is crucial to note, though, that across the centuries US leaders have often resisted the temptation to make such declarations. The aversion was not dictated by simple lack of opportunity. For example, the United States quarreled in its infancy with the Muslim Barbary pirates—a sort of gunboat diplomacy writ small and now remembered in the "Marines' Hymn" line "to the shores of Tripoli." The decades-long intermittent conflict possessed the right ingredients for any holy war: a Christian nation in the throes of a religious awakening arrayed against the Islamic dey of Algiers. Yet US leaders strove to define the escalating conflict in secular terms. The eleventh article of the 1797 Treaty of Tripoli proclaimed as much: "As the government of the United States of America is not in any sense founded on the Christian Religion . . . it is declared . . . that no pretext arising from religious opinions shall ever produce an interruption of the harmony existing between the two countries."[4] The harmony between the United States and the Barbary states was later sundered by ransomed seamen, naval battles, and ship-to-shore bombardments, but the battles turned, at least officially, on free commerce and national honor rather than on cross and crescent.[5]

Less than a century later, US warships once again stared down a distant power, this time the ailing Spanish Empire. Spain was not only undemocratic but Catholic as well, and more than a few Protestant clergymen in the United States publicized this religious difference. But any hope that war against the Spanish would create a crisis between Catholicism and Protestantism disappeared with the first roars of Commodore George Dewey's guns in Manila Harbor. America's "imperialism of righteousness," as one historian called the nation's late nineteenth-century expansionist urges, was notable not for religious difference but for religious concurrence. US Catholics applauded the Spanish-American War with such alacrity that all but the most hardened Protestant nativists abandoned hopes of framing the conflict in divisive religious terms. The nation's leaders cast it instead as a confrontation between despotism and democratic freedom.[6]

Recently, US policy makers were presented anew with the opportunity to view a conflict through the lens of religious difference. The attacks of September 11, 2001, brought the world's foremost Christian republic into confrontation with Islamic terrorists. From the suffocating clouds of debris over Manhattan, Washington, and Pennsylvania, a holy battle cry might have risen. Many US leaders did their best to ensure that it did not. When President George W. Bush announced America's inchoate plans for the coming "War on Terror" in an address before a joint session of Congress on September 20, he enjoyed the support of arguably the most united populace in a generation. He used the occasion to speak directly to the Muslim world, pausing in the middle of his address to proclaim, "We respect your faith. Its teachings are good and peaceful. . . . The terrorists are traitors to their own faith."[7] US leaders were reluctant to fight a holy war, notwithstanding neoconservatives who labeled the enemy "Islamo-fascism." The Bush administration even forced a lieutenant general who called the Second Gulf War a battle against Satan to make a series of embarrassing apologies before a worldwide audience.[8]

Not so with the early Cold War, when America's political and military leadership consciously constructed their Communist antagonists as not only evil but also spiritually incongruous. The nation's religious leaders were instrumental in laying the groundwork for such a view. From across a wide spectrum of faith traditions and denominations, they had spent the better part of two decades portraying Communism as a spiritual threat and bemoaning the secularization sapping US society of its sacred vigor. In the decades between the Bolshevik Revolution and the end of World War II, relatively few Americans were well versed in Communist writings and theory. As a result, a handful of opinion makers—many of them religious leaders—exerted a strong influence on the way that policy makers assessed the aims and threats of Soviet doctrine.[9] They saw in Communism not only a rival political and economic system of belief, but also an entire religious scheme complete with martyrs and missionaries, saints and sinners, sacred texts and dogma, dreams of redemption, and even an implied eschatology. The Cold War was in this sense a rare moment when Americans faced a theologically alien enemy. Although they could defeat political regimes with the usual implements of warfare, the annihilation of a religious system would require something more. To fight Communism, Americans would have to fight faith with faith.

One of the earliest and most complete US examinations of Communism as a religion came in the spring of 1931 from the theologian Reinhold Niebuhr, then a professor at Union Theological Seminary in New York. On the surface, he admitted that Communism appeared to be nothing more than a "highly scientific and irreligious social philosophy." But on deeper examination, Niebuhr realized it was a new religious movement. To him, Marx's works were the Communist bible, and the writings of Lenin achieved "a dogmatic significance for [Communism] comparable to that which the thought of Thomas Aquinas had for the medieval church." Having established a doctrinaire faith, Communists could expect a sea of converts. "The world is still looking for workable combinations of the certainty which encourages action," Niebuhr wrote, presaging the spiritual and psychological attraction to Communism that would worry US policy makers several years later.[10]

Throughout the 1930s, a string of analyses of Communism, written mostly by theologians, followed in Niebuhr's wake. After spending several months in a US Communist labor school, one religious writer was struck by the psychological similarities between zealous Christians and converted Communists. Communists had their missionaries, theologians, and even doubters. They wrote and sang their own songs, developing a hymnology akin to that of mainline faiths. Most important, the Communists he met shared the unflinching belief that theirs was the one true faith. Another theologian argued that Communism was actually an offshoot of Calvinism since its followers believed in a predetermined and inevitable historical process. "Marxism is, in fact, Calvinism secularised," he argued, "for submission to a process may have something of the mystic quality of submission to the will of God." Others disagreed, contending that "the vital principle in Marx's system is that man is sufficient for himself"—a stance with profound implications, since if humans were entirely self-sufficient, they would have no need for God.[11]

US Catholic leaders contributed significantly to this distillation of Communism into a religious system.[12] Catholic writers looked beyond the economic and political facets of Communism and readily saw a "social convulsion," "an awful disease," and a "false messianic idea." They considered Communism a mass religious neurosis. How else could one explain conversions by men and women with the most to lose in a Communist political or economic system? "If it were merely political or economic," wrote one contributor to *Commonweal*, "its appeal to individuals living in a state of comparative liberty and security would be inexplicable; but it is really the . . . arch-heresy of our age." The need for religion rested deep within the soul of all humans. Communism tapped this spiritual root, perverting it.[13] Those seduced by Communism no longer acknowledged the power and sovereignty of God. "A new world is rising," observed a monsignor in 1937, "a mechanical world peopled by soulless machines. The God-man shall be replaced by the Man-god."[14]

Two US Catholics were particularly instrumental in laying down this framework. Fulton Sheen—the intellectual priest who hosted a popular radio show beginning in the 1930s—made Communism a favorite target of his broadcasts. Sheen noted that Karl Marx was an atheist before he became a Communist, a significant observation since it inverted traditional conceptions of Communism and religion. Most religious intellectuals in the 1920s and 1930s observed that Communism bred an undying hostility to religion in the minds of its followers. But Sheen argued that Communism merely invaded spiritually weak hosts: the seductive promises of Marx would fail to penetrate the psyche of religiously grounded men and women. According to Sheen, America's increasingly liberal, materialistic, and secularized culture lowered resistance to Communist infection by enervating religious authority and diluting spiritual meaning. In 1935, he called for the creation of a "Catholic proletariat" and nearly got his wish three months later when four thousand Catholic employees from the New York Department of Sanitation rallied at the Astor Hotel, proclaiming that faith had inoculated them against Communism.[15]

Sheen's superior, Francis Cardinal Spellman, made his home at the nexus of religion and politics from the 1930s (while assisting President Franklin D. Roosevelt) until his death in 1967.[16] His political connections, sharp intellect, and public relations savvy made him the undisputed star of the US Catholic hierarchy during the early Cold War. When Communist puppet governments in Eastern Europe began imprisoning Catholic clergy in 1946, Spellman placed himself at the forefront of US outrage. In rallies around the Northeast, he claimed that the Communist mistreatment of church leaders in Europe proved that America was involved in a battle for its very soul against "satanic Soviet sycophants." In one New Jersey rally alone, an estimated 140,000 Catholics marched against Communist religious persecution. He also wrote letters of protest to politicians, teamed up with anti-Communist government officials like FBI director J. Edgar Hoover to write pamphlets, worked to influence Catholic policy makers, and used the power of the pulpit to convince all who would listen that the nascent Cold War was a holy battle. The pith of Spellman's rhetoric was evident in a 1949 sermon from St. Patrick's Cathedral: "A new god has come to you, my people. His fiery eyes do not flash through clouds of incense or from altar candles. They do not gleam from gold-framed darkened pictures of saints. . . . This is the red god. The Seine shudders at his impact and tries to break its banks. Westminster trembles before him like Jericho, and across the green ocean his shadow falls on the walls of the White House. Hosanna!"[17]

Although Jewish leaders in the United States joined the battle against Communism later than Catholics and mainline Protestants, by the early Cold War they too had thrown down the spiritual gauntlet. Some regarded the battle against an alien religious system as a unique opportunity to unite America's faiths in common indignation. Several of New York's rabbis, believing that spiritual conflict with Communism was unavoidable, sought alliance with

Catholics and Protestants. "It will not do," declared a rabbi from Temple Emanu-El, "if Catholics, Protestants and Jews eagerly petition the support of all men of faith when their own are touched, and remain silent and aloof, when others walk in the valley of the shadow."[18] Although Catholic and Protestant leaders often framed the religious threat of Communism in Christian terms, they welcomed Jewish cooperation at anti-Communist rallies at Madison Square Garden and the Hollywood Bowl.

Given the attention they attract in the modern US religious landscape, it may come as a surprise that evangelical Protestant leaders were not always at the forefront of the holy war against Communism. But once committed, evangelical leaders took up the torch of religious anti-Communism and carried it furthest into the conflict.[19] In 1946, the evangelical author Verne Paul Kaub did not construe the Cold War as a battle between Christianity and Communism. He, like most US political leaders, labeled it a conflict between Communism and the American way of life. But Kaub argued that Christianity undergirded the American way. Free enterprise, the doctrine of free will, republican government, and the sanctity of individuals were each a Christian doctrine. In short, as he insisted, "The rock upon which America was founded is the Christian faith." Even the American concept of history implied progress through providence, Kaub wrote, whereas Communists believed in economic determinism. Each person had to choose between one of these worldviews. "These two philosophies, Christianity and Communism, cannot logically exist in one heart and mind," he reasoned. "Either one or the other can be accepted, or both rejected, but both cannot consistently be accepted."[20] Other evangelicals took up this cause. In the 1950s, the psychiatrist-turned-preacher Fred Schwarz held religiously centered schools of anti-Communism in major cities around the nation. Meanwhile, in Tulsa, Oklahoma, the young evangelist Billy James Hargis built a radio and print empire called Christian Crusade, pioneering in the name of religious anti-Communism the grassroots communication and fund-raising techniques that conservative politicians would later employ to great effect.[21]

In US evangelical leadership during the early Cold War, the figure of Billy Graham towers over other preachers. Indeed, for a time, the North Carolina preacher's name seemed synonymous with the movement he led through revivals across America and throughout the world. His ascendancy began following a 1949 Los Angeles revival when the devout Christian anti-Communist and press lord William Randolph Hearst cabled to his newspaper editors a two-word order: "Puff Graham." The preacher made national sin and repentance a keystone of his message, warning audiences that unless America was reborn it risked destruction by the Soviets. Although he urged Americans to convert, Graham also believed in the power of Communist conversion. "Rather than try to shut up a Communist, I would try to bring him to Christ," Graham explained to a crowd in the Rose Bowl.[22] During a revival in London, he managed to convert a prominent British Communist leader, and he dreamed of launching a crusade in the heart of the Soviet Union, bringing Christ to the Russian workers and ending the Cold War with Bibles rather than bombs.[23] In books and pamphlets, on radio and television, and during revivals and rallies across the nation, religious leaders like Graham had defined Communism and, by extension, lighted a pathway toward its defeat. But implementation in the realm of foreign policy would depend on public servants.

If the rhetoric, insight, and umbrage of US religious leaders had gone no further than the conceptualization of the Cold War as a religious struggle, their contributions would still have been significant. Although they began laying the groundwork for a spiritual solution to the Communist menace in the early years of the Soviet Union, it took the exigency of conflict for many of their ideas to attain widespread acceptance in policy circles. The process by which messages from sermons became strategies for the nation is understandably muddled. Still, on examining the assumptions of national security directives, the words and deeds of US political leaders, and the protocol governing psychological warfare operations, it is clear that foreign policy implementation flowed in part from religious convictions. One can detect the language, ideas, and arguments of religious leaders within a number of foreign policy features, and this magnified considerably the consequence of America's holy war against Communism.

By January 1946, members of the US security community were beginning to conclude that the battle against Communism would be unprecedented and, to say the least, strange. One of the earliest formulations came from Edward F. Willett, who penned a top-secret report on January 14 called "Dialectical Communism and Russian Objectives." In it, he delved beyond the everyday machinations of state interest to examine the crux of Communist philosophy. Like Niebuhr two decades earlier, Willett concluded that Communism was more than a political movement: it was at once hostile to religion and itself quasi-religious. "Any relaxation in Communist opposition to religion," he wrote, "should probably be regarded more properly as a temporary departure to allay opposition rather than as a change in basic philosophy." He believed that Communist enmity toward religion was animated by a deeper moral impetus that justified any action, no matter how violent or evil, if it brought about the ideal Communist society.[24]

When applied to US national security, the full ramifications of the Communist faith crystallized. "It should be clear at the outset that under these circumstances the United States is laboring under a severe disadvantage," Willett warned. "Russia is a nation with the Messianic goal, the driving force around which a crusading spirit can be built up. Our driving force is only the somewhat passive concept of self-defense."[25] The United States would be at a severe disadvantage in a battle of asymmetric zeal—a conflict in which the fanatical war cries of Communist faith would drown out the American chants of simple state interest. Desperately needed, then, was a counterfaith—something to channel American fervor into the impending conflict.

Five weeks later, George F. Kennan, a State Department official in Moscow and the soon-to-be-proclaimed "father of containment," transmitted his famous "Long Telegram." He contended that the US policy makers' assumptions of Soviet behavior were flawed and dangerous. The Soviets could not be bridled with encomiastic expressions or bribed with promises of territory and monetary aid. The prophetic certainties of Marxism had found refuge in the traditional insecurities of the Russian soul, producing a nation that combined irrational hostility with deadly capability. The Soviet Union was being driven by an illogical internal engine, and external forces like foreign diplomacy could not shape its action.[26]

Although Kennan's work is often celebrated as a fresh breath of realpolitik in an age of ideological hyperbole, he, like Willett, could not avoid the psychological or even spiritual facets of any confrontation with the Soviets.[27] He viewed Communism as a seductive philosophy. Like Catholic commentators, he drew on the metaphor of disease to explain the Communist menace. Diseases rarely struck perfectly healthy bodies, he argued. They fed instead on weakened tissue. "Much depends on [the] health and vigor of our own society," Kennan explained. "This is [the] point at which domestic and foreign policies meet. Every courageous and incisive measure to solve [the] internal problems of our own people is a diplomatic victory over Moscow worth a thousand diplomatic notes and joint communiqués." In the vein of Willett a month earlier, Kennan believed that victory in the mounting Soviet conflict depended on internal vitality. Militarily, the Soviets were weak. But like Edmund Burke, who centuries earlier had grasped the true danger of French republicanism, Kennan understood that America was dealing with an armed doctrine whose greatest power was psychological. Against this new enemy, national self-confidence and preservation of the American way counted.[28]

These same assumptions continued to inform national security, most notably in the Cold War document NSC 68. Written in 1950 by Paul Nitze, who followed Kennan in the State Department's Policy Planning Department, it formed a blueprint for American assumptions into the fifties. Nitze broke with Kennan by advocating a perimeter defense, which would challenge Soviet encroachment worldwide, rather than a selective application of force. He also intensified the religious and spiritual concerns first voiced by Willett and Kennan. At times, NSC 68 resembled less a security document than a philosophical and spiritual treatise. The Soviets were "animated by a fanatical faith." They found existential meaning only by "serving the ends of the system." In this "perverted faith," Nitze wrote, Communist society "becomes God, and submission to the will of God becomes submission to the will of the system." Likewise, Americans drew strength from the "contagious" concept of freedom, thought by many military and political leaders in 1950 to flow from religion. Nitze summed up America's fundamental purpose with a quote from the Declaration of Independence: "With a firm reliance on the protection of Divine Providence, we mutually pledge to each other our Lives, our Fortunes, and our sacred Honor." The logic of force was joined with the logic of faith.[29]

In a sense, documents like NSC 68 merely formalized ideas that were already widely accepted by the US military command. In 1948, a year before he became the nation's first chairman of the Joint Chiefs of Staff, Omar Bradley delivered an Armistice Day speech in Boston that reflected on the acute need for spiritual guidance in the Cold War. "Man is stumbling through a spiritual darkness with the precarious secrets of life and death," he said. "The world has achieved brilliance without wisdom, power without conscience. Ours is a world of nuclear giants and ethical infants." A year later, Brigadier General C. T. Lanham, director of the Staff and Personnel Policy Board for the Defense Department, worried that US military prowess alone would be insufficient in winning a battle against a spiritually energized Soviet Union. "Over and over again," he said, "gigantic concentrations of physical power have gone down in defeat before a lesser strength propelled by conviction; . . . the Goliaths have perished at the hands of the Davids." He continued: "Therefore, without deprecating our armed might and the evil circumstances that make it necessary, I contend that we must be increasingly vigilant lest we come to evaluate our strength and our security exclusively in terms of material power. . . . To do otherwise is to build a colossus of straw."[30] Americans possessed the bomb, a powerhouse economy, and an unparalleled culture of technological achievement. But for policy makers, physical power in the face of spiritual zeal was no power at all.

US political rhetoric underscored in the public arena the conclusions reached privately in Washington's corridors of power. President Harry S. Truman would never have been mistaken for an overtly religious man, but he and his administration readily tapped into the spiritual perceptions of Communism circulated by the nation's religious leaders and security analysts. He often contrasted a US system grounded in religious faith with the Soviet system where "men exist merely to strengthen the state or to be cogs in the economic machine." During a speech on Christmas Eve, 1950, he called Communism "godless" and noted that "democracy's most powerful weapon is not a gun, a tank, or a bomb. It is faith—faith in the brotherhood and dignity of man under

God." Within the Truman administration, Attorney General Tom C. Clark traveled the nation parroting lines from religious leaders. Warnings against Communism's "false prophets" and "black bible" became popular parts of his public-speaking repertoire, and for him, the Cold War could be reduced to the "choice between God and Mammon."[31]

The Truman administration went further than rhetoric. In the summer of 1947, the president began cultivating an alliance with the Vatican. US diplomatic relations with the Holy See had been historically poor, and for long periods nonexistent. In 1940, Roosevelt had dispatched Myron C. Taylor to Rome to establish closer ties with the pope during World War II. Taylor, an Episcopalian, had conveyed Roosevelt's pleas for Pius XII to soften the Catholic Church's stance on Communism. Truman sent FDR's emissary back to Rome following World War II, much to the consternation of some Protestant leaders.[32] But this time the envoy was not ordered to smooth over religious tensions between Moscow and the Vatican. He was charged with inflaming them.

Truman began the flirtation with an extraordinary letter on August 6, 1947. "Your Holiness, this is a Christian Nation," he announced, proposing an alliance of moral and religious forces and a crusade by men of goodwill across the world against the evil encroachments of Communism. "I believe that the greatest need of the world today," he confided, "is a renewal of faith." On August 26, Pius XII wrote back. "Certainly," the pope asserted, "Your Excellency and all defenders of the rights of the human person will find wholehearted cooperation from God's Church."[33] In the spring of 1948, Truman began a new round of correspondence with the pope, his language peppered with biblical allusion and prophetic imagery. He pledged America to the cause of bringing about the kingdom of God on Earth. Truman also argued that the basic acceptance of Christ underlay all of secular society, from schools and marketplaces to town halls and world parliaments. Pius was skeptical, for understandable reasons. In the end, America's alliance with the Vatican remained in spirit only. Still, the White House publicized the letters to Pius, giving Americans and Soviets alike a whiff of Truman's religious convictions.[34] Although some Protestants objected to their president's sudden chumminess with Rome, few could take offense at his larger message.[35]

If Americans wondered whether or not Dwight D. Eisenhower had imbibed the same conceptualization of Communism, they needed to wait no longer than Inauguration Day, 1953. Eisenhower began the ceremony with a self-composed prayer, delivered a speech that meditated on good and evil in the world, and kicked off his inaugural parade with a religious float bearing the motto In God We Trust. His administration often made Truman's rhetoric seem tame by comparison. "What is our battle against Communism if it is not a fight between anti-God and a belief in the almighty?" asked one of his campaign statements.[36]

Perhaps the ultimate emblem of the influence of religious conceptions of Communism within the Eisenhower administration was the secretary of state. A prominent Protestant layman, John Foster Dulles had largely accepted the religious construction of Communism developed by other religious leaders. As the US secretary of state, he had ample opportunity to translate his beliefs into policies. The son of a Presbyterian preacher, Dulles was a moralist not unlike the crusaders of a generation earlier. He was instrumental in convincing Eisenhower to open his inauguration with a public prayer, and he was convinced that the doctrine of containment was too morally and religiously bankrupt to win a holy war. Dulles was so deeply influenced by religious interpretations of the Cold War that the historian William Inboden has argued he "took the strategic architecture of containment and sacralized it."[37]

The influence of religious leaders on foreign policy was also notable in America's psychological warfare operations, programs approved by Truman and strengthened by Eisenhower. Soviet leaders had grasped the power of propaganda even before the Bolshevik Revolution, and by the beginning of the Cold War, US leaders recognized the tremendous advantage that such psychological enterprises afforded their chief adversaries. The Soviets framed their chief message simply and effectively: they offered change at a time when for millions the status quo seemed agonizing. US propaganda concentrated on a wide array of differences between the free world and the Communists, but religious difference proved to be one of the sharpest contrasts between the two systems.

By December 1947, Truman's newly created National Security Council (NSC) had decided that America was losing the battle of information and ideas. NSC 4 reported that the Soviets were "employing psychological, political and economic measures designed to undermine non-Communist elements in all countries." The US psychological response, on the other hand, was uncoordinated and in many cases nonexistent. "The present world situation," the report concluded, "requires the immediate strengthening and coordination of all foreign information measures of the US government designed to influence attitudes in foreign countries in a direction favorable to attainment of its objectives."[38] In early 1948, Congress passed the US Information and Educational Exchange Act, which gave US psychological operations legal cover and funding.

NSC 68 reaffirmed previous mandates for psychological operations, and one year later, in April 1951, Truman created the Psychological Strategy Board (PSB). Comprising the CIA, Departments of State and Defense, and Joint Chiefs of Staff, the PSB would coordinate all US psychological operations.

Afforded a broad mission, the PSB wasted little time before investigating the potential role of religion in psychological warfare. In its first few months of existence, the PSB compiled an "Inventory of Instrumentalities" that cataloged all possible avenues of psychological attack against the Soviets. Religion had a central role:

> The potentialities of religion as an instrument for combating Communism are universally tremendous. Religion is an established basic force which calls forth men's strongest emotions. Because of the immoral and un-Christian nature of Communism and its avowed opposition to and persecution of religions, most of the world's principal religious organizations are already allied with the cause of the free nations. Our over-all objective in seeking the use of religion as a cold war instrumentality should be the furtherance of world spiritual health; for the Communist threat could not exist in a spiritually healthy world.[39]

The PSB released two major reports in May 1952, one estimating the efficacy of psychological operations and the other establishing a future strategic framework. Both underscored the important role religion could play in achieving US strategic interests. Religion was one of the few values uniting the world that the Soviets could not co-opt. If the United States could define the global conflict as a holy war between traditional religious faiths and Communism rather than an economic and political struggle between the oppressed and powerful, the Soviets would be at a severely disadvantage. "The United States can retain its allies," the PSB concluded, "only by persuading them that the US position is to their best interests and comes within the framework of their moral and spiritual beliefs as well as the interests and moral and spiritual beliefs of the United States." Future psychological operations would portray US policy as a "truly Christian approach . . . characteristic of the American people." In a holy war, simply lauding one's own beliefs was never enough, and the PSB suggested a direct attack on the Soviet faith, calling for psychological operations that would refute the teachings of prophets like Lenin and Stalin and cast doubt on their "deification" and creed.[40]

The State Department took these findings seriously. It operated 165 "information centers" around the world—special libraries where foreigners could obtain books, newspapers, and pamphlets. Beginning in 1952, the department ensured that each information center contained "balanced collections of US publications which portray America's spiritual heritage and religious values in true perspective." Ample quantities of the Bible began arriving, along with subscriptions to religious periodicals like *Christian Century*, *Commonweal*, and *Commentary*. The State Department also sent periodic religious news dispatches to its embassies, complete with analyses of each event's implications for Communism. The Voice of America (VOA) enlisted the aid of US religious leaders, who broadcast messages into nations under Communist control. The archbishop of Baltimore, for example, addressed the Eastern bloc in a 1951 Christmas message. "These feasts have special meaning for everyone throughout the Christian world, but they have special meaning for you, dear friends in Hungary and Czechoslovakia who languish under a tyrant's rule," he said. "Take courage from the example of St. Stephen, who gave his life in its very prime rather than deny Christ."[41]

Roger Lyons, VOA's director of religious programming, oversaw the spiritual offensive. Assisted by a panel of religious advisers, he used his lineup to paint two portraits. The first depicted the importance of religious freedom and attacked the Communist animus toward religion directly. But Lyons also tried to emphasize the importance of religion in US society. "Spiritual and moral factors enter into every phase of our output, and not just into specifically religious services," he reported in 1952. "They permeate all our programs whether we are trying to give a picture of the life of a farmer in the mid-West, covering a meeting of the American Foreign Policy Association, or a village church service." Lyons went beyond merely combating the "colossus of straw" image; he created in the minds of foreigners a righteous American state permeated with religious zealotry. In this ideation, the United States seemed the perfect foil for Communist designs—a nation ready to martyr itself so that others could worship God.[42]

While Voice of America focused its religious propaganda on the masses, the PSB decided to target the Communist elite. In 1952, the agency initiated the US Doctrinal Program to "create confusion, doubts and loss of confidence in the accepted thought patterns of convinced Communists, captive careerists . . . and others under Communist influence susceptible to doctrinal appeals." Rather than broadly assaulting Communism with generalities, the Doctrinal Program would pierce the intellectual apparatus holding Communist ideology together. It did not take long for analysts to realize that the Communist intolerance of religion and rejection of individual morality were major Soviet vulnerabilities. They drew up detailed plans for doctrinal warfare, and charged various government agencies with carrying them out.[43]

The Eisenhower administration provided US psychological operations with a much-needed second wind, in part to define the Cold War in religious terms. The president created two new agencies to coordinate and implement the psychological strategies in discussion since 1951: the US Information Agency (USIA), which pulled propaganda operations out from underneath the State Department's complex bureaucracy, and the Operations Coordinating Board (OCB), which was designed to implement the broad recommendations of the National Security Council.[44] The USIA and the OCB cooperated closely on psychological operations, and both continued their predecessor agencies' work on religious matters. NSC 162/2, which laid out Eisenhower's initial security plan, cited the need for "mobilizing the spiritual and material resources necessary to meet the Soviet threat."[45] In response, the OCB created the Ideological Subcommittee on the Religious Factor and charged it with developing a "spiritual factor" in Cold War national security.[46] In the years of Eisenhower's presidency that followed, psychological warfare operations would continue to exploit the perceived religious fissures between Communist states and the West.

When the first Bible balloons floated upward in 1953, they represented the culmination of a process. US religious leaders had spent the previous decades building a narrative of Communism that emphasized its spiritual strengths and weaknesses. When the Soviet Union emerged from the ashes of World War II as America's chief adversary, US policy makers drew on this narrative. Given its dominant conclusion—that faith must be combated with a counterfaith—the balloon projects and others like it were not far-fetched or irrational. Just as Eisenhower and Truman had presided over the creation of a military-industrial complex, so too did they supervise the creation of a spiritual-industrial complex—a fusion of religious ideas, national resources, and state policy.

The last US Bible balloon made its way past the Iron Curtain in 1959. No one knows what became of it. In the end, it proved no more effective than other religiously inspired programs of foreign policy in turning the tide of war—a tide dictated then, as it is now, by the application of earthly power. Whether its contents were spilled in the wilderness by some Russian-made bullet or collected furtively by a schoolchild, the contrast between that simple balloon and the latent fury of the atomic age borders on the inexplicable. When thinking about the Cold War, it is easy to envision the red telephones, nuclear submarines, and backyard fallout shelters. But we would do well to think also of those rubber balloons borne aloft on a wing and a prayer.

## Notes

1. The Crusade for Freedom was the creation of General Lucius D. Clay, the US military governor of Germany, who in 1950 envisioned a "spiritual airlift" in Eastern Europe to complement the Berlin Airlift then under way. Clay's program boasted an impressive board of directors that included twelve US senators, and it funded both a religiously themed liberty bell for West Berlin as well as the fledgling Radio Free Europe. See "A Spiritual Airlift," *New York Times*, October 22, 1950; and

National Crusade for Freedom Council, report, July 24, 1950, Library of Congress, Washington, DC, Henry Luce Papers, Box 33, Folder 11.

2. "Balloon Barrage Grows," *New York Times*, August 19, 1951; "Reds Shoot at Balloons," *New York Times*, August 28, 1951; "U.S. Ban on Sending Bibles to Reds by Air Reported," *New York Times*, August 31, 1953; and "Bible 'Airlift' Lauded: Eisenhower Approves Plan to Send Them over Iron Curtain," *New York Times*, September 5, 1953.

3. Andrew J. Rotter, "Christians, Muslims, and Hindus: Religion and US-South Asian Relations, 1947–1954, *Diplomatic History* 24, no. 4 (2000): 593–94; Seth Jacobs, "'Our System Demands a Supreme Being': The U.S. Religious Revival and the 'Diem Experiment,' 1954–1955," *Diplomatic History* 25, no. 4 (2001): 589–624; William Inboden, *Religion and American Foreign Policy, 1945–1960: The Soul of Containment* (New York: Cambridge University Press, 2008); David S. Foglesong, *The American Mission and the "Evil" Empire* (New York: Cambridge University Press, 2007); and Andrew Preston, "Bridging the Gap between the Sacred and the Secular in the History of American Foreign Relations," *Diplomatic History* 30, no. 5 (2006): 783–812. For an example of another attempt to merge religious history and foreign policy history, albeit during a different time period, see David Zietsma, "Building the Kingdom of God: Religious Discourse, National Identity, and the Good Neighbor Policy, 1930–1938," *Rhetoric and Public Affairs* 11, no. 2 (2008): 179–214. For a wide collection of essays on the influence of religion during the Cold War, see Diane Kirby, ed., *Religion and the Cold War* (New York: Palgrave Macmillan, 2003). It is also important to note that some historians have examined the religious war against Communism from a domestic perspective. See Donald F. Crosby, *God, Church, and Flag: Senator Joseph R. McCarthy and the Catholic Church, 1950–1957* (Chapel Hill: University of North Carolina Press, 1978); T. Jeremy Gunn, *Spiritual Weapons: The Cold War and the Forging of an American National Religion* (Westport, CT: Praeger, 2009); and Robert Jewett, *Mission and Menace: Four Centuries of American Religious Zeal* (Minneapolis: Fortress Press, 2008).

4. "Treaty of Peace and Friendship, Signed at Tripoli November 4, 1797." Available at Lillian Goldman Law Library, *The Avalon Project: Documents in Law, History and Diplomacy*, avalon.law.yale.edu (accessed July 26, 2010).

5. In his history of the Barbary Wars, Frank Lambert argues that the conflicts "were primarily about trade, not theology, and rather than being holy wars, they were an extension of America's War of Independence." See Lambert, *The Barbary Wars: American Independence in the Atlantic World* (New York: Hill and Wang, 2005), 8.

6. Perhaps the best short account of religious leaders in the Spanish-American War is in Julius Pratt's *Expansionists of 1898* (Chicago: Quadrangle Books, 1964), 279–316. Winthrop Hudson, in his essay "Protestant Clergy Debate the Nation's Vocation, 1898–1899," *Church History* 42, no. 1 (1973): 110–18, departs from the "imperialism of righteousness" argument and contends that key Protestant leaders only reluctantly embraced the war with Spain.

7. "President Bush's Address on Terrorism before a Joint Meeting of Congress," *New York Times*, September 21, 2001.

8. Michael R. Gordon, "The Struggle for Iraq," *New York Times*, April 24, 2007; Sheryl

Gay Stolberg, "Islamo-Fascism Had Its Moment," *New York Times*, September 24, 2006; and Douglas Jehl, "U.S. General Apologizes for Remarks about Islam," *New York Times*, October 18, 2003.

9. Of course, secular scholars, journalists, and analysts contributed to this conceptualization of Communism as well. See Jonathan Herzog, "The Hammer and the Cross: America's Holy War against Communism" (PhD diss., Stanford University, 2008).

10. Reinhold Niebuhr, "The Religion of Communism," *Atlantic Monthly*, April 1931, 462–70. For an outstanding examination of Niebuhr's life and the evolution of his theology, see Richard Wightman Fox, *Reinhold Niebuhr: A Biography* (New York: Pantheon Books, 1985). One year later, Niebuhr refined some of these views in *Moral Man and Immoral Society* (New York: Scribner, 1932). He argued that Marxism combined a powerful sense of moral cynicism with equalitarian social idealism—a potent and intoxicating but altogether untenable formula. His 1932 work was more critical of Marxism than was his 1931 article, demonstrating that his stance was hardening already. Niebuhr's early writings on Communism shared many arguments with the Russian intellectual Nicholas Berdyaev, who wrote at the same time.

11. Henry Black, "Religion and Communism—a Parallel," *Christian Century*, June 27, 1934, 861–62; H. G. Wood, *Christianity and Communism* (New York: Roundtable Press, 1933), 3–4; and F. J. Sheed, *Communism and Man* (New York: Sheed and Ward, 1938), 155.

12. In fact, the church had taken a stand against Communism before even a fraction of Americans had even heard of Karl Marx. In 1846, Pope Pius IX had issued an encyclical addressing "that infamous doctrine of so-called Communism which is absolutely contrary to the natural law itself," and Pope Leo XIII had referred to Communism as a "fatal plague" in 1878; both quoted in Pius XI, "Divini Redemptoris: Encyclical of Pope Pius XI on Atheistic Communism to the Patriarchs, Primates, Archbishops, and Other Ordinaries in Peace and Communion with the Apostolic See," *www.vatican.va* (accessed November 21, 2011; also in Pius XI, *Atheistic Communism* [New York: Paulist Press, 1937]).

13. The *Commonweal*, a liberal Catholic journal, provided a platform for critiques of Communism. Rarely did an issue pass without some reference to Communism. See William Thomas Walsh, "Is Communism Dangerous?" *Commonweal*, February 8, 1935, 421. See also Catherine Radziwill, "Bolshevism—a Universal Danger," *Commonweal*, April 22, 1925, 653–55; Paul Scheffer, "Moscow and the Churches," *Commonweal*, April 23, 1930, 701–3; and F. J. McGarrigle, "The Soviet Religion," *Commonweal*, February 8, 1935, 177–79.

14. Eugene Kevane, "The Depths of Bolshevism," *Commonweal*, September 3, 1937, 433–35.

15. Kathleen Riley Fields, "Bishop Fulton J. Sheen: An American Catholic Response to the Twentieth Century" (PhD diss., University of Notre Dame, 1988); Michael J. Epple, "American Crusader: Bishop Fulton J. Sheen's Campaign against Communism" (PhD diss., University of Akron, 2001), 53; Fulton Sheen to Martin Dies, December 1, 1938, Catholic University, Washington, DC, National Catholic

Welfare Conference Papers, Box 23, Folder 21; "Communist 'Faith' Defined by Sheen," *New York Times*, March 25, 1935; and "Religion Is Held Antidote to Reds," *New York Times*, June 3, 1935.

16. John Cooney, *The American Pope: The Life and Times of Francis Cardinal Spellman* (New York: Times Books, 1984).

17. "Text of Spellman Plea on Mindszenty," *New York Times*, February 7, 1949.

18. "Power of Religion Urged as War Bar," *New York Times*, March 6, 1949.

19. The best account of the relationship between religious constructions of the Cold War and the US evangelical movement is Angela M. Lahr's *Millennial Dreams and Apocalyptic Nightmares: The Cold War Origins of Political Evangelicalism* (New York: Oxford University Press, 2007).

20. Verne Paul Kaub, *Collectivism Challenges Christianity* (Winona Lake, IN: Light and Life Press, 1946), 2, 43, 70–75, 84, 125.

21. Frederick Schwarz, *Beating the Unbeatable Foe: One Man's Victory over Communism, Leviathan, and the Last Enemy* (Washington, DC: Regnery Publishing, 1996), 15–16, 21–22, 104; Billy James Hargis, *Communist America . . . Must It Be?* (Tulsa: Christian Crusade, 1960), 154; and Billy James Hargis, *The Far Left* (Tulsa: Christian Crusade, 1964), 227.

22. "Billy Graham Arrives for Rose Bowl Rally," *Los Angeles Times*, September 9, 1950.

23. For more on Graham's rhetoric, see Roger Bruns, *Billy Graham: A Biography* (Westport, CT: Greenwood Press, 2004); "Graham Sees Peril; Says 'Atheistic Nation' Could Destroy Unrepentant U.S.," *New York Times*, July 4, 1957; "Graham Wins a Communist," *New York Times*, May 31, 1954; and "Graham Proposes Russian Crusade," *New York Times*, June 10, 1957.

24. Edward F. Willett, "Dialectical Materialism and Russian Objectives," January 14, 1946, in *Documentary History of the Truman Presidency*, ed. Dennis Merrill (Bethesda, MD: University Publications of America, 1996), 7:23–24.

25. Ibid., 49–50.

26. George F. Kennan, "Telegram 511" (hereafter "Long Telegram"), in *Documentary History of the Truman Presidency*, ed. Dennis Merrill (Bethesda, MD: University Publications of America, 1996), 7:68–103.

27. John Lewis Gaddis, who proffered perhaps the single best treatment of Kennan's "Long Telegram," also emphasizes its psychological aspects. See Gaddis, *Strategies of Containment* (New York: Oxford University Press, 1982), 36–37.

28. Kennan, "Long Telegram," 84–85, 91. Similarities between Kennan's formulation and Edmund Burke's observations during the French Revolution are surprisingly similar. Both men likened their opponent to a disease, both believed that alliance with their respective enemies was ideologically impossible, and both believed that domestic zeal could ensure victory. See Edmund Burke, "First Letter on a Regicide Peace," in *Empire and Community: Edmund Burke's Writings and Speeches on International Relations*, ed. David P. Fidler and Jennifer M. Welsh (Boulder, CO: Westview Press, 1999), 287–320.

29. "A Report to the National Security Council" (NSC 68), April 14, 1950, Harry S. Truman Library (hereafter HSTL), Independence, MO, Secretary's Files. John Lewis Gaddis's treatment of NSC 68 is still the most useful; see *Strategies of Containment*,

90–117. For a discussion of the ways in which NSC 68 transcended the boundaries of a strategy document to frame the Cold War politically, socially, and culturally, see Ernest R. May, ed., *American Cold War Strategy: Interpreting NSC 68* (Boston: Bedford Books, 1993), 152–64.

30. "Science without Conscience Menaces Man, Bradley Says," *Washington Post*, November 11, 1948; C. T. Lanham, "The Moral Core of Military Strength," February 16, 1949, HSTL, Records of the President's Committee on Religion and Welfare in the Armed Forces, Box 33, Folder 2-c.

31. Harry S. Truman, "Annual Message to the Congress on the State of the Union," January 7, 1948, in *Public Papers of the Presidents of the United States: Harry S. Truman, 1948* (Washington, DC: US Government Printing Office, 1964), 4:1–10; "Truman Says Faith Is Best U.S. Weapon," *New York Times*, December 25, 1950; and Tom C. Clark, "Address before the International Sunday School Convention," July 24, 1947, HSTL, Tom C. Clark Papers, Box 18.

32. The Federal Council of Churches, led by Bishop G. Bromley Oxnam, protested Taylor's reappointment vigorously. See Merlin Gustafson, "Religion and Politics in the Truman Administration," *Rocky Mountain Social Science Journal* 3 (1966): 125–34.

33. This initial round of correspondence was reprinted by the White House in a press release, August 28, 1947, HSTL, Secretary's Files, Box 196.

34. Harry S. Truman to Pius XII, March 26, 1948; Truman to Pius, April 24, 1948; Pius to Truman, July 19, 1948; and Truman to Pius, August 11, 1948: all in HSTL, Myron C. Taylor Papers, Box 3.

35. "Baptists Blast Truman-Pope Letter Writing," *Chicago Daily Tribune*, August 31, 1947.

36. Eisenhower campaign statement, n.d., Ann Whitman File, Campaign Series, Box 7, Dwight D. Eisenhower Library (hereafter DDEL), Abilene, KS; and Eisenhower, "Speech at Fort Worth," October 15, 1952, DDEL, Stephen Benedict Papers, Box 6.

37. Inboden, *Religion and American Foreign Policy*, 231.

38. "Memorandum from the Executive Secretary (Souers) to the Members of the National Security Council" (NSC 4), December 9, 1947, HSTL.

39. Quoted in Edward P. Lilly, "Religious Factors in OCB," 1954, DDEL, Operations Coordinating Board Central Files, Box 2, Folder 000.3, File 2. See also Gordon Gray, Oral History, n.d., HSTL, Truman Oral Histories Files; and Mallory Browne to Gordon Gray, February 15, 1952, HSTL, Psychological Strategy Board (PSB) Files, Box 1, Folder 000.3.

40. Report, "Preliminary Estimate of the Effectiveness of U.S. Psychological Operations," 1952, HSTL, PSB Files, Box 15, Folder 091.412, File 2; draft report, "Over-all Strategic Concept for Our Psychological Operations," 1952, HSTL, PSB Files, Box 15, Folder 091.412, File 2; and E. P. Lilly to William Gibbons, September 25, 1952, HSTL, PSB Files, Box 1, Folder 000.3.

41. Department of State, Press Release 94, February 4, 1952, DDEL, Operations Coordinating Board (OCB) Secretariat Series, Box 5; and Francis P. Keough, "Remarks for the Voice of America Broadcast by Archbishop Keough," November 8,

1951, Catholic University, Washington, DC, National Catholic Welfare Conference Papers, Box 35, Folder 11.

42. Roger Lyons, "The Problem of Religious Broadcasting to an International Audience," February 5, 1952, National Archives and Records Administration (hereafter NARA), College Park, MD, USIA Records, Box 17; and Roger Lyons, "The Role of Religion on the Voice of America," n.d., NARA, USIA Records, Box 17.

43. PSB, "U.S. Doctrinal Program," 1953, DDEL, Operations Coordinating Board Secretariat Series, Box 1; Agenda, Panel for Doctrinal Warfare, January 23, 1953, DDEL, OCB Secretariat Series, Box 2; Stefan T. Possony to Edward P. Lilly, January 12, 1953, DDEL, OCB Secretariat Series, Box 2; T. B. Larson, "Vulnerabilities of Soviet-Communist Ideology," 1952, DDEL, OCB Secretariat Series, Box 2; Edward P. Lilly to PSB, May 1, 1953, DDEL, OCB Secretariat Series, Box 2, Folder 5; and PSB Doctrinal Warfare Panel, "National Doctrinal Program to Reduce Communist Influence," 1953, DDEL, OCB Secretariat Series, Box 2, Folder 5.

44. Although the USIA was initially subject to State Department guidelines and policies, it would gain greater bureaucratic independence in the coming years. Murray G. Lawson, *The United States Information Agency: A History* (Washington: United States Information Agency, 1970); *Operations Coordinating Board Handbook*, 1955, DDEL, OCB Central Files, Box 100, Folder OCB 334; and Kenneth Osgood, *Total Cold War: Eisenhower's Secret Propaganda Battle at Home and Abroad* (Lawrence: University of Kansas Press, 2006), 85–90. For an insider's perspective on the founding of the USIA, see Richard T. Arndt, *The First Resort of Kings: American Cultural Diplomacy in the Twentieth Century* (Washington, DC: Potomac Books, 2005), 264–87.

45. "A Report to the National Security Council" (NSC 162/2), October 30, 1953, DDEL. The same basic phrasing reappears in NSC 5440/1, released December 1954, and in NSC 5602/1, released March 1956.

46. Edward P. Lilly to Elmer B. Staats, March 3, 1954, DDEL, OCB Central Files, Box 2, Folder 000.3.

## References

ARCHIVES
Catholic University, Washington, DC
Dwight D. Eisenhower Library, Abilene, KS
Harry S. Truman Library, Independence, MO
Library of Congress, Washington, DC
National Archives and Records Administration, College Park, MD

PERIODICALS
*Atlantic Monthly*
*Chicago Daily Tribune*
*Christian Century*
*Commonweal*

*Los Angeles Times*
*New York Times*
*Washington Post*

**PUBLISHED GOVERNMENT DOCUMENTS, REPORTS, AND SERIALS**

Kennan, George F. "Telegram 511" (the "Long Telegram"). In *Documentary History of the Truman Presidency*, ed. Dennis Merrill, 7: 68–103. Bethesda, MD: University Publications of America, 1996.

"Memorandum from the Executive Secretary (Souers) to the Members of the National Security Council" (NSC 4), December 9, 1947, Harry S. Truman Library, Independence, MO

"A Report to the National Security Council" (NSC 68), April 14, 1950, Harry S. Truman Library, Independence, MO

"A Report to the National Security Council" (NSC 162/2), October 30, 1953, Dwight D. Eisenhower Library, Abilene, KS

Willett, Edward F. "Dialectical Materialism and Russian Objectives," January 14, 1946. In *Documentary History of the Truman Presidency*, ed. Dennis Merrill, 7:23–24. Bethesda, MD: University Publications of America, 1996.

## Selected Published Works

Gaddis, John Lewis. *Strategies of Containment*. New York: Oxford University Press, 1982.

Gunn, T. Jeremy. *Spiritual Weapons: The Cold War and the Forging of an American National Religion*. Westport, CT: Praeger, 2009.

Hargis, Billy James. *Communist America . . . Must It Be?* Tulsa, OK: Christian Crusade, 1960.

———. *The Far Left*. Tulsa, OK: Christian Crusade, 1964.

Herzog, Jonathan. "The Hammer and the Cross: America's Holy War against Communism." PhD diss., Stanford University, 2008.

Inboden, William. *Religion and American Foreign Policy, 1945–1960: The Soul of Containment*. New York: Cambridge University Press, 2008.

# CHAPTER 4

# Hewlett Johnson

## *Britain's Red Dean and the Cold War*

*David Ayers*

Hewlett Johnson, widely known as the "Red Dean," was a famous supporter of Communism from the mid-1930s to his death in 1966.[1] Johnson served for five years as dean of Manchester Cathedral before being appointed dean of Canterbury Cathedral as the choice of Prime Minister Ramsay MacDonald in 1929. The dean of Canterbury should not be confused with the archbishop of Canterbury, a mistake occasionally made by the Communist regimes that hosted Johnson's visits; the archbishop is the primate of all England, while the dean performs merely local functions at the cathedral itself. Nonetheless, Canterbury is the most important cathedral in England and Johnson's public projection was certainly aided by his status. Yet his influence in the public sphere was mainly built by his speaking in Britain, the United States, Canada, Australia, and elsewhere; by his role in pro-Communist bodies such as the Society for Cultural Relations; by his journeys to Communist countries; by his extensive book, pamphlet, and periodical publications; and by the press reports of the controversy occasioned by his opinions and actions. The challenge that Johnson presented to the public was not only his assertion that Communism was the practical realization of Christianity, despite its avowed atheism, but also his endorsement of Communist regimes, which seemed not merely to ignore the widely reported abuses of authoritarian states but to mask or endorse them. Johnson was never a member of the Communist Party, and he could honestly deny this at a hearing for which he volunteered at the US

Hewlett Johnson greeted by Nikita Khrushchev upon his arrival in Moscow for the All-Union Congress for Peace, August 1949. *This photograph is held as part of the Hewlett Johnson Papers in Special Collections at the Templeman Library, University of Kent, and is used with the permission of Johnson's family.*

embassy in 1954. Yet it seems that in effect he accepted party discipline, no more so than in his funeral oration for Stalin in London: delivered in April 1953, it was published as a pamphlet that reproduces, section by section, the claims of the official biography of Stalin, frequently verbatim. Although he avoided the topic of revolutionary violence in his public statements, Johnson can be found endorsing it in his written works, where he caricatures landlords and similar groups who were the targets of such violence and defends political show trials. While Johnson may have taken as true things that were not, and while his technocratic ignorance of political process was at times breathtaking, it is important to understand that in his political Communism and direct support for Communist regimes, he was quite conscious of questions both of revolutionary violence and internal repression.

Johnson's politics contrast with those of most other prominent British clergy in the period in question. Certainly in the 1930s a range of clergy could be found expressing an interest in Communism, and of course many clergy were socialists and supported the Labour Party.[2] A strand of politically liberal Anglicans achieved an important voice in the interwar period, exemplified by William Temple, archbishop of York (1929–1942) and briefly of Canterbury (1942–1944), but while Johnson shared their interest in poverty and issues of unemployment, he did not share their communitarian approach to social cohesiveness. While such Anglicans were anti-authoritarian and firmly opposed to Adolf Hitler and Nazism, they were not pro-Communist.[3] From the 1940s, few clergy could be found to support Communism, and some senior Anglican clerics were actively anti-Communist, portraying the Cold War as a Manichaean struggle between good and evil, a defense of the West and of Christianity.[4] Others were reluctant to align themselves with an uncritical anti-Communism but took positive lessons for Christianity from the inability of Communist governments to extinguish faith among their own people.[5] From the 1940s on, Johnson was a relatively unusual figure among British clergy in his open support of Communism, while his presence as a pro-Communist speaker in the United States contrasted sharply with the more familiar brand of anti-Communism preached by Billy Graham and other evangelicals.[6] Johnson was an unusual figure, but it is important to remember that the Anglican Church was (and is) an established church. The relationship between church and state was not, during his tenure, of merely notional or formal importance. Christianity remained an important force in Britain until the 1960s. The politically liberal, communitarian Anglican clergy sought to equate Anglicanism and Englishness with a view to creating national cohesiveness, a rhetorical strategy also embraced by Conservative politicians such as Stanley Baldwin and Winston Churchill.[7] Johnson did not adopt this strategy but, like these liberal Anglicans, he knew that he spoke from within an establishment in which the authority of state and church subtly but definitely converged. Johnson went further than most Anglo-Catholic socialists in supporting Communism, and we might expect to find that he had examined important precedents in the revolutionary history of Christianity in Britain as exemplified by such groups as the Levellers.[8] Leading Marxist intellectuals considered this a key approach at that time, but Johnson was simply not reliant on this history either politically or theologically.[9] In some ways, his position anticipates that of what later became "liberation theology" in Latin America, with its emphasis on social change and activism. Johnson was interested in changing society, not in changing the church. He was arguably more interested in societies that had changed than in changing Britain or America.

Johnson's position in the church is remarkably singular, and for this reason he cannot be regarded as the representative of any religious movement or any general tendency within the church itself. Nevertheless, Johnson was both famous and notorious as a catalyst for reactions to Communism both in Britain and America, where he commanded large audiences. The Communist countries well understood his usefulness, which stemmed both from his own actively achieved presence in the public sphere, as well as from the apparent authority of his position as part of the establishment. They routinely invited him to their embassies, and his numerous visits served both internal and external propaganda purposes. In the 1930s, Johnson was merely one of a number of figures supporting Communism in a wave of anti-Nazism and appeared unusual only in the context of his position in the church; during the war, his pro-Soviet position at first clashed and then harmonized with popular opinion regarding Russia; and after the war, he came to appear increasingly anomalous and isolated—a catalyst for sentiments about the Cold War, perhaps, but one whose pro-Communism did not chime with the more straightforwardly antiwar attitudes of the audiences he still attracted. This chapter maps the pattern of Johnson's political activities across three periods—prewar, war, and postwar—and articulates some of the roots of political-religious debate during the Cold War proper in terms of the already-existing framework of discussion and activity established in the 1930s. It thereby advances a theory in which the war against Germany can be viewed as merely an episode in a longer struggle that had begun in 1917. Indeed, following Johnson's trajectory from the 1930s through the early 1960s, it is impossible not to notice that while his political and theological convictions remained basically unchanged, the social and political situations in which he found himself fluctuated dramatically.

Johnson's attitude toward Communism was partly conditioned by his background as an engineer, and his approach to politics was highly technocratic. Before turning to Communism, Johnson had been one of the few supporters of the monetary theory Social Credit expounded by Major C. H. Douglas.[10]

Like Johnson, Douglas was an engineer. His theories are simple and do not withstand scrutiny. Social Credit attracted cranks, and Johnson's adherence to it might at first glance seem to identify him as an eccentric—a common view of Johnson in later years, when his pro-Communism was depicted as naive. Yet Johnson's correspondence with Ezra Pound shows him to be cool and serious, and cautious of his correspondent's inflammatory rhetoric and apparently disjointed thinking.[11] This is important because it confirms a degree of political lucidity in Johnson. It is worth mentioning, too, that adherents of credit reform, who sought a monetary response to questions of social injustice, were frequently anti-Communists and anti-Semites who desired a Third Way—an alternative to both socialism and capitalism. Johnson was interested in practical solutions to questions of social justice but otherwise did not share these attitudes. He had become vice president of the Society for Cultural Relations in 1935, and in 1937 made his first visit to the Soviet Union, a trip that is only thinly documented. The advent of the Spanish Civil War confirmed to Johnson that greater things were afoot in the world than credit reform, and over a short period, which involved a visit to the front in Spain at a critical moment, he moved to a position of ardent support for Soviet Communism.

The religious dimension of the war in Spain is important because the rebels, supported by the Germans, depicted the "reds" as godless and claimed that the struggle against the Spanish government was a struggle for Christianity. While in Spain as part of an ecumenical Christian delegation, Johnson witnessed a bombardment by German aircraft that preceded Guernica by a month. The multi-authored report of the delegation contains Johnson's account of this attack and of his own involvement in it. The attack had resulted in the destruction of churches, for which the rebels blamed the "reds"; Johnson was outraged by this and rushed to make a broadcast, giving his eyewitness account and claiming that it was the rebel forces that had destroyed the churches.[12] How this broadcast from Bilbao was enabled and to whom it was made remains obscure, but Johnson's text survives. As well as reporting the air attack, Johnson is effusive about the victims on the ground: "There is wonderful bravery among these deeply religious peasant people. . . . I do not wonder that their churches are full. . . . Their religion gives them wonderful courage."[13] This view of "the people" reflects a liking on Johnson's part for religious orthodoxy and also reflects the distanced and objectified view of communities that he would take on most of his foreign travels—perhaps inevitably so: unable to speak the languages, and reliant on translators and guides, Johnson seems always to project a collectivized view of the foreign others. Johnson was not sole author of the delegation's report, but in addition to providing firsthand testimony regarding Durango, the report takes some trouble to claim that there is freedom of religious practice in government-controlled Spain and, while acknowledging that the churches and monasteries are mainly empty, blames this on the political machinations of the clergy and asserts that if they were allowed to return, they would in all likelihood resume their "disloyal intrigue."[14] The delegates seem to have accepted much of what they were told about the closure of the great majority of religious establishments and make a great deal of the few examples of religious practice they do find. That this is a collective report is a reminder that at this time Johnson was not alone as a churchman in his sympathy for Communism, but the document very much bears the mark of his authorship and of his future defense of the Soviet Union, in that it glosses over the facts of religious repression, accepts official accounts if presented in socialist rhetoric, and celebrates the material accomplishments of socialism even where religious freedom is absent.

Johnson's experience in Spain, and the particular configuration of the wider public discussion concerning religion and Communism that was triggered on his return, predicted in important ways the course of the confrontation between religion and politics in the British and international public spheres in which Johnson would continue to play a key part. Johnson learned practical lessons in Spain about the necessity of defending Communism and socialism against their own atheism. When the right-wing rebels accused the "reds" of attacking churches, Communism's express atheism seemed to give veracity to their claim. Later, when Germany invaded the Soviet Union, the Nazis attempted to present themselves as the defenders of Russian religion against the Soviet state. In the Cold War, Johnson frequently revisited the accusations against the Soviet Union in the wake of the many concessions Stalin made in response to the difficulties that assertive state atheism had created both with wartime allies and with the peoples of the newly Russian-occupied countries. The connections between religion, politics, foreign policy, and propaganda were all made for Johnson during his visit to Spain, which did much to set the model for his future activities as a public figure.

Johnson's actions in Spain were reported in the British press, and on his return he gave a sermon on Spain in the cathedral. An almost apoplectic response from a local vicar who was present at the sermon identifies the central intellectual claim that Johnson would make about Communism throughout his life: "You say that denial of God is not irreligious!!!! You say it does not matter what they say with their lips; it is what they mean in their hearts (that matters)!!!!"[15] That Communism was the real-world realization of Christianity, regardless and in spite of the beliefs of individual Communists and notwithstanding the atheist policies of Communist authorities, remained a central plank of Johnson's arguments for decades to come. The angry responses of some believers in private communications and letters to newspaper editors would echo the frustration of this early correspondent. Others, though, were grateful that Johnson had spoken out. In fact, Johnson had been committed to support for the Spanish government before his participation in the delegation. He was the treasurer of the Christian Foodship Committee formed in early April 1937 to send supplies to Bilbao.[16] In an apparently unsent letter to the *Times*, Johnson responded to an article titled "Religion in Spain" with a rebuttal of the claim that the republican government had "liquidated the Catholic clergy," having been assured by his contact in Barcelona that this was not true.[17] Johnson's reliance on his church colleagues abroad would become a prominent strain in his publicly presented arguments. He distrusted the capitalist press and tended to prefer the testimony of churchmen whom he felt he could trust. During the Cold War, the degree to which such sources might be contaminated by political selection and monitoring was never acknowledged by Johnson. This reliance on the authority and testimony of usually senior church figures remained a key part of his rhetoric of witness throughout his life.

Another consequence of Johnson's foray into the public sphere, which would be repeated in an amplified form both before and after the war, was the ritual attempt to get him to resign. The form of Johnson's appointment—his selection from a restricted field of candidates by the prime minister acting on behalf of the monarch—meant that he could not be fired for procedural reasons. Following the outcry over his Spanish visit and sermon, the archbishop of Canterbury hinted to Johnson that he should resign; but the archbishop had no authority to remove him, and Johnson got used to resisting such pressure, which later reached much greater proportions.[18] The platform that his role guaranteed for him allowed him to be outspoken and made his position in the public sphere absolutely secure, since in effect the authority of his personal religious stance was indissociable from the authority of the established church and of the state that guaranteed his livelihood.

Johnson's relationship with Russia predated his visit to Spain. Johnson's diaries show that he periodically dined with the Soviet ambassador after the war, as well as with the ambassadors of the other Eastern European Communist states. Letters to Johnson from Ivan Maisky, the Soviet ambassador to the United Kingdom from 1932 to 1943, show that the two were comfortably familiar with each other, although the contents of Maisky's letters are always innocent, ready for the eye of the British intelligence officer who might be expected to intercept them. Johnson was not formally a member of the Communist Party, nor is there evidence he was a paid agent (in any case, he did not need money and made no effort to conceal his support for Communist countries), but his pro-Communist interventions reveal not simply a general adherence to the ideal of an imagined, future Communism but a practical adherence to the foreign policy and international propaganda purposes of the Soviet Union and later its Eastern European satellites, China and Cuba.

Johnson's 1937 visit to the Soviet Union included travel to Russia, Ukraine, Crimea, the Caucasus, and Georgia. Afterward, Johnson was approached by the socialist publisher Victor Gollancz. Gollancz initially asked for a book based on Johnson's experiences, but what resulted was a more thoroughgoing theoretical and statistical account of the Soviet Union, *The Socialist Sixth of the World* (1939). Johnson would subsequently claim that the book had been translated into any number of languages and had sold in the millions, although practical evidence for this is so far wanting. Nevertheless, it became a well-known point of reference, was sold widely at Johnson's frequent appearances on public political platforms, and generated a warm correspondence from enthusiastic readers. In 1938, Johnson had undertaken a tour, speaking at large political rallies around England at Gollancz's request. This pattern of speaking at large rallies was something that he would repeat later in the United States, Canada, and elsewhere. The arrival of *Socialist Sixth* in the wake of this speaking tour and following the controversy over his visit to Spain ensured Johnson's prominence as an advocate of Communism.

In *Socialist Sixth*, Johnson states that Communism and Christianity can be reconciled. He sets out the basic case for viewing Christianity and Communism as convergent. While Johnson would later spell out other elements, the core of his thinking is the claim that Christ, like Communism, always advocated for the poor.[19] The case he makes here does not really vary throughout his career. While many Soviet supporters, such as Victor Gollancz, became disillusioned after the signing of the Molotov-Ribbentrop Pact in August 1939, Johnson not only remained loyal to the Soviet Union, but also maintained his intellectual and spiritual commitment to Communism. In this respect, it is a little short of the mark to see Johnson as a "fellow traveler."[20] Indeed, what is remarkable about Johnson is not only his unflinching commitment to practical support of Communism, but also the consistency of his theological position. While we might expect to find in Johnson's writing evidence of some struggle of conscience, at least in his private works, there is nothing but dogmatic certainty.

Johnson was strongly impressed by what he believed to be Stalin's anti-racism and frequently expressed his approval of Stalin's nationalities policy. Taking notes some years later on Corliss Lamont's *Soviet Civilization* (1952), Johnson wrote: "That is the gift and contribution of Stalin. His crown."[21] In the light of this, it is probably necessary to assert that Johnson was a Stalinist. This emerges not just in his later willingness to speak favorably of turns in Soviet policy, but also in his enthusiasm for the Soviet Constitution of 1936, for which Johnson adopted the official Soviet name, the Stalin Constitution. It is given the strongest possible recommendation in *Socialist Sixth*. Later, it is the subject of an entire pamphlet where Johnson gives it a blanket endorsement while brushing aside concerns about religious freedom: "In tone and content the new Constitution may be described as the most liberal the world has yet seen."[22] Johnson also did not acknowledge the existence of the Terror and completely disregarded the growing anti-Stalinist literature on the left, including the writings of Trotsky. Finally, it should be noted that Johnson often claimed that Communism allowed freedom of religion, occasionally accompanying it with a defense of anticlericalism and its historical roots: "Outrages were committed on the church in proportion as the church had become corrupt and wealthy. . . . No great revolution, alas, was ever carried through without bloodshed, violence, and brutality."[23]

While in later years Johnson would appear a rather atypical figure, during this period he was one of a number of British clergy keen to connect Communism and Christianity.[24] Alongside the broader clerical debate, there were the works and activities of the pro-Communist cleric Stanley G. Evans, who, like Johnson, traveled, spoke, and published widely on many of the same topics: the church in the Soviet Union and Eastern Europe, the relationship between Communism and Christianity, the Soviet Union's thorny claim of the right to access US nuclear technology, and the severe embarrassment to Christian Communists of the Cardinal Mindszenty trial.[25] Among the theologians who dealt with the relationship between Christianity and Communism, John MacMurray was a particular influence on Johnson; *Creative Society* (1937) gave a strong fillip to Johnson's own sense of Communism was the realization of Christianity. Johnson underlined passages in his copy of MacMurray's book that found their way into his own repertoire, notably the central claim that "Communism . . . has recovered that essential core of a real belief in God, which organized Christianity in our day has largely lost."[26]

While the writings of Evans and MacMurray reflect and accompany the practical and theological aspects of Johnson's mission, reminding the historian that Johnson was not simply a maverick, as the press often portrayed him, he was nevertheless a unique figure in terms of his extraordinary national and international public profile. Johnson could have ignored the Soviet invasion of Finland in November 1939, but instead he wrote for the *New Statesman and Nation* on December 16, justifying the action. Controversial in itself, Johnson's stance resulted in an awkward situation only two weeks after the article was published. A service titled "Prayers for the Finns" was to be held at the cathedral, led by the archbishop but with Johnson present, against a background where "prominent citizens" were said to be boycotting services on account of Johnson's politics and where "little Finland" was seen straightforwardly as the victim of a huge bully.[27] Sensing weakness, and inflamed that Johnson's passion for Russia remained undimmed even while Britain stood alone against Hitler, the canons of Canterbury Cathedral moved against Johnson in a campaign to have him ousted, which was prominently reported in the press and occasioned sustained debate. He was not the man for the job, they asserted, for he "condones the offences of Russia against humanity and religion" and he offended Christians locally and throughout the world.[28] Johnson's response appeared three days later in the *Times*, even though he had no need to mount a defense of his position at the cathedral, as he knew that he could not be dismissed. This widely reported incident confirmed Johnson's role in the public sphere; it was wartime, though, and the questions it raised were no more than a noisy sideshow.

Johnson gained a new platform from which to defend the Soviet Union with Hitler's invasion of Russia on June 22, 1941. The routine anti-Communism of most of the British press was quickly replaced by praise for the new ally. While some predicted the imminent collapse of the Soviet Union, Johnson believed that the Soviets were strong enough to resist the Nazis because of their period of extraordinary industrial growth throughout the 1930s. Johnson was back in demand as a public speaker, now able to link Russian strength in war to the economic and psychological benefits of Communism. This message held particular potency for working-class audiences. When Johnson spoke on the topic "Russia's Heroic Struggle" at the Queen's Hall in the industrial town of Derby, an event organized by the Russia To-day Society, the hall attracted a capacity crowd of seven hundred with as many again reportedly turned away. The June 1942 bombing raid on Canterbury (a reprisal for an Royal Air Force attack on Cologne) in which the cathedral library sustained damage was widely reported as an outrage and indirectly contributed a different kind of authority to Johnson's message. Johnson took the opportunity to begin publishing again, issuing a book intended to explain Russia's capacity for military resistance, *Soviet Strength* (1942); a short theoretical pamphlet, *Marxism and the Individual* (1943); and a pamphlet praising the formal British-Soviet treaty signed in May 1942, *Hitler's Death Warrant* (1943). *Soviet Strength* advances arguments already set out in *Socialist Sixth*, with renewed emphasis on Stalin's nationalities policy and on the "new life" of the individual in the Soviet state, with a final section asserting that the war will end in a "Socialist Europe."[29] Most interesting here in light of the eventual Cold War is *Hitler's Death Warrant*, which celebrates Soviet war achievements in a propagandistic style and aligns itself closely with Soviet foreign policy goals. Johnson praises the British war effort for the level of commitment from munitions workers, airmen, and most notably the seamen, who sailed in the famously dangerous Arctic convoys and had become an emblem of Anglo-Russian solidarity, but he criticizes the tardiness of Britain and the United States in creating a second front against

Nazi Germany. Anglo-Soviet friendship is high on the pamphlet's agenda, with warm endorsement for the welcome given to Ivan Maisky, Soviet ambassador to the United Kingdom, at the Anglo-Soviet Friendship Week in Manchester. The outcome of all these developments was that British eyes had been opened to the new Soviet Man and the path to peace and prosperity that Russia had demonstrated.[30] The pamphlet was entirely political in character and made no mention of religion.

As Johnson exploited his opportunities to convey the Soviet message, his task of defending Soviet atheism became somewhat easier. The newfound patriotic role of the Orthodox Church had already resulted in a large collection of essays and other documents called *The Truth about Religion in Russia*, which had been issued in 1942 and promptly translated into English, outlining the patriotic stance of the church, listing Nazi outrages, rebutting reports that the Nazis were opening closed churches, and asserting the advantages of the church's independence from the state.[31] Ivan Maisky sent a copy to Johnson.[32] While this publication might have been important to individual churchmen in Britain and America defending the Soviet system in order to boost the war effort, a more important event came in its wake. The restoration of the Moscow Patriarchate after a meeting between Stalin and Orthodox bishops in September 1943 had several outcomes: it harnessed the already notable patriotic efforts of the church, deflected the Nazis' claims of liberating Orthodoxy, and helped Western churchmen such as Johnson who had been prominent in advocating support for the Russian war effort.[33] The main effect of the Stalin Concordat (as it is sometimes known) came after the war, when the newly occupied or liberated territories of Eastern Europe were able to take some comfort from the recently normalized relations of state and church in Russia, where once again new priests could be trained and church literature be printed.

When Johnson visited Russia for the victory celebrations in May 1945, he and other British representatives witnessed an impressive Orthodox ceremony staged for their benefit, and Johnson himself was tossed into the air by soldiers in Red Square.[34] The itinerary also included Poland, where Johnson was among the early visitors to Auschwitz. The trip culminated in an interview with Stalin that Johnson later documented in his book *Soviet Success* (1947), an account inserted verbatim into his posthumously assembled autobiography, *Searching for Light* (1968).

In 1945, Johnson was motivated not simply by the desire to celebrate Russia's victory, but also by the need to maintain Russia's good relations with the West. To this end, he undertook a short visit to Canada and the United States, where he spoke at a major rally in Madison Square Garden in December 1945 alongside Dean Acheson, then undersecretary of state; Nikolai Novikov, the Soviet chargé d'affaires; and Paul Robeson, the African American singer and activist. Johnson used this visit to advertise the Soviet claim that the United States should share nuclear weapons technology with Russia in the interests of peace. He made this claim at the rally and at every opportunity when interviewed. Although Acheson's presence made the rally an official event, Robeson also took the opportunity to praise Communism, challenging the United States and the United Nations to "accomplish on a world-wide scale precisely the kind of democratic association of free peoples which characterises the Soviet Union today."[35] Although Johnson's presence represented an obvious strategy of political intervention, coverage in the US press was comparatively benign.[36]

His speaking tour of the United States and Canada in 1948 came as a relief to him, following another campaign against him in the press at home—this time waged by his own archbishop and once again successfully deflected. The audiences were reported to be huge. Once again Johnson spoke at Madison Square Garden, this time alongside Henry Wallace, the recently defeated Progressive Party presidential candidate, who took the opportunity to demand a summit meeting between Stalin and Truman in the interests of peace. The rally was attended by twenty thousand people, and the Garden was decorated with the Stars and Stripes interspersed with the hammer and sickle.[37] Johnson spoke at length on familiar themes—he was by all accounts a compelling public speaker—and impressed the audience with his claim that God was not interested in whether you said your prayers, but in whether you had helped others.[38] Having struggled to obtain a visa, Johnson toured widely, speaking at sixteen venues in the United States and four in Canada. The crowds were universally reported to be large.

This tour, however, took place in a far different climate than Johnson's 1945 appearances; he would never again be as well received as he had been right after the war. On his arrival at LaGuardia airport in 1948, he was mobbed by at least a hundred reporters, who seem above all to have been keen to ask him questions about religion. The *New York Herald Tribune* said Johnson had been "patient and friendly but dodged some questions. He managed to convey the impression that in spite of his ecclesiastical gaiters and the silver cross on his bosom he did not think it mattered too much whether the Russians believed in God. . . . Asked whether he thought Stalin was an atheist or a Christian he said: 'I never asked Stalin that, but he was very kind to me when I talked to him.'"[39] Johnson consciously avoided debate, being evidently interested in persuasion but not in any kind of intellectual negotiation. The consistency with which his views were reported in the press shows that he was as aware of the role of the prepared sound bite and the noncommittal answer to questions as any modern politician. One of his sound bites was the claim that the United States had encircled Russia with 434 airbases. This was widely albeit skeptically reported, and the (mis)information made rapid progress through the media. His witty claim that the Iron Curtain did not extend from the Adriatic to the Mediterranean but from one end of Fleet Street to the other also appeared in many reports.[40] While the major newspapers kept a patrician, critical distance from Johnson, some local papers were robust in their condemnation. They claimed that Johnson was peddling the "commie line" and the United States might as well have invited Stalin.[41]

In 1949, the trial of Cardinal Mindszenty in Hungary would focus the issues surrounding the treatment of the church in the Eastern bloc. József Mindszenty was the head of the Roman Catholic Church in Hungary. The Hungarian government depicted him as a right-wing traitor, while the Western press portrayed his case as an attack on religion, one in which new psychotropic drugs had been used to extract a confession.[42] Asked to comment, Johnson unequivocally took the line of the Hungarian government, with which he had ties. Manifesting once again his distrust of the church's reactionary past, Johnson argued that what was at stake here was not the fate of a mistried individual, but of a "new kulturkampf" in which "the two great totalitarian systems meet and wrestle together," phrasing that identifies the church with reaction and capital.[43] Johnson had seen the documentation of the case, which he regarded as damning, before it was published in English, probably because of his privileged connections with the Hungarian embassy.[44] Johnson's later book *Eastern Europe in the Socialist World* (1955) revisited the cases of Mindszenty and other clerics in a chapter titled "Subversion," reiterating the evidence against Mindszenty in detail, insisting that religion did not even enter into the case, and affirming the Hungarian government's claim that Mindszenty had sought US support for its overthrow and planned on restoring the great estates appropriated by the government to the former owners.[45]

In effect, Johnson argued both that the action of the Hungarian government was not anticlerical, and that in any case the Catholic Church was reactionary and therefore should expect retribution. What is significant is not that his argument was internally contradictory, but that he robustly maintained the line of the Hungarian government and was absolutely unfazed by what he regarded as the propagandistic efforts of the Western press to defend Mindszenty. Neither the 1948 attack by his archbishop nor the Mindszenty debate seemed to affect Johnson's commitment to Communism, even though one consequence was an increased hostility on his international speaking tours. His visits to Canada and Australia in early 1950 occasioned some protests, and on one occasion a police escort was necessary to protect him from an angry crowd.[46]

With the outbreak of the Korean War, Communism and Johnson were presented with new problems. It is unclear what mechanisms lay behind Johnson's 1952 visit to China, through which he traveled extensively, but when he returned, he immediately began a highly publicized propaganda campaign against the alleged use of germ warfare by the Americans in Korea. Johnson traveled with his wife to China, and they used a carefully staged photograph of the two with a long scroll to announce that they had proof of the practice.[47] Photographs from their press conference appeared in many national newspapers in Britain. The London *Evening Standard* for July 8, 1952, features a photo of Johnson with the huge scroll under the headline "Presenting the Evidence—According to Dr. Johnson," with the subheading "I Saw Germ War Insects—Says the Red Dean." Johnson's assertion, which he would repeat many times, is set out: "The facts about germ warfare are conclusive and irrefutable. . . . The facts cannot be hidden." He claimed to have a large ledger of documents supplied by Beijing and to have consulted scientists in China who had trained in England and the United States and whose opinion could therefore presumably be trusted. Johnson also cited the evidence of the two US airmen named Enoch and Quinn, who were said to have "described their methods of training in germ warfare, their missions and where they dropped the bombs." Johnson had read their statements and heard their voices on a recording. He had visited sites of three attacks and been shown insects said to have been infected with "diseased germs." Johnson quoted a Chinese pastor who had seen insects in his garden "unknown in his locality." The "germ carriers," according to one source Johnson quoted, were said to include flies, mosquitoes, spiders, rats, and other insects. Johnson later set out these claims in more detail and with supporting documentation in a pamphlet titled *I Appeal*, but it was the press conference itself that had the most impact, both for Johnson's claims and also for the fantastic visual prop in the form of the scroll. The press conference was widely mocked in cartoons, such as one that depicted Johnson with the scroll, the Chinese characters replaced mainly by hammers and sickles, the exception being two vertical lines that said "Canterbury Tales" and "Gullible's Travels."[48] Another, "The Germ," covered Johnson's face in hammers and sickles resembling the measles, with the crumpled scroll as the background.[49]

Even before Johnson's return, prominent figures had been moved to answer him. Once again, his archbishop, Dr. Geoffrey Fisher, intervened, this time speaking in the House of Lords about Johnson's germ warfare allegations. The allegations, which had been made by the Chinese since mid-1951, were grave enough that General Matthew Ridgway, supreme commander of the Allied Powers in Europe, issued a rebuttal to the effect that "no element in the United Nations command at any time has employed germ warfare."[50] This issue was already being taken seriously, and consequently there were calls in the Lords and the Commons for Johnson's dismissal from his post. The *Daily Worker* dissented, reporting that cheering crowds had welcomed the dean to London on his return, and that his talk on China had been packed. The paper claimed that although Johnson had addressed germ warfare, the major part of his speech had been on "the modern miracle of China."[51] This would be the subject of Johnson's ensuing book, *China's Creative Upsurge* (1953), but the story of China's regeneration was eclipsed by the germ warfare argument. Perhaps it was the *Daily Herald*, with its front-page coverage of Johnson and his scroll, which correctly identified how the attempt at propaganda by the dean and his Chinese mentors had backfired: "Dr. Hewlett Johnson, the 'Red Dean' of Canterbury, has unwittingly killed Communism's biggest propaganda lie."[52] Prime Minister Winston Churchill was perhaps wise enough to understand that the actions of Johnson and the Chinese had been self-defeating when he ruled that there should be no special tribunal to investigate Johnson's role as a propagandist for a foreign power.[53] It is no more than a belated historical irony that while Johnson's claims about germ warfare were at the time presented as evidence of his folly, historians have since found evidence of clandestine germ-warfare experiments that took place in Korea.[54]

The year 1952 marked both the height of Johnson's public presence and the effective loss of his significant influence. His new political tracts did not find major independent publishers. *China's New Creative Age* (1953) and *Eastern Europe in the Socialist World* (1955) were published in Britain by the Moscow-funded publisher Lawrence and Wishart. *The Upsurge of China* (1961) was published in Beijing. A book on the Cuban Revolution remained unfinished. The 1956 Russian invasion of Hungary had perhaps demonstrated to most onlookers that Johnson's defense of Eastern European Communism was a propagandistic sham, and Johnson himself had been forced to criticize the Russians for their actions, albeit in equivocal terms. Johnson never seems to have wavered from his support of Communism. In acting as a mouthpiece for the views of the Russian and Chinese regimes, Johnson seems to have behaved as a dutiful Communist, even though he was not a party member, as he could honestly testify at a voluntary hearing at the US embassy in London in 1954.

Johnson's speech on the death of Stalin was published in pamphlet form as *Joseph Stalin*.[55] The very format of the talk (including its section headings) is taken directly from the official biography of Stalin, as are all the factual claims, the rhetoric, and many specific phrases and sentences.[56] Johnson did not at any moment use his text to open up questions regarding the relationship between Communism and Christianity. In fact, it is in no sense his own text, as there is virtually no remark in it clearly attributable to him. While there is no evidence that Johnson was ordered to give this speech, or that he was presented with the text, it is clear that he knew the protocols of Soviet propaganda and in no way attempted to depart from them. There was significant anti-Stalinist literature circulating in England at that time, not least Trotsky's various book-length attacks and Isaac Deutscher's *Stalin: A Political Biography* (1947), but the claims of the left-wing opposition to Stalin are never even fleetingly recognized in anything Johnson wrote, least of all in the printed speech.

*The Upsurge of China* (1961) was Johnson's final completed work about a Communist country.[57] While his earlier books had found English and US publishers, this one was published by the New World Press in the People's Republic of China. In contrast to the halcyon days of *Socialist Sixth*, it is negligible in terms of its likely influence but interesting as an artifact for what it reveals about the propaganda strategy of Johnson and his mentors. The book is based on the Johnsons' extensive family holiday in China in 1956, which was wholly paid for by the host government, and the rest is based on data regarding China's industrial and agricultural upsurge in the period 1959–1960. The aim of the book was to emphasize that China had entered a new era of peace and prosperity in which different nations and religions were all accommodated, education was a priority, individuals (especially women) were liberated, life had regained color, and culture was open to all. In the second and shorter section of the book, Johnson dutifully reports production statistics. The general tenor and many specifics of the book are drawn from a journal called *People's China*, published in Beijing and prepared for English-language readers. The journal featured articles on the continued struggle for progress, the party and the army, and industrial and agricultural accomplishments narrated in terms both of colossal quantities of data and local stories intended to individualize the otherwise sublime grandeur of the reports. Johnson's library contains copies of *People's China* from the first issue in January 1950 to December 1951, collected into four volumes. The uniform binding suggests that these were supplied to Johnson to assist in the preparation of his book. While Johnson never claims that his information is firsthand, he writes in a manner that suggests that it is personal testimony.

It is probable that Johnson considered his sources to be reliable and treated it as a duty to transmit the facts to a wider readership under the authority of his own name. The lack of intellectual tension in these texts seems remarkable, and this continues to be so even in *Christians and Communism* (1956), a late collection of essays that sets out Johnson's view of Communism as a kind of achieved Christianity and defends Communist states against the charge of anticlericalism by reminding readers of the degenerate state of the (unreformed) Orthodox Church on the eve of the Bolshevik Revolution. The arguments in this book, far from being the culmination of a lifelong intellectual quest, are straightforward reiterations of arguments that Johnson had expressed often in print and in person. In a way, Johnson's Communism is as orthodox as his Christianity. His belief seems to have been not a process of searching but of affirming that which he identified as the truth. However, the question of truth regarding Communism itself and the prospective outcome of world-historical processes cannot be settled by reference to the types of facts that appear in principle to be ascertainable. Johnson's mentors in Russia and China well understood that he brought religious authority to their cause in a complex and highly mediated fashion, but his own view of the relationship between religion and reality enacted something complicated, even if it did not receive a complex articulation in his written work. While Johnson seems to have known little about Marx and almost nothing about Hegel, in his life and practice he took seriously the concept of reality as the actualization of the progress of rationality. Having been exposed to violence in Spain and in England, he did not misunderstand it; he realized that violence could at times be rationalized and at other times be absolutely necessary. While he probably overestimated the independence and credibility of the many church leaders he dealt with in Communist countries, his general stance did not really depend on them but on the notion that the highest form of individual realization had to come through technological and social progress. In this respect, for Johnson the question of liberty of religious practice was purely secondary, and it is likely that for this reason he did not display much skepticism about claims that Communist governments protected freedom of religion. Although he never quite said as much, he essentially regarded religious freedom as secondary to the progression toward Communism (which he always distinguished from the achieved socialism of "Communist" countries). Seen in this light, the contingencies of Johnson's life and career show a high degree of consistency as the manifestation of a philosophical singularity.

From 1936 to 1939, when he was supported and promoted by Victor Gollancz, Johnson appears to have had an important role in developing public interest in and support for Soviet Communism, but no discernible role in recruiting members for the Communist Party of Great Britain, of which he was not in any case a member. After that period, his influence waned, though he still served both British and Russian war policy goals from 1941 to 1945, when Anglo-Soviet friendship was of key importance. His prominence and popularity as a speaker may well have worked against the interests he attempted to serve once the Cold War got under way. While he continued to be often loudly welcomed as an antiwar speaker, his pro-Communism had little impact. In Britain, socialist tradition was upheld by the parliamentary Labour Party and their backers in the trade unions, both dominant forces with a gradualist agenda, while in America neither socialist nor Communist tradition was strong. At key moments, Johnson was portrayed by conservative newspapers and politicians as the embodiment of the dangers of a naive support of Communism. That said, while it might be easy to view Johnson in this light as an

English eccentric, and an elderly one at that (Johnson was ninety-two when he died in 1966), it would be a mistake to lose sight of the fact that the forces for which he spoke were undefeated in his time, and that he could point to the example of Cuba as evidence of a continued world progression to Communism. Johnson visited Cuba in 1964, where he was photographed meeting Castro as part of the fifth anniversary celebrations of the revolution. From 1959, the decolonization process had moved rapidly, and while Johnson was no longer a conduit for feelings of global solidarity, the interview he gave to a Cuban newspaper expresses forward-looking sentiments that belong as fully to the era of the New Left as they do to the period of anti-Nazi struggles of the 1930s: "Christians must be at the heart of revolutionary struggles for freedom, which can give them their inspiration. For me, every honest Christian must feel as his own each one of the liberation struggles which the people support. Each liberation movement must be welcomed by all Christians."[58]

## Notes

1. My thanks are due to Jane Gallagher and the staff of Special Collections at the Templeman Library of the University of Kent for their generous help and close interest in this work. Further thanks are due to the earlier readers of this piece, especially Ian Jones and Antoine Capet, for their generous and detailed comments. The research was made possible by a Leverhulme Trust Research Fellowship.

2. For a contemporary collection of essays on this topic, authored by clergy and theologians, see H. Wilson Harris, ed., *Christianity and Communism* (Oxford: Blackwell, 1937). For a broad view of the clerical politics of the 1930s, see Adrian Hastings, *A History of English Christianity: 1920–1985* (London: Collins, 1986), 319–29.

3. See Matthew Grimley, *Citizenship, Community, and the Church of England: Liberal Anglican Theories of the State between the Wars* (Oxford: Clarendon, 2004); see especially 172–73, on Anglican opposition to Hitler.

4. See in this regard the work of Dianne Kirby, particularly her discussion of Cyril Garbett in "The Archbishop of York and Anglo-American Relations during the Second World War and Early Cold War, 1942–1955," *Journal of Religious History* 23, no. 3 (October 1999): 327–45; her survey of the role of the churches in building the Cold War alliance in "Divinely Sanctioned: The Anglo-American Cold War Alliance and the Defence of Western Civilization and Christianity, 1945–48," *Journal of Contemporary History* 35, no. 3 (July 2000): 385–412; and finally her "Harry Truman's Religious Legacy: The Holy Alliance, Containment and the Cold War," in *Religion and the Cold War*, ed. Dianne Kirby (Basingstoke, UK: Macmillan, 2003), 77–102.

5. See Ian Jones, "The Clergy, the Cold War, and the Mission of the Local Church: England ca. 1945–60," in *Religion and the Cold War*, ed. Diane Kirby (Basingstoke, UK: Macmillan, 2003), 188–99.

6. On Graham, see Stephen J. Whitfield, *The Culture of the Cold War* (Baltimore: Johns Hopkins University Press, 1996), 77–100.
7. Grimley, *Citizenship, Community, and the Church*, 11–12.
8. The Levellers were a political group arguing for freeborn rights and suffrage extension during the English Civil War.
9. For attempts in the immediate wake of the Russian Revolution to grasp the historic significance of radical protestant groups for English political history, see the work of the leading German Social Democrat, Eduard Bernstein, *Cromwell and Communism: Socialism and Democracy in the Great English Revolution* (London: Allen and Unwin, 1930); Trotsky's comparison of the Red Army to Cromwell's army in *Where Is Britain Going?* (London: Allen and Unwin, 1926); and an early study under the auspices of the new Soviet historiography, I. L. Popov-Lensky's *Lilburnei Levellery: Sozialnye dvizheniya i klassovayaborba v epokhu angliiskoi revolyutsii XVII veke* [Lilburne and the Levellers: Social movements and class struggle at the time of the seventeenth-century English Revolution] (Moscow: Rabochii, 1928). Despite the intense international theoretical interest in the Protestant roots of the English Revolution and its implications for the Hegelian-Marxist analysis of world history, Johnson seems unaware of this legacy and can hardly be considered to belong to it.
10. Social Credit was a monetary theory based on the goal of distributing purchasing power to consumers and preventing hoarding. See C. H. Douglas, *Social Credit* (London: Palmer, 1924).
11. See Leon Surette, *Pound in Purgatory: From Economic Radicalism to Anti-Semitism* (Urbana: University of Illinois Press, 1999), for a thorough exploration of forms of Social Credit theory as well as of Pound's relation to them. Johnson's correspondence with Pound (UKC/JOH/COR 755–80) is found in the Hewlett Johnson Papers (hereafter HJP), Special Collections, Templeman Library, University of Kent, Canterbury, Kent, United Kingdom (references to this archive without item numbers indicate documents that were not fully catalogued at the time of access). Outside this archive and Johnson's own published writings, including his *Searching for Light: An Autobiography* (London: Joseph, 1968), a further source for information is the biography by Robert Hughes, *The Red Dean: The Life and Riddle of Dr. Hewlett Johnson, born 1874, died 1966, Dean of Canterbury 1931–1963* (Worthing, UK: Churchman Publishing, 1987).
12. See Dean of Canterbury [Hewlett Johnson] et al., *Report of a Recent Religious Delegation to Spain, April 1937* (London: Gollancz, 1937), 12–13. Johnson's testimony on the bombing of Durango can also be found in his diary for 1937 and in a letter to Sherwood Eddy, April 17, 1937, HJP, UKC/JOH/COR 241.
13. HJP, UKC/JOH/COR 171. The undated document is a manuscript that was very likely the text of the broadcast Johnson made from Bilbao for an unidentified radio station.
14. Dean of Canterbury et al., *Report*, 32.
15. Letter from S. E. Cottam, vicar of Wootton Church, to Hewlett Johnson, April 19, 1937 [the day after Johnson's sermon], HJP, UKC/JOH/COR 173.

16. Letter from Hewlett Johnson to Fenner Brockway, chairman of the Independent Labour Party, April 11, 1937, HJP, UKC/JOH/COR 128.

17. HJP, UKC/JOH/COR 116.

18. Letter from Hewlett Johnson to Sherwood Eddy, May 14, 1937, HJP, UKC/JOH/COR 242.

19. Hewlett Johnson, *The Socialist Sixth of the World* (London: Gollancz, 1939), 63–66.

20. See David Caute, *The Fellow Travellers: Intellectual Friends of Communism* (New Haven, CT: Yale University Press, 1988).

21. HJP, UKC/JOH/Sermons 1. This is a notebook in which Johnson recorded material for use in sermons. In *Soviet Strength: Its Source and Challenge*, 2nd ed. (London: Frederick Muller, 1943), Johnson noted that the Soviet Union had 150 nationalities and claimed that national autonomy was "the basis of the Soviet Constitution" (78–79).

22. Dean of Canterbury [Hewlett Johnson], *The Soviet Constitution and the Rights of the Soviet Citizen* (London: National Council for British-Soviet Unity, n.d.), 2, 6, 7.

23. Johnson, *Socialist Sixth*, 357.

24. Harris, *Christianity and Communism*.

25. Stanley G. Evans's numerous book and pamphlet publications include *Christians and Communists* (London: S.S.C.M., 1949), *Christians in the World Struggle* (Birmingham, UK: Council of Clergy and Ministers for Common Ownership, 1944), *The Churches in the USSR* (London: Cobbett Publishing, 1943), *Hungary's Churches Today* (London: Hungarian News and Information Service, 1952), *Russia and the Atomic Bomb* (London: British Soviet Society, 1949), and *The Trial of Cardinal Mindszenty: An Eye Witness Account* (Birmingham, UK: Religion and the People Publication, 1949.)

26. John MacMurray, *Creative Society: A Study of the Relation of Christianity to Communism* (London: Student Christian Movement, 1935), 24.

27. As reported in the *Sunday Dispatch* (London), December 31, 1939, HJP, UKC/JOH/Cuttings 7651.

28. Letter to the *Times* (London), March 13, 1940. A collection of relevant material is found in HJP, UKC/JOH/CANONS.

29. Johnson, *Soviet Strength*, especially 78–79, 96–102, 123.

30. Hewlett Johnson, *Hitler's Death Warrant: The British-Soviet Treaty* (London: Russia Today Society, 1943).

31. Nicholas Yarusevich, Gregory Petrovich Georgievsky, and Alexander Pavlovich Smirnov, eds., *The Truth about Religion in Russia* (London: Hutchinson, 1942), 5.

32. Letter from Soviet Ambassador to the United Kingdom Ivan Maisky to Hewlett Johnson, January 7, 1943, HJP, UKC/HJ/COR 7242.

33. See Tatiana A. Chumachenko, *Church and State in Soviet Russia: Russian Orthodoxy from World War II to the Khrushchev Years*, trans. Edward E. Roslof (London: Sharpe, 2002), 4–8; and Steven Merritt Miner, *Stalin's Holy War: Religion, Nationalism, and Alliance Politics, 1941–1945* (Chapel Hill: University of North Carolina Press, 2003), 8.

34. A. T. D'Eye, *Russia Revisited: With the Dean of Canterbury through the USSR* (London: Russia Today Society, 1945). My colleague John Butler has pointed out to me the instructive tone of some of D'Eye's letters to Johnson and speculates that he

may have been a conduit between Moscow and Canterbury, not least as he had lived in Russia for some years.

35. Quoted in "U.S., Soviet Gov't Leaders Stress Close Ties at Garden Rally Here," *Daily Worker* (New York), November 15, 1945.

36. See "Canterbury Red," *Time*, November 26, 1945, and "The Red Dean," *Newsweek*, November 26, 1945, both in HJP, UKC/JOH/ALBUSA.

37. "Wallace and 'Red Dean' Urge End of Cold War with Soviets," *New York Post*, December 1948, HJP, UKC/JOH/CUT 6655.

38. Alistair Cooke, "Bronx and Brooklyn Hail the Dean," *Glasgow Herald*, January 13, 1949, HJP, UKC/JOH/CUT 7942.

39. John Chabot Smith, "Canterbury's Dean Asks Red Understanding," *New York Herald Tribune*, November 13, 1948, HJP, UKC/JOH/CUT 6645.

40. "Overflow Crowd Spellbound by Magic of Dean's Oratory," *Vancouver News Herald*, December 6, 1948, HJP, UKC/JOH/USACAN. Johnson parodies a phrase used by Churchill in "The Sinews of Peace" (also known as his "Iron Curtain speech"), given at Fulton College in 1946.

41. "'Red' Dean, Peddling Commie Line, Undeserving of Courtesy," *Brooklyn Eagle*, November 17, 1948. HJP, UKC/JOH/CUT 6647.

42. Leslie Laszlo, "Religion and Nationality in Hungary," in *Religion and Nationalism in Soviet and East European Politics*, ed. Pedro Ramet (Durham, NC: Duke University Press, 1984), 145.

43. "The Pope and the Cardinal," *New Statesman and Nation*, February 12, 1949.

44. Letter from Hewlett Johnson to "Dear Sir," probably intended for the *Times* (London), January 16, 1949, HJP, UKC/JOH/COR 2279.

45. Hewlett Johnson, *Eastern Europe in the Socialist World* (London: Lawrence and Wishart, 1955), 60–64.

46. "Eggs, Tomatoes and Rock Fly at Dean but Miss," *Globe and Mail* (Toronto), May 16, 1950, HJP, UKC/JOH/USACAN.

47. The scroll can be located neither in the archive at the University of Kent nor in the library of Canterbury Cathedral, and appears to be lost.

48. Unidentified newspaper clipping dated July 11, 1952, HJP, UKC/JOH/KOREA.

49. Unidentified clipping, July 1952, HJP, UKC/JOH/KOREA.

50. Report, *News Chronicle* (London), July 1, 1952.

51. "Cheering Crowds Welcome the Dean to London," *Daily Worker*, July 17, 1952.

52. "The Astonishing Dean—Not a Germ of Proof," *Daily Herald* (London), July 9, 1952.

53. See, for example, "Will the Dean Take Note?" *Daily Graphic* (London), July 16, 1952, HJP, UKC/JOH/Cuttings 7473.

54. See Stephen Endicott and Edward Hagerman, *The United States and Biological Warfare: Secrets from the Early Cold War and Korea* (Bloomington: Indiana University Press, 1998).

55. Hewlett Johnson, *Joseph Stalin: Memorial Address to the British Soviet Friendship Society, Beaver Hall, London, April 18th 1953* (London: British Soviet Friendship Society, 1953).

56. The text of the official biography is available at the Marxist Internet Archive, *www.marxists.org* (accessed May 4, 2010).

57. Hewlett Johnson, *The Upsurge of China* (New World Press: Peking, 1961).
58. The text is from an interview in an unidentified Cuban newspaper clipping, HJP, UKC/JOH/CUBA. The translation from Spanish is my own. In a longer interview for *Revolución*, January 4, 1964, accompanied by several photographs of Johnson, he describes Fidel Castro as a "Man of Steel" and "one of my heroes," states again at length that socialism is Christian, and criticizes organized churches in the West for not following the way of Christ. Asked about his sobriquet the "Red Dean," Johnson states that he is proud of it, as red is the color of blood, vitality, and church renewal, and it has always been the color of progress and of revolutionaries.

## References

ARCHIVES

Hewlett Johnson Papers, Special Collections, Templeman Library, University of Kent, Canterbury, Kent, United Kingdom

SELECTED PUBLISHED WORKS

Ayers, David. "Literary Criticism and Cultural Politics." In *The Cambridge History of Twentieth-Century English Literature*, ed. Laura Marcus and Pete Nicholls, 379–95. Cambridge: Cambridge University Press, 2005.

Dean of Canterbury. See Johnson, Hewlett.

D'Eye, A. T. *Russia Revisited: With the Dean of Canterbury through the USSR*. London: Russia Today Society, 1945.

Grimley, Matthew. *Citizenship, Community, and the Church of England: Liberal Anglican Theories of the State between the Wars*. Oxford: Clarendon, 2004.

Harris, H. Wilson, ed. *Christianity and Communism*. Oxford: Blackwell, 1937.

Hastings, Adrian. *A History of English Christianity: 1920–1985*. London: Collins, 1986.

Hughes, Robert. *The Red Dean: The Life and Riddle of Dr. Hewlett Johnson, born 1874, died 1966, Dean of Canterbury 1931–1963*. Worthing, UK: Churchman Publishing, 1987.

Johnson, Hewlett. *Act Now! An Appeal to the Mind and Heart of Britain*. London: Gollancz, 1939.

———. *Christians and Communism*. London: Putnam, 1956.

———. *Eastern Europe in the Socialist World*. London: Lawrence and Wishart, 1955.

———. *Hitler's Death Warrant: The British-Soviet Treaty*. London: Russia Today Society, 1943.

———. *Joseph Stalin: Memorial Address to the British Soviet Friendship Society, Beaver Hall, London, April 18th 1953*. London: British Soviet Friendship Society, 1953.

———. *Marxism and the Individual*. London: Lawrence and Wishart, 1943.

———. *Searching for Light: An Autobiography*. London: Joseph, 1968.

———. *The Socialist Sixth of the World*. London: Gollancz, 1939.

———. *The Soviet Constitution and the Rights of the Soviet Citizen*. London: National Council for British-Soviet Unity, n.d.

———. *Soviet Strength: Its Source and Challenge*, 2nd ed. London: Frederick Muller, 1943.

———. *The Upsurge of China*. Beijing: New World Press, 1961.

Johnson, Hewlett [Dean of Canterbury] et al. *Report of a Recent Religious Delegation to Spain, April 1937.* London: Gollancz, 1937.

Jones, Ian. "The Clergy, the Cold War, and the Mission of the Local Church: England ca. 1945–60." In *Religion and the Cold War*, ed. Dianne Kirby, 188–99. Basingstoke, UK: Macmillan, 2003.

Kirby, Dianne. "The Archbishop of York and Anglo-American Relations during the Second World War and Early Cold War, 1942–1955." *Journal of Religious History* 23, no. 3 (October 1999): 327–45.

MacMurray, John. *Creative Society: A Study of the Relation of Christianity to Communism.* London: Student Christian Movement, 1935.

Miner, Steven Merritt. *Stalin's Holy War: Religion, Nationalism, and Alliance Politics, 1941–1945.* Chapel Hill: University of North Carolina Press, 2003.

Morrison, Simon. *The People's Artist: Prokofiev's Soviet Years.* Oxford: Oxford University Press, 2009.

Popov-Lensky, I. L. *Lilburne i Levellery: Sozialnye dvizheniya i klassovaya borba v epokhu angliiskoi revolyutsii XVII veka* [Lilburne and the Levellers: Social movements and class struggle at the time of the seventeenth-century English Revolution]. Moscow: Rabochii, 1928.

Surette, Leon. *Pound in Purgatory: From Economic Radicalism to Anti-Semitism.* Urbana: University of Illinois Press, 1999.

Trotsky, Leon. *Where Is Britain Going?* London: Allen and Unwin, 1926.

Whitfield, Stephen J. *The Culture of the Cold War.* Baltimore: Johns Hopkins University Press, 1996.

Yarusevich, Nicholas, Gregory Petrovich Georgievsky, and Alexander Pavlovich Smirnov, eds. *The Truth about Religion in Russia.* Translation supervised by E. N. C. Sergeant. London: Hutchinson, 1942.

# CHAPTER 5

# Rising to the Occasion

## *The Role of American Missionaries and Korean Pastors in Resisting Communism throughout the Korean War*

*Kai Yin Allison Haga*

The Cold War is often perceived as a political conflict, an ideological competition, or a military tension between the Soviet Union and the Western world. Yet, in a recent study of the relations between religion and the Cold War, William Inboden argues that religion functioned both as a cause that could explain the rationale of the United States' opposition to the Soviet Union, and also as an instrument to strengthen anti-Communism at home and to undermine the influence of Communism abroad. Since Presidents Truman and Eisenhower both, according to Inboden, viewed the Cold War as "nothing less than a religious war," their efforts to form a "civil religion" in America were motivated by political objectives.[1] Inboden did not analyze the Korean War, however, despite its crucial role in both presidencies and in the formation of the Cold War.

The Korean War was a mini-theater of the Cold War struggle in which the two opposing camps competed not only for military domination, but also in the political, social, and ideological realms. The war threatened to wipe out the last mission field in East Asia, yet the destruction of war ironically allowed Christianity to expand in the Southern zone. Religious actors—mostly Christian clergymen (Catholic and Protestant), both inside and outside of

Korea—were active on all fronts of the conflict: military, political, social, and ideological. The war ushered in a time of intimate collaboration between state and nonstate actors that would be critical to not only the war, but also the future development of US-Korean relations.

This chapter examines the influence of Christianity and missionaries in the Korean War, showing how religious factors (including ideas, activities, and actors) shaped the early development of the Cold War. It addresses two major questions: why did religion matter in Korea, and how did religious factors play out in the course of the war? The main goal of this analysis is to show how the course and the final outcome of the war amplified the relevance of religion as an ideological alternative to the Communist utopia.

## Christianity in Korea and the Rise of Korean Nationalism

Korea was originally dominated by Buddhism and Confucianism. Christianity arose in the 1700s when Korean tributary missions brought Catholic religious texts back from China.[2] The first American Protestant missionary, Dr. Horace N. Allen (a Presbyterian), came as the physician of the US legation in Seoul in 1884. His ability to heal Queen Min's nephew, Prince Min Yŏng-ik, earned him the respect of the royal court and led the king to permit missionaries to build hospitals and schools.[3] By 1910, American missionaries were running 1,623 schools of all types, enrolling more than 130,000 students. These American schools accounted for about 93 percent of all foreign mission schools.[4] Religious schools and Christian-run schools graduated about a third of the country's high school students.[5] Meanwhile, Christianity grew rapidly during the final decade of the Chosŏn Dynasty (1898–1907).[6]

Meanwhile, Japan's colonial aggression in Korea incited deep anti-Japanese sentiment among young Korean intellectuals and diverted traditional anti-foreign sentiment away from Christianity. Missionary activities, especially the establishment of mission schools, gave rise to a new generation of Korean elites that included such renowned nationalists as Syngman Rhee, Yŏ Un-hyŏng, Kim Kyu-sik, and Ahn Chang-ho. These men all explicitly espoused Christian ideals in their nationalist struggle against Japan. Syngman Rhee became the first president of the Korean Provisional Government (KPG), which was established by Korean exiles in Shanghai in April 1919. For two decades, Rhee lived as a political exile in America, seeking recognition for the KPG. Ahn Chang-ho, Yŏ Un-hyŏng, and later Cho Man-sik were well-respected Christian educators who sought to build up Korea through Christian education.[7] Yŏ and Cho remained in Korea and each enjoyed a wide following. Cho was a cofounder of Sin'ganhoe (New Korea Society or New Trunk Society) in P'yŏngyang, with a membership of thirty thousand.[8] His nonviolent approach to resisting Japanese colonial control earned him the nickname "the Gandhi of Korea."[9]

Japanese aggression also incited Korean Protestant church leaders to preach a message of national deliverance. Church buildings became secret meeting places for anti-Japanese nationalists. Kim Il-sung, whose parents were Protestants, recounted his father's role in organizing anti-Japanese activities in Manchuria through local church gatherings.[10] Christian churches were gaining members despite Japanese pressure.[11] The growth was particularly significant in P'yŏngyang, which, because of its concentration of various Protestant institutions, was known as the Christian capital of Korea. When he first arrived in 1923, Father Patrick Byrne, an American Catholic missionary, exclaimed that P'yŏngyang was "the most Protestant city [he] was ever in, in America or elsewhere."[12]

As church membership grew, so did the influence of American missionaries. In 1939, Americans represented more than 76 percent of all Protestant missionaries and had influence over 72 percent of all the Korean Protestants who were under the care of foreign mission stations.[13] The churches' positive public image and the American missionaries' influence at this time would pave the way for their involvement in post–World War II Korean politics. Yet conflicts between the Christians and the Communists, which had begun in the 1920s, also further intensified.[14]

Following the surrender of Japan, the People's Republic was declared on September 6, 1945, under the leadership of Yŏ Un-hyŏng in the South and Cho Man-sik in the North.[15] While the leftists had a dominant position in the South, the rightists commanded a large following in the North, precisely the opposite of the ideologies of the northern and southern occupiers. In the North, supported by Soviet troops, Kim Il-sung succeeded in seizing power and purging the rightists; in the South, the rightists rose to power with the blessings of the Americans. Two governments in two zones, with two different visions for Korea's future and supported by two opposing patrons, competed for national domination. As the historian Allan R. Millett has pointed out, even if there had been no foreign occupations, the Koreans themselves would still have fought bitterly against each other to have their competing agendas adopted.[16]

## Conditions in the Soviet Occupation Zone

When Russian troops entered Korea in late August, they found immediate resistance to their Communist message. Korean leaders had already formed the Committees for the Preparation of Korean Independence (CPKIs). The

P'yŏngyang delegation had only two Communists among its twenty members and the popular Christian leader, Cho Man-sik, was in charge. According to Charles K. Armstrong, "The [People's Committees] in the northern provinces were usually dominated by conservative nationalists."[17] In South P'yŏngan Province, for example, Cho drew his strongest support from both Christians and non-Christians.[18] Likewise, almost all northern CPKIs were under non-Communist leadership (the exceptions being North and South Hamgyŏng Provinces).[19] The Russians chose to work with Cho because the high concentrations of Christians in major northern cities made immediate Communist assimilation impossible.

Instead of waiting passively for the Koreans to work out their own political destiny, the Soviet army began taking over all Japanese enterprises, including railroads, radio stations, and banks. They placed Communist red guards in charge of all provincial police stations because they feared that pro-Americans and anti-Communists might have taken root in them.[20] Outwardly, the Soviets advocated a coalition government and encouraged rightists to set up political parties. Secretly, they were biding their time while they tightened their military grip.[21] When Cho resisted that tightening, they brought in Kim Il-sung, the leader of the Kapsan faction of anti-Japanese guerrilla fighters in Manchuria. He was chosen for his informal connection with both the Soviet Union and the Chinese Communist Party, and for his appeal among the Korean people as an anti-Japanese fighter with a Christian family background in P'yŏngyang.

Religious groups, especially Christians and Ch'ŏndogyo followers, posed the greatest obstacles to a Communist revolution. Ch'ŏndogyo's political wing, the Young Friends' Party (YFP), worked against Communist efforts among farmers in the countryside.[22] In Sinŭiju, where Christians dominated the CPKI, two Presbyterian pastors, Rev. Yun Ha-yŏng and Rev. Han Kyŏng-jik, organized the Social Democratic Party (SDP) in September 1945.[23] Later, Cho Man-sik and Rev. Yi Yun-yong formed the Chosŏn Democratic Party (CDP) in November 1945. Launched with three hundred thousand official members, it grew to five hundred thousand by early 1946.[24]

Violent confrontations began in November when the executive members of SDP spoke up in their district meeting against the tightening control of the Red Army. Communists stirred up local workers to disrupt the meeting. They destroyed the church where the meeting was held, beat one church elder to death, wounded several others, and later attacked the homes of various SDP executive members.[25] A few days later, about five thousand Christian high school students held a mass demonstration against Communist violence. The Red Army put down the demonstration with machine guns. Twenty-three students were killed, about seven hundred were wounded, and more than a thousand were arrested.[26] Rev. Yun Ha-yŏng and Rev. Han Kyŏng-jik escaped the purge by fleeing south. It was the beginning of a Christian exodus southward. In the North, a Christian family background was declared to be a sign of political "unreliability."[27]

Matters deteriorated further after the Moscow Conference in December 1945. The foreign ministers of the three major Allied powers (United States, Soviet Union, and United Kingdom) decided to form a US-Soviet joint commission to assist the establishment of a provisional Korean government. It called for a four-power trusteeship of Korea for up to five years. Cho Man-sik and the CDP rejected the trusteeship because they found it insulting: it indicated that the foreign powers looked down on the Korean people and doubted their capacity for self-government. Dramatically, Cho and his supporters resigned from the South P'yŏngan Provincial People's Political Committee (SPPPC). In response, the Russians put Cho under house arrest.[28]

The rise and fall of Cho Man-sik revealed the significance of Christian nationalists and the influence of churches in politics. In the first three months of postwar Korea, Cho had been the political head of the Northern zone. Cho's fall ended any possibility of a peaceful unification. With Kim Il-sung now in charge, Christians and members of Ch'ŏndogyo had to decide whether to compromise or flee.

## Conditions in the US Occupation Zone

Meanwhile, below the thirty-eighth parallel, the Americans made several early missteps that caused serious problems for the US occupation. First, they refused to recognize the popular People's Republic. Second, for expediency, they chose to maintain former Japanese collaborators in their government positions. This sowed distrust of US intentions. Third, the Americans were not well prepared for the occupation, which allowed leftists from the better-organized northern regime to infiltrate the South and to spread propaganda.

The rightists' cause got its first boost with the appointment of Commander George Z. Williams as an adviser to General John R. Hodge, the commander of the US occupation forces. Williams, the son of Rev. Franklin E. C. Williams, a Methodist missionary to Korea, was chosen simply because he was the only US military employee who spoke fluent Korean.[29] The general urgently asked Williams to advise him on the political conditions in Korea, to hire Koreans for the United States Army Military Government in Korea (USAMGIK), and to speak on behalf of the USAMGIK to Korean leaders.[30] Williams hired many Christians to work in the USAMGIK. Of the top fifty Koreans in the USAMGIK, 70 percent were Christians: Choson Christian College (later Yonsei University) professors, graduates, clergymen, or church laymen.[31] Moreover, six Korean doctors, all personally trained by American medical missionaries, were appointed vice governors.[32]

The return of American missionaries and their children in the employment of the USAMGIK and the US Army also further boosted the influence of Christianity.[33] A good example was the Underwood family. Rev. Horace H. Underwood, a second-generation missionary to Korea, worked as a civilian officer in the USAMGIK. His youngest son, Lt. Richard Underwood, was assigned to the American liaison team in P'yŏngyang, collecting intelligence information through his church connections.[34] His oldest son, Lt. Horace G. Underwood, was later put in charge of reorganizing Seoul National University.[35] Williams's father, Rev. Frank Williams, was an agricultural adviser to the USAMGIK. The USAMGIK depended on these missionaries; every Friday morning at ten o'clock, General Archer Lerch, the military governor, met with them and listened to their advice.[36]

Williams also trusted the conservative leaders of the Korean Democratic Party and appointed many of them as officials of the USAMGIK.[37] Cho Pyŏng-ok, a well-known Christian nationalist and an active KDP member, was later appointed head of the national police. These rightists urged Williams to allow the famous nationalists Kim Ku and Syngman Rhee to return as a way of offsetting the influence of Yŏ Un-hyŏng's People's Party.[38] General Hodge was persuaded; Rhee returned in October and Kim in November. It was a decision the general would later deeply regret.

Rhee and Kim did have the effect of weakening Yŏ Un-hyŏng. Yŏ's popularity began to drop when he came out in support of the Moscow Agreement. Then, as rumors of Communist persecution of Christians began to reach the South, the southern church community became less willing to compromise and began moving away from Yŏ. To make matters worse, Yŏ's appeasement policies had enabled Communist spies to infiltrate his People's Party and eventually tear it apart. As a result, Yŏ's political fortunes collapsed and attention shifted to Rhee and Kim.[39]

Rhee soon surpassed Kim in political influence when he gained the support of northern refugees, repatriates from Japan, and Christians because of his staunch anti-Communism. These refugees set up anti-Communist organizations such as the National Salvation Young Men's Federation, the Northwest Young Men's Association, and the Korean National Youth Corps, which later became Rhee's street squads against the leftists.[40] He enlisted churches and other Christian institutions into his local political network.[41]

Rhee was not only a shrewd politician, but also a skillful diplomat. He understood the important role of Christianity for building a Westernized Korea and his political success. A young Rhee had argued that without a clear commitment to Christian faith, Korea would not be able to "reap [the] true benefits" of learning from the Western world and that deep friendship with it would not be possible.[42] He strongly believed that Korea was "Christianity's greatest bastion in the Orient."[43] Therefore, to achieve his political ambition, he cultivated friendships with some influential US church leaders, such as Rev. Frederick Brown Harris, the chaplain to the US Senate, and Bishop Francis Spellman of New York, during his exile in America. Prior to Rhee's return to Korea, Bishop Spellman praised Rhee as the US Catholic Church's choice for leadership in Korea against the forces of godless Communism.[44]

When Christian refugees from the North began to concentrate in the South, it infused the southern churches with a radical anti-Communism. New refugee churches sprang up rapidly.[45] Missionaries were kept busy offering relief to the refugees.[46] Their interactions with refugees shifted the opinions of many missionaries and church leaders. Whereas the church community was originally divided, with some clergymen supporting Yŏ Un-hyŏng and Kim Kyu-sik, many now saw the Soviet Union and the Communist regime above the thirty-eighth parallel as the "two most anti-Christian powers" of their time.[47] They supported Korean independence and unity, but their stronger desire was for a free and democratic government.[48] Syngman Rhee was praised as "the chief bulwark against the communization of Korea."[49]

An opportunity to form a new government in the South came in mid-1947, when the United Nations authorized a separate election in the Southern zone to form a National Assembly to write a Korean constitution and establish an executive branch of government for the South. In May 1948, Syngman Rhee was elected by the National Assembly as the first president of Korea. The South was moving away from its Buddhist-Confucian traditions and toward a new society built in the American image, adopting a US-model presidential system and Christianized ceremonies at government events.[50] Religious freedom was guaranteed by the Korean Constitution and the principle of separation of church and state was respected by Rhee's government.[51] By early 1950, Rhee's government had eradicated most of the Communist guerrilla activities and gained firm control over the Southern zone.

Meanwhile, back in the North, Kim Il-sung was gathering his power. He launched his revolution in early 1946 with land reforms, new regulations on labor and equality between the sexes, and the nationalization of major industries. Opposition to these initiatives and several attempted assassinations of Kim Il-sung resulted in tougher reprisals. Many churches and seminaries were closed and Christian workers were arrested.

As the Cold War grew colder, ice was forming in Korea between its two inflexible governments. They held opposing visions of modernism, but a common ambition to unify the country according to their own terms. When Kim Il-sung saw that the guerrilla activities were ineffective in subverting Rhee's government, his desire to invade the South became stronger. Simultaneously, the growing stability of the Southern zone and the wish of many North Korean refugees to return home also motivated Syngman Rhee to pursue a more aggressive policy. The peninsula was filled with fear, either that Rhee might march north or that Kim might march south. Each side used this fear to tighten control and to plead for more aid from its patron.[52]

## American Missionaries in South Korea

America's interest in missionary activities in Korea grew as anti-Communist sentiment was settling in America. Religious journals, pamphlets, and letters brought news about Korea and the condition of the Korean churches.[53] In a 1948 report, missionaries not only urged US churches to send more workers to the field, they also portrayed the "New Korea" as a country that "holds the centre of the stage in international politics in the East."[54] In another report, from 1949, missionaries spoke positively about political and religious developments because "many Christians [had] distinguished themselves as officials in the new government," and because the churches were packed.[55] They were hopeful for the future, and not ready to "lose the field of battle to heathenism, or Communism, or materialism."[56] The American Methodist Church viewed the ideological battle in Korea as a struggle "between Soviet and Christian concepts of democratic progress."[57] Thoburn T. Brumbaugh, the associate secretary of the Methodist Division of Foreign Missions, asserted that Christianity would be "a great factor" in the internal political struggle in South Korea.[58]

The domestic religious environment in America at that time also favored missionary activities. To many preachers, the stories of the persecution of Christians in Eastern Europe and in Asia fit the premillennialists' view of the end times.[59] The biblical term *Armageddon* was frequently used to describe the possibility of a nuclear war. President Truman envisioned building an informal Western Christian alliance—"a common religious and moral front"—to counter the Communist ideological expansion in Europe and Asia.[60] He also encouraged the American people to put their freedoms and rights into practice by attending religious activities and paying more attention to religion.[61] Meanwhile, Rev. Billy Graham's crusades were breaking attendance records and his anti-Communist religious sermons found resonance across the entire religious spectrum.[62] Missionaries and their activities in this Cold War environment were perceived by both politicians and the public as a strategic and important means to spread pro-American information and contain Communism.[63]

While the US army was withdrawing its troops from Korea, US churches were sending more missionaries to Korea. The number of American missionaries increased from about a dozen in 1945 to more than two hundred by the end of 1949. When tensions rose with the North in early 1950, missionaries wrote to their patrons at home, telling them to pray for Korea so that "atheistic Communism may not succeed" and that "Christ and Christian Democracy may win" because if "democracy of a Christian nature wins, America and all democratic nations will have an important foothold in the heart of Asia."[64] The fate of South Korea was tied to US policy but also the "Christian forces of America."[65]

President Rhee understood the importance of US support to the survival of his government. To secure the passage of the Korean Aid Bill, which was under debate in Congress in June 1949, the National Christian Council of Korea (NCC) organized nationwide public demonstrations, pleading for US support. In Seoul alone, more than fifty thousand Christians carried signs with slogans such as "We Christians will defend our native land from Communist attack," "The insecurity of Korea is a threat to world peace," "All Asia is watching America's action in Korea in defense of democracy," and "Let the churches of the world unite their strength to protect the churches of Korea." The NCC even issued a proclamation, declaring that only in the atmosphere of Christian ideals could democratic government survive in Asia, and arguing that if the Christian world refused to protect and help South Korea, the whole of Asia would be lost.[66]

The Koreans' desire for US protection was not simply orchestrated propaganda. As recorded in the letters of missionaries, Korean Christians were genuinely afraid of a Communist invasion. Two weeks before the outbreak of the Korean War, President Rhee met with Dr. Bob Pierce, an American evangelist and a close friend of Billy Graham. Rhee told him that every Christian in Korea knew that they were prime targets, especially those who served in the South Korean government. Rhee warned that there was not much time left if they did not get military protection from the United States.[67]

Fears of invasion also encouraged Korean Christians to seek religious means for national deliverance. In March 1950, Protestant churches under the sponsorship of the Korean National Council of Churches (KNCC) conducted a campaign entitled the "Save the Nation Evangelical Crusade." The American missionaries Rev. Harold Voelkel and Rev. Otto De Camp were involved in the interdenominational preparation committee. Pierce was the major speaker of the crusade. From April to June 1950, the crusade visited all the major cities of the South. Pierce reported that more than twenty-five thousand new converts made public confessions.[68] The average number of converts gained in each meeting was higher than the crusades led by Billy Graham in Los Angeles (1949) or any other Youth for Christ rallies in the United States during the same period of time.

During the crusade period, the South Korean military also invited Pierce to preach to their soldiers. The implication was clear: in the Cold War, Christianity emerged as a dominant ideological force against Communism in South Korea (also known as the Republic of Korea, or ROK). The real impact of the crusade was hard to measure because within weeks after Pierce's departure, the Korean War broke out.

On June 25, 1950, North Korea launched an all-fronts attack. After five hours, the city of Kaesŏng fell. Six Methodist missionaries were captured there—the first group of US POWs.[69] Later, some Catholic priests and nuns were also taken. For the next three years, their internment served as a rallying cry among the American religious groups who sought their release.

## Missionaries and the War Effort

Missionaries in other areas of Korea had more warning, and most evacuated to Japan or to Pusan. Still, some missionaries chose to remain and offer their services. John and Horace G. Underwood, for instance, headed back north immediately after they sent their families off to Japan. Horace Underwood first tried to find General John H. Church, who was the head of US military survey group, so that he might assist the US Army. Horace found Major General William F. Dean instead and volunteered to be a civilian adviser to the 24th Division.[70] John Underwood helped the military by guiding Army scouts in the Taejŏn area.[71]

Other missionaries also offered their services to the military during this early stage of the war. On July 6, Rev. Francis Kinsler (Northern Presbyterian) went to Taegu as an interpreter for UN officials. The officials asked Rev. Harry Hill, who had lived in P'yŏngyang, to help them interrogate North Korean POWs and to provide religious services to the war-weary US troops.[72] Rev. William Linton (Southern Presbyterian) and Rev. Kinsler volunteered to lead religious services as well.[73]

Up to this point, these missionaries received no compensation from the US government. But US churches were willing to provide them with financial support, because their presence in the war zone was considered "very important to the future of the work in Korea" and crucial to the development of the US-Korean relationship. Therefore, their patrons in the United States promised to "push very hard" and "do everything" needed for full-scale relief work in Korea and for the return of missionaries to the war zone.[74]

The army, however, was not willing to let the evacuated missionaries return from Japan unless the war subsided and conditions improved, and unless the applicants were able to guarantee their own food and shelter.[75] For missionaries who had served in the US military before, there was a quicker option: reenlisting. By August, Dr. Howard Moffett (Naval Medical Corps), Dr. Horace H. Underwood (Department of the Army Civilian), Rev. William Shaw (Civilian Chaplains), and Rev. Harold Voelkel (Civilian Chaplains) all returned in this way.

## Among the Refugees

The war caused great civilian suffering. By mid-July, there were about four hundred Christian workers taking refuge in Taegu, with more heading to Pusan. Rev. Han Kyŏng-jik gathered a number of northern pastors in Taejŏn and formed the Christian National Salvation Assembly to promote and coordinate patriotic relief activities among Christians.[76] The assembly also tried to use human networks for intelligence gathering and relief work.[77]

Although the Korean Christians had a structure for relief operations, they lacked the means for a large relief campaign. This situation gave American missionaries an opportunity to have a real impact on saving lives, because the missionaries had resources and special privileges: they were the only civilians who still had vehicles, external means of support, connections with local churches to organize workers, and influence within the US Army to obtain permission for their activities. Also, they secured some funds from banks and material supplies from the Church World Service for relief work.[78] Establishing Taegu as their main relief center, the missionaries sent truckloads of food to other crowded cities, like Yŏngdong and Kimch'ŏn. Later in September, they received new supplies from Tokyo through the Economic Cooperation Administration (ECA).[79]

Once transported from Taegu, the aid was distributed through church channels. The missionaries would contact local pastors and laymen ahead of time, to get the word out. Once a crowd had gathered, relief workers distributed food together with some Christian tracts to the non-Christians. To Christians, they offered copies of the gospels or New Testaments in addition to the relief materials. The missionaries often left behind additional supplies at local churches. Churches thus became known as places to get help.[80] As a result, Christian influence continued growing, even though many leaders and buildings had been lost.

After three months, the United Nations began to coordinate relief work. It is unknown how many people survived those first months as a result of the missionaries' efforts, because no data was collected. The efforts, however, aroused public interest around the world. News about the missionaries and the Korean refugees was frequently reported in various religious magazines.

Evacuated missionaries in Japan regularly published the letters and reports of missionaries and Christians in the war zone in a pamphlet called *Korea Letters*. Retired missionaries, church leaders, Korean churches in America, and interdenominational organizations distributed the publication across the United States, encouraging people to pray and to donate money and goods.

Christian propaganda also greatly assisted the relief efforts. During the Korean War, Dr. Bob Pierce founded World Vision Inc. and made two documentaries on Korea. The first one, *The 38th Parallel*, chronicled his "Save the Nation Evangelistic Crusade." One local American newspaper described the film a telling "the story of [Korea's] tragedies as well as its hopes found in the Christian way of life."[81] In October 1950, US church leaders recognized that "Christian concerns must find expression in an organized effort for Christian relief in Korea."[82] Drives for cash donations and clothing began in November among individual denominations.

Later, Pierce's second film, *The Flames*, was released in 1952 and shown to churches across America.[83] His graphic depiction of suffering women and children shocked people. Churches and individuals throughout the United States and Canada (and later England and Australia) sent money to the Presbyterian boards, the Methodist boards, the Church World Service (CWS), the Salvation Army, the Catholic Relief Service, the Maryknoll Sisters, and other organizations, often expressly to support the Christian refugees in Korea. Whenever the label "Korea" was attached to a drive, public response was exceptionally generous.

Most religious groups participated in the UN relief effort, voluntarily collecting and distributing supplies on behalf of the United Nations.[84] During the first two years of the war, materials (worth about US $4,856,446) from Christian groups accounted for about 44 percent of overall US voluntary donations.[85] Later, when the war became stabilized along the thirty-eight parallel, private groups were allowed to control the distribution of their own relief materials. US Protestant churches sent $271,341.70 in cash, $1,599,752.82 worth of clothing, and 5,469,882 pounds of relief supplies in 1953 through CWS alone.[86]

American donations helped Christian refugees not only survive but also build churches, orphanages, temporary schools, technical institutes, shelters for widows, and clinics.[87] These social services benefited all refugees and strengthened the church's positive image. Missionary efforts were therefore crucial not only to the survival of the Christian community in Korea, but also its future expansion.

In addition to giving relief materials to Korean refugees, missionaries also offered emergency evacuation to Christian leaders, who were certain to be killed if captured. When the Chinese "volunteers" entered the Korean conflicts and forced the United Nations to evacuate from the North, missionaries organized what they called Operation Heartbreak, to save Christian leaders and their families.[88] Korean drivers carried notes from the missionaries declaring that the passengers were Christians and asking for assistance from the US military.[89] Similar efforts were carried out by missionaries and Korean Christian leaders collaborating with each other in Hŭngnam, Inch'ŏn, and Seoul. The estimated number of all refugees on the road to the South by February 1951 was more than one million.[90] These refugees had survived Communist control, and their testimonies and evangelical zeal were strong tools to counteract Communist propaganda.

## Inside the POW Camps

When fighting stabilized above the thirty-eighth parallel and UN forces reestablished control over the Southern zone, new frontiers for missionary activity emerged, in the prisoner of war (POW) camps and at the truce table. The evangelical work among POWs caused problems for the negotiations.[91]

Missionaries had actually been involved with POWs since the beginning of the war. US intelligence depended heavily on the voluntary services of American missionaries like Rev. Harry Hill. (Since Rev. Hill had worked in the North before World War II, his background helped him to verify the claims of prisoners.) In return for their help, the military allowed these missionaries to preach to the prisoners.[92] Later, in August 1950, the US authorities sent two civilian chaplains, Rev. William Shaw and Rev. Harold Voelkel, to look after the Korean troops and POWs. They soon found that there were Christians among the prisoners; forcibly conscripted by the Korean People's Army (KPA), they had surrendered at their first opportunity.[93]

By December 1950, there were nearly 150,000 prisoners being held by UN forces.[94] General MacArthur saw an opportunity. He believed that since Communism grew by terrorism, subversion, and deceit, it would lose its power in an open atmosphere.[95] The Far Eastern Command hired Dr. William C. Kerr and Dr. Dexter Lutz in Tokyo, both missionaries from the Presbyterian Mission, to prepare a reorientation program, which was later called "CI&E" (Civilian Information and Education).[96]

The pilot program began in early October 1950, at Yŏngdŭng-p'o (near Seoul). Five hundred North Korean inmates were selected for classes designed to correct their distorted ideas about Western democracy and to teach Western values. They also attended Protestant and Roman Catholic religious services held by missionary chaplains. Although the retreat from Seoul caused this pilot program to be cut short, it did lay down the premise for the later reeducation program begun on Kŏje Island.[97]

The United Nations implemented a religious program in all their Kŏje POW camps. In addition to Chaplain Voelkel, two more missionary chaplains, Rev. John E. Talmage and Rev. Bruce A. Cumming, were transferred there.[98] Initially, there were only about three thousand Protestants and one thousand Catholics among the 147,000 Korean POWs.[99] In addition to weekly worship services and prayer gatherings, the chaplains also set up Bible institutes in the compounds. The first one began with only thirty-eight prisoners. By 1953, however, there were 3,883 prisoners per week in fifteen different institutes.[100] After about a year of ministry, 2,266 Korean POWs were baptized. More than 1,500 others became catechumens (people who had finished their doctrinal instructional courses and were waiting to be baptized) and 11,000 were preparing for the catechumenate.[101]

US commanders introduced a similar program into the Chinese camps. Unlike the case of the North Koreans, there were very few Christians among the Chinese POWs. The US Army asked Rev. Earle Woodberry and Father Thomas O'Sullivan, two senior ex-China missionaries, to be chaplains for the Chinese POWs. US churches took notice, and Rev. Woodberry was asked for information "about the experiences" and "the attitude of some of these Chinese" prisoners, because the American people had great interest in his ministry. The secretary of the Presbyterian Church (USA), Dr. John Smith, promised that his stories would "be given wide publicity" in the United States.[102]

During the first month of ministry, Woodberry reported that about six hundred Chinese soldiers came forward to receive Christ as their Savior. Among them, seventy-five were officers. Three months later, nearly five hundred more officers had come forward. The worship attendance increased to six or seven thousand per gathering. At least six thousand expressed "a purpose to believe in Christ," and some wanted to be baptized.[103] The growth was so rapid that Chaplain Woodberry and his staff had to "hold them back from recording their decisions in order to be sure they were genuine."[104] About a year later, in June 1952, the chaplain and his Korean staff held between eight and twelve worship services a month, with an average of more than four thousand attendees at each.[105] Even after the Chinese prison camps moved from Kŏje Island to Cheju Island, the attendance in the nonrepatriate camp (camp no. 3) did not drop.[106] Chaplain Woodberry and his fellow American officers were "astounded at the spontaneous outburst of Christian evangelism," especially when they knew the services were voluntary.[107]

The number of conversions alarmed the Communist prisoners and prompted them to fight back. Some sought to ban chaplains from preaching.[108] Others vented their feelings by attacking Christian prisoners. In August 1951, the murder of a deacon in a Korean POW church congregation stirred more violence between Communist and Christian prisoners. In response, Christians in Compound 85 drew up a petition, signed in their blood, asking to be put to death rather than returned to North Korea. Within days, Christians in every compound of North Korean POWs had written blood petitions.[109] These blood petitions, according to a newspaper report, "eventually became the mightiest propaganda weapon in the peace talks."[110] Christians POWs also organized anti-Communist protests and signed blood petitions against repatriation.[111]

Religion strengthened the moral case for voluntary repatriation, and thus hampered the truce talks. The missionaries' ministry among POWs and the mass conversions within the camps became well known to US churchgoers. For the general public, the implication was more important than the details of exactly how many converted or whether the confessions of faith were sincere. What mattered was that droves of people who had lived under Communism and even fought under its banner were now choosing the side of Christianity and of America. It inspired a sense of righteousness and provided a boost to the moral case for US intervention. Religious freedom, church leaders believed, was the antidote to Communism's hold on people's minds.[112]

Truman's administration, in fact, explored the political value of religion in the POW controversy. In a telegram to the US ambassador in Pusan, Secretary of State Dean Acheson instructed the US embassy to "corroborate and furnish [the State Department] enough material for [a] pamphlet."[113] Truman even considered releasing all the nonrepatriates unilaterally if he could gain the support of President-elect Dwight D. Eisenhower and other US allies. Eisenhower, however, rejected the suggestion because he did not want to associate himself with Truman's policy. Later, in early 1953, to impress on President Eisenhower the importance of voluntary repatriation, Billy Graham brought back from Korea one of the North Korean Christians' blood-signed petitions.[114] Eisenhower ordered the petition book to be preserved and thanked Graham for the special gift.[115] Five months later, an agreement was reached and the remaining 22,604 nonrepatriates in UN custody were able to go or to stay in the land of their choice (27,451 North Korean prisoners had already escaped with the help of the ROK government).

Though the war was a draw, freedom—and in particular, religious freedom—seemed to have won a sizeable victory. "Liberation comes through the Christian faith," Harold E. Fey, managing editor of the *Christian Century*, proclaimed, "brought to this place by missionaries and Korean pastors. . . . Under these circumstances Communists are being converted by tens of thousands. Here where the ideological struggle is conducted fairly, truth triumphs as it has always done, as it will always do."[116] Perhaps his observations sound exaggerated, but they reflected popular religious opinion.

US officials repeatedly emphasized the large number of Korean and Chinese nonrepatriates. The idea of a psychological victory was vital. After suffering 140,000 US and 15,431 UN casualties, the US government and the United Nations needed a legitimate claim of achievement in Korea to maintain its credibility as a peacekeeping body.[117]

## Christian Gains in the Midst of War

In addition to its impact on North Korean prisoners, Christianity also influenced South Korean soldiers. Having witnessed how ROK troops collapsed quickly before the North Korean Army and the poor morale of ROK soldiers, American missionaries petitioned US authorities and the ROK government to set up a chaplains corps for the Korean military.[118] Both the Republic of Korea and the United States agreed, and Rev. William Shaw and Monsignor George M. Carroll were hired by the US Army to minister to Korean soldiers in August 1950.[119] Another missionary, Rev. Archibald Campbell, translated the US Army regulations concerning chaplains into Korean and modified them to include representatives of other traditional religions.[120]

President Rhee originally favored a civilian Christian chaplain corps, because he was concerned about the budget and the potential opposition from the military.[121] Yet, to his surprise, the Korean National Assembly approved the plan in early 1951. The initial order called for seventy-seven Christian clergymen, with no other religions represented.[122] Churches in America donated money to support their families. Chaplain Shaw and Chaplain Carroll were responsible for recruitment and training. Another forty-three graduated in April 1951.[123] By June 1953, the training school in Taegu had graduated a total of 113 trainees that year.[124] As a result, hundreds of thousands of Korean soldiers encountered the Christian faith through their chaplains during the war. These soldiers, regardless of whether or not they remained in the military, emerged as the backbone of Korean society in the decades that followed the war.[125] Through the corps, Christianity became more firmly entrenched within the Korean ruling class.

The influence of Christianity was further strengthened by Christian relief programs. Relief efforts by Korean churches, foreign missionaries, and the United Nations shaped a positive image of Christianity to the Korean public. Partly through the relief agencies' influence and partly through the evangelizing efforts of the Korean church, Christianity expanded rapidly during and after the war. New seminaries, Christian colleges and schools, orphanages, and widows' houses sprang up. Foreign funds allowed the training of new clergymen and the expansion of Christian institutions in postwar Korea. A new, more intimate, US-Korean church relationship had begun.

Today, the Cold War has long subsided. Yet, in Korea at least, it lives on.

US soldiers continue to be stationed in the South, and in the North, children are still taught to sing the old songs in praise of Communism. Both Koreas have seen remarkable religious transformations: Kim's cult of personality is omnipresent in the North, and traditional religions have faded in the South. In 1950, there were only about 600,000 Protestants in South Korea. A decade later, the number had risen to 1,140,000.[126] In 1970, it had grown to nearly four million. In 1981, the number reached nine million.[127] These statistics show that during the Cold War period, the Christian population doubled every decade. Since then, the rise has been slower: 12.7 million in 1995 and 13.7 million in 2005. This number accounts for about 29 percent of the overall population.[128] In fact, Christianity has had such a strong impact on South Korea's social development, internal politics, and foreign relations that five decades later, South Korea has emerged as one of the most Christianized of nations. It now sends out more missionaries than any nation other than the United States.

Following the war, Christians have remained politically active. Christians opposed General Park Chung-hee's military government and collectively served as one of the leading forces in the movement to democratize South Korea. Since the 1990s, every one of Korea's elected presidents has been a Christian. Even today, churches are still major voices for reunification efforts. But with North Korea now a nuclear power, it is unclear when, if ever, this final chapter of the Cold War can be closed.

## Notes

1. William Inboden, *Religion and American Foreign Policy, 1945–1960: The Soul of Containment* (New York: Cambridge University Press, 2008), 1–6.
2. W. J. Kang, "Early Korean Contact with Christianity and Korean Response: An Historical Introduction," in *Korea's Response to the West*, ed. Yung-Hwan Jo (Kalamazoo, MI: Korea Research and Publications, 1971), 43.
3. Horace N. Allen, *Things Korea: A Collection of Sketches and Anecdotes, Missionary and Diplomatic* (New York: Fleming and H. Revell, 1890), 70.
4. In Soo Kim, *Protestants and the Formation of Modern Korean Nationalism, 1885–1920* (New York: Peter Lang, 1996), 65. See also Takayoshi Matsuo and S. Takiguchi, "The Japanese Protestants in Korea, Part 1: The Missionary Activity of the Japan Congregational Church in Korea," *Modern Asian Studies* 13 (1979): 419.
5. Chung-shin Park, *Protestantism and Politics in Korea* (Seattle: University of Washington Press, 2003), 122.
6. Jongsuk Chay, *Diplomacy of Asymmetry: Korean American Relations to 1910* (Honolulu: University of Hawaii Press, 1990), 5.
7. Kenneth M. Wells, *New God, New Nation: Protestants and Self-Reconstruction Nationalism in Korea, 1896–1937* (Honolulu: University of Hawaii Press, 1990), 41.

8. The US government document translated "Sin'ganhoe" as the "National Foundation Association." See US Department of State, *North Korea: A Case Study in the Techniques of Takeover* (Washington, DC: US Government Printing Office, 1950), 13. Sin'ganhoe was founded by Yi Sang-jae and Kwŏn Tong-ji in Seoul in February 1927, while Cho Man-sik was the cofounder of the branch in P'yŏngyang.

9. Andrei Lankov, *From Stalin to Kim Il Sung: The Formation of North Korea, 1945–1960* (New Brunswick, NJ: Rutgers University Press, 2002), 10.

10. Yong-ho Choe, "Christian Background in the Early Life of Kim Il-song," *Asian Survey* 26 (October 1986): 1087.

11. For details of Catholic and Protestant mission works, see Donald N. Clark, *Living Dangerously in Korea: The Western Experience, 1900–1950* (Norwalk, CT: EastBridge, 2003), 137–40.

12. Quoted in ibid., 137–38.

13. Edward Adam, "Information of Christian Work in Korea, October 12, 1945," Presbyterian Church Archives (hereafter PCA), Presbyterian Historical Society, Philadelphia, PA, Record Group (RG) 140, Folder 29.

14. Among native religions, only Ch'ŏndogyo, a nationalistic religious sect that developed from the Tonghak movement (1894), had the potential to compete with Christianity and Communists. See R. Pierce Beaver, "Chondogyo and Korea," *Journal of Bible and Religion* 30 (April 1962): 116.

15. Lankov, *From Stalin to Kim Il-sung*, 11. See also Erik van Ree, *Socialism in One Zone: Stalin's Policy in Korea, 1945–1947* (Oxford: Berg, 1989), 62–64.

16. Allan R. Millett, *The War for Korea, 1945–1950: A House Burning* (Lawrence: University Press of Kansas, 2005), 5.

17. Charles K. Armstrong, *The North Korean Revolution, 1945–1950* (Ithaca, NY: Cornell University Press, 2003), 50.

18. Ibid., 67n118.

19. According to a Counter Intelligence Corps (CIC) document (US intelligence), the Soviet forces found that Cho Man-sik had formed a "Nation Reconstructing Preparatory People's Committee composed primarily of Christians, businessmen, and educators." They forced Cho to form a new committee that would include fifteen members from the People's Committee and fifteen other members from the Community Party. See "Weekly Information Bulletin 20," September 4, 1947, in 美軍政期情報資料集 [Document collections of the period of the US military government in Korea: CIC, September 1945–January 1949] (hereafter *Document Collections CIC*) (Seoul: Hallym University, Institute of Asian Culture Studies, 1995), 2:381.

20. Ree, *Socialism in One Zone*, 100–101.

21. "Weekly Information Bulletin 20."

22. Armstrong, *North Korean Revolution*, 116–19.

23. Allen D. Clark, *A History of the Church in Korea* (Seoul: Christian Literature Society of Korea, 1971), 240.

24. Armstrong, *North Korean Revolution*, 122; and US Department of State, *North Korea*, 14.

25. A. D. Clark, *History of the Church in Korea*, 240.

26. Ree, *Socialism in One Zone*, 117.

27.  US Department of State, *North Korea*, 97.
28.  Bruce Cumings, *The Origins of the Korean War: Liberation and the Emergence of Separate Regimes, 1945–1947* (Princeton, NJ: Princeton University Press, 1981), 217.
29.  "Conditions in Korea," September 13, 1945, in 美軍政期情報資料集 [Document collections: John R. Hodge, June 1945—August 1948] (Seoul: Hallym University, Institute of Asian Culture Studies, 1995), 3:8.
30.  "Notes on address by Commander George Tsur Williams to Korea secretaries and missionaries in the Methodist Chapel, January 30, 1946," PCA, RG 140, Box 16, Folder 29: 1.
31.  Edward Adams, "Report on Korea," January 15, 1946, PCA, RG 140, Box 16, Folder 29. See also Arthur J. Moore, *The Church Cradled in Conflict: A Report of an Episcopal Visit to Korea in 1946* (New York: Methodist Church, 1946), 8.
32.  R. Manton Wilson, "Dear Friends" letter, January 23, 1946, Presbyterian Church (USA) archives (hereafter PCUSA), Department of History, Montreat College, Montreat, NC.
33.  John Hooper, "Letter from the Board to the Korea Mission," October 22, 1945, PCA, RG 140, Box 2, Folder 28.
34.  Richard F. Underwood, "Memories and Thoughts" (unpublished manuscript, 2002), 56–58.
35.  Horace G. Underwood, *Korea in War, Revolution, and Peace: The Recollections of Horace G. Underwood*, ed. Michael J. Devine (Seoul: Yonsei University Press, 2001), 103.
36.  *History of the Korean Mission Presbyterian Church in the USA, Vol. 2 1935–1959*, ed. Harry A. Rhodes and Archibald Campbell (New York: United Presbyterian Church in the USA, 1964), 379–80.
37.  "Notes on address by Commander George Tsur Williams," 2–5. See also James I. Matray, "Hodge Podge: American Occupation Policy in Korea, 1945–1948," *Korean Studies* 19 (1995): 21.
38.  "Notes on address by Commander George Tsur Williams," 2–5.
39.  See Robert T. Oliver, *Syngman Rhee and American Involvement in Korea, 1942–1960* (Seoul: Panmun Book Company, 1978), 35.
40.  *Document Collections CIC*, 1:469–94.
41.  C. Park, *Protestantism and Politics in Korea*, 170.
42.  Syngman Rhee, *The Spirit of Independence: A Primer of Korean Modernization and Reform*, trans. Han-kyo Kim (Honolulu: University of Hawaii Press, 2001), 282–83.
43.  Letter from Syngman Rhee to Dr. Hoo, December 5, 1942, National Archives and Records Administration (NARA), Political Affairs: Korean Independence Movement, 1941–1944, RG 59, Records of the US Department of State relating to internal affairs of Korea, 1940–1944, File 895.
44.  D. N. Clark, *Living Dangerously in Korea*, 349.
45.  Maie Borden Knox, "Dear Friends across the Pacific" (letter), March 7, 1949, PCUSA.
46.  R. F. Underwood, "Memories and Thoughts," 110–11.
47.  Letter from Marion E. Hartness to Dr. J. L. Hooper, February 2, 1946, PCA, RG 140, Box 16, Folder 29.

48. "Churches Demand Immediate Freedom for Korea: Separate Government Idea Oppose [sic]," *Voice of Korea* 6 (February 15, 1947): 1, Harry S. Truman Library, Independence, MO, Vertical File: Truman Subject File—Religion.

49. "Report on Korea," *New York Times*, November 10, 1946.

50. See C. Park, *Protestantism and Politics in Korea*, 173–74.

51. Myeong-su Park, "대한민국의 건국, 기독교, 그리고 이승만" [Syngman Rhee, Christianity, and the formation of the Republic of Korea], 성결교회와 신학 제20호 [The Theological Study of the Holy Church] 20 (2008): 114–15.

52. Kim Il-sung was, however, restrained by Stalin. See Evgueni Bajanov, "Assessing the Politics of the Korean War, 1949–51," *Cold War International History Project Bulletin* 6–7 (Winter 1995–1996): 54. In the case of Syngman Rhee, the United States refused to give him any offensive weapons. See Oliver, 271–77.

53. Moore, *Church Cradled in Conflict*, 3.

54. S. Dwight, "Korea Mission," *Annual Report of the Executive Committee of Foreign Missions, 1948*, Presbyterian Church in the U.S. (Nashville: Executive Committee of Foreign Missions, 1948), 78–79.

55. Joe B. Hopper, "Korea Mission," in *Annual Report of the Executive Committee of Foreign Missions, 1949*, Presbyterian Church in the U.S. (Nashville: Executive Committee of Foreign Missions, 1949), 86. In 1950, about half of Rhee's cabinet members were Christians. Forty out of the newly elected 210 legislators in the National Assembly were Christians. The vice chairman of the assembly was a Presbyterian elder. The mayor of Seoul and three of the eight provincial governors were Christians. See letter from Harold Voelkel to Dr. John C. Decker, July 29, 1950, *Documents of the WCC Library: The Korean War*, ed. Kim Heung Soo (Seoul: Institute for Korean Church History, 2003), 61.

56. Hopper, "Korea Mission," 86.

57. Thoburn T. Brumbaugh, "Which Way Korea?," *World Outlook*, April 1950, 798.

58. Ibid., 800.

59. Dean C. Curry, "Where Have All the Niebuhrs Gone? Evangelicals and the Marginalization of Religious Influence in American Public Life," *Journal of Church and State* 36 (Winter 1994): 104.

60. Harry S. Truman, *Mr. Citizen* (New York: Popular Library, 1960), 99. See also *Off the Record: The Private Papers of Harry S. Truman*, ed. Robert H. Ferrell (New York: Harper and Row, 1980), 44–45.

61. Harry S. Truman, "Annual Message to the Congress on the State of the Union," January 7, 1948, in *Public Papers of the Presidents of the United States: Harry S. Truman, 1948* (Washington, DC: US Government Printing Office, 1964), 3.

62. Patricia Daniels Cornwell, *A Time for Remembering: The Story of Ruth Bell Graham* (San Francisco: Harper and Row, 1983), 86.

63. Remarks to a group of Baptist missionaries, February 3, 1950, in *Public Papers of the Presidents of the United States: Harry S. Truman, 1950*, 146.

64. William E. Shaw, *Korea at the Crossroads* (New York: Methodist Church Editorial Department, 1950), 5–7.

65. Ibid., 6.

66. Marion Conrow, "Christian Rally, Seoul, Korea, June 23, 1949," United Methodist

Archives and History Center (hereafter UMAHC), Madison, NJ, Missionary Collection 3, File Name: Conrow, Marion L. (1946–1949).

67. Franklin Graham, *Bob Pierce: This One Thing I Do* ([Boone, NC?]: Samaritan's Purse, 1983), 146.

68. Bob Pierce, *The Untold Korean Story* (Grand Rapids, MI: Zondervan, 1951), 29.

69. For the details of their imprisonment, see Larry Zellers, *In Enemy Hands: A Prisoner in North Korea* (Lexington: University Press of Kentucky, 1991).

70. R. F. Underwood, "Memories and Thoughts," 136.

71. Ibid., 135–37.

72. Letter from Rev. Harry Hill, August 22, 1950, PCA, RG 140, Box 18, Folder 14.

73. Letter from Charlotte Linton to her children, August 13, 1950, PCUSA.

74. Letter from Dr. John Smith to Ned Adams, August 5, 1950, PCA, RG 197, Box 1, Folder 2.

75. Letter from Harold Voelkel, November 12, 1950, PCA, RG 140, Box 18, Folder 15.

76. Letter from Rev. Han Kyŏng-jik, August 12, 1950, PCA, RG 140, Box 16, Folder 37.

77. John C. Smith, "Our Stake in Korea," *Presbyterian Life*, September 2, 1950, 13.

78. Church World Service (CWS) was founded to provide relief regardless of nationality, party, or religion. From 1946 to 1950, the agency helped mainly refugees from North Korea with supplies sent by churches in the United States.

79. Letter from Grace H. Wood to friends, September 21, 1950, PCA, RG 140, Box 16, Folder 37.

80. Letter from Edward Adams, July 21, 1950, PCA, RG 140, Box 18, Folder 14.

81. "Korean Movies at Youth for Christ," *Walla Walla* (WA), December 7, 1951. See also "Korean Film Listed for Youth Rally," *Gettysburg (PA) Times*, April 13, 1951, and "Speaks and Shows Film," *Mansfield (OH) News-Journal*, April 9, 1952.

82. C. W. Randon, "Korean Relief," in *Documents of the WCC Library*, 136–37.

83. Graham, *Bob Pierce*, 170.

84. Letter from T. T. Brumbaugh to William Shaw, October 6, 1950, UMAHC, Missionary Collection 4.

85. This amount does not include cash distributed through private church channels, which the United Nations did not control. See Heung-soo Kim, "한국전쟁 시기 기독교 외원단체의 구호활동" [Relief activities of foreign Christian voluntary agencies during the Korean War], 한국기독교와 역사 [History of Korean Christianity] 23 (2005): 107–8.

86. Rhodes and Campbell, *History of the Korean Mission Presbyterian Church*, 323.

87. Letter from Dr. John Smith to Rev. Edward Adams, January 3, 1951, PCA, RG 140, Box 18, Folder 15.

88. "The World Scene: From Hope to Snowy Death," *Presbyterian Life*, January 6, 1950, 15. See also letter from Rev. Edward Adams to Dr. John Smith, January 1, 1951, PCA, RG 197, Box 1, Folder 3.

89. Chulho Awe, *Decision at Dawn: The Underground Christian Witness in Red Korea* (New York: Harper and Row, 1965), 163–64, 168.

90. Gertrude Samuels, "Korea's Refugees—Misery on the March," *New York Times*, February 11, 1951, 156.

91. According to Rosemary Foot, a wide range of factors (including the domestic

situation and the international environment) also influenced the outcomes of the negotiations. See Rosemary Foot, *Substitute for Victory: The Politics of Peacemaking at the Korean Armistice Talks* (Ithaca, NY: Cornell University Press, 1990), x–xi.

92. See letter from Rev. Harry Hill, August 22, 1950, PCA, RG 140, Box 18, Folder 14.

93. Interview with Jeong Chun-Seop, an ex-North Korean POW who resided in South Korea, May 18, 2004, College Park, MD.

94. Outgoing message from Commander in Chief, Far East (CINCFE), Tokyo, Japan, to Commanding General (CG) Army Eight Korea, December 4, 1950, MacArthur Memorial (hereafter MM), Norfolk, VA, RG 9, Box 37, Folder: "Army 8—out, Dec 50."

95. From MacArthur to Mr. George Djamgaroff, chairman of the Organizational Committee of the Fourth Anti-Communist Convention, February 22, 1951, MM, RG 16a, Box 4, Folder 7.

96. Letter from William C. Kerr to Dr. John C. Smith, April 11, 1951, PCA, RG 140, Box 18, Folder 17.

97. Military History Office, Office of the Assistant Chief of Staff, "The Handling of Prisoners of War during the Korean War" ([San Francisco?]: United States Army, Pacific, 1960), 102–3.

98. George Thompson Brown, Mission to Korea ([Richmond, VA?]: Board of World Missions, Presbyterian Church US, 1962), 198.

99. Ibid.

100. Harold Voelkel, *Behind Barbed Wire in Korea* (Grand Rapids, MI: Zondervan, 1953), 15–16.

101. Data provided by Chaplain Harold Voelkel in "Chaplain's Report: Kojedo Prisoner of War Camp, March 1951–April 1952," PCA, RG 140, Box 16, Folder 40.

102. Letter from John Smith to Chaplain Earle Woodberry, April 18, 1951, PCA, RG 197, Box 1, Folder 3.

103. Letter from Rev. Earle Woodberry to "Dear Praying Friends," undated (received July 10, 1952), PCA, RG 360, Folder: Earle J. Woodberry.

104. "Six Months in the Chinese POW Camps" (Resume#1–Abridged), PCA, RG 360, Folder: Earle J. Woodberry.

105. "Copies of EJW's reports for April, May, and June, 1952," received on November 19, 1952, PCA, RG 140, Box 18, Folder 17.

106. Memo from Dr. Wysham to the Secretary Council, June 29, 1953, PCA, RG 360, Folder: Earle J. Woodberry.

107. "Six Months in the Chinese POW Camps."

108. See testimony by Chuen-sang Wu in *Meijun Jizhongying Qinli Ji* [Personal records in the US prison camps], ed. Zhe-shi Zhang (Beijing: Chinese Archives Press, 1996), 134–36.

109. Ibid.

110. "Missionary Tells of Red Brutality in War Camp," *Syracuse (NY) Post-Standard*, October 15, 1953.

111. Voelkel, *Behind Barbed Wire*, 29.

112. See Eugene Carson Blake, "Barbed-Wire Prayer Meetings," *Presbyterian Life*, February 2, 1952, 27.

113. Telegram from Dean Acheson, Department of State, to US Embassy in Pusan, April 7, 1952, NARA, 695A.0024/7-1951—5-2825, Problem of POW's related international issue, 1951–1952/Acheson, Dean/US Dept of State, Records of the U.S. Department of State relating to Korea: International political relations, 1950–1954.

114. Rodger R. Venzke, *Confidence in Battle, Inspiration in Peace: The United States Army Chaplaincy, 1945–1975* (Washington, DC: US Government Printing Office, 1977), 5:95.

115. Letter from Dwight D. Eisenhower to Billy Graham, November 3, 1953, Dwight D. Eisenhower Library, Abilene, KS, Billy Graham Files, Box 996, Papers of Dwight D. Eisenhower as President, 1953–1961.

116. Harold E. Fey, "Korea Must Live!," *Christian Century* 75 (February 20, 1952): 217.

117. See also Callum A. MacDonald, "'Heroes Behind Barbed Wire'—The United States, Britain and the POW issue in the Korean War," *The Korean War in History*, ed. James Cotton and Ian Neary (Atlantic Highlands, NJ: Humanities Press International, 1989), 144.

118. See "Chaplaincy Needs Are Revealed," *United Presbyterian*, November 6, 1950, 7. See also "Chaplains' Corps to Be Increased," *Presbyterian Life*, September 2, 1950, 13.

119. Letter from Adeline H. Shaw, September 14, 1950, UMAHC, Missionary Collection 4.

120. Rhodes and Campbell, *History of the Korean Mission Presbyterian Church*, 345.

121. Letter from Rev. William Shaw to T. T. Brumbaugh, October 24, 1950, UMAHC, Missionary Collection 4.

122. The quota was thirty-two Presbyterian, seventeen Methodist, twenty Catholic, seven Holiness, and one Salvation Army. Letter from Chaplain William Shaw to T. T. Brumbaugh, March 19, 1951, UMAHC, Missionary Collection 4. The same letter is also in PCA, RG 140, Box 16, Folder 39.

123. The breakdown here was fifteen Presbyterians, eleven Catholics, seven Methodists, and four Holiness. The second class graduated on April 13. There were six Catholics, two Methodists, and one Holiness. See "Excerpts from letters from Chaplain William E. Shaw," PCA, RG 140, Box 16, Folder 39.

124. "Chaplains for ROK," *Time*, June 1, 1953.

125. C. Park, *Protestantism and Politics in Korea*, 175–83.

126. Young-ik Yoo, "이승만과 한국의 기독교" [Syngman Rhee and the Korean Church], 성결교회와 신학 제13호봄 [Holiness Church and Theology] 13 (2005): 25.

127. See James Huntley Grayson, *Early Buddhism and Christianity in Korea: A Study in the Emplantation of Religion* (Leiden, Netherlands: Brill, 1985), 126.

128. For the 1995 figure, see the CIA web page on Korea: *www.cia.gov* (accessed May 14, 2010). For the 2005 figure, see US State Department, "International Religious Freedom Report 2008," *2001-2009.state.gov* (accessed May 14, 2010).

# References

## ARCHIVES
Dwight D. Eisenhower Library, Abilene, KS
Harry S. Truman Library, Independence, MO
John Foster Dulles Papers, Seeley Mudd Library, Princeton, NJ
Korean Christian Museum (숭실대학교 한국기독교박물관), Soongsil University, Seoul, Korea
MacArthur Memorial, Norfolk, VA
National Archives and Records Administration, College Park, MD
National Assembly Library of Korea (국회도서관), Seoul, Korea
Presbyterian Church Archives, Presbyterian Historical Society, Philadelphia, PA
Presbyterian Church (USA), Department of History, Montreat College, Montreat, NC
Syngman Rhee Collection, Center for Korean Classics Collection (학술정보원 국학자료실), Yonsei University, Seoul, Korea
United Methodist Archives and History Center, Drew University, Madison, NJ

## PERIODICALS
*Christian Century*
*Gettysburg (PA) Times*
*Mansfield (OH) News-Journal*
*New York Times*
*Presbyterian Life*
*Syracuse (NY) Post-Standard*
*Time*
*United Presbyterian*
*Voice of Korea*
*Walla Walla (WA)*
*World Outlook*

## SELECTED PUBLISHED WORKS
Armstrong, Charles K. *The North Korean Revolution, 1945–1950*. Ithaca, NY: Cornell University Press, 2003.
Clark, Allen D. *A History of the Church in Korea*. Seoul: Christian Literature Society of Korea, 1971.
Clark, Donald N. *Living Dangerously in Korea: The Western Experience, 1900–1950*. Norwalk, CT: EastBridge, 2003.
Cumings, Bruce. *The Origins of the Korean War: Liberation and the Emergence of Separate Regimes, 1945–1947*. Princeton, NJ: Princeton University Press, 1981.
Graham, Franklin. *Bob Pierce: This One Thing I Do*. [Boone, NC]: Samaritan's Purse, 1983.
Inboden, William. *Religion and American Foreign Policy, 1945–1960: The Soul of Containment*. New York: Cambridge University Press, 2008.
Kim, Heung-soo. "한국전쟁 시기 기독교 외원단체의 구호활동" [Relief activities of foreign Christian voluntary agencies during the Korean War]. 한국기독교와 역사 [History of Korean Christianity] 23 (2005): 97–124.

Kim, In Soo. *Protestants and the Formation of Modern Korean Nationalism, 1885–1920*. New York: Peter Lang, 1996.

Lankov, Andrei. *From Stalin to Kim Il Sung: The Formation of North Korea, 1945–1960*. New Brunswick, NJ: Rutgers University Press, 2002.

Oliver, Robert T. *Syngman Rhee and American Involvement in Korea, 1942–1960*. Seoul: Panmun Book Company, 1978.

Moore, Arthur J. *The Church Cradled in Conflict: A Report of an Episcopal Visit to Korea in 1946* (pamphlet). New York: Methodist Church, 1946.

Park, Chung-shin. *Protestantism and Politics in Korea*. Seattle: University of Washington Press, 2003.

Park, Myeong-su. "대한민국의 건국, 기독교, 그리고 이승만" [Syngman Rhee, Christianity, and the formation of the Republic of Korea]. 성결교회와 신학 제20호 [The Theological Study of the Holy Church] 20 (2008): 98–116.

Pierce, Bob. *The Untold Korean Story*. Grand Rapids, MI: Zondervan, 1951.

Ree, Erik van. *Socialism in One Zone: Stalin's Policy in Korea, 1945–1947*. Oxford: Berg, 1989.

Rhodes, Harry A., and Archibald Campbell, eds. *History of the Korean Mission Presbyterian Church in the USA*, vol. 2, *1935–1959*. New York: United Presbyterian Church in the USA, 1964.

Truman, Harry S. *Public Papers of the Presidents of the United States: Harry S. Truman, 1945–1963*. Washington, DC: US Government Printing Office, 1964.

Underwood, Horace G. *Korea in War, Revolution, and Peace: The Recollections of Horace G. Underwood*. Ed. Michael J. Devine. Seoul: Yonsei University Press, 2001.

US Department of State. *North Korea: A Case Study in the Techniques of Takeover*. Washington, DC: US Government Printing Office, 1950.

Venzke, Rodger R. *Confidence in Battle, Inspiration in Peace: The United States Army Chaplaincy, 1945–1975*. Vol. 5. Washington, DC: US Government Printing Office, 1977.

Voelkel, Harold. *Behind Barbed Wire in Korea*. Grand Rapids, MI: Zondervan, 1953.

# CHAPTER 6

# The Campaign of Truth Program

## *US Propaganda in Iraq during the Early 1950s*

*Ahmed Khalid al-Rawi*

Sensing the danger of the spread of Communism in the Middle East during the late 1940s and early 1950s, the US government worked hard to counter Soviet attempts to find and expand a breeding ground for its ideology. To influence the hearts and minds of people, US propaganda endeavored to expose the negative aspects of Marxism-Leninism in order to convince the Arab masses that Communism represented a common enemy for both America and the Arab world. In this chapter, the discussion is mainly focused on Iraq, since Communism flourished in that country during this period. The Iraqi Communist Party (ICP) gained wide popular appeal that frequently exceeded the popularity of other Communist parties in the Arab world.

US propaganda targeted a variety of sectors of Iraqi society but focused especially on the molders of opinion, many of whom were religious leaders. As for means, the US Information Bureau provided financial assistance; distributed magazines, pamphlets, and posters; manipulated news and radio broadcasts; and promoted books, libraries, music, movies, cartoons, and educational activities. But among the most effective strategies was involving religion in propaganda activities, because of its importance to Iraqis' daily lives. The US propaganda efforts concentrated on portraying Communism as an atheist ideology that was the sole enemy of Islam, and featured stories of persecution of

Muslims within the Soviet bloc. At the same time, the US embassy in Iraq tried to project the idea that unlike the Soviet Union, America was a friend to all Muslims, as both were united against a godless enemy.

Like the US State Department, the Iraqi monarchy opposed Communism because it called for establishing a republic, overthrowing the capitalist feudal system, and giving Kurds independence in northern Iraq—hence, the Iraqi penal code prohibited the propagation of the Communist ideology. The Iraqi, British, and US governments were thus joined in their propaganda efforts to stop the spread of Communism.

This chapter argues that the US government used all the propaganda tools at its disposal—playing especially on Muslims' religious sentiments to counter the Communist threat—for two reasons: its fear that the Soviet Union might establish in Iraq a basis of ideological expansion in the Middle East, and its concern over the future domination of the rich oil fields of Iraq and the rest of the Persian Gulf region if Moscow supplanted US hegemony.

## US Propaganda in the Early Cold War

Propaganda was a basic tool used by the US government during the Cold War. In the late 1940s and early 1950s, the US government supported various European institutions and bodies that played a role in propaganda. For example, the New York–based National Committee for a Free Europe, officially founded in June 1949, supported Eastern Europeans in getting rid of Communism. Also, the Berlin-based Congress for Cultural Freedom, a gathering of intellectuals and writers who started working in June 1950 to counter Communism, was supported by the CIA. The US government created Radio Free Europe, which advocated capitalism and attacked Communist ideology; it started broadcasting in Czechoslovakia on July 4, 1950, and then in Romania, Hungary, and Poland.[1] US propaganda activities went through four main stages in the 1940s and 1950s. The first phase, from 1945 to 1947, was headed by the US Interim International Information Service, later renamed the Office of International Information and Cultural Affairs. The second stage, from 1947 to 1949, was run by the Office of International Information and Educational Exchange. In the third stage, from 1950 to 1951, President Harry Truman expanded overseas propaganda activities under the Campaign of Truth program. Building on the work of his predecessor, President Dwight Eisenhower established the US Information Agency (USIA), which started a new phase in US propaganda activities overseas.[2]

However, Communist propaganda was frequently more effective than US efforts to win the hearts and minds of people in many places around the world.

In light of this, two committees were established during Truman's administration to review the work of the US information programs: the President's
Committee on Governmental Organization and the President's Committee
on International Information Activities. The two committees "agreed that two
years of hard-hitting anti-Communist propaganda under the Campaign of
Truth had been ineffective, if not counterproductive."[3]

During Eisenhower's administration, the use of propaganda was greatly
enhanced with the creation of the USIA in June 1953. While Truman had
established the National Security Council and used the term "US national
security policy," Eisenhower expanded this concept and established the New
Look policy. Among its aims was that the "United States should rely more on
collective security in the future. Allied unity and allied acceptance of their
responsibilities for regional defense were alike essential, not only to protect the
world against Communist aggression, but also to achieve American national
security goals."[4] In general, the New Look policy was based on a distinction
between overt and covert propaganda. In relation to overt propaganda, the
president emphasized that materials directly linked to the US government
must "abandon the brazenly anti-Communist tone that marked the Campaign
of Truth." Covert propaganda activities included the use of "independent news
media, nongovernmental organizations, and private individuals as surrogate
communicators to convey propaganda messages."[5]

Efforts to infiltrate the Communist bloc included the use of the Voice of
America service (VOA), US embassies' affiliated libraries and other information centers, exchange programs, publishing houses, the motion picture industry, television and the press, exhibitions, and tourism. The real aim of USIA
was "to persuade foreign peoples that it lies in their own interest to take actions
which are consistent with the national objectives of the United States."[6]

In March 1953, the US administration refused to consider military intervention as an option because it feared that the Soviet Union might inflict great
losses on the United States. Instead, psychological warfare, especially radio
broadcasting, was considered the best choice for winning the allegiance of the
Eastern European people and in the end to "undermine Soviet control over
the Eastern bloc."[7] US propaganda efforts later intensified with the advice and
guidance of Charles D. Jackson, Eisenhower's special assistant in psychological warfare, who wanted to "get into 'the real guts' of the matter" by directing
continuous CIA propaganda activities against Communist countries and even
against other moderate governments. Some coups were planned by the United
States, and the result was the installation of pro-US governments in Iran in
1953 and Guatemala in 1954.[8] US propaganda activities in Eastern Europe
were instrumental in supporting a worker-led revolt in East Germany in June
1953. Although it was quashed by the Soviet Union, the revolt was used as a

propaganda tool by the US government, which provided covert logistical assistance to the workers.[9] In Poland, US propaganda encouraged riots organized by Polish students in Poznan on June 28, 1956.[10] The United States also assisted Eastern European refugees, who provided a great deal of useful intelligence on political, social, and cultural aspects of conditions in their countries.[11]

The New Look policy adopted by Eisenhower, which focused on what was called "polite propaganda," proved more effective than Truman's. It included more emphasis on overt methods like direct news, exchange programs, and various exhibitions. Also, the US magazine *Amerika* and the VOA's jazz show significantly improved the image of the United States. In the end, such efforts, combined with covert activities, allowed the US government to part the Iron Curtain slightly by early 1960, as the Eisenhower administration neared its end.[12] To understand US propaganda activities in the Arab world, the following section focuses on the spread of Communism in Egypt and Iraq because of their geopolitical importance.

## The Political Background

After the rise of Communism in the Soviet Union, many Arab youths became fascinated with the idea of introducing its ideology into their own countries. The impetus behind this admiration was the dream of applying the ideals of economic equality and socialism to societies used to a harsh feudal system that separated the elite upper class from the downtrodden lower class.[13] Communism also gave some Arab youths hope in a revolution that would allow them to achieve economic and political independence from Western powers, especially Britain and France, which had colonized the region and maintained a commanding influence in the area even after the end of colonialism. As the issue of Palestine was instrumental to the majority of the Arab masses, it played another important part in swaying the public against the Western powers that actively supported the establishment of Israel. In various publications, the Iraqi Communist Party called for establishing a free and independent Palestinian state, and it frequently accused Britain and the United States of standing against this objective. The ICP used Western support of Israel to its favor, stating in one report that "the British, American, and Zionist imperialists who were supported by some Arab countries especially [Iraq's Prime Minister] Nuri al-Said created a very tense environment which ultimately led to the division of Palestine."[14]

Despite early policy tensions between the United States and the United Kingdom over the Middle East because of their rival oil ambitions in Saudi Arabia and Iraq, the two governments cooperated in the early 1950s in "psychological warfare directed at the Arab world" to convince the Arab masses to support pro-Western Arab governments and counter Communism.[15] In the beginning, the US and British governments were not overly concerned about the spread of Communism in the Arab world because they saw no obvious or immediate threat. This was partially because many Arab governments had banned Communist parties. The Egyptian government, for example, had outlawed Communist activities in the country and arrested many activists since the 1930s. In June 1931, Ismael Sidqqi Pasha, chair of the Egyptian Cabinet Council and prime minister of Egypt, succeeded in amending the Egyptian Civil Law (Article 13) to state that any Egyptian found to be involved in a revolutionary activity—an indirect reference to Communism—could have his citizenship revoked. Hence, on August 23, 1931, King Fuad of Egypt issued a royal decree that stripped Egyptian citizenship from eight Communists.[16] As a result, a CIA report from May 1949 mentioned that the Communist influence in Egypt would remain "negligible" unless the political and social situation changed and "US and UK influence rejected." But the two most important factors of unrest were the issues of Palestine and economic hardship.[17] However, Communism did not spread in Egypt even after the toppling of the monarchy and the establishment of a republic in 1953. Gamal Abdel Nasser, who ruled Egypt following the coup, overtly opposed Communism because it threatened his control over the country. For example, Mustapha Taiba and Mustapha Kamal Khalil were arrested before the Egyptian Revolution that began on July 23, 1952, but they remained in custody after the revolution and were later tried for allegedly attempting to stage a coup d'état. Some US officials expressed their satisfaction with the formation of a military committee to prosecute Communists after the revolution.[18] In May 1955, the Egyptian government held about 252 Communists in prisons, sentencing some of them to hard labor. In an official meeting on November 29, 1961, Nasser accused Egyptian Communists of being agents of foreign powers and taking their orders from Sofia and stated that they could never be regarded as nationalists.[19] Communist parties thus remained banned in Nasser's Egypt.

As for Iraq, the Iraqi Communist Party had been banned since its establishment in 1934. The reasons for outlawing the party ranged from its plans to spread socialism in the country and to its revised national charter of 1953, which called for creating an independent state in Iraqi Kurdistan for the Kurds.[20] The usual stance of the ICP was to oppose the imperialism represented by Western powers, and from the start, party members were followed by the police. In November 1935, Iraqi security forces arrested the party's leader, Asim Flayyih, who later pledged that he would abandon his political activity.[21]

Between 1945 and the 1958 Revolution, Iraqi parties became very actively involved in politics, and the ICP "significantly expanded its social base."[22]

Although the party remained under police scrutiny, it was instrumental in agitating the public against Iraqi Prime Minister Salih Jabr's decision to sign the Portsmouth treaty with Britain in December 1947. This led to the al-Wathbah riots. As a result, the leaders of the ICP were arrested in October 1948, among them Yousif Salman Yousif (Comrade Fahad), and most of them were executed on February 14, 1949.[23] Fahad was responsible for introducing the concept of the national front in Iraqi politics in order to unify the opposing voices to achieve higher political aims.[24] He was also an anticolonialist who rejected any kind of foreign intervention in Iraq and the Arab world.

Jassim al-Halwa'i, a Shiite member of the ICP, recalled in his memoirs that party members were greatly persecuted by the Iraqi government despite the fact that they had strong support from the people. The Iraqi government banned classic Communist publications (such as the works of Vladimir Lenin, Joseph Stalin, and Maurice Thorez) that had been translated into Arabic. Even listening to Radio Moscow's Arabic service was prohibited; however, many people listened to the radio and disseminated Communist books in secret.[25] According to Article 89 in the Iraqi Penal Code at the time, anyone who possessed Communist publications was to be imprisoned. In fact, Baquba Prison in Diyala Province was dedicated to the Communists: prisoners were routinely and harshly tortured until they signed a paper stating their renouncement of the Communist party.[26] Prisoners who refused to sign this document were threatened by the police and risked losing their Iraqi citizenship, which happened to some ICP members.[27] Police officers asked Shiite prisoners in particular to curse Lenin. If they refused, they were then ordered to curse Imam Hussein, the prophet Muhammad's grandson and one of the most venerated Shiite reference, to prove to the other bystanders that the Communists had no respect for their most dignified figures.[28]

Ironically, the Iraqi General Police–Directorate of Criminal Investigation published an overview of the ICP after the arrest of its members in 1948. The book, published in Baghdad in 1949, was entitled *The Secret Encyclopedia of the Iraqi Communist Party*, and it contained the hierarchal structure of the party and information on its leadership and cadre. The Iraqi government meant to initiate an anti-Communist propaganda campaign in publishing this book; however, according to al-Halwa'i, the work instead became a propaganda tool for the ICP, especially after the 1958 Revolution, since new party members needed information on their political system and there were no other available publications.[29]

As mentioned earlier, the British and United States governments were initially not greatly concerned about Communism's influence in the region, given the strong stance of Arab governments against the ideology. However, with the success of the Chinese Communist Revolution in October 1949, the two governments were forced to consider the possibility that some Arabs might be inspired to organize similar revolutions. Ernest Bevin, the British secretary of state for foreign affairs, sensed the danger of the Communist threat. According to the historian Peter Hahn, Bevin warned the cabinet in 1949 that Britain had to "prevent the Middle East [from] falling behind the iron curtain."[30]

After the 1948 Arab-Israeli conflict, the British and US governments understood the magnitude of the growing dangers of nationalism in the Arab world and agreed that they should work together to counter their common enemies. In 1949, the US assistant secretary of state for Near Eastern affairs, George C. McGhee, met with Michael Wright, the British assistant undersecretary of the Foreign Office. They confirmed that the two governments' interests in the Middle East were "basically the same," and that it was not "sufficient just to ward off Communism in the Middle East. It was essential to assist the peoples of the Middle East to improve their living standards and social and political institutions and to acquire self-respect."[31]

After the attack on and the burning of the United States Information Service (USIS) office in Baghdad in 1952, the US embassy became certain that more propaganda efforts should be directed at Iraqis, many of whom favored Communism as a new political system.[32] As part of the US campaign to stop the spread of Communist influence in the Middle East, some conservative pro-Western governments in the region were persuaded to join Western-backed military treaties or alliances. For instance, Washington made a concerted effort to unite the so-called northern tier countries of Iraq, Turkey, Pakistan, and Iran into an anti-Communist defense pact with the United Kingdom. The United States felt that creating the northern tier would be the best "indigenous regional defense arrangement in the Near East," one that would achieve "political and psychological rather than military" gains.[33] In other words, the northern tier concept would bring these diverse countries together to influence their people and stop the Communist threat.

Hence, the Truman administration pressured these countries to join the Middle East Command (MEC), an organization whose sole aim was "to build a series of interlocking alliances along the peripheries of the Soviet Union."[34] Such efforts continued during the Eisenhower administration, but MEC got a great deal of negative reception in the Arab world mainly because of its name, which was interpreted in terms of colonial control.[35] It was soon replaced with the Middle East Defense Organization (MEDO), which was organized by the British and US governments in June 1952. Unlike MEC, MEDO was to be a "planning organization with no military forces at its disposal," so many Western analysts believed that many Arabs states would accept it. However, during King Farouk's regime, the Egyptian government refused to sign the treaty because of its concern over public reaction. In 1952, the Egyptian military coup toppled the monarchy and introduced the new republic.[36] Egypt's ambassador to Washington, Ahmed Hussein, then revealed that MEDO remained "completely unacceptable" in Egypt because nationalists in the country would reject it.[37] After visiting eleven countries in the Middle East in May 1953, US Secretary of State John Foster Dulles shelved the idea of MEDO in July. Dulles confirmed that the United States government would "promote increasingly close cooperation with those states of the Middle East which were most conscious of the Soviet threat and most disposed to cooperate with the Western Powers."[38] The states Dulles referred to were Iraq, Iran, Turkey, and Pakistan.

It is important to note Britain's rivalry with the United States over Iraq, especially in light of the latter's increasing influence in postcoup Iran and postrevolutionary Egypt.[39] Britain had several military bases in the country, but it did not offer the financial support the Iraqi government needed to pursue its various projects. Hence, in early 1953, Baghdad started to seek US assistance, especially in relation to military aid. However, the United States' role was restricted because of its other commitments in Korea and Europe. In a meeting on March 22, 1953, Iraq's foreign minister, Tawfiq Suwaidi, met with the US ambassador to Iraq, Burton Berry. Suwaidi stressed to Berry that Iraq needed financial assistance and weapons, claiming that "Communism would arise in Iraq" if Iraq had to reassign money from economic development to defense On the other hand, according to the historian Daniel C. Williamson, Berry "expressed pleasure that Iraq was taking the Communist threat seriously and seemed willing to participate in a regional defense pact."[40] Despite Berry's subsequent request to the State Department, however, no major military aid was given to Iraq, since some US politicians felt that the Iraqi government was using Communism merely as a justification for more assistance.

In 1955, the government of the United Kingdom introduced a new treaty called the Baghdad Pact, a direct result of the efforts Dulles made in May 1953.[41] The pact was created because of fears of possible Communist control of the region. In fact, the governments of the United States and the United Kingdom thought that the oil riches of Iraq might motivate the Soviets to extend their influence to other vital parts in the Middle East.[42] Iraq was chosen as the first Arab country to sign the pact because its government strongly opposed Communism, which represented a direct threat to the existence of the Iraqi monarchy. In 1955, Iraq's prime minister, Nuri al-Said, broke off diplomatic relations with the Soviet Union because the latter criticized Baghdad for signing the pact. It was only in 1958, after the toppling of the monarchy, that diplomatic relations between Moscow and Baghdad were normalized.[43]

In fact, the Baghdad Pact and the tripartite aggression by the British, French, and Israelis against Egypt during the Suez Crisis were used as a pretext by ICP members to intensify a fierce pro-Communist propaganda campaign, though they had been "threatening" the Iraqi government with their activities since the Second World War.[44] ICP members frequently accused the British and US governments of being responsible for their plight and other miseries in the Arab world, a charge that was greatly enhanced by the Suez Crisis of 1956. In a report issued by the ICP's Central Committee after the party's second conference in September 1956, there was much praise for China and the Soviet Union for defending the Arab cause. On the other hand, the report condemned "the imperialist countries that adopted the tripartite declaration which protected Israel against the interests of the Arabs. [The aggression against Egypt] was a threat to the independence of Arab countries and peace in the Middle East."[45] The report clearly accused Britain and the United States of disrupting the national movements in the region: "Arab liberation movements are facing the fiercest kind of resistance by the imperialists who encounter them with various conspiracies and plots. They use the Baghdad Pact and Israel as two spears pointing toward the heart of the Arab cause. The dirty role played by the Anglo-American imperialism that uses Baghdad Pact as a weapon against the Arabs is quite clear."[46]

Furthermore, the Iraqi Communist newspaper, *Attihad al-Shaab* (People's Unity) published an editorial in October 1957 on the infamous Baquba Prison, stating: "Behind the black gate of this prison, the worst kinds of humiliation are practiced against the opponents of the Baghdad Pact and Eisenhower's doctrine. The prisoners are tortured because they want to protect the constitutional rights of the Iraqi people and the freedom and unity of the Arab nation."[47]

Other Arab countries like Saudi Arabia, Egypt, and Syria opposed the Baghdad Pact and decided to make their own alliance, which was called the Riyadh-Cairo-Damascus Axis. They harshly criticized the Iraqi government and waged a propaganda war against it. For example, the Egyptian and Saudi governments established radio channels to convince the Iraqi masses that their government had made a big mistake by joining the pact. In April 1955, "Radio Free Iraq" started broadcasting from Cairo a few days after Baghdad broadcast a radio show called "The Voice of Truth," which attacked Nasser's government for its stance against the Baghdad Pact. However, the Egyptian-run radio station stopped transmitting after the beginning of the Suez Crisis.[48]

As a result of the increase in anti-Iraqi sentiments, the governments of Britain and the United States intervened to help the Iraqi government strengthen its anti-Communist radio propaganda against other Arab countries and to discredit Nasser's regime in Egypt, by using "local broadcasting facilities as a substitute for direct broadcasts by the BBC and the VOA." The two governments offered similar support to other Arab nations for the same objective.

However, it later appeared that their efforts had not "resulted in anything more than resounding failure."[49]

## US Propaganda in Iraq

In January 1956, the former Iraqi prime minister Mohammed Fadhel Jamali attacked Saudi Arabia, Egypt, and Syria for their rejection of the Baghdad Pact, accusing them of being manipulated by the Communists: "The Arabs are threatened by Communist activity supported by Egyptian propaganda and Saudi riyals. That Egypt and Saudi Arabia could align themselves with Communist propaganda is a matter which makes the heart of every loyal Arab bleed."[50] In fact, Jamali, who was married to an American woman, was one of the most active Iraqi politicians to oppose Communism, and he tried hard to join US efforts to counter Communist ideology.[51] As a supervisor of the education sector in Iraq, he authorized the Ministry of Education to coordinate anti-Communist lectures with the USIS in response to protests led by Iraqi students against their government, which had begun in late 1952.[52] Thus, an American academic was sent by the Fulbright Scholarship Committee to document and analyze the Communist propaganda methods employed in Iraq.[53] In 1953, Jamali himself went to a Reserve Officers Training Corps (ROTC) camp in northern Iraq to present a series of anti-Communist lectures to over four thousand Iraqi students, speaking as the president of the Iraqi Parliament.[54] Because of his extraordinary services to the United States, Jamali was greatly favored by Washington; Burton Berry described him as "one of the few politicians in Iraqi life today willing to support such an anti-Communist campaign."[55] Finally, Jamali employed both the police and propaganda to counter Communist activities, but in doing so, he was used as a tool to implement US anti-Communist policies in Iraq. The United States found him especially convenient for highlighting US nonintervention in Iraq's internal affairs and emphasizing that Iraq was independent from any foreign power since he himself had played a role in disseminating such ideas.[56] When Nuri al-Said was reelected prime minister in 1954, new laws were introduced against active Communists, who were persecuted further in different ways. Al-Halwa'i remembers 1955 as the harshest and most difficult year for ICP members.[57] The official line was clearly hostile toward any socialist or Communist tendencies that blatantly opposed the very foundation on which the Iraqi monarchy was built.

Through USIA, the US government toiled to change the negative view of the majority of Arabs toward America. The prime reason behind the then-prevalent anti-Americanism in the Arab world was America's active role in supporting Israel. In fact, when Israel was established in 1948, the event was perceived by most Iraqis to be directly linked to US political efforts to attack Islam and Muslims in the region.[58] The aim of US propaganda was to make the Arab masses detest pro-Communist governments, Cold War neutralism, and the pan-national policies of Egypt's Nasser. In fact, one of the basic goals of US propaganda in the region was to "eliminate neutralist tendencies by exposing the realities of Soviet life and the basically hostile intentions of the USSR toward the area."[59] Also, the US government initiated a propaganda campaign to persuade the Arab people of the validity of the Baghdad Pact.[60]

In Iraq, the US embassy in Baghdad routinely collected intelligence, located potential cooperators to counter Communism, identified Communist sympathizers, and disseminated anti-Communist propaganda. The Campaign of Truth program was made up of two phases and funded with an initial budget of $2,150. It primarily emphasized the concept of "collective security" in the sense that the security of Iraq and neighboring countries was deemed a part of America's own security. The United States Information Service had seventy employees working in its bureau in Baghdad, and in 1956 the agency received its highest level of funding in the 1950s.[61] The US propaganda program included publishing five thousand copies of a magazine called *Al-Urwa* (The Bond). The name of the magazine itself was significant because it echoed the title of the famous pan-Islamic *Al-Urwa al-Withqa* magazine published in France during the nineteenth century by Jamal al-Deen al-Afghani. *Al-Urwa al-Withqa* had called on Muslims to rise up and unite against the injustice caused by British imperialism, stressing the validity of siding with the Muslim Turks, whereas *Al-Urwa* was intended to call on Arabs and Muslims to unite against the Communists, emphasizing the goodness of America and the Western world. As for the US advertising campaign, it consisted of two or three inserts per week in thirteen Iraqi newspapers. This changed monthly to include "either a pamphlet, a premium, a map carrying the central theme, or some similar item."[62]

The US propaganda efforts also targeted different ethnic groups, including the Turkish minority in Iran. The Kurds of Iraq received a weekly bulletin written in Kurdish that was issued by the USIS.[63] The US government feared that Communists would infiltrate Iraq from the North given the vulnerable situation in Iraqi Kurdistan. Hence, it paid extra attention to them and somehow "manipulate[ed] Kurdish nationalist sentiment in Northern Iraq" to make them side with the United States rather than the Soviet Union.[64] In the early 1940s, ICP's leader, Fahad, observed that the US government had sent a journalist named Mr. Harold who met with Kurdish leaders: "Compromises were made and promises were given to the Kurds to unify the Kurdish regions" in return for abandoning and halting the advance of Communism.[65] Fahad commented on this journalist's visit to Kurdistan by referring to the new US "imperialist" policy in the Middle East, saying: "The American imperialist rivalry has lately appeared in the form of economic interests—the takeover of oil resources in the Arab countries and the defense of the Zionist cause. It is now manifesting itself in a new form: the Americans want to establish a social basis in Iraq by exploiting the Kurds' situation."[66]

Edward S. Crocker II, the first US ambassador to Baghdad, feared that the Soviets might invade Iraq from the North. He wanted to prepare for that contingency by building up a cadre of pro-US Iraqis, but he was not impressed with the kind of contacts the embassy had with prominent figures in Iraqi society, believing that the United States "should endeavor to reach leaders who represent a wider range of political opinion than those persons already cooperating closely with the United States—leaders who are not yet beyond the pale of potential cooperation with the West." Crocker, however, cited practical difficulties in approaching potential leaders such as Yahia Qasim, the editor of *Attihad al-Shaab*; Hussein Hadid, a journalist; and Hussein Jamil, the former minister of justice; and inviting them to visit the United States. The problems stemmed from whether such persons could get the security clearances necessary to enter the United States, given their past Communist associations. Crocker therefore advised that there was "little purpose in inviting leftists [to the United States], even as mildly pinkish as these men are—or may have been in the past because they are probably not eligible to receive visas for the United States." He further concluded that such moderate leftists would probably align themselves with Moscow in the event of a Soviet occupation of Iraq anyway. The US ambassador was more hopeful of the prospects of influencing members of the Istiqlal (Nationalist) Party but doubted that such men would jeopardize their nationalist credentials by openly aligning themselves with the United States.[67]

The activities of the USIA in Iraq were scattered across different areas. For instance, support was given only to publications that advanced pro-US stances. In one incident, the famous Iraqi diplomat, Amin al-Mumayiz, asked the US embassy to publish his book *America as I Saw It*, which narrated his experiences as a diplomat in the Iraqi embassy in Washington. However, al-Mumayiz's book proposal was rejected because it contained "sensational" elements, such as discussions of "the Negro problem" and anti-Semitism in the United States.[68]

Propaganda efforts included films, which were shown using mobile units. The US embassy in Baghdad rejected a film script titled "When the Communist came," deeming it unsuitable for Iraqi audiences because of its references to the feudal system, which was still prevalent in Iraq during this period of monarchical rule.[69] Conducting opinion surveys was another way to reach a clearer understanding of the ways Iraqis thought and felt. Two Iraqi academics, Nuri Jafar and Ali Wardi, proposed a study that would cover three hundred persons through questionnaires and personal interviews. Given Iraqi suspicion toward anything foreign, the USIA preferred that the two Iraqis conduct the project themselves rather than involving US academics in it.[70]

Finally, the most important method employed by the US embassy was the distribution of monthly pamphlets to reveal the reality of "Communist Imperialism." In contrast with the US propaganda in Eastern Europe, which heavily depended on radio transmission because radio devices were readily available, US propagandists in Iraq relied on the publication of fifteen thousand to twenty thousand pamphlets, because they were constrained by the "limited and unsympathetic press, lack of access to radio facilities, the backward state of the book publishing business, and the relatively few available anti-Communist films."[71] Six themes were to be emphasized in the publication; the most important was viewing Communism as an "international conspiracy" aimed at destroying the Arab nation and its culture.

## Islam and US Propaganda

One of the most important tactics in US propaganda efforts was playing on Muslim religious feelings. Despite the fact that some voices inside the State Department regarded Islam's influence on the region as "reactionary," the US government tried to show itself in alignment with Muslims to win their support.[72] In 1952, a US intelligence report identified Islam as the defining factor in shaping the Arab culture because it provided common ideas and aspirations and a comprehensive way of living. One of the earliest attempts to use religion in US propaganda took place in 1952: when a regional airline left 3,800 Muslim pilgrims stranded in Beirut due to overbooking, the US government arranged for the US Air Force to airlift the pilgrims to Mecca in Operation Magic Carpet.[73]

The US Psychological Strategy Board (PSB) published a report in 1953 that discussed the influence of Islam on Arab culture. It mentioned that "no consideration of the traditional Arab mind is possible without taking into consideration the all pervading influence of the Muslim faith on Arab thinking."[74] According to Matthew F. Jacobs, some US experts viewed Islam's role in US foreign policy in the Middle East between 1945 and 1955 as very significant, given the increasing influence of pan-Islamic movements (which organized conferences and gatherings) and the anti-Western sentiments that accompanied them.[75] Sensing the importance of Islam in the Arab and Muslim world, US propagandists sought to find ways to turn people against Communism by manipulating their religious sentiments. Charles D. Jackson pointed out the main shortcoming of the US propaganda efforts in the Arab world at the time, saying: "All our speeches and proposals are made as if we are talking to Anglo-Saxons. They are based on reason with no emotion. The Arabs don't give a damn about that."[76] New arguments and strategies were needed to exert more influence on the Arab masses. The basic argument was that Communist states opposed religion and that Muslims were persecuted and had no rights in Communist countries.[77] The other idea hammered through the different media channels was that Islam and Christianity, two monotheistic religions, stood united against the atheistic doctrine of Communism, which was depicted as the "common enemy of all religions."[78] This idea was emphasized in the US Operations Coordinating Board report internally circulated among US diplomatic circles in 1957.[79]

The US diplomat William Eddy believed that "from the point of view of psychological warfare alone, we need desperately some common ground to which we welcome the Muslims and the Arabs as respected and valued friends." Eddy argued that religion could provide that common ground between the West and the Arab world. In pursuit of such a possibility, Eddy met with the Palestinian anti-British Muslim figure Haj Amin al-Husseini in Damascus in May 1951. According to Eddy, al-Husseini viewed Communism "with the deepest hate" and claimed that the United States had fought on the wrong side during World War II, arguing that Washington should have sided with Nazi Germany against the Soviet Union. Al-Husseini believed that "all historic religion" would be destroyed if the Soviet Union conquered the world; thus, despite his overt political differences with the policies of Britain in Palestine and the Middle East, he proposed an alliance between Islam and Christianity against international Communism.[80] Some Arab politicians suggested other ways to counter Communism with an Islamic-Christian alliance. On February 22, 1952, an Iraqi businessman and former military attaché with the Iraqi embassy in Washington, Chefik Haddad, met in Beirut with Iraqi Foreign Minister Jamali, Lebanese Prime Minister Sami Solh, and the Pakistani foreign minister. According to John H. Bruins, Haddad revealed that there was a suggestion to create "healthy public opinion" in the three countries by explaining the "Moslem religion on the basis of tolerance" and to "condemn terrorism, Communist or otherwise, by close cooperation mainly among Moslem religious societies or with any other cultural societies, including Christian organizations, in those areas."[81]

The US propaganda interest in Islam was manifested in different ways, but there was no indication to suggest that the USIA directed some programs exclusively at Sunnis and others at Shiites. Instead, the propaganda programs were rather unified. Efforts were made in Iran to develop "specialized materials which tend to instill among religious elements a friendly attitude toward the West and antipathy for Communism."[82] The VOA, for example, was scheduled to air thirty religious programs about the danger of Communism directed to Muslims living in different areas.[83] Also in Iran, a four-page brochure entitled "Voices of God" was published with a religious dimension—it showed a mosque on its cover and cited quotations from the Quran, Hafez, Jesus Christ, the prophet Isaiah, Mo-tzu, Buddha, the Bhagavad Gita, Abraham Lincoln, and Mahatma Gandhi. The aim was to show that all the religions and sublime ideological and philosophical doctrines of the world were similar because they preached the same morality, which was contrasted with the supposedly immoral and debased ideology of Communism.[84]

One US scheme for improving relations with the Muslim world was inspired by the thousandth anniversary of the birth of the Persian scholar Avicenna. According to the proposal, it was very important to show the "negativism" of the Soviet claim that Avicenna was Uzbek (since Uzbekistan was part of the Soviet Union). Hence, US officials should promote the idea that the Soviets wanted to prove that the "most important elements in the Islamic culture were inspired by the Uzbeks" as a slight to other Muslims.[85] Another prospective US propaganda effort was to stress the inauguration of a mosque in Washington, to show that the US government respected Islam and was encouraging its growth in America. To add an emotional side to the story, the State Department proposed having schoolchildren from Washington compete to paint a picture of the new mosque.[86] However, the USIA in Baghdad rejected the mosque-related proposals because they were out of context. The idea of celebrating Avicenna, who did not originally live in Iraq, was not very popular, and the opening of the Washington mosque was negatively received in Iraq because of rumors that Egyptians from the embassy in Washington had reaped financial benefits from building it. Furthermore, according to the US embassy in Baghdad, the mosque story served only to illustrate how few mosques there were in the United States. Instead, the USIA wanted propaganda efforts to be directed toward highlighting "the plight of Muslims in the USSR."[87]

In both Iran and Iraq, the US embassy tried to reach different segments of society, including anti-Communist religious leaders and mullahs who were regarded as important opinion molders. The US government also held a colloquium on Islamic culture in September 1953 in coordination with the Library of Congress and Princeton University. According to Wilson Compton, an administrator of the International Information Administration (IIA) within the State Department, the colloquium was intended to look "on the surface . . . like an exercise in pure learning. This in effect is the impression that we desire to give. IIA promoted the colloquium along these lines and has given it financial and other assistance because we consider that this psychological approach is an important contribution at this time to both short term and long term United States political objectives in the Moslem area."[88] Leading Islamic intellectuals were invited to attend the colloquium, and some were given three-month grants to visit different places in America.[89] Among the figures invited were the Iraqi Shiite scholar Muhammad el-Husayn Kashif al-Ghata, because of his alleged religious influence. The main arguments to be highlighted were the negative attitude of Communism toward Islam and the ongoing persecution of Muslims by the Soviets.[90] In Iran, the US government continued to monitor the situation and was pleased to learn that mullahs in two mosques were preaching against the dangers of Communism.[91] Also, the USIA supported local printers with the help of a US government contractor, Franklin Publishers Inc. One of the first books published by this company was George Orwell's *Animal Farm*.[92] It was supposed to target the "conservative intellectual community who have received a traditional Muslim rather than Western education" because of their wide public reach and influence.[93] However, it was recommended that the kind of propaganda directed to this group should be cautious rather than direct so that it would not "arouse the deeply ingrained distrust and suspicion of foreign influence."[94]

In its Baghdad office, the USIA exhibited several photographs of the new Washington mosque on Massachusetts Avenue. It also showed four posters that attracted crowds. One of these posters involved religion by referring to the idea that the Soviet Union dealt negatively with Muslims. It stressed that the Communists were like a "big bully maltreating a man labeled 'Religion.'" It implied that religion was freely practiced in the United States, in contrast with the Soviet Union.[95] But the most infamous poster showed a greedy red pig with a Red Star armband and a hammer-and-sickle tail, telling the story of "how he came to a bad end." The red pig poster was drawn by an Iraqi artist and captioned by a US public affairs officer,; it was later distributed throughout the country as a two-color poster with text in both Arabic and Kurdish. The symbol of a pig was intentionally used to fan hatred of Communism. The Quran mentions the pig in four places—Al-An'am (The Graces), verse 145; Al-Baqara (The Cow), verse 173; Al-Ma'ida (The Table), verse 3; and Al-Nahal (The Bees), verse 115—to emphasize that Muslims must abstain from eating pork and nonslaughtered dead animals. The Muslim scholar Abu Abdullah al-Qurtubi believes that the devil encourages people to err. Based on Surat al-Nass (The People), verse 5, the devil itself is pictured in the form of a pig.[96] Furthermore, in one interpretation of Surat al-Teen (The Fig), verses 1–5, Muslims who strayed in their lives and committed bad deeds would enter hell in the form of a pig as punishment for what they had done on Earth.[97] In other words, in Islam, the pig is a symbol of the devil, filth, and ugliness, and is completely detested all over the Muslim world. Hence, the use of its image in the poster is highly significant because Muslims would unconsciously associate Communism with a taboo. The US ambassador to Iraq, Edward Crocker, reported on the success of the poster:

> The fact that the pig is wearing a Red Star in his armband and has at his rear end instead of the normally piggy curl a hammer-and-sickle tail has not escaped the observers. If we can make the Soviet-Communist state ridiculous as well as frightening to the ordinary Arab, we shall certainly stimulate his resistance." Crocker heard people talking about "the suitability of making the Communist villain a pig because of the resistance appeal it has for Moslems.[98]

It was further suggested that a "whole series of cartoon-posters can be developed, using the Red Pig as the central figure."[99] George C. Cameron, a professor at the University of Michigan, later commented on the effectiveness of the "greedy red pig" propaganda effort. Cameron lived for a short time with Iraqi Kurds in the area of Baradost. In the tent of a Kurdish tribal leader responsible for over five thousand Kurds, Cameron saw a "little tract with pictures representing a pig with hammer and sickle tail, the pig intent upon gobbling up various quarters of the world." The caption was written in the Kurdish language, but the chieftain expressed his indignation about the money wasted on such propaganda, saying: "I know the Baghdad man who is producing this sheet for your Government. I know how much he is being paid yearly to produce it. If one fourth of that was to be made available in medicines or in some other more tangible product of your country which could be used to lessen the poverty or to better the health of my people, would it not be a far more successful propaganda approach?"[100]

The chieftain raised an important question about the validity of the US propaganda efforts in Iraq. To use today's expression, "winning the hearts and minds" of people does not come through propaganda; instead, it is earned by providing humanitarian assistance to the most vulnerable groups. The Kurdish chief was right in his assessment, given that most Iraqis continued to view direct US propaganda with doubt and suspicion.

After the July 1958 Revolution in Iraq, in which a group of nationalist officers toppled the monarchy, the US and British governments "seriously considered the possibility of reversing the outcome by military force."[101] Even the Iraqi Communists detained in Baquba Prison expected a swift Anglo-American military intervention to reverse the revolution.[102] Indeed, the toppling of the monarchy and the popular appeal that the new republic subsequently gained showed the extent of the regime's isolation and its alienation from the masses. It also indicated that many Iraqis did not take the anti-Communist government propaganda as seriously as the monarchy wanted them to. Britain and the United States later altered their decision to intervene after realizing that Abdul Karim Qasim, the new president of the republic, did not stand as a threat to their political and economic interests. Besides, Qasim opposed Nasser's expansionist policies since he did not want to be under Nasser's influence. However, Qasim had many Iraqi Communists on his side. When Salam Adel led the ICP after 1958, its members agreed that they must support Qasim's rule instead of toppling it.[103] By the end of November 1958, the CIA assessments indicated that there was, in Stephen Blackwell's words, "increasing concern about the growth of Communist influence in Iraq."[104] Put another way, the previous anti-Communist propaganda efforts by the Iraqi government and the USIS did not lead to tangible results; instead, they probably backfired because they did not correspond with the US foreign policy in the region, especially in relation to the United States' overt support for Israel and its economic ambitions in the area.

The Western world and in particular the United States remained popular among the educated people in Iraq. As Saddam Hussein declared during his detention, the number of people who wanted to get visas to the United States in the 1950s greatly surpassed the number of applicants who wanted to go to other countries like the Soviet Union.[105] Politics and ideology had little if nothing to do with this popularity; they were instead a result of the advanced technology and scientific development in the United States, which made it look like a land of opportunity to the majority of educated Iraqis. What is certain is that Communism in Iraq failed to lead any government, and the Iraqi authorities throughout the twentieth century frequently used brutal force to silence Communist voices.

The Campaign of Truth and the other US propaganda programs that followed it are important today for two reasons. First, they show how much time and effort the US government invested in directing the public's attention toward supporting pro-Western governments and drawing it away from dangerous nationalism and Communism. This was done in Iraq mainly by playing on people's religious sentiments. Second, it provides researchers the chance to compare the propaganda methods employed by the US government in Iraq during the 1950s and after the War on Terror and the US invasion of Iraq in 2003. The similarity is astounding—it is no coincidence that the US government allocated a budget of $49 million before the beginning of the 2003 war to create its own media plan. It was later revealed that the United States had intended to make use of Iraqi religious sentiments and stress the internal divisions in Iraqi society to achieve its political aims.[106] For example, a Department of Defense white paper suggested publishing an Iraqi newspaper with sections for "Shia news, Kurd news, and Sunni news."[107] In 2005, the US Information Operations Task Force worked with Lincoln Group, a US contractor, to plant "storyboards" in the Iraqi media. With a budget of $300 million devoted to public diplomacy (propaganda), the US government wanted to influence "the local population to support United States policy" in Iraq.[108] In both eras, the United States assisted an Iraqi government that was too weak to function alone, and worked hand in hand with it to combat their common enemies—Communists during the Cold War era and Islamic fundamentalists after 9/11. Most importantly, they used propaganda in both periods as a basic tool to counter the rhetoric of their opponents.

## Notes

1. Walter L. Hixson, *Parting the Curtain: Propaganda, Culture, and the Cold War, 1945-1961* (New York: St. Martin's Press, 1998), 58–60.
2. Nicholas Cull, *The Cold War and the United States Information Agency: American Propaganda and Public Diplomacy, 1945–1989* (New York: Cambridge University Press, 2008), 22–23.
3. Kenneth Osgood, *Total Cold War: Eisenhower's Secret Propaganda Battle at Home and Abroad* (Lawrence: University Press of Kansas, 2006), 76.
4. Saki Dockrill, *Eisenhower's New-Look National Security Policy, 1953–61* (London: Macmillan, 1996), 2.
5. Osgood, *Total Cold War*, 77, 78.
6. Hixson, *Parting the Curtain*, 26, xv.
7. Chris Tudda, *The Truth Is Our Weapon: The Rhetorical Diplomacy of Dwight D. Eisenhower and John Foster Dulles* (Baton Rouge: Louisiana State University Press, 2006), 83–87.
8. Hixson, *Parting the Curtain*, 57.
9. Tudda, *Truth Is Our Weapon*, 84–85.
10. Hixson, *Parting the Curtain*, 95.
11. Tudda, *Truth Is Our Weapon*, 89; and Hixson, *Parting the Curtain*, 59.
12. Hixson, *Parting the Curtain*, xiv, ix.
13. Hanna Batatu, *The Old Social Classes and the Revolutionary Movements of Iraq* (Princeton, NJ: Princeton University Press, 1978), 396.
14. Quoted in Malik Saif, *Lil Tarikh Lisan: Al-Hizb al-Shiu'i al-Iraqi Munthu Ta'sisah hata al-Yawm* [History has a tongue: The Iraqi Communist Party from its establishment until this day] (Baghdad: Dar al-Hurria, 1983), 324.
15. Memorandum from Shepard Jones to G. Lewis Jones, "Anglo-American Cooperation in the Psychological Field in the Arab States and Iran," March 30, 1951, National Security Archive (hereafter NSA), Washington, DC, *www.gwu.*

*edu/~nsarchiv.* For a discussion of US and UK interest in the Saudi and Iraqi oil industries, see Henry B. Ryan, *The Vision of Anglo-America: The US-UK Alliance and the Emerging Cold War, 1943–1946* (Cambridge: Cambridge University Press, 2004), 65–66.

16. Mahmood Azmi, *Khabayya Siyasiah* [Political secrets] (Cairo: Mattabi' Jaridat al-Masri, 1950), 78.

17. Peter L. Hahn, *The United States, Great Britain, and Egypt, 1945–1956: Strategy and Diplomacy in the Early Cold War* (Chapel Hill: University of North Carolina Press, 2004), 89–90.

18. Abdul A'dhim Ramadhan, *Qussat Abdul Nasser wa al-Shiyu'een* [The story of Abdul Nasser and the Communists] (Cairo: Al-Hay'ah al-Masriah lil Kitab, 1998), 1:277.

19. Ibid., 29–33.

20. Ilario Salucci, *A People's History of Iraq: The Iraqi Communist Party, Workers' Movements and the Left, 1924–2004* (Chicago: Haymarket Books, 2005), 30.

21. Tareq Y. Ismael, *The Rise and Fall of the Communist Party of Iraq* (New York: Cambridge University Press, 2008), 23.

22. Eric Davis, *Memories of State: Politics, History, and Collective Identity in Modern Iraq* (Berkeley: University of California Press, 2005), 82.

23. Ismael, *Rise and Fall*, 39–40.

24. Davis, *Memories of State*, 98.

25. Jassim al-Halwa'i, *Al-Haqiqa Kama 'Ashttuha* [The reality as I lived it] (Baghdad: Iraqi Communist Party, 2008), 19–20, 31. Available at *www.iraqicp.com* (accessed May 10, 2011).

26. Ibid., 40–43.

27. Cull, *Cold War*, 73; and al-Halwa'i, *Al-Haqiqa Kama 'Ashttuha*, 43. Al-Halwa'i also asserts that the prison contained a solitary confinement unit that had been built under the supervision of the US Point IV program, a "key element in the output of USIS [United States Information Service] posts across the region" (*Al-Haqiqa Kama 'Ashttuha*, 43).

28. Al-Halwa'i, *Al-Haqiqa Kama 'Ashttuha*, 39.

29. Ibid., 20, 65.

30. Hahn, *United States, Great Britain, and Egypt*, 90.

31. Ibid., 91.

32. Telegram from Burton Berry, US ambassador to Iraq, to Secretary of State Dean Acheson, November 23, 1952, NSA, *www.gwu.edu/~nsarchiv.*

33. National Security Council report, "United States Objectives and Policies with Respect to the Middle East," July 6, 1954, NSA, *www.gwu.edu/~nsarchiv.*

34. Alan R. Taylor, *The Superpowers and the Middle East* (Syracuse, NY: Syracuse University Press, 1991), 58.

35. Elie Podeh, *The Quest for Hegemony in the Arab World: The Struggle over the Baghdad Pact* (Leiden, Netherlands: Brill, 1995), 55.

36. Podeh, *Quest for Hegemony*, 55.

37. Quoted in Hahn, *United States, Great Britain, and Egypt*, 158.

38. Quoted in Behçet Kemal Yeşilbursa, *The Baghdad Pact: Anglo-American Defence Policies in the Middle East* (London: Routledge, 2005), 24.

39. Roby Carol Barrett, *The Greater Middle East and the Cold War: US Foreign Policy under Eisenhower and Kennedy* (London: Tauris, 2007), 19.

40. Daniel C. Williamson, *Separate Agendas: Churchill, Eisenhower, and Anglo-American Relations, 1953–1955* (Lanham, MD: Lexington Books, 2006), 49–50.

41. Taylor, *Superpowers*, 59.

42. Ara Sanjian, "The Formulation of the Baghdad Pact," *Middle Eastern Studies* 33, no. 2 (1997): 232.

43. Oles M. Smolansky and Bettie Moretz Smolansky, *The USSR and Iraq: The Soviet Quest for Influence* (Durham, NC: Duke University Press, 1991), 15–16.

44. Waldemar J. Gallman, *Iraq under General Nuri: My Recollections of Nuri al-Said, 1954–1958* (Baltimore: Johns Hopkins University Press, 1964), 68.

45. Quoted in Saif, *Lil Tarikh Lisan*, 325.

46. Ibid., 323.

47. Editorial, *Attihad al-Shaab* (Baghdad, Iraq), October 1957.

48. Khalid H. al-Rawi, *Methods of Foreign Propaganda in the Arab World* [in Arabic] (Amman: Al-Warraq Printing Press, 2010), 194.

49. James Vaughan, "Propaganda by Proxy? Britain, America, and Arab Radio Broadcasting, 1953–1957," *Historical Journal of Film, Radio and Television* 22, no. 2 (2002): 170.

50. Mohommed [Mohammed] Fadhel Jamali, "Arab Struggle; Experiences of Mohammed Fadhel Jamali," Special Collections, Widener Library, Harvard University. Available as "Experiences in Arab Affairs, 1943–1958" at *www.physics.harvard.edu.*

51. Memorandum from John H. Bruins, US Legation in Lebanon, February 26, 1952, NSA, *www.gwu.edu/~nsarchiv.*

52. The name "USIS" was later changed to "USIA."

53. Telegram from Philip W. Ireland, US Embassy in Baghdad, to Department of State, March 30, 1953, NSA, *www.gwu.edu/~nsarchiv.*

54. Telegram from Burton Berry, US ambassador to Iraq, to Department of State, May 26, 1953, NSA, *www.gwu.edu/~nsarchiv.*

55. Telegram from Burton Berry, US ambassador to Iraq, to Department of State, January 13, 1954, NSA, *www.gwu.edu/~nsarchiv.*

56. Telegram from Burton Berry, US ambassador to Iraq, to Secretary of State John Foster Dulles, January 19, 1954, NSA, *www.gwu.edu/~nsarchiv.*

57. Al-Halwa'i, *Al-Haqiqa Kama 'Ashttuha*, 32.

58. See Department of State circular airgram from Secretary of State Dean Acheson, May 1, 1950, NSA, *www.gwu.edu/~nsarchiv*; and telegram from Burton Berry, US ambassador to Iraq, to Secretary of State Dean Acheson, September 11, 1952, NSA, *www.gwu.edu/~nsarchiv*; and telegram from Burton Berry, US ambassador to Iraq, to Department of State, October 1, 1952, NSA, *www.gwu.edu/~nsarchiv.*

59. National Security Council report, "United States Objectives and Policies with Respect to the Near East," July 23, 1954, 42, NSA, *www.gwu.edu/~nsarchiv.*

60. See Hixson, *Parting the Curtain*, 128, and Hahn, *United States, Great Britain, and Egypt*, 183.

61. Osgood, *Total Cold War*, 405.

62. Telegram from Edward S. Crocker II, US ambassador to Iraq, to Department of State, May 16, 1952, NSA, *www.gwu.edu/~nsarchiv*.

63. Telegram from Henry F. Grady, US ambassador to Iran, to Department of State, July 6, 1950, NSA, *www.gwu.edu/~nsarchiv*, and telegram from Edward S. Crocker II, US ambassador to Iraq, to Department of State, April 27, 1950, NSA, *www.gwu.edu/~nsarchiv*.

64. Sanjian, "Formulation," 232.

65. Fahad (Yousif S. Yousif), *Mu'lafat Fahad: Min Wathai'q al-Hizb al-Shiu'i al-Iraqi* [Fahad's writings: From the documents of the Iraqi Communist Party] (Baghdad: Mattba'at al-Sha'b, 1973), 134.

66. Ibid.

67. Telegram from Edward S. Crocker II, US ambassador to Iraq, to Department of State, March 26, 1951, NSA, *www.gwu.edu/~nsarchiv*.

68. Telegram from Dean Acheson, secretary of state, to US Embassy in Iraq, August 29, 1951, NSA, *www.gwu.edu/~nsarchiv*.

69. Telegram from Philip W. Ireland, US Embassy in Iraq, to Department of State, July 8, 1952, NSA, *www.gwu.edu/~nsarchiv*.

70. Telegram from Edward S. Crocker II, US ambassador to Iraq, to Secretary of State Dean Acheson, February 6, 1952, NSA, *www.gwu.edu/~nsarchiv*.

71. Telegram from Harry L. Smith, first secretary of the US Embassy in Baghdad, "Arabic Anti-Communist Pamphlet Program," September 9, 1952, NSA, 511.8021/10-752, *www.gwu.edu/~nsarchiv*.

72. Department of State report, "Conference of Middle East Chiefs of Mission," February 21, 1951, NSA, *www.gwu.edu/~nsarchiv*.

73. Ibid., 74.

74. Quoted in Matthew F. Jacobs, "The Perils and Promise of Islam: The United States and the Muslim Middle East in the Early Cold War," *Diplomatic History* 30, no. 4 (September 2006): 711–12.

75. Ibid., 724, 737–38.

76. Quoted in Vaughan, "Propaganda by Proxy," 160.

77. Telegram from Burton Berry, US ambassador to Iraq, to Department of State, October 1, 1952, NSA, *www.gwu.edu/~nsarchiv*.

78. National Security Council staff study, "United States Objectives and Policies with Respect to the Arab States and Israel," April 7, 1952, NSA, *www.gwu.edu/~nsarchiv*, and National Security Council report, "United States Objectives and Policies with Respect to the Near East," July 23, 1954, NSA, *www.gwu.edu/~nsarchiv*.

79. Jacobs, "Perils and Promise," 732.

80. Letter from William A. Eddy to Dorothy Thompson, June 7, 1951, NSA, *www.gwu.edu/~nsarchiv*.

81. John H. Bruins, counselor of legation, American Legation, Beirut, February 26, 1952, NSA, *www.gwu.edu/~nsarchiv*.

82. Telegram from Henry F. Grady, US ambassador to Iran, to Department of State, July 6, 1950, NSA, *www.gwu.edu/~nsarchiv*.

83. Telegram from Foy Kohler, US Embassy in Egypt, to Voice of America Representative Sabbagh, US Legation in Lebanon, November 2, 1952, NSA.

84. Telegram from Loy Henderson, US ambassador to Iran, to Department of State, May 29, 1953, NSA, *www.gwu.edu/~nsarchiv*.

85. Letter from G. H. Damon to Richard H. Sanger, Department of State, March 25, 1952, NSA.

86. Ibid.

87. Telegram from Burton Berry, US ambassador to Iraq, to Department of State, October 1, 1952, NSA, *www.gwu.edu/~nsarchiv*.

88. Memorandum from Wilson S. Compton of the International Information Administration to Under Secretary of State David K. E. Bruce, January 16, 1953, NSA, *www.gwu.edu/~nsarchiv*.

89. Letter from Helen M. Anderson, organizer of the Colloquium on Islamic Culture, to Richard H. Sanger, Department of State, May 8, 1953, NSA, *www.gwu .edu/~nsarchiv*, and telegram from Jefferson Caffery, US ambassador to Egypt, to Department of State, July 27, 1953, NSA, *www.gwu.edu/~nsarchiv*.

90. Telegram from Henry F. Brady, US ambassador to Iran, to Secretary of State Dean Acheson, October 19, 1950, NSA, *www.gwu.edu/~nsarchiv*, and telegram from Harry Smith, US Embassy in Iraq, to Department of State, October 7, 1952, NSA, *www.gwu.edu/~nsarchiv*.

91. Telegram from Henry F. Grady, US ambassador to Iran, to Secretary of State Dean Acheson, October 19, 1950, NSA, *www.gwu.edu/~nsarchiv*.

92. Cull, *Cold War*, 73.

93. Letter from Dan Lacy, International Information Administration, to Datus C. Smith Jr., president of Franklin Publications, October 27, 1952, NSA, *www.gwu. edu/~nsarchiv*.

94. Telegram from Henry F. Grady, US ambassador to Iran, to Department of State, July 6, 1950, NSA, *www.gwu.edu/~nsarchiv*.

95. Telegram from Edward S. Crocker II, US ambassador to Iraq, to Department of State, March 10, 1951, NSA, *www.gwu.edu/~nsarchiv*.

96. Abu Abdullah al-Qurtubi, *Tafssir al-Qurtubi* [Al-Qurtubi's interpretation] (Cairo: Dar al-Katub al-Massryya, 1964), 263.

97. Abu Mohammed al-Baghawi, *Maaliym al-Tanzil* [The features of revelation] (Riyadh: Dar Tybba lil Nashir wa al-Tawzi', 1997), 277.

98. Telegram from Edward S. Crocker II, US ambassador to Iraq, to Department of State, March 10, 1951, NSA, *www.gwu.edu/~nsarchiv*.

99. Ibid.

100. Quoted in letter from George C. Cameron, University of Michigan, to Assistant Secretary of State Edward W. Barrett, October 4, 1951, NSA, *www.gwu.edu/~nsarchiv*.

101. Stephen Blackwell, "A Desert Squall: Anglo-American Planning for Military Intervention in Iraq, July 1958–August 1959," *Middle Eastern Studies* 35, no. 3 (July 1999): 3.

102. Al-Halwa'i, *Al-Haqiqa Kama 'Ashttuha*, 62.
103. Samir Abdul Karim, *Adwa' a'la al-Harkah al-Shiu'iah fi al-Iraq* [Aspects of the Communist movement in Iraq] (Beirut: Dar al-Mirsad), 2:230.
104. Blackwell, "Desert Squall," 5.
105. Memorandum from the US Department of Justice Baghdad Operations Center, May 13, 2004. NSA.
106. Joyce Battle, "Pentagon 'Rapid Reaction Media Team' for Iraq," May 8, 2007, NSA, *www.gwu.edu/~nsarchiv*. See also Jim Lobe, "Pentagon Moved to Fix Iraqi Media before Invasion," *Inter Press Service*, May 9, 2007.
107. US Department of Defense, 2003, "White Paper: 'Rapid Reaction Team Concept," NSA, *www.gwu.edu/~nsarchiv*.
108. Karen de Young and Walter Pincus, "U.S. to Fund Pro-American Publicity in Iraqi Media," *Washington Post*, October 3, 2008; and Mark Mazzetti and Borzou Daragahi, "U.S. Military Covertly Pays to Run Stories in Iraqi Press," *Los Angeles Times*, November 30, 2005.

## References

**ARCHIVES**
National Security Archive, Washington, DC

**PERIODICALS**
*Attihad al-Shaab*
*Inter Press Service*
*Los Angeles Times*
*Washington Post*

**SELECTED PUBLISHED WORKS**
Abdul Karim, Samir. *Adwa' a'la al-Harkah al-Shiu'iah fi al-Iraq* [Aspects of the Communist movement in Iraq]. Vol. 2. Beirut: Dar al-Mirsad.
Azmi, Mahmood. *Khabayya Siyasiah* [Political secrets]. Cairo: Mattabi' Jaridat al-Masri, 1950.
Baghawi, Abu Mohammed al-. *Maaliym al-Tanzil* [The features of revelation]. Riyadh: Dar Tybba lil Nashir wa al-Tawzi', 1997.
Batatu, Hanna. *The Old Social Classes and the Revolutionary Movements of Iraq*. Princeton, NJ: Princeton University Press, 1978.
Blackwell, Stephen. "A Desert Squall: Anglo-American Planning for Military Intervention in Iraq, July 1958–August 1959." *Middle Eastern Studies* 35, no. 3 (July 1999): 1–18.
Cull, Nicholas. *The Cold War and the United States Information Agency: American Propaganda and Public Diplomacy, 1945–1989*. New York: Cambridge University Press, 2008.

Davis, Eric. *Memories of State: Politics, History, and Collective Identity in Modern Iraq.* Berkeley: University of California Press, 2005.

Dockrill, Saki. *Eisenhower's New-Look National Security Policy, 1953–61.* London: Macmillan, 1996.

Fahad [Yousif S. Yousif, pseud.]. *Mu'lafat Fahad: Min Wathai'q al-Hizb al-Shiu'i al-Iraqi* [Fahad's writings: From the documents of the Iraqi Communist Party]. Baghdad: Mattba'at al-Sha'b, 1973.

Gallman, Waldemar J. *Iraq under General Nuri: My Recollections of Nuri al-Said, 1954–1958.* Baltimore: Johns Hopkins University Press, 1964.

Hahn, Peter L. *The United States, Great Britain, and Egypt, 1945–1956: Strategy and Diplomacy in the Early Cold War.* Chapel Hill: University of North Carolina Press, 1991.

Halwa'i, Jassim al-. *Al-Haqiqa Kama 'Ashttuha* [The reality as I lived it]. Baghdad: Iraqi Communist Party, 2008. *www.iraqicp.com* (accessed May 10, 2011).

Hixson, Walter L. *Parting the Curtain: Propaganda, Culture, and the Cold War, 1945–1961.* New York: St. Martin's Press, 1998.

Jacobs, Matthew F. "The Perils and Promise of Islam: The United States and the Muslim Middle East in the Early Cold War." *Diplomatic History* 30, no. 4 (September 2006): 705–39.

Jamali, Mohommed [Mohammed] Fadhel. "Experiences in Arab Affairs, 1943–1958." *physics.harvard.edu* (accessed December 23, 2009).

Osgood, Kenneth. *Total Cold War: Eisenhower's Secret Propaganda Battle at Home and Abroad.* Lawrence: University Press of Kansas, 2006.

Podeh, Elie. *The Quest for Hegemony in the Arab World: The Struggle over the Baghdad Pact.* Leiden, Netherlands: Brill, 1995.

Qurtubi, Abu Abdullah al-. *Tafssir al-Qurtubi* [Al-Qurtubi's interpretation]. Cairo: Dar al-Kutub al-Massryya, 1964.

Ramadhan, Abdul A'dhim. *Qussat Abdul Nasser wa al-Shiyu'een* [The story of Abdul Nasser and the Communists]. Vol. 1. Cairo: Al-Hay'ah al-Masriah lil Kitab, 1998.

Rawi, Khalid H. al-. *Asalib al-Di'ayah al-Ajnabiah al-Muwajaha alla al-Wattan al-Arabi* [Methods of foreign propaganda in the Arab world]. Amman: Al-Warraq Printing Press, 2010.

Saif, Malik. *Lil Tarikh Lissan: Al-Hizb al-Shiu'i al-Iraqi munthu Ta'sisah hata al-Yawm* [History has a tongue: The Iraqi Communist Party from its establishment until this day]. Baghdad: Dar al-Hurria, 1983.

Salucci, Ilario. *A People's History of Iraq: The Iraqi Communist Party, Workers' Movements, and the Left, 1924–2004.* Chicago: Haymarket Books, 2005.

Sanjian, Ara. "The Formulation of the Baghdad Pact." *Middle Eastern Studies* 33, no. 2 (1997): 226–66.

Taylor, Alan R. *The Superpowers and the Middle East.* Syracuse, NY: Syracuse University Press, 1991.

Tudda, Chris. *The Truth Is Our Weapon: The Rhetorical Diplomacy of Dwight D. Eisenhower and John Foster Dulles*. Baton Rouge: Louisiana State University Press, 2006.

Vaughan, James. "Propaganda by Proxy? Britain, America, and Arab Radio Broadcasting, 1953–1957." *Historical Journal of Film, Radio, and Television* 22, no. 2 (2002): 157–72.

# CHAPTER 7

# Religion and Cold War Politics in Ethiopia

*Wudu Tafete Kassu*

For more than 1,500 years (AD 430 to 1959), the Ethiopian Orthodox Church was governed by the Coptic Orthodox Church of Alexandria, Egypt, which consecrated and appointed Coptic bishops to preside over the Ethiopians. The Coptic Church did not allow Ethiopians to be bishops of their own church. There were several attempts to get an Ethiopian national appointed as bishop, but none of them succeeded.

In the 1920s, a nationalist religious movement demanded the appointment of an Ethiopian bishop and the independence of the Ethiopian Church. This chapter briefly investigates the emergence of this nationalist consciousness, which argued against Coptic suzerainty in terms of race, slavery, serfdom, economic exploitation, and colonial domination. It then summarizes the prolonged negotiations between the Ethiopian Church and the Coptic Church. It emphasizes that local and regional as well as religious and political determinants had a great impact on the negotiations between the two churches. Local ethnonationalist rebellions from the 1940s, supported by Arab and Islamic governments, threatened to destabilize the Ethiopian government. During the Cold War, Egypt opposed that government because it was the region's major supporter of the West. Egypt also disliked Ethiopia's leaning in favor of Israel, which was based on scriptural as well as ancient and medieval Ethiopian traditions. Moreover, Egypt was nervous about Ethiopian attempts to construct a dam on the Nile River. Finally, the establishment of a US military base in Asmara (present-day Eritrea) was threatening to Egypt and the other Middle Eastern countries that had developed strong political and military ties with the Soviet Union.

Thus, the Egyptian government under Gamal Abdel Nasser backed the ethnonationalist struggle in Ethiopia, training and arming local dissident groups. Moreover, Nasser's pan-Islamist image was strong among Ethiopian Muslims, who saw him as an ally. Cairo became a hub of radical nationalism, attracting young educated people from Ethiopia who espoused socialism and viewed Nasser as a radical and a supporter of their cause. Nasser's regime was revolutionary and socialist but used Islam to further its own political objectives.

The government of Ethiopia was threatened by the involvement of neighboring Muslim countries in its internal political affairs. It received intelligence reports from the United States and Great Britain about what these countries were doing against Ethiopia. Cold War politics and regional rivalry clouded the religious negotiations between Ethiopia and Egypt. As a minority in a predominantly Muslim Egypt, the Coptic Church was subject to strong political pressure from the Egyptian government and therefore could not bargain freely with the Ethiopian Church.

As we will see, the negotiations between the two churches stalled, prolonged by the intervention of the Islamic Egyptian government. At one point in its attempt to control the Coptic Church, the Nasser government removed the Coptic patriarch, who had given autonomy to the Ethiopian Orthodox Church, and changed the patriarchal election rule. Its aim was to frustrate the bold Ethiopian demand for greater representation in the Coptic Synod, in patriarchal elections, on the patriarchal electoral committee, and in terms of candidates for the throne of St. Mark. The Ethiopian Synod threatened to sever its relations with the Coptic Church and refused to participate in the election of the next patriarch. To maintain the relationship between the Coptic Church and the Ethiopian Orthodox Church, the Coptic patriarch raised the Ethiopian archbishop to the status of patriarch. Until that time, the independence of the Ethiopian Orthodox Church and the discussions leading to its autocephalous status had been marred by Cold War politics between the two governments and by the pan-Islamist and pan-Arab policies of Nasser.

## Religious Nationalism in the Ethiopian Orthodox Church

The Ethiopian Orthodox Church is the bastion of Ethiopian tradition and culture. It is also a way of life. It contributed to the development of the country in the fields of education, literature, bookbinding, architecture, building, painting, and music. Beginning with its establishment in the fourth century, it was the largest single diocese under the Coptic Church of Alexandria. The head of the Ethiopian Orthodox Church was an Egyptian national, consecrated and appointed as bishop of the Ethiopian Orthodox Church by the Coptic patriarch. The main job of the resident Coptic bishop in Ethiopia was to anoint kings, to consecrate *tabots* (replicas of the Ark of the Covenant), and to ordain priests and deacons. Except for these functions, the administration of the Ethiopian Church was not in the hands of the Coptic metropolitan.

Since the fifteenth century, the echage—the abbot of the Dabra-Libanos monastery and the top-ranked Ethiopian monk—had been responsible for the administration of the church. The supreme head of the church was the king, and various clerics assisted him in its administration. The office of the Coptic bishop was attached to the royal court. The king could exile the bishop, ask the Alexandrian patriarch for a replacement, call religious councils, and preside over them. The king was the final arbitrator of doctrinal differences, and he appointed clerics to important churches and monasteries. The bishop's only power was excommunication, and this power was not fully exercised.[1]

The Coptic bishops in Ethiopia were somewhat isolated figures because they neither spoke the local languages nor did they know the culture and traditions of the country to which they were appointed. Preaching and understanding the spiritual needs of the people were impossible for them; official and private communications took place only through interpreters. The Coptic bishop had little interaction with his religious followers and the clergy, and he was not in a position to offer religious leadership. The expansion of Christianity, the development of church education, and the literary and other achievements of the Ethiopian Orthodox Church were therefore the work of the Ethiopian clergy.[2]

Ethiopian kings sent costly gifts and slaves to the Egyptian sultan and the Coptic patriarch to gain their consent to import Coptic bishops, gifts Ethiopia could ill afford. Coptic bishops in Ethiopia lived a rich life, administering their *gults* (nonhereditary right of the clergy and the nobility to collect tribute from tenants) like regional governors. They also received gifts for consecrating altars and ordaining priests and deacons. The office of the Coptic bishop was so economically attractive that during periods of vacancy, pseudo-bishops from Egypt and Syria came to Ethiopia, trying to take advantage of the opportunities; when their identities became known, they were either deported or put to death.[3]

The early twentieth century marked the beginning of discussions on the backwardness of the country and the need for reform, as intellectuals began to address the issue of modernity and of safeguarding the country's independence. Even after Ethiopia's astounding victory at Adwa against the Italians in 1896, these individuals were aware of the dangers of hostile colonial expansion to the survival of Ethiopia's independence. They believed that education was the key to adopting Western technology, and hence modernization. In this regard, they judged Japan the best example. They published their ideas in newspapers, enlightening their readers and calling on Ethiopian rulers to speed up the expansion of education and administrative reforms. It was in light of this background that the opposition against the Coptic Church reemerged in 1926.[4]

The debates of the early 1920s dealt with race, slavery, serfdom, economic exploitation, and colonial domination.[5] The circulation of the first newspapers in the country helped the religious nationalists publicize their ideas—*Berhanena Salam* (Light and Peace), established in 1925, had a wide circulation in the provinces and in foreign countries where Ethiopians were studying. Thus, a large number of people participated in the discussion.

The main demand of the religious nationalists was the appointment of Ethiopians as bishops of their own church. They denounced the practice of simony and other payments to the bishop. They argued that forcing young boys to travel to Addis Ababa for ordination (because that was where the bishop lived) put them at risk for diseases (contracted on their way to the capital) and other difficulties. Some of the boys drowned in the Abbay River (Blue Nile) while trying to travel to Addis Ababa. This was a criticism of the Coptic bishop at the time, who was regarded as a moneymaker indifferent to the suffering of children. The religious nationalists also denounced the Coptic forgery of a Council of Nicaea (AD 325) canon that had ostensibly forbidden Ethiopians from holding the Episcopal office and the refusal of the Coptic Church to appoint any Ethiopian as metropolitan of their church. There were conservative individuals who defended the age-old relations between the two churches and who argued for their continuation. This group included the more established clergy. Only a small number of this group published their views, but they were strongly condemned by the religious nationalists and thus never participated in the debate with vitality.[6]

One of the contentious issues between the two churches was the question of Ethiopian monasteries in Jerusalem. The Egyptians had controlled the monasteries since the second half of the nineteenth century, when the number of Ethiopian monks declined as a result of epidemic diseases. Ethiopia's attempt to get back the control of these monasteries was frustrated by the Coptic Church of Alexandria. In 1902, the Coptic bishop in Ethiopia, Abuna Matewos (Matthew), was sent to Jerusalem to resolve the dispute. Rather than protecting Ethiopian rights, he concluded a backdoor deal that gave ownership directly to the Alexandrian Church. This betrayal so angered the Ethiopian authorities that they considered severing relations with the Egyptians and importing Syrian bishops instead.[7] The question of Ethiopian monasteries in Jerusalem became so contentious that there were later reports that Ethiopia was contemplating taking the case to the League of Nations.[8] While the issue did not go that far, it indicated that Addis Ababa prepared to take legal action in an international forum.

It was in the 1920s that the Coptic Church agreed to ordain Ethiopians as bishops of their church. Thus, four Ethiopian monks were consecrated in Cairo in June 1929 (Abunas Abreham, Petros, Mikael, Yeshaq), and the fifth (Abuna Sawiros) was consecrated in Addis Ababa in January 1930. The appointment of these Ethiopian bishops was a historic occasion for the Ethiopian Church. It was a milestone in the development of the first national hierarchy of the church; its first diocesan structure was organized in 1931. Ethiopia, however, was then invaded by the fascist Italians in 1935. Abunas Petros and Mikael were murdered during the war of resistance against the invaders. Abuna Yeshaq was taken as a prisoner to Italy and later brought back to his country. Abuna Sawiros had died a few years before the war.

Abuna Abreham submitted to the Italians and was appointed as the first archbishop of the Ethiopian Orthodox Church under the Italian colonial administration. The administration also appointed more Ethiopian bishops and established more dioceses. Above all, the Italians separated the Ethiopian Orthodox Church from its mother church and declared its independence. As a result, the ancient relationship between the Ethiopian Church and the Alexandrian Church was disrupted during the period of the occupation, 1936–1941.

With the restoration of the Ethiopian government in 1941, the old relationship between the two churches was gradually rebuilt. The question of the Ethiopian Church's independence again became a complicated issue, and the protracted negotiations often involved the governments of Egypt and Ethiopia.

## Cold War Politics and Religion

The long negotiation for the independence of the Ethiopian Orthodox Church took place between 1941 and 1959. The Ethiopians demanded the independence of the church and the appointment of an indigenous archbishop with the power to consecrate other bishops. The discussions revolving around such issues widened the rift between the two churches. During two separate meetings, in July 1941 and November 1945, the Ethiopian Synod overwhelmingly voted in favor of declaring the independence from Alexandria. The Coptic Church regarded the synod as a body that represented only the pro-separation intelligentsia—Ethiopian clerics who had enjoyed the short-lived independence of the church under the Italians and were resolutely opposed to the Coptic resumption of power now that the country was liberated from colonial rule. The Ethiopian clergymen built their argument for independence on the Italian legacy.

However, the Ethiopian government was edgy about the militant eagerness of the Ethiopian clergymen to sever relations with the Alexandrian church.

The government was uneasy about the effect religious nationalism might have on its political administration. Thus, the government wanted to broker a peaceful settlement. The emperor, Haile Selassie, sent several letters and delegations to the Coptic Church, calling on the Alexandrian patriarch to solve the long-standing demands of his church. He also warned that he would be forced to support his clergy unless a satisfactory settlement was reached.

When the Ethiopian delegation came back from Cairo in March 1946 with no conclusive settlement, the *Ethiopian Herald* declared that "Ethiopia is a free country. It is natural that she should seek religious as well as political freedom and independence. Self-determination can not be restricted to only a selected field of national life, but must embrace also the field of religion."[9] The paper was referring to the Atlantic Charter, which supported the self-determination of nations, and it tried to present its argument in light of world political events. In response to the Coptic press, which had criticized Ethiopia and alleged that Ethiopian religious nationalists were extremists who wanted to separate their church from Alexandria, the *Ethiopian Herald* commented that the "Coptic Church is uncompromising, even ultra radical, her attitude is inspired by human selfish considerations, the Ethiopian church is inspired by pure ecclesiastical reasons claiming only her natural rights."[10] Another weekly newspaper, *Sadaqqalamačen*, strongly questioned whether it was spiritually right for one million Egyptian Copts to dominate ten million Ethiopian Christians.[11] The presses in both countries were involved in the debate, supporting the ideas of their respective churches.

Political issues marred the discussions of independence. In 1946, at the Paris Peace Conference, Egypt put a claim on Eritrea while Ethiopia demanded its return to its motherland. The Egyptians had occupied parts of Eritrea in the 1870s, fighting and losing two major battles in 1875 and 1876. A treaty of 1884 recognized the sovereignty of Ethiopia over its territories, which the Egyptians departed from in 1885. Eritrea became an Italian colony from 1890 until 1941, when the British controlled it as occupied enemy territory. The new Egyptian claim was a major shock to Ethiopia and it darkened the religious negotiations.[12]

Local and regional political factors interfered with and obstructed the religious negotiations as well. The pan-Africanist and pan-Arabic policy of Egyptian president Nasser and other Islamic leaders destabilized Ethiopia's internal affairs. Egypt trained, armed, and financially supported dissident Ethiopian groups, opposing the imperial regime's religious policy against its Muslim subjects. Egyptian and Ethiopian rulers claimed that they were the protectors of religious minorities in each other's countries; along with the issue of the Ethiopian monasteries in Jerusalem, this strained the relations between Ethiopia and Egypt in particular, and between Addis Ababa and its Muslim neighbors in general. The hydropolitics of the Nile River was another key factor that created tension. When Nasser came to power in 1952, the Revolutionary Command Council of Egypt planned to construct the Aswan High Dam. Egypt wanted to strengthen its position by making sure that Ethiopia could never construct a dam that would affect the flow of the Nile. Nasser was also supporting ethnonationalist groups to weaken Ethiopia in order to maintain Egypt's hydropolitical position. Moreover, the Muslim world in general resented Ethiopia's traditionally close relations with Israel and the claim of the Ethiopian ruling classes as descendants of the "Solomonic dynasty" of Israel. Ethiopia's close alliance with the United States and the presence of a US intelligence base in Asmara contributed further to the regional dislike of Ethiopia. In contrast with Ethiopia's alliance with the United States, Egypt became closely aligned with the Soviet Union.[13]

One of the major outcomes of the religious negotiations was the consecration of the five Ethiopian bishops in Cairo in July 1948. However, the appointment of the first Ethiopian archbishop was delayed until January 1951. With this appointment, the Ethiopian Church gained a limited autonomy. However, some Coptic clergy and the Maglis al-Milli (council of lay leaders in the Coptic Church of Alexandria) resented these developments. The Maglis al-Milli had been reconstituted by Nasser's government as part of strategy for controlling the affairs of the Coptic Church. The Maglis al-Milli did not accept the autonomy of the Ethiopian Church, even though the Ethiopian archbishop remained accountable to the Coptic patriarch. The friendly attitude of the Coptic patriarch, Abuna Joseph (also called Abuna Yosab; patriarch from 1946 to 1956), toward the Ethiopian Orthodox Church earned him the hostility of these Coptic clerics and lay leaders. Because of this, a group of Coptic bishops—who were actually a minority in the Coptic Synod—deposed him in September 1955 with the support of the Egyptian government. The Ethiopian Church, which was neither consulted nor invited to discuss any of the allegations made against the patriarch it shared with the Coptic Church, considered his removal illegal. At first, it sought to find a peaceful solution; it sent a delegation to Cairo that was not received well. The bishops who had removed Joseph were uncompromising, rejecting the Ethiopian demand to restore Joseph to his holy seat. The Ethiopian delegates stayed in Cairo for three months and, frustrated, came back home in February 1956. Four months later, another Ethiopian delegation traveled to Cairo. After a lot of wrangling, the Egyptian and Ethiopian supporters of Joseph held a synod in June 1956 and decided to take Joseph back to his patriarchate themselves. On the agreed date, however, none of the Coptic bishops turned up; only the Ethiopian delegation accompanied him back to his residence. Unfortunately, it had been locked by his opponents and was heavily guarded. Joseph was kidnapped from the Ethiopians and taken to a hospital, where he was under the constant watch of spies designated by the Egyptian government and his other opponents.[14]

The Ethiopian Synod convened in August 1956 to examine its relations with the Coptic Church. It denounced the illegal acts of the minority of Coptic bishops and their stubborn refusal to return their common father—the connection between the two churches—to his seat. Joseph died in the hospital in November 1956. After his death, the Ethiopian Synod refused to acknowledge the acting Coptic patriarch and declined to participate in the election and installation of his successor. The Ethiopian Synod also discovered that the Egyptian government had changed the rules for electing the Coptic patriarch, which had previously been agreed on by the two churches. This was to frustrate the Ethiopian demands for more rights and to maintain its strong influence in Coptic affairs. Thus, the Ethiopian Synod decided to isolate itself from the Coptic Church.[15]

The main reason the Ethiopian Church was disappointed was because the Coptic Church had drafted a new law for the election of the Coptic patriarch, replacing the law of 1946. The new law was approved and published by President Nasser in November 1957. Article 3 stipulated that the patriarch must be a Copt and an Egyptian national. Article 14 allowed a small number of Ethiopian electors. The Ethiopian Church complained about the unequal number of electors. The Ethiopian Church wanted to have equal representation in the Coptic Synod and on the patriarchal electoral committee. Above all, the Ethiopian Orthodox Church refused to be governed by a religious law issued by an Egyptian Islamic government.[16]

Emperor Haile Selassie, however, was not interested in an immediate and hasty split. As he and his ministers deliberated with the Ethiopian Synod, they were troubled by the politics of Ethio-Egyptian relations. Nasser, the leader of a revolution and a pan-Arab, pan-Islamic, and socialist government, was seeking to bring other countries under his political influence. Emperor Haile Selassie was conscious of his own historical legacy and considered himself the protector of Coptic religious minorities in Egypt, just as President Nasser considered himself the protector of Ethiopian Muslims.[17] The emperor thus strongly argued against plans for separation, which would leave the Copts at the mercy of Nasser's Islamic government. Haile Selassie told his synod that he would not let down the Copts. He was pragmatic; rather than intervening directly in Coptic affairs, he wanted to put diplomatic pressure on Egypt. Ethiopian secular officials supported his stance, but the Ethiopian bishops were eager for a complete break from Alexandria and downplayed the political and regional issues, disregarding Nasser's ambitions.

In the 1940s, various separatist ethnonationalist and religious movements directed against the centralizing policy of the government of Haile

Selassie had emerged in several regions, particularly in Eritrea and Somalia. The first major threat had come from the Ogaden, who aimed to unite all the Somali language-speaking peoples into one state. They had established an office in Harar and prompted the Adaré (Harari) and the Somali to join their struggle. One of the Adaré leaders, Shaykh Yusuf ʻAbd al-Rahman, was also a leader of the Wahhabi movement, which wanted to establish an Islamic state in Harar.

ʻThe Adaré, claiming religious oppression by the Ethiopian government, launched an underground movement, Kulub Hannolatoa (Long live the movement), which sent delegates to Mogadishu to present their wish to join the future independent Somalia to a United Nations commission. The popular slogan among Kulub Hannolatoa activists was "Long live Somalia, death to Ethiopia." The commission came to Mogadishu in 1948 to investigate the former Italian colonies.[18]

The Ethiopian government reacted swiftly to this and imprisoned the members of the movement it was able to apprehend in Harar. On receiving the news, the delegates to the UN commission, who had traveled to Mogadishu earlier, moved to Jedda, Saudi Arabia, and then to Egypt. In Cairo, they were received by leaders of the Wafd Party, the Arab League, and the Egyptian Muslim Brotherhood. A secret letter from the Ethiopian minister of foreign affairs to the deputy governor of Harar relayed that people in Cairo were spreading propaganda against the government about the plight of Muslims in eastern Ethiopia. Security reports also indicated that Ethiopian Muslim communities were organizing a major rebellion. The government was forced to control Muslim religious schools in Harar, which it believed were engaged in spreading antigovernment propaganda. At about the same time, local papers reported that Muslims from various regions, fearing government measures, had come to the capital to express their allegiance to the emperor and to demand that the Adaré perpetrators be punished. These incidents increased government anxiety about things going out of control if they were not properly handled, and thus shaped its future attitude toward Egypt.[19]

By the mid-1950s, the Ethiopian political authorities were greatly worried by the disruptive propaganda that Nasser's government was directing against their country in the form of radio broadcasts in local and regional languages. Nasser also gave Ethiopian Muslims material and moral support as he tried to stir them up into revolting against their government. In 1956, a US diplomatic report indicated the involvement of Nasser's Islamic government in Ethiopian political affairs. The report emphasized that the radio broadcasts in Amharic and Somali from Cairo were destabilizing the security of the region and constituted a major threat to Ethiopia:

> The Egyptian Embassy has stated that a break up of the Ethiopian
> Empire is inevitable unless these minorities are given political privi-
> leges. Broadcasts from Cairo in Amharic attack the present regime in
> Addis Ababa. Other broadcasts in the long-neglected Somali tongue
> appeal to Somali nationalism. Egyptian officials have carried out
> propaganda and political action program in Ethiopia and Eritrea
> designed to organize the large Muslim minorities against the ruling
> Christian Amhara dynasty.[20]

Three crucial issues are mentioned here. The Egyptians carried out political propaganda to destabilize the government. They were broadcasting daily on the radio to incite the Muslim population against the Ethiopian government. They wanted to organize a large Muslim League against the Ethiopian Empire. They also sought to unify the large Muslim population of eastern Ethiopia and the Somalis under one state. This would entail the breakup of the Ethiopian Empire.

In the 1940s, at the very time the two churches were negotiating over the appointment of an Ethiopian archbishop, Egypt had announced in the United Nations its goal of regaining control of Eritrea, part of which it had conquered in the 1870s. Later, in 1950, Egypt had dropped the claim. However, in the 1950s and 1960s, Egypt was heavily engaged in subversive activities, support-ing Eritrean guerrilla fighters against the Ethiopian government. The Eritrean Liberation Front (ELF) was established in Cairo in 1960.[21] The Egyptian Islamic government continued to fund, train, and arm other Eritrean freedom fighters throughout the 1970s and 1980s. As the historian Haggai Erlich summed up: "Their prominent leader (later the father figure of Christian-Tigrean Eritrean-ism), the Protestant Walda-Ab Walda-Mariam, was invited in 1955 to broad-cast daily anti-Ethiopian messages on Radio Cairo to Eritreans. The Nasserist regime remained the main pillar of support for the Eritrean separatist move-ment until 1963. The Nasserist-installed myth of Eritrea's Arabism, adopted and advanced by Eritrean Muslims, was to survive until the 1960s."[22]

United States diplomatic sources continued to note the subversive activi-ties of Egypt in the region, and the concern that these evoked in the Ethiopian government. The Saudi Arabian government likewise supplied money to the Eritrean fighters for purchasing arms, and its Voice of Islam radio station car-ried propaganda condemning Ethiopia for mistreatment of its Muslim sub-jects.[23] Moreover, since the 1940s, the Society of the Muslim Brothers of Egypt had been enacting its plans to extend its reach to other countries. One sec-tion, Liaison with the Islamic World, was entrusted with spreading Islam and the ideals of the Muslim Brothers by "compiling files on each country which include relevant political economic, social, and cultural data, as well as information on the course of 'Islamic movement' therein."[24] One of the permanent committees was in charge both of East Africa and Ethiopia; its main duty was to contact and work with national Muslim organizations. The society also supported dissident students from other countries attending Egyptian schools.

Other Arab and Islamic countries (such as Syria, Saudi Arabia, Iraq, Pakistan, Sudan, and Somalia) were engaged in similar activities, providing logistical support and military training to Eritrean secessionists. In 1962, the Arab League passed a resolution calling on member states to support Eritrean freedom fighters. Egyptian newspapers such as *Al-Shaab* had always claimed that Ethiopia was "joining the imperialist bloc to encircle the United Arab Republic and Arab nationalism," an allusion to Ethiopia's close relations with the United States.[25] The Saudi government, for its part, resented Ethiopia's close relations with Israel. Its paper, *Al-Da'wa*, declared that "Ethiopia is a tool of imperialism. . . . Haile-Selassie and his gang [Israel and America] are acting against you, Arab, and against your religion and your existence."[26] A decade later, in a May 1972 Organization of African Unity summit meeting, Colonel Muammar al-Qadafi of Libya called Ethiopia "a colonial empire in the service of the United States, South Africa, Portugal, Rhodesia, and Israel."[27]

The spread of Nasserist influence among Ethiopian Muslims and the control of Coptic affairs by the Nasser government was a concern for Ethiopia. To pursue the demands of the Ethiopian Synod for separation would have left the Copts without support when they looked to the government of Ethiopia, just as the Ethiopian Muslims looked to the government of Nasser. No matter how the religious negotiations were stalled, Ethiopia had to weigh the political implications of its steps carefully.

In 1957, when the rules regulating the election of the Coptic patriarch were issued, they continued to limit candidates to Copts and Egyptian nationals and to ignore the Ethiopian Synod's demands for significant representation on the election committee, a permanent place in the Coptic Synod, and candidacy to the throne of St. Mark. Ethiopia's aspiration to the throne of St. Mark was greatly alarming to the minority Copts. Approval of candidates from all followers of St. Mark meant that Ethiopian bishops might get elected and thereby shift the holy seat of St. Mark from Alexandria to Addis Ababa. At one point during this round of religious negotiations, the Ethiopians agreed to the sole Coptic candidate for patriarch in the election to be held in 1958 (which was delayed until April 1959), because the Copts insisted to the Ethiopians both in public and private that they had to accept this term. For their part, the Copts feared that the Islamic Egyptian government would consider them traitors if they allowed Ethiopians to compete for the throne of St. Mark.

The Egyptian government disliked Ethiopia's involvement in Coptic affairs and its continued aspiration for more rights; the Majlis al-Milli opposed the revision because it feared that the law of candidature would favor Ethiopians in the future. Thus, Egypt annulled the revised electoral law the two churches had drafted. Ethiopia vehemently opposed the unilateral abrogation of the protocol of 1958. The election of the Coptic patriarch was held in April 1959 without Ethiopian participation. Since Ethiopian demands were not met, Ethiopia boycotted the election and the enthronement of the patriarch. However, as an act of reconciliation, the newly elected patriarch of the Coptic Church agreed to raise the Ethiopian archbishop to the status of patriarch of the Ethiopian Church in 1959.[28] The Ethiopian archbishop was formally crowned as patriarch in June 1959 in Cairo. This was the final and formal achievement of independent autocephalous status for the Ethiopian Orthodox Church.

A few years earlier, with the increase in ethnonationalist and religious movements against the imperial regime, and in light of the destabilizing activities of neighboring Muslim governments, the government of Haile Selassie had tried to promote national unity through two homogenizing processes: imposing the Amharic language over other languages, and defining of the nation in terms of Orthodox religion. These notions had been crystallized in the revised constitution of 1955, which defined Amharic as the national language of Ethiopia and Orthodoxy as the official religion of the state. The language policy was promoted everywhere, including in schools and government offices. The religion policy was directed at non-Christian subjects: The government pursued the homogenizing process of getting them to embrace Orthodoxy since 1941. The push for a culturally homogeneous society grew from the fear of the spread of Islam and the growing militancy of its followers, the spread of missionary churches even in the traditionally Christian regions, and the weakness of the Orthodox Church in active evangelization. The government aimed to build a homogeneous society based on three main concepts: religious homogeneity, linguistic uniformity, and ethnic intermixing.[29]

In the postliberation period, Muslims and other religious groups began to lobby vigorously for their rights. Religious identity was on the rise, and government support for the Orthodox Church became a point of conflict. The grievance of non-Orthodox organizations turned into armed struggle. Some Muslim activists protested the support given to Orthodox religious schools. In 1948–1949, the government had granted educational taxes collected from church lands to the church for the expansion of religious education. Muslims complained that Muslim religious schools were not given any financial support. They objected to the neglect of Islamic schools, and to the taxes collected from Muslims going to Orthodox religious schools. Activists also pointed out that no Muslim holidays were publicly observed, that the government had not recruited Muslims into its civil service, and that the government had not granted *waqf* (land specifically for a mosque) to their mosques. Muslim schools resisted the use of Amharic and refused to accept Christian clergymen as teachers of the language. Instead, they wanted to continue using Arabic as the main instructional medium. They used Arabic in their religious preaching and regarded it as part of their religious identity.

There were also several reports that Muslims were establishing associations to spread the influence of Islam. Muslim clerics from Harar were allegedly converting people in Arsi, reconverting those baptized into the Orthodox Church, and influencing back those who were about to be converted to Christianity. Graduates of Al-Azhar University of Cairo were playing a leading role in organizing and inciting Muslims against the Ethiopian government.[30]

Ethiopian Muslims believed that Nasser was their protector. Nasser's portrait was displayed in the houses of almost all Muslims in urban areas as a demonstration of the hope they placed in him as their protector. In 1963, when Nasser came to Addis Ababa for the founding conference of the Organization of African Unity (now the African Union), the government was shocked by the turnout of Muslims to receive him, even though the government had recognized the strength of Nasser's pan-Islamist and pan-Africanist reputation among its Muslim subjects.[31] Bereket Habte-Selassie, who was then attorney general of the imperial regime, went to Bole International Airport to receive President Nasser:

> The airport was filled with literally hundreds of thousands of people. Most of them were turbaned country folks, so it was obvious that they were Ethiopian Muslims who had come from Harar, Jimma, Arsi, Sidamo, and other districts. This was not "in the books" of the government, and was an immense surprise. It was an emphatic demonstration of solidarity with the Muslim/Arab world at a time when Muslims felt excluded from government affairs in a country ruled by a Christian king.[32]

Habte-Selassie also described how, as soon as Nasser's tall figure emerged from the plane, "the multitude voiced their feelings, shouting 'NASSER! NASSER! NASSER!' I could feel the ground shaking. Nasser waved with supreme pleasure, as I could see from his smiling, charismatic face."[33] Berket further noted that the Ethiopian prime minister, Aklilu Habta-Wald, was greatly distressed by the spectacle of the Muslims' welcome.

On the other hand, a confidential report from the British embassy some years earlier had concluded that the Ethiopian government and the church had no major threat to fear from Islam in the near future, because the Muslims would not gain by collaborating with another Muslim power against their own country. This conclusion was based on an assessment of the government's tolerance toward Islam.[34] The study itself explains that Western governments shared the government's concern about the politicization of its Muslim subjects. The government was not ready to treat such threats carelessly, and it would devise other measures to integrate Muslims.

The government and the church had defined the identity of the country as a Christian state surrounded by unfriendly Muslim countries. On many occasions, the emperor and the church leaders emphasized this. Prime Minister Aklilu Habta-Wald confided to the director general of the Foreign Ministry of Israel in March 1968 that "Ethiopia is a Christian island in a Muslim sea, and the Muslims make no distinction between religious and political goals. Their aim is to destroy Ethiopia."[35] The Ethiopian prime minister was referring to the pan-Africanist and pan-Islamist policy of Nasser as well as those of other Arab governments.

The trauma of the wars of Ahmed Gran in the sixteenth century still lingered in the minds of Christians, church leaders, and the government. One could argue that Christian Ethiopia had developed a strong siege mentality while dealing with political Islam. The rebellion of the Adaré in 1948, the secessionist tendencies in the Ogaden, the widespread Arab support of Eritrean secession until 1991, the political problems in Bale in 1968, and the different wars against the Somali in the 1960s and 1970s contributed to this mentality.

When the Ethiopian Revolution broke out and the military government came to power in 1974, the relations between Ethiopia and Egypt were further strained. The conflict had a religious and political dimension. When the military rulers deposed the second patriarch of the Ethiopian Orthodox Church, Abuna Tewoflos, in 1976, the Coptic Church continued to regard him as the legitimate patriarch of Ethiopia. The Coptic Church viewed the deposition as contrary to the traditions and laws of the Ethiopian Orthodox Church, and believed the patriarch had been removed because of political reasons. The Synod of the Coptic Church of Alexandria refused to participate in the enthronement of the newly elected third patriarch of the Ethiopian Orthodox Church or to recognize him. Both the Ethiopian and the Egyptian governments carefully watched religious developments in each other's country.[36]

Amid this controversy, there was also a political problem. The Ethiopian socialist military government was establishing closer ties with the Soviet camp, and also building relations with Libya against their common enemy, the Sudan. From 1975 to 1977, the Soviet Union supported Libya against the Sudan and other pro-Western conservative Arab governments such as Egypt and Saudi Arabia. In 1976, President Anwar Sadat of Egypt and President Ja'far Numeiry of the Sudan signed a military agreement to ensure the flow of the Nile River to Egypt. Egypt had also stationed a large army in the Sudan, mainly as a warning to the Ethiopian socialist military government. After the Camp David Accord of September 1978, Sadat became aligned with the United States while the Ethiopian socialist military government was allied with the Soviet Union. The Ethiopian rulers regarded these Arab states as their country's historical enemies, whose reactionary governments were supporting the secessionist movement in Eritrea and an irredentist Somali state. Sadat and his Arab colleagues similarly viewed the Soviet-backed Ethio-Libyan alliance as a threat to their governments.[37]

## Conclusion

The Coptic Orthodox Church of Alexandria ruled the Ethiopian Orthodox Church for more than 1,600 years, but the Coptic bishops assigned to Ethiopia did not know the language or the traditions of the country. Because of this, they had very limited interaction with their followers. The Alexandrian church did not allow Ethiopians to hold the office of the bishop. Religious nationalism emerged at various times, but it was only in 1928 that Ethiopians were ordained as bishops of their own church. When the Italians invaded the country in 1935, they appointed several bishops, expanded the dioceses, and separated the Ethiopian Church from Alexandria, thereby declaring the independence of the Ethiopian Church. After the liberation of the country in 1941, negotiations with the Coptic Church for the autonomy of the Ethiopian Church began.

The negotiations were arduous and marred by Cold War politics between the Egyptian and Ethiopian governments. Nasser adopted a policy of political intervention in support of Ethiopian Muslims. Haile Selassie likewise considered himself the protector of Coptic religious minorities in Egypt. Egypt and other Muslim governments interfered in the internal politics of Ethiopia by supporting ethnonationalist and religious rebellions. They also trained and armed dissidents fighting against the imperial government. Ethiopia's close relations with the West and with Israel, the issue of the Nile River, and the question of religious minorities in both countries were major issues in its strained relations with Egypt in particular and with other Arab and Islamic states in general. These political areas of contention clouded the religious negotiations until the Ethiopian Orthodox Church gained its independence from the Alexandrian church in 1959. However, the Cold War politics continued through the fall of the imperial government in 1974, up until the socialist military government was overthrown in 1991, which coincided with the end of the Cold War.

## Notes

1. Stuart C. Munro-Hay, *Ethiopia and Alexandria: The Metropolitan Episcopacy of Ethiopia* (Warsaw: Bibliotheca Nubica et Aethiopica, 1977), 174; and Shiferaw Bekele, "The Shadowy Bishops of the Ethiopian Church in the First Millennium of Its History (4th to 14th Centuries): A Review Article," *Journal of Ethiopian Studies* 34, no. 1 (June 2001): 103–11.
2. Heruy Walda-Selassie, *ä-həywät tarik: bähʷala zämän läminäsu ləǧǧočč mastawäqiya* [Biography: A guide to future generations] (Addis Ababa: Berhanena Salam Printing Press, [1915 EC] 1922/1923), 85; and see Otto F. A. Meinardius, *Christian Egypt, Faith, and Life* (Cairo: American University in Cairo Press, 1970), 390.
3. Menelik to Patriarch Cyril (Qerelos), Genbot 7, 1981 EC (May 1898), Institute of Ethiopian Studies Archives (hereafter IES), Addis Ababa, Ethiopia, MS 162; and see Gorgoreyos, *Ya Ityopiya Orthodox Beta-Kresitiyan Tarik* [The history of the Ethiopian Orthodox Church], 4th ed. (Addis Ababa: Tensae Za-Gubaé Printing Press, 1974), 33–34.
4. See Bahru Zewde, *Pioneers of Change in Ethiopia: The Reformist Intellectuals of the Early Twentieth Century* (Oxford: James Currey, 2002), and his "The Concept of Japanization in the Intellectual History of Modern Ethiopia," *Proceedings of the Fifth Seminar of the Department of History* (Addis Ababa: Addis Ababa University Press, 1990; also, Abebe Fisseha, "Education and the Formation of the Ethiopian Modern State, 1896–1974" (PhD diss., University of Illinois at Urbana-Champaign, 2000), 22–47.
5. Wudu Tafete Kassu, "The Ethiopian Orthodox Church, the Ethiopian State, and the Alexandrian See: Indigenizing the Episcopacy and Forging National Identity, 1926–1991" (PhD diss., University of Illinois at Urbana-Champaign, 2006), ch. 2.
6. Taddesse Tamrat, *Church and State, 1270–1527* (Oxford: Clarendon Press, 1972), 114n2; *Berhanena Salam*, no. 24 (June 27, 1926): 191; and Kassu, "Ethiopian Orthodox Church," 28–42.
7. Mr. J. L. Baird to the Marquess of Lansdowne, Addis Ababa, September 30, 1902, National Archives (hereafter NA), Kew (London), UK, FO 1/40; cf. An-gen report, November 6, 1907, NA, FO/371/192/1957; Tigab Bezie, "The Ethiopian Claim on the Monastery of Deir Es-Sultan in Jerusalem, 1850s–1994" (MA thesis, Addis Ababa University, 2001), 41–42.
8. Cf. *A'emro*, no. 257 (September 7, 1929): 2–3.
9. *Ethiopian Herald*, April 8, 1946.
10. *Ethiopian Herald*, July 22, 1946.
11. *Sadaqqalamačen*, Sane 26, 1938 EC (July 1946); see also Kassu, "Ethiopian Orthodox Church," 143–48.
12. *Ethiopian Herald*, October 14, 1946, December 9, 1946, and March 31, 1947; and *Addis Zemen* (an Amharic weekly), Magabit 20, 1939 EC (March 1947).
13. Kassu, "Ethiopian Orthodox Church," 220–21. See also Haggai Erlich, *The Cross and the River: Ethiopia, Egypt and the Nile* (Boulder, CO: Lynne Rienner, 2002); Yacob Arsano, *Ethiopia and the Nile: Dilemmas of National and Regional Hydro-Politics* (Zurich: Center for Security Studies, 2007); and Daniel Kendie, "Egypt and the

Hydro-Politics of the Blue Nile River," *Northeast African Studies* 6, nos.1–2 (1999): 141–69.

14. *Zena Beta-Krestiyan* (newspaper of the church), no. 11, Maskaram 30, 1948 EC (October 1955); Basliyos to Patriarch Joseph, Private Office of the Ethiopian Patriarch, Addis Ababa, Ethiopia, Folder 551/48, Genbot 28, 1948 EC (June 1956), Folder 3384-3400, File 3385/94; notes of the Ethiopian bishops on June 24, 1956, Private Office of the Ethiopian Patriarch; and *Addis Zemen*, Sane 2, 1948 EC (June 1956).

15. Resolution of the Synod, Hamle 27, 1948 EC (August 1956), Private Office of the Ethiopian Patriarch, Folder 3384-3400, File 3385/94; *Zena Beta-Krestiyan*, no. 9, Hamle 30, 1948 EC (July 1956); and *Ethiopian Herald*, August 11, 1956.

16. A translation from the Arabic paper *Al-Misriya* (Egypt), November 3, 1957, National Library and Archive, Ministry of Culture, Addis Ababa, Ethiopia, Marse'-Hazan Walda-Qirqos File, File 05-02.

17. Meeting notes, Genbot 23, 1949 EC (June 1957), Private Office of the Ethiopian Patriarch, Folder 3384-3400, File 3385/94.

18. Tim Carmichael, "Approaching Ethiopian History: Addis Ababa and Local Governance in Harar, c. 1900 to 1950" (PhD diss., Michigan State University, 2001), 194–218; see also Rahji Abdella, "The Kulub-Hannolato Movement by the Harari" (BA thesis, Addis Ababa University, 1994), and Haggai Erlich, *Saudi Arabia and Ethiopia: Islam, Christianity and Politics Entwined* (Boulder, CO: Lynne Rienner, 2007), 81–83, 91.

19. Top-secret letter from Zawde Gabra-Heywat, Director of the Ministry of Foreign Affairs, to Ayala Gabre, Hedar 27, 1941 EC (December 1948), IES, MS 1800, A and B; report of 1953–1954, IES, MS 13367; *Sandaqallamachen*, Miyaziya 27, 1940 EC (May 1948); Carmichael, *Approaching Ethiopian History*, 219–24.

20. James S. Lay, memorandum for the NSC planning board, section 6 (pages 2–3), October 8 and 18, 1957, IES, MS 2287; note from the executive secretary to the National Security Council on US policy toward the Horn of Africa, NSC 9503, sections 7–13 (pages 4–13), February 4, 1959, IES, MS 1187B, US Department of State, Ethiopia, 1957–1967, 1–19; and George A. Lipsky et al., eds., *US Army Area Hand Book for Ethiopia*, 2nd ed. (Washington, DC: Human Relations Area Files, 1964), 436–37.

21. Lipsky et al., *US Army Area Hand Book*, 98.

22. Erlich, *Cross and the River*, 130.

23. Erlich, *Saudi Arabia and Ethiopia*, 107, 109–10.

24. Richard Mitchell, *The Society of the Muslim Brothers* (London: Oxford University Press, 1969), 172–73.

25. Quoted from the *Ethiopian Herald* (January 1959) in Lipsky, *US Army Area Hand Book for Ethiopia*, 436.

26. Quoted in Erlich, *Saudi Arabia and Ethiopia*, 112–13.

27. Ibid., 115.

28. Ibid.

29. Abebe, "Education and the Formation," 165.

30. Ethiopian Government Security report about Muslim plots, Hamle 23 and 27, 1945

EC (August 1953) and Maskaram 5 and 11, 1946 EC (September 1953), IES, MS 13367; the echage (abbot) to Asrat Kassa, 1943–44 EC 8th central register, entry 404/4, Magabit 20, 1943 EC (March 1951), Private Office of the Patriarch; and security report (author unknown) dated Sane 10, 1957 EC (June 1965), IES, MS 2396/02/1.

31. Security report dated Sane 10, 1957 (1965). The government daily, *Addis Zemen* did not report the turnout, though.
32. Bereket Habte-Selassie, *The Crown and the Pen: The Memoirs of a Lawyer Turned Rebel* (Trenton, NJ: Red Sea Press, 2007), 185.
33. Ibid.
34. Confidential report from the British Embassy in Addis Ababa to the Foreign Office, July 27, 1954, NA, FO 371/10827.
35. Erlich, *Cross and the River*, 150; see also *Ethiopian Herald*, July 1, 1959.
36. Resolution of the Coptic Synod, August 14, 1976: sent to the Ethiopian Church by the Ethiopian Ministry of Foreign Affairs, File 136; by Pope Shenouda to Abuna Yohannes, August 16, 1976; and by telegram from Shenouda to Yohannes, August 18, 1976; all in the Ethiopian Orthodox Church Archive, Addis Ababa, Ethiopia, File 4382.
37. Marina and David Ottaway, *Ethiopia, Empire in Revolution* (New York: Africana Publishing, 1978), 169; Erlich, *Ethiopia and the Middle East* (Boulder, CO: Lynne Rienner, 1984), 179, and Erlich, *Cross and the River*, 199.

## References

ARCHIVES

Ethiopian National Library and Archive, Addis Ababa, Ethiopia
Ethiopian Orthodox Church Archive, Addis Ababa, Ethiopia
Institute of Ethiopian Studies Archives, Addis Ababa, Ethiopia
Ministry of Culture, Addis Ababa, Ethiopia
National Archives, Kew (London), United Kingdom
Private Office of the Ethiopian Patriarch, Addis Ababa, Ethiopia

PERIODICALS

*Addis Zemen*
*A'emro*
*Berhanena Salam*
*Ethiopian Herald*
*Sadaqqalamačen*
*Sandaqallamachen*
*Zena Beta-Krestiyan*

SELECTED PUBLISHED WORKS

Arsano, Yacob. *Ethiopia and the Nile: Dilemmas of National and Regional Hydro-Politics.* Zurich: Center for Security Studies, 2007.

Erlich, Haggai. *The Cross and the River: Ethiopia, Egypt, and the Nile*. Boulder, CO: Lynne Rienner, 2002.

———. *Ethiopia and the Middle East*. Boulder, CO: Lynne Rienner, 1984.

———. *Saudi Arabia and Ethiopia: Islam, Christianity, and Politics Entwined*. Boulder, CO: Lynne Rienner, 2007.

Kassu, Wudu Tafete. "The Ethiopian Orthodox Church, the Ethiopian State, and the Alexandrian See: Indigenizing the Episcopacy and Forging National Identity, 1926–1991." PhD diss., University of Illinois at Urbana-Champaign, 2006.

Munro-Hay, Stuart C. *Ethiopia and Alexandria: The Metropolitan Episcopacy of Ethiopia*. Warsaw: Bibliotheca Nubica et Aethiopica, 1977.

# CHAPTER 8

# Soviet Policies toward Islam

## *Domestic and International Considerations*

*Eren Murat Tasar*

The Soviet Union commenced its history in 1922 under the direction of a political party devoted to the liquidation of religion.[1] By late 1991, when the country collapsed, religion existed as a tolerated and even vibrant force in political and social life. How did such a radical transformation occur in the space of less than seventy years? Through the prism of Soviet policy toward Islam, this chapter argues that historical events, and in particular the cataclysm of World War II, compelled the Communist Party to completely reframe its struggle with religion. Stalin's decision to open up religious life in 1943–1944 constituted an unexpected historical development that reshaped the context and framework of religious policy for the remainder of Soviet history.[2] World War II, and more specifically Stalin's response to it, relegated the nation's struggle with religion to the realm of ideas, with irreversible consequences for state and society.

An examination of Islam in the Soviet Union highlights the Cold War's importance in Soviet domestic politics. Considerations of international public diplomacy played a significant role in making the religious policy reforms of 1943–1944 possible. Although Stalin principally had the Russian Orthodox and Catholic Churches in mind, Soviet Muslims benefited greatly from the reforms. From the mid-1950s on, the status of Islam in the Soviet Union became a significant point of contention in Cold War propaganda. The evolution of policy toward Islam therefore merits examination in the context of

Cold War rivalries, particularly the Soviet government's decades-long drive for influence and favor in the Muslim and developing worlds.

From the perspective of ideology, if not actual policy, the Communist Party remained committed to eradicating religion throughout its entire history. Thus, party officials and bureaucrats dealing with religion from 1917 until the onset of World War II believed they could make religion vanish among Soviet people. To achieve this objective, they relied on two instruments: antireligious propaganda and mass repression.[3] This entire period of prewar Soviet history witnessed the uneasy coexistence of these two elements of the antireligious struggle in radically varying measure, depending on the year in question.[4]

If Soviet history as a whole represented a debate over the meaning of the revolutions of 1917, then the postwar period arguably constituted a debate over how to properly interpret Stalin's wartime reforms. As of 1943, a legally sanctioned institutional framework existed in the Soviet Union to protect almost all the major faiths observed by the country's citizenry. Stalin decided to create a legal space for religion in the Soviet Union.[5] He permitted the reopening of the Moscow patriarchate, as well as the establishment of four Islamic organizations, known as muftiates, spanning the country. For the remainder of Soviet history, any and all antireligious initiatives would take place in the shadow of these reforms. Postwar policy debates concerning religion revolved around the question of how best to contain religion, rather than how best to annihilate it. Mass repression vanished as a viable policy option, giving way to the more limited avenues of administrative and restrictive measures targeting specific religious figures and institutions.

The departure from an explicitly revolutionary attack on all religion toward a posture of toleration and even a striking degree of reliance on certain religious figures reflected a substantial fault line within the party-state after World War II. A segment of officialdom advocated a stable, statist mode of regulation, while encouraging the party to win the populace over to atheism. This impulse constituted the moderate line toward religion. Concurrently, a vocal constituency called for aggressive pressure against religion in the form of denial of applications to register prayer houses, curtailment of legal religions organizations, and the expansion of propaganda. This general understanding that religious figures should not get too "comfortable" constituted the hard line toward religion.[6] Proponents of the hard and moderate lines sparred until the two groups coalesced in the aftermath of Nikita Khrushchev's antireligious campaign (1959–1964). Their disagreement speaks to a chasm between two strands in Bolshevik history, revolutionary and statist, that in turn echo the conflicting legacies of early Soviet history—the popular revolutionary impulse that marked the late 1920s and early 1930s, and the statist mode of rule that found its reflection in the cult of Stalinism.

The existing bodies of scholarly literature on Soviet policy toward Islam, as well as religious policy in the Soviet Union more generally, have not acknowledged the extent of the moderate line's influence after World War II. Instead, they have tended to characterize hard-line rhetoric and policy implementation as representative of Soviet religious policy throughout the postwar decades. During the Cold War, Western analyses of Islam in the Soviet Union emphasized resistance and mutual suspicion as the defining features of the country's policy toward Muslims.[7] In significant advances for the literature, Mark Saroyan and later Yaacov Ro'i posited the Soviet muftiates as organizational actors capable of advancing their own institutional interests in the context of Soviet religious policy; however, they did not identify the moderate line as a powerful constituency within the party-state that facilitated the numerous institution-building measures undertaken by religious organizations.[8] The more general scholarship on Soviet religious policy, much of which deals with the Russian Orthodox Church, has often presented Soviet leaders as adopting a consistently hard line throughout the history of the Soviet Union.[9] In fact, official deliberations concerning religious policy during the first decade of Bolshevik rule, and in the fifty years following World War II, witnessed rigorous debate. Soviet bureaucrats dealing with religious affairs all accepted that religion must eventually disappear, but they fiercely disagreed on how to effect such a change while remaining true to Communist ideals.

## An Attack in Halts and Spurts (1917–1941)

Policy toward Islam during the first two decades of Bolshevik power stemmed from a uniform conceptual framework. The Soviet leadership believed that it could eradicate religion from society. Within a realistic time frame, virtually the entire population could be won over to atheism. Two strategies would serve this objective. First, the state would employ mass violence to wipe out the social and economic bases of Islam in society. The leadership felt that it could plausibly destroy Islam's institutional infrastructure in the form of prayer houses, educational establishments, charitable endowments (*waqf*), and Islamic figures enjoying influence among the Muslim population based on erudition or descent. Second, it would use propaganda and agitation to convince Muslims of the shallowness of faith in God and reliance on the clergy. The goal of liquidating religion complemented other revolutionary initiatives of early Soviet history: disenfranchisement of *kulaks* (rich peasants), collectivization, the purging of nationalists from state power structures, and the overwhelmingly rapid drive toward industrialization that transformed the country's economy in the space of less than half a decade.[10]

Very roughly speaking, the largest Muslim populations in the Soviet Union fell within six general cultural spaces. First, Islam in western Russia was traditionally centered on the major urban centers of Moscow and Kazan. Muslim communities had inhabited these cities since before the time of the Mongol invasion; Kazan had been a center of Islamic culture and learning until the ravages of Ivan the Terrible in the mid-sixteenth century.[11] Second, the vast expanses of Siberia boasted their own brand of Islamic civilization. Many central and eastern Siberian settlements featured Muslim communities of varying sizes throughout the imperial and Soviet periods.[12] Third, central Asia hosted historical capitals of Islamic civilization such as Samarqand and Bukhara that enjoyed renown in the entire Muslim world.[13] Fourth, nomads— predominant in central Asia's northern expanses (e.g., modern-day Kazakhstan)—fell somewhere between the political and cultural influence of Siberian and central Asian Islamic influences while retaining their own distinct culture and nonsedentary brand of Muslim civilization.[14] Fifth, the northern Caucasus exhibited the predominantly Shafi'i influences of the Arab Middle East. This region, which includes the modern Russian republics of Chechnya and Dagestan, mustered the most prolonged and fierce resistance to Moscow's rule in the nineteenth century.[15] Finally, the southern Caucasus, and especially Azerbaijan, were inhabited by Shiite Muslims who looked to the South—to the Iranian holy city of Qom, the Iraqi pilgrimage centers of Najaf and Karbala, and Iranian Azerbaijan—for erudition and guidance, while hosting their own brand of Azeri Shiite culture.[16]

Such remarkable diversity in Islamic culture and practice among the Soviet Union's Muslims carried little significance for the Communist Party's leadership during this first phase of religious policy. After seizing control of most of the former Russian Empire in October 1917, the party under Lenin's leadership had no strategy other than to survive in power. The first decade of Bolshevik rule, from 1917 to 1927, witnessed a strikingly moderate posture toward Islam.[17] This stemmed from an attempt in the early 1920s to promote Bolshevism as a version of anticolonial nationalism for the former Russian Empire's Muslims. This trend embraced an array of Soviet Muslims, from the Tatar Bolshevik Mirsaid Sultan-Galiyev (1892–1940) to the prominent Bukharan Jadid Abdurauf Fitrat (1886–1938), but it lost favor with Lenin's descent into illness and subsequent death in 1923–1924. After asserting control over central Asia, Lenin hastened to introduce conciliatory measures designed to win the support of the Muslim population for Bolshevik rule. While fashioning the Communist Party as an instrument of social liberation from tsarist colonial subjugation, he took dramatic steps to reverse some of the restrictive measures enacted by the wartime tsarist authorities. Throughout 1918–1922, formerly confiscated *waqf* lands were returned to Muslim communities.[18] A law issued in December 1922 provided for the creation of a main *waqf* administration, staffed by Muslims, to oversee charitable endowments.[19] From 1920, the Statute on the United People's Court allowed for shari'a courts implementing Islamic law to operate parallel to Soviet courts. As of late 1922, the authorities permitted the establishment of regional Muslim administrations (*mahkama-i shari'a*) based in central Asia's major cities. These bureaus enjoyed a degree of autonomy from the state until 1927.[20]

The first radical change in direction toward religious policy was signaled in 1926, on the very question of Bolshevik cooperation with central Asia's reformist Islamic scholars, the Jadids. Akmal Ikromov, a prominent Uzbek Communist, attacked the Jadids as "bourgeois nationalists."[21] The parting of ways with the Jadids indicated a radical departure from the stability and moderation of the New Economic Policy (NEP) period.[22] A new, harsh approach toward religion stemmed from Stalin's objective of transforming society politically, socially, and economically through mass repression and intimidation, a goal which the Communist Party began implementing in 1927. Stalin's "Great Breakthrough" of 1928–1930 emphasized de-kulakization, rapid industrialization, state mobilization of the population in all walks of life, and the reorganization of the peasantry and remaining nomadic population into collective farms, the output of which the government would monitor and control. In line with their goal of utterly transforming and modernizing society, the Bolsheviks placed special emphasis on the settlement of nomads, an aspiration to which they had committed themselves upon coming to power in 1917.[23] Whereas only a quarter of the Qazaq population in neighboring Kazakhstan lived a consistently sedentary life in 1926, this figure rose to nearly 100 percent by the end of collectivization.[24] The famine of 1932–1933, which wiped out a quarter of the nonsedentary Qazaq population and had an indelible impact on Kyrgyzstan as well, dealt a final blow to the seminomadic lifestyle (a combination of subsistence agriculture and livestock breeding accompanied by seasonal migration) that had prevailed during the NEP era.[25] The consequences for the nomadic Islamic civilization of northern central Asia are easily fathomed.

The period from 1927 to 1930 in many respects saw an all-out attack on religion. Bolshevik officials clearly believed they had acquired a sufficient degree of capacity to effect the eradication of religion from society. Much in the way it had violently cleansed the landscape of rich peasants, the Communist Party proceeded to demolish or seize mosques, target Islamic practices, and exile, imprison, and execute religious figures. In 1927, the authorities launched a campaign against the Islamic veil, during which they pressured Muslim women—especially the wives of party officials—to remove their coverings and burn them in public ceremonies. The chief result of this initiative was the retaliatory murder of hundreds of these women by enraged men in

Muslim communities.[26] Religious courts were rapidly dismantled throughout the first half of the 1930s. In 1936, an article of the new Stalin Constitution reaffirmed the freedom of conscience guaranteed to all Soviet citizens by previous Soviet constitutions, but it arguably did not receive serious attention by the state until after World War II. The Great Terror of 1937–1938 saw even more state violence directed toward religion than the Cultural Revolution and the Great Breakthrough of 1928–1930.[27] Shoshana Keller estimates that during these two intervals, "more than 14,000 Muslim clergy were arrested, killed, exiled from their homes, or driven out of the USSR."[28] Especially during the Great Terror, it appears that local authorities compiled lists of revered religious figures in their regions and simply rounded them up for arrest. For example, a report on religious life in one district in Tajikistan noted that thirty influential clergy members were active in the area until 1937.[29] Ziyovuddinxon ibn Eshon Boboxon (1908–1982), central Asia's future mufti, gave up his job as a teacher at a madrassa in 1937 to work as a gardener.[30] Even this precautionary step, however, did not prevent the secret police from jailing him for eight months that same year.[31] The documentation suggests that Islamic figures living near the Soviet Union's international boundaries were subject to precautionary repression with little or no evidence of any criminal activity on their part. In 1937, for example, a group of mullas in Kyrgyzstan was accused of trying to take advantage "of the wars in China and Spain, which will soon have an impact on the USSR" to bring about "the end of Soviet power."[32] During the Great Terror, the authorities similarly became concerned about the Ismailis, a Muslim sect whose members were concentrated on the Soviet border with Afghanistan. Local officialdom claimed that the Ismailis' spiritual leader in Bombay, the Agha Khan, sought to stir up a broad-based anti-Soviet rebellion in the border region from 1937 to 1939, even though other sources offer no indication of such an occurrence.[33] Religious figures implicated in these alleged anti-Soviet plots faced incarceration in the prison colony system and the possibility of death from disease, exhaustion, torture, or execution.

The late 1930s greatly reduced the visible manifestations of religious life in the Soviet Union. If World War II had not diverted Stalin's attention, and fundamentally reshaped his thinking on religious policy, there is no telling what further steps he might have taken. It is clear, though, that the threat the Nazi invasion posed to the Communist Party and to the Stalinist political system required a fundamental rethinking of the way ideological goals were to be transformed into reality. After 1938, the party-state never again resorted to mass repression as a strategy for combating ideological foes, real or imagined. Although Stalinism in many respects marked a statist consolidation of power and a departure from the revolutionary zeal of the early years of Bolshevik rule, the antireligious policies of 1917–1938 merit characterization as revolutionary. Collectively, they represented an attempt to eradicate religion—to fundamentally rebuild society from the bottom up. It was a goal that a humbled postwar state would abandon, seeking instead to contain and regulate religious life.

## Interpreting the Legacy of World War II, 1942–1964

During the war, the Communist Party relegated the task of liquidating religion to the end of history. Stalin introduced a legal and institutional framework for protecting religion in Soviet society. This framework became so embedded into the political system that a return to antireligious revolutionary initiatives proved impossible for the remainder of Soviet history.

The significance of Stalin's religious reforms of 1943–1944 cannot be overstated. They entailed the establishment of legally recognized religious bodies and, equally significantly, two bureaucracies within the Soviet government charged exclusively with overseeing them. The Russian Orthodox patriarchate in Moscow was reinstated for the first time since its abolishment by Peter the Great more than two centuries earlier. Stalin permitted the creation or reestablishment of four Islamic bodies (known as "muftiates") to oversee mosques, shrines, and other aspects of legally sanctioned Muslim life.[34] These muftiates held responsibility for central Asia, the northern Caucasus, the southern Caucasus, and the pairing of Russia and Siberia.[35] The central Asian muftiate, formally known as the Religious Board of the Muslims of Central Asia and Kazakhstan, was commonly referred to by the Russian acronym SADUM.[36] It was by far the largest and most prominent in the country, perhaps by virtue of its ties with influential Islamic scholars and institutions in the historical cities of Bukhara and Samarqand. It was headed by a mufti belonging to an ancient family of Naqshbandi Sufi sheikhs.[37] Stalin permitted SADUM to operate the single legally permitted Islamic educational establishment for most of Soviet history, the Mir-i Arab madrassa in Bukhara, which has functioned without interruption to the present day.[38] However, all Muslim life occurring beyond the auspices of these muftiates, including prayer and education, was considered illegal by the state.[39] Mosques and Islamic figures (e.g., imams) working for the muftiates were referred to as "registered" in official parlance. The much larger number of "unregistered" mosques, prayer groups, and individual mullas technically violated the law.

Concurrently, Stalin created two bureaucracies exclusively to monitor and supervise these newly legalized entities. They became the strongest advocates in the party-state on behalf of the moderate line toward religion. One of them, the Council for the Affairs of the Russian Orthodox Church (CAROC), dealt solely with the Russian Orthodox Church.[40] The other, the Council for the Affairs of Religious Cults (CARC), held responsibility for all the other legally recognized religions in the country. These included Baptism, Buddhism, Catholicism, Islam, Judaism, and a number of smaller faiths. In 1965, the two bureaucracies were combined into a single Council for Religious Affairs (CRA).[41] Although they were staffed by party members, these bureaucracies rapidly developed into the staunchest proponents of a legally regulated and inviolable space for religion in the Soviet Union. They promoted the view that the antireligious struggle must solely constitute a battleground of ideas.

From 1943 to 1958, it was this view that carried the day within the party-state. Over the outraged objections of party members who called for harassment and restriction (although, generally speaking, not repression) of religious figures and institutions, the Communist Party's senior leadership adopted the moderate line. In the years immediately following the end of World War II, Muslims reopened thousands of mosques that had been closed or seized by local authorities during the 1920s and 1930s. They did so illegally, insofar as the muftiates had official permission to open and run not more than several hundred mosques throughout the entire country.[42] These illegal mosque openings did not encounter systematic opposition.[43] Numerically, illegal Muslim life far exceeded the modest offerings of the legal muftiates. The bureaucrats thus had no way of ascertaining the precise scope of Muslim life occurring beyond the purview of the muftiates. One central Asian bureaucrat reported to Moscow, "As it turns out, there are [illegal] groups practicing Islam in almost every substantial population point."[44]

While the second half of the 1940s saw the moderate line toward religion crystallize, the period from 1950 to 1958 became the heyday of the politics of moderation. During this period, CARC became a proactive entity within the Soviet party-state, calling for increased autonomy for the four muftiates and for a posture of lethargy toward illegal religious life.[45] This line received approval from the party leadership with the publication of a decree on November 10, 1954, that highlighted the sanctity of freedom of conscience as a constitutional right enjoyed by all Soviet citizens.[46] Throughout the decade, CARC went to great lengths to secure reprimands for local government officials who violated the rights of religious groups or otherwise caused offense to the faithful.[47] Under these conditions, illegal Muslim figures and prayer groups felt increasingly secure in facilitating rites and services for the population.[48] At the same time, the four legally sanctioned muftiates enjoyed a degree of leeway and autonomy from the state that became more enhanced with each passing year. The Islamic scholars staffing these bodies successfully convinced CARC not only of their political loyalty and ideological innocuousness, but also of their potential utility.[49] CARC took no action when the central Asian muftiate,

SADUM, proceeded to assert administrative and dogmatic authority over hundreds—and perhaps thousands—of illegal mosques throughout the decade.[50]

The bureaucrats at CARC and in the Communist Party's senior echelons did not adopt this attitude because they were now assigning a positive role to religion. Quite the contrary: they genuinely believed that their actions would hasten its atrophy. Strict observance of freedom of conscience and of the legal rights of believers on the part of officialdom would highlight the moral superiority of Communism over religion. Placed next to this lofty objective, the existence of illegal prayer groups seemed a small price to pray.[51] Aggressive enforcement of the moderate line also allowed CARC to consolidate its organizational authority in relation to local government and other bureaucracies.

Not everyone in the party-state agreed with this approach, however. Throughout the 1950s, hardliners regarded the existence of religion in the Soviet Union in any form as proof that the Bolsheviks had lost their way under the Stalinist cult of personality. A powerful constituency within the Communist Party gathered around Nikita Khrushchev (the party secretary from 1953 to 1964) in an attempt to thwart the moderate line.[52] Khrushchev, the one-time party secretary of the city of Moscow and the republic of Ukraine, held a special animus toward religion.[53] During the mid-1950s, he engaged in a power struggle with a number of protégés of the late dictator.[54] Throughout the decade, Khrushchev and like-minded Communists bristled at what in their view amounted to an extraordinary and inappropriate degree of leverage granted to religious institutions.

Khrushchev successfully sidelined his opponents in 1957 and, two years later, proceeded to inaugurate a series of policy initiatives commonly referred to as "the antireligious campaign." Initially, the Soviet leader principally had the Russian Orthodox Church in mind. CAROC, the bureaucracy responsible for supervising the Russian Orthodox Church, had developed a relationship with the church very similar to the ties between CARC and the four muftiates in the postwar period. Georgii Karpov, CAROC's chairman, fashioned his organization as a partner to the church. In a 1957 speech, he declared:

> Principally, the main goal for which this council was established . . .
> is the facilitation of stable, normalized relations between church
> and state . . . to ensure that the church, as a religious organization
> in the country, and the clergy, as its cadres, do not roll back and
> return to the position of reactionary politics in relation to the state.
> And absolutely, it would not only be unacceptable, but criminal, if
> this occurred as a result of incorrect, ill-conceived, hurried, or other
> mistaken actions on our part.[55]

For Karpov, this represented a rational formulation of the obligations placed on his bureaucracy by the Communist Party. If the bureaucrats were charged with monitoring a legal religious organization, then, by implication, religion must enjoy freedom from harassment.

Khrushchev disagreed with this line of reasoning. While the party engaged in mass propaganda to enlighten the people, it must also not let up administrative restrictions against religious figures. He saw room to introduce violations of the law such as exorbitant taxation, reduction in the number of legal prayer houses based on dubious pretexts (e.g., "sanitation" or "fire safety"), and the occasional arrest. Khrushchev lost no time in forcing Karpov to retire at the outset of the campaign.[56] A blitz of personal attacks ensued on senior religious figures at the union, republican, and provincial levels. From 1958 to 1959, ninety places of worship associated with the Russian Orthodox Church lost their registrations.[57] At the end of 1958, the Communist Party of Ukraine proposed closing thirteen of the republic's forty monasteries.[58]

The antireligious campaign, which began at the end of 1958 and lasted until Khrushchev's forced removal from power in late 1964, was less of an attack on religion than an intensive attempt to contain it. The treatment of Islam closely mirrored that meted out to the Orthodox. The number of registered mosques in Tajikistan, for example, went from thirty-three in 1957 to eighteen in 1963.[59] In late 1958, a Communist Party of the Soviet Union (CPSU) Central Committee decree targeted pilgrimages to shrines and other holy sites across the Soviet Union, singling out central Asia. Whereas CARC's apparatus had compiled a list of 210 such shrines in Tajikistan in early 1958, by January 1, 1960, 170 of these had been closed.[60] In the first half of 1959, the authorities shut down thirty-one shrines in Uzbekistan, sixty-two in Tajikistan, and four in Turkmenistan, not to mention twenty in Azerbaijan, one in Tatarstan, and one holy site affiliated with an unspecified confession (perhaps Islam) in Ukraine.[61] Such closures took place in a variety of ways. Kazakhstan's Communist Party planned to transform the mausoleum of Qoja Akhmat Yassawi into a museum, while the authorities in the city of Osh eventually bulldozed an historical structure at the holy mountain, the Throne of Solomon, and transformed its affiliated mosque first into a university lecture hall, then into living quarters, and finally into an athletic facility. (They later used dynamite to blast a cavity into the mountain for a museum of atheism that is still open to visitors today.)[62] The documentation also suggests that a widespread forced exile of unregistered religious figures (usually to the outskirts of a locality) took place on the basis of declarations condemning shrine pilgrimage that were adopted at community gatherings. This occurred, for example, at the Throne of Solomon, at the Ismamut Ata shrine in northern Turkmenistan, and even to a group of Orthodox prophets at the Kievo-Pecherskaia Lavra in Ukraine.[63]

The authorities also proceeded to demolish or take over holy sites under the control of the Culture Ministry's Architecture Directorate. For example, the number of sites on the directorate's list in Uzbekistan went from 132 in 1957 to 112 in 1965.[64]

Muslim figures not affiliated with the muftiates encountered a broad-based strategy of intimidation. In most cases, this apparently consisted of visits to individual mullas' homes or mosques by local government representatives. The figure in question would receive directly worded threats making it clear that he was to abandon his religious activities and adopt a "socially useful profession" (as the jargon of the era went).[65] Sometimes, though, the restrictive measures against illegal figures went as far as punitive fines and even temporary exile from a given town or district.[66] Arrests occurred only here and there, occasionally as a reflection of the zeal of an individual bureaucrat, but mostly with the objective of setting a resonant and frightening example.[67]

Khrushchev's antireligious campaign bears no comparison to the Cultural Revolution or the Great Terror. The political will to seriously envision stamping out religion did not exist, Khrushchev's visceral pronouncements to this effect notwithstanding. For all its antireligious rhetoric, the hard line on religion most pressingly questioned the depth and extent of Stalin's normalization of religious policy, rather than the normalization itself. Poorly implemented, the campaign had little impact on the everyday lives of most Muslims. The muftiates faced enhanced pressure and restrictions, but their existence was never in question.[68]

So secure was their position, in fact, that they began to play a visible role in the Soviet Union's international propaganda efforts for the first time during the Khrushchev years—that is, at the height of the antireligious campaign. Khrushchev's personal dislike of religion coincided with his passionate commitment to the anticolonial struggle.[69] The CPSU's twentieth party congress in 1956 emphasized the need to support national liberation movements throughout the colonial territories of Asia and Africa.[70] Thus, ironically enough, the muftiates' ties with Islamic figures and organizations abroad skyrocketed for the first time during the years of the antireligious campaign.[71] The existence of Islamic organizations staffed by religious scholars, and in particular a formidable body such as SADUM, proved too formidable a public relations asset for the party-state to ignore.[72] In formulating ways to use SADUM to advance its image and ties abroad, the party-state considered both the muftiate's status as an Islamic organization and the origins of its members in central Asia, a region that had experienced colonialism. While the four muftiates withstood severe and unprecedented restriction of their affairs at home, they enthusiastically heralded the freedoms enjoyed by Muslims in Soviet central Asia before foreign audiences at home and abroad.[73]

Even Khrushchev's antireligious campaign confirmed the interpretation of the wartime religious reforms as a total shift in the party's approach. Although the hard line against religion remained a presence in the party-state throughout the decades after World War II, Stalin's institutionalization of Islam stood beyond question. The heyday of the moderate line, from 1943 to 1958, came to an abrupt end in 1959. Even in power, though, the hardliners could only launch a haphazard curtailment of religion at home, while assigning greater importance to the muftiates' contributions abroad. This speaks to the overwhelming importance of the wartime religious reforms and their subsequent interpretation in setting the tone of religious policy until 1991 and beyond.

## The Hard and Moderate Lines Coalesce, 1965–1991

In the second half of the 1960s, the party-state determined that its religious policy would reject the perceived excesses of both the moderate and hard lines. It would combine elements of both to yield a regulatory policy that embraced administrative pressure mechanisms while upholding the principles of stability, consistency, and the rule of law. This balance between two extremes— the moderate line that reigned supreme from 1943 to 1958, and the hard line of 1959–1964—yielded a more marked distinction in policy implementation with respect to registered and unregistered religious figures.

Under the leadership of Leonid Brezhnev (party secretary from 1964 to 1982), the party-state sought to rescind most of the restrictive measures applied to the four muftiates during the antireligious campaign. Government officials treated the muftis with great esteem.[74] In the aftermath of the antireligious campaign, officialdom permitted them to reassert control over the finances and staffing of mosques.[75] However, the muftiates never again achieved the autonomy from Soviet bureaucracy they had enjoyed during the 1950s. Official meddling in their internal finances by the CRA—once considered taboo— remained commonplace throughout the 1970s and 1980s.[76] The three muftiates outside central Asia—those responsible for Russia, the northern Caucasus, and the southern Caucasus—faced additional disadvantages. They had little choice but to send their imams to the two SADUM-run madrassas in Uzbekistan for an Islamic education recognized by the state. Given their relatively low international profile, they also lacked political breathing room to issue their own publications, such as copies of the Quran.[77]

Throughout the Brezhnev, Andropov, and Gorbachev years, the muftiates promoted the Muslim faith as a force for the greater good in Soviet society. They called on agricultural laborers to eschew fasting during the month of Ramadan, a requirement of the Muslim faith (on the twin grounds that it would cause undue hardship to the Muslims and that it would decrease agricultural productivity, causing detriment to the state and society as a whole).[78] They conducted domestic propaganda to align themselves with the party-state; for example, SADUM lambasted the dissident Andrei Sakharov as "humanity-reviling" and organized celebrations of the millennium of Russian Orthodox Christianity.[79] The central Asian muftiate also stepped up its rhetorical campaign against unregistered religious figures—that is, the imams, mullas, and others whom it did not employ.

The muftiates' engagement of Islamic organizations overseas, which had already acquired impressive dimensions during the campaign years, expanded under Brezhnev. This principally took the form of mutual visits, which went smoothly because many of the muftiates' senior staff spoke Arabic fluently. More often than not, Muslim delegations visiting the Soviet Union were directed to Uzbekistan, to showcase the successful modernization of a historically Islamic territory. The central Asian muftiate therefore played an important role in serving as guide and interlocutor to high-profile visitors from nations as diverse as Burkina Faso, Indonesia, and Turkey. By the mid-1970s, SADUM played a strikingly formal role in the conduct of pro-Soviet diplomacy abroad. Notwithstanding its status as a religious organization, it began hosting members of foreign Communist parties at the request of the Communist Party of Uzbekistan.[80] Its members met with numerous heads of state both at home and abroad; SADUM's deputy chair, Abdulgani Abdullaev, even gave a press conference in the main hall of the US Capitol.[81] Most substantively, the party-state used SADUM as a channel for exploring the reestablishment of diplomatic relations with Saudi Arabia.[82]

The Soviet invasion of Afghanistan in 1979 greatly complicated this approach, pitting the party-state against a resilient, internationally funded opponent that legitimized its resistance almost exclusively through the vocabulary of Islamic justice.[83] Afghanistan presented Soviet propaganda organs abroad with a public relations crisis. It did not take long for sentiment to turn overwhelmingly against the invasion, both in the Muslim world and elsewhere.[84] The party-state clearly appreciated that the invasion of Afghanistan had complicated the avowedly pro-Muslim image it had sought to cultivate internationally throughout the 1960s and 1970s. At the twenty-sixth CPSU congress in 1981, Brezhnev addressed this problem directly, noting that "we Communists respect the religious beliefs of those practicing Islam, or any other religion. The important thing is to question the motives of those powers propounding this or that slogan."[85] As under Khrushchev, the four muftiates offered Soviet propagandists a means of partly addressing the misgivings of Muslims overseas. The party-state required them to assist in the conduct of Soviet public diplomacy on behalf of the invasion, as well as the fledgling, pro-Soviet Democratic Republic of Afghanistan (DRA). They were meant to promote the DRA's legitimacy and its policies abroad, and to lend support to pro-DRA Islamic figures inside Afghanistan. A delegation representing all four muftiates first arrived in Kabul in April 1981.[86] SADUM took the lead in establishing a presence in Afghanistan, first because of central Asia's historical and cultural ties with the country, and second because its senior staff all spoke Persian fluently.[87]

SADUM's prominent role in Afghanistan speaks to the increasing stability and even esteem it enjoyed at home. The concept of a legal, viable religious organization, staffed by religious figures meriting political confidence, constituted the central pillar of policy toward Islam under Brezhnev. Although the party-state would apply restrictions to the muftiates (e.g., limiting the number of legal mosques), it would continue to rely on them as the basic unit of regulating Islam in the Soviet Union. A return to the tactics of constriction and even humiliation favored by Khrushchev was out of the question.

By contrast, policy makers of the 1970s and 1980s regarded unregistered religious figures (that is, those not employed by the muftiates) as alien to the panorama of normalized church-state relations. In this respect, they did not differ from Khrushchevian officialdom. Unlike Khrushchev, however, they did not advocate a sustained and harsh attack on religious figures. Instead, they sought to limit and contain the scope of unregistered activity through a variety of low-key pressure mechanisms. Thus the 1970s witnessed the emergence of "prophylaxis" (*profilakticheskie mery*) as a favored policy measure in central Asia. This consisted of written and verbal warnings to individuals, threatening them with punishment should they continue facilitating religious rites. Other measures included punitive fines of a moderate character. Arrests picked up somewhat with Andropov's rise to power—particularly with respect to the illegal sale of religious literature—but remained modest in scope. Prison sentences rarely exceeded one year and were often commuted to fines.[88]

As in other areas, Brezhnev-era religious policy was fashioned as a rejection of Khrushchev's model of revolutionary rejuvenation. Officialdom sought to contain unregistered religious life and remain true to the party's antireligious struggle—without, however, causing dramatic disruption in people's lives. Policy measures with respect to the unregistered were neither volatile nor potent. Since the fundamental impulse of Brezhnev's religious policy was regulatory rather than revolutionary, many unregistered figures apparently experienced little more than a warning from local officials. This explains why illegal study circles proliferated in the 1970s and 1980s, while widely known unregistered jurisconsults (renowned Islamic scholars) accepted students with little or no obstruction.

Especially in central Asia, a large network of such scholars not affiliated with the muftiates taught study circles in their homes. Such study circles existed throughout the Soviet period, but very likely occurred in a climate of secrecy during tense periods such as Khrushchev's antireligious campaign, and had perhaps ceased functioning entirely during the Great Terror of 1937–1938. Although the names of only some of the most prominent of these scholars have come down to us, the oral history of the Soviet period testifies to their influence. During the 1970s and 1980s, the most renowned jurisconsult was without doubt a man named Muhammadjon ibn Rustam al-Hindustoniy (1892–1989).[89] While enjoying a scholarly affiliation with the Oriental Studies Institute of Tajikistan's Academy of Sciences, he cultivated a group of young Islamic scholars who now enjoy prominence as revered authorities in their own right in modern-day central Asia. Many of the young men who ended up in these illegal study networks had completed the program at the Mir-i Arab madrassa; they viewed additional study at the foot of a master as the equivalent of graduate school. Furthermore, many (perhaps most) of them went on to accept employment in mosques run by SADUM. Thus, the Brezhnev years saw significant interaction between legal and illegal Muslim life, even as the distinction between the two remained quite rigid on paper.[90]

The final years of Soviet history under Gorbachev brought significant changes to Muslim life. Increasingly, the muftiates found their legitimacy challenged by a small number of Islamic scholars, as well as by Muslim youth groups. In line with Salafi (i.e., puritan) thought elsewhere, they called for rethinking the foundations of the traditional Hanafi jurisprudence rooted in much of the Soviet Union, especially central Asia.[91] Individual Salafi figures such as Rahmatullo 'alloma and Abduvali Mirzoyev acquired strong followings in the Farg'ona Valley during the second half of the 1980s. Not all or even most of the criticism directed at the muftiates during the perestroika years stemmed from Salafis or from Islamic puritans. For example, SADUM's third mufti was forced to resign in 1989 after widespread public outcry over his personal lifestyle.[92] Religious life became opened to such an extent, that even the heyday of moderation in the 1950s paled in comparison. Muslims set up alternate religious organizations lacking legal sanction with no retaliation from the authorities.[93] Mosques and churches opened in the thousands in the face of official inertia.[94] In 1990, Kazakhstan became the first central Asian republic to cease recognizing SADUM's authority, setting up its own national muftiate even before the breakup of the Soviet Union.[95] For its part, the Communist Party under Gorbachev attempted to facilitate communication between atheism and religion as two legitimate worldviews coexisting on the basis of mutual understanding.[96] Atheists faced little in the form of retaliation from believers and aspiring politicians throughout the late Soviet and early post-socialist eras, but also found that their philosophical views no longer enjoyed currency or esteem.

## Conclusion

The Communist Party could not sustain an organized antireligious drive for the majority of its history. With the right degree of acumen, most Soviet citizens could continue practicing their faith without fearing retaliation. World War II stands out as the single most important turning point in the party's policy, a sea change that signaled the unspoken but resounding abandonment of the tactics of the 1920s and 1930s. From 1943 on, the bulk of officialdom—including even those party members who most loathed religion—recognized the imperative of constructing a stable society built in part on predictable church-state relations. This meant that the struggle with religion would be relegated to a body of antireligious propaganda that featured almost no innovation in form or content.

Although the majority of Soviet Muslims did not become atheists, the short Soviet century had a profound impact on every sphere of religious life. The muftiates became ingrained as a permanent and central feature of the landscape of church-state relations, with readily apparent implications for religious policy across the post-Soviet space today. Ironically enough, the central legacy of Soviet policy toward Islam has been the promotion of centralized, stable, and viable religious organizations operating under official scrutiny but in many respects boasting independence from state meddling. It is improbable that this mechanism will undergo a fundamental revision any time soon.

## Notes

1. I would like to thank Philip Muehlenbeck and three anonymous reviewers for their comments on an earlier draft of this chapter.
2. Historians of Soviet Russia have emphasized the importance of international relations—particularly the Soviet Union's image in Allied countries during World War II—as well as concerns over Russian nationalism as primary considerations behind Stalin's decision to open up religious life. See Tatiana A. Chumachenko, *Church and State in Soviet Russia: Russian Orthodoxy from World War II to the Khrushchev Years*, trans. Edward Roslof (Armonk, NY: M. E. Sharpe, 2002), 190; Nathaniel Davis, *A Long Walk to Church: A Contemporary History of Russian Orthodoxy* (Boulder, CO: Westview Press, 1995), 16–25; Steven M. Miner, *Stalin's Holy War: Religion, Nationalism, and Alliance Politics, 1941–1945* (Chapel Hill: University of North Carolina Press, 2003); and M. V. Shkarovskii, *Russkaia*

*pravoslavnaia tserkov' pri Staline i Khrushcheve: Gosudarstvenno-tserkovnye otnosheniia v SSSR v 1939–1964 gg* [The Russian Orthodox Church under Stalin and Khrushchev: Church-state relations in the USSR, 1939–1964] (Moscow: Krutitskoe Patriarshee Podvor'e, Obshchestvo liubitelei tserkovnoi istorii, 1999). Except where otherwise indicated, all translations of non-English-language quotations in this chapter are mine.

3. The Bolshevik Party witnessed early debate between those favoring repression as a means of liquidating religion and those advocating greater reliance on "persuasion" (*ubezhdenie, raz'iasnitel'naia rabota*) through propaganda. This latter argument for a "conciliatory religious policy" was associated with Nikolai Bukharin and the New Economic Policy (NEP) era. Arto Luukkanen, *The Party of Unbelief: The Religious Policy of the Bolshevik Party, 1917–1929* (Helsinki: SHS, 1994), 235.

4. The Central Standing Commission on Religious Questions constituted the earliest institutional voice within the party-state promoting the politics of persuasion over repression. Unlike the postwar religious affairs bureaucracies, however, it had no power outside Moscow. Arto Luukkanen, *The Religious Policy of the Stalinist State: A Case Study; The Central Standing Commission on Religious Questions, 1929–1938* (Helsinki: SHS, 1997), 102.

5. Technically speaking, of course, Soviet citizens always enjoyed freedom of conscience, starting with the issuance of Lenin's January 1918 decree on the separation of church and state. This remained the case during the Cultural Revolution of 1928–1931 and the Great Terror of 1937–1938. Report 1949, Central State Archive of the Republic of Kyrgyzstan (hereafter KR BMA), Bishkek, 2597/1s/12/20.

6. Daniel Peris, *Storming the Heavens: The Soviet League of the Militant Godless* (Ithaca, NY: Cornell University Press, 1998).

7. Hélène Carrère d'Encausse, "Islam in the Soviet Union: Attempts at Modernization," *Religion in Communist Lands* 2, nos. 4–5 (1974): 12–19; Chantal Lemercier-Quelquejay, "Sufi Brotherhoods in the USSR: A Historical Survey," *Central Asian Survey* 2, nos. 4–5 (1983): 1–35; Alexandre Bennigsen and Marie Broxup, *The Islamic Threat to the Soviet State* (New York: St. Martin's Press, 1983); Alexandre Bennigsen and S. Enders Wimbush, *Mystics and Commissars: Sufism in the Soviet Union* (Berkeley: University of California Press, 1985); Alexandre Bennigsen and S. Enders Wimbush, *Muslims of the Soviet Empire: A Guide* (London: Hurst, 1985); and Marie Broxup, "Political Trends in Soviet Islam after the Afghanistan War," in *Muslim Communities Reemerge: Historical Perspectives on Nationality, Politics, and Opposition in the Former Soviet Union and Yugoslavia*, ed. Edward Allworth, 304–21 (Durham, NC: Duke University Press, 1994).

8. Mark Saroyan, "Reconstructing Community: Authority and the Politics of Islam in the Soviet Union" (PhD diss., University of California, Berkeley, 1990); and Yaacov Ro'i, *Islam in the Soviet Union: From Gorbachev to the Second World War* (New York: Columbia University Press, 2000).

9. Otto Luchterhandt, "The Council for Religious Affairs," in *Religious Policy in the Soviet Union*, ed. Sabrina P. Ramet, 55–83 (Cambridge: Cambridge University Press, 1993); Dimitry Pospielovsky, *The Russian Church under the Soviet Regime,*

*1917–1982, vol. 2* (Crestwood, NY: St. Vladimir's Seminary Press, 1984); and Gerhard Simon, *Church, State and Opposition in the U.S.S.R.*, trans. Kathleen Matchett (London: Hurst, 1974).

10. Lynn Edgar, *Tribal Nation: The Making of Soviet Turkmenistan* (Princeton, NJ: Princeton University Press, 2004), 197–220; Hamdam Sodiqov, ed., *O'zbekiston Sovet mustamlakachiligi davrida* [Uzbekistan under Soviet subjugation] (Tashkent: Sharq, 2000), 346–59; and Rustambek Shamsutdinov, *Qishloq fojiyosi: Jamoalashtirish, quloqlashtirish, surgun* [The tragedy of the village: Collectivization, de-kulakization, exile] (Tashkent: Sharq, 2003).

11. Charles Halperin, *Russia and the Golden Horde: The Mongol Impact on Medieval Russian History* (Bloomington: Indiana University Press, 1985); and Andreas Kappeler, *The Russian Empire: A Multiethnic History*, trans. Alfred Clayton (New York: Longman, 2001), 21–55.

12. Robert D. Crews, *For Prophet and Tsar: Islam and Empire in Russia and Central Asia* (Cambridge, MA: Harvard University Press, 2006); A. P. Iarkov, ed., *Islam na kraiu sveta: Istoriia Islama v zapadnoi Sibiri* [Islam at the edge of the world: The history of Islam in western Siberia], vol. 1 (Tiumen', Russia: Koleso, 2007); and I. K. Zagidullin, *Islamskie instituty v Rossiiskoi imperii: Mecheti v evropeiskoi chasti Rossii i Sibiri* [Islamic institutions in the Russian Empire: Mosques in the European part of Russia and Siberia] (Kazan', Russia: Tatarskoe knizhnoe izdatel'stvo, 2007).

13. Richard N. Frye, *Bukhara: The Medieval Achievement* (Costa Mesa, CA: Mazda, 1996).

14. Virginia Martin, *Law and Custom in the Steppe: The Kazakhs of the Middle Horde and Russian Colonialism in the Nineteenth Century* (London: Curzon, 2001).

15. Charles King, *The Ghost of Freedom: A History of the Caucasus* (Oxford: Oxford University Press, 2008); and Michael Kemper, *Herrschaft, Recht und Islam in Daghestan: Von den Khanaten und Gemeindebünden zum gihad-Staat* [Rule, law, and Islam in Dagestan: From the khanates and local societies to jihad-states] (Wiesbaden: Reichert, 2005).

16. Hüseynqulu Mämmädil, *Qafqazda Islam va şeyxülislamlar* [Islam and the shaykh ul-islam in the Caucasus] (Baki, Azerbaijan: MBM, 2005).

17. This stemmed entirely from the Leninist approach toward minorities during the early years of Bolshevik rule. In stark contrast, Orthodox churches in Russia suffered harassment, theft, and destruction during the Civil War and in its immediate aftermath. Robert H. Greene, *Bodies Like Bright Stars: Saints and Relics in Orthodox Russia* (DeKalb: Northern Illinois University Press, 2009), 103–95. Also Dimitry Pospielovsky, *Soviet Antireligious Campaigns and Persecutions* (New York: St. Martin's Press, 1988).

18. Shoshana Keller, *To Moscow, Not Mecca: The Soviet Campaign against Islam in Central Asia, 1917–1941* (Westport, CT: Praeger, 2001), 41.

19. Niccolò Pianciola and Paolo Sartori, "*Waqf* in Turkestan: The Colonial Legacy and the Fate of an Islamic Institution in Early Soviet Central Asia, 1917–1924," *Central Asian Survey* 26, no. 4 (December 2007): 475–98.

20. Keller, *To Moscow*, 119, and Paolo Sartori, "An Overview of Tsarist Policy on Islamic Courts in Turkestan: Its Genealogy and Its Effects," *Cahiers d'Asie Centrale* 17–18 (2009): 481.

21. Quoted in Adeeb Khalid, *Islam after Communism: Religion and Politics in Central Asia* (Berkeley: University of California Press, 2007), 75.

22. The period of the NEP lasted from 1921 to 1928 and saw an easing of restrictions on the peasantry's economic activity, among other policy changes. Its objective was to form an alliance between the Bolshevik state and the middle peasantry, and to create a grain surplus. Alec Nove, *An Economic History of the USSR* (New York: Penguin, 1969); and Roger Pethybridge, *One Step Backwards, Two Steps Forwards: Soviet Society and Politics in the New Economic Policy* (Oxford: Oxford University Press, 1990).

23. Pethybridge, *One Step Backwards*, 396.

24. Ibid., 390.

25. Martha Brill Olcott, *The Kazakhs* (Stanford, CA: Hoover, 1995), 174.

26. Douglas Northrop, *Veiled Empire: Gender and Power in Stalinist Central Asia* (Ithaca, NY: Cornell University Press, 2004).

27. Rustambek Shamsutdinov, ed., *Repressiia, 1937–1938 gody: Dokumenty i materialy* [Repression, 1937–1938: Documents and materials] (Tashkent: Sharq, 2005); and Rustambek Shamsutdinov, *Qatag'on qurbonlari: 1937 yil 10 avgust–5 noyabr* [Victims of oppression: August 10–November 5, 1937] (Tashkent: Sharq, 2007).

28. Keller, *One Step Backwards*, 241.

29. Report, April 5, 1955, Central Archive of the Republic of Tajikistan (hereafter BM JT), Dunshabe, 1516/1/44/27.

30. Report, June 12, 1954, Central State Archive of the Republic of Uzbekistan (hereafter O'zR MDA), Tashkent, r-2456/1/166/7.

31. Ashirbek Muminov, "Shami-damulla i ego rol' v formirovanii 'Sovetskogo Islama'" [Shami damulla and his role in the formation of a "Soviet Islam"], in *Islam, identichnost' i politika v postsovetskom prostranstve: Materialy mezhdunarodnoi konferentsii "Islam, identichnost' i politika v postsovetskom prostranstve"— sravnitel'nyi analiz tsentral'noi Azii i Evropeiskoi chasti Rossii' 1–2 aprelia 2004 g.* [Islam, identity and politics in the post-Soviet space: Materials of the international conference "Islam, identity, and politics in the post-Soviet space"—a comparative analysis of central Asia and the European part of Russia, April 1–2, 2004], ed. R. S. Khakimov and R. M. Mukhametshin (Kazan', Russia: Master Lain, 2005), 231–47.

32. Report, November 12, 1937, KR BMA 2678/1/4/22.

33. Report, March 24, 1959, BM JT 1516/1/77/137.

34. Crews, *For Prophet and Tsar*; Alan W. Fisher, "Enlightened Despotism and Islam under Catherine II," *Slavic Review* 27, no. 4 (December 1968): 542–53; and Kelly O'Neill, "Between Subversion and Submission: The Integration of the Crimean Khanate into the Russian Empire, 1783–1853" (PhD diss., Harvard University, 2006), 63–77.

35. Eren Murat Tasar, "Soviet and Muslim: The Institutionalization of Islam in Central Asia, 1943–1991" (PhD diss., Harvard University, 2010).

36. Its formal name was O'rta Osiyo va Qozog'iston Musulmonlari Diniya Nazariyati in Uzbek and Dukhovnoe Upravlenie Musul'man Srednei Azii i Kazakhstana in Russian.

37. The Naqshbandiyya is a Sufi order and intellectual tradition originating from the

teachings of Bahovuddin Naqshband (1318–1389). Much of SADUM's leadership claimed affiliation with the Naqshbandiyya.

38. Ro'i, *Islam in the Soviet Union*, 163.
39. Tasar, "Soviet and Muslim," 88–103.
40. Its role and function within the party-state did not differ from those of CARC.
41. This occurred on December 8, 1965. Luchterhandt, "Council for Religious Affairs," 59.
42. In 1981, SADUM had control of 180 registered (i.e., legal) mosques. Report, December 1–2, 1981, O'zR MDA r-2456/1/637/8. The total number of illegal mosques in the Soviet Union at any given point is not known, but it surely ran into the thousands. The corresponding figure for illegal Muslim prayer groups—meeting in private homes, cemeteries, and elsewhere—was surely even higher.
43. Tasar, "Soviet and Muslim," 91, 109–21.
44. Report, September 27, 1961, KR BMA 2597/2s/51/8.
45. Tasar, "Soviet and Muslim," 78–103.
46. Postanovlenie TsK KPSS ot 10 noiabria 1965 g [CPSU Central Committee resolution of November 10, 1965]. "Ob oshibkakh v provedenii nauchno-ateisticheskoi propagandy sredi naseleniia" [Errors in spreading scientific and atheistic propaganda to the people], in A. M. Zalesskii and T. G. Kupcheniia, eds., *O religii i tserkvi: Sbornik vyskazyvanii klassikov marksizma-leninizma, dokumentov KPSS i Sovetskogo Pravitel'stva* [On religion and the church: A collection of quotations from the classics of Marxism-Lenism and documents of the Communist Party of the Soviet Union and the Soviet government] (Minsk: Belarus, 1983): 62–63.
47. Tasar, "Soviet and Muslim," 88–97.
48. Ibid., 109–21.
49. Ibid., 122–38.
50. Ibid., 236–46.
51. Aleksei Puzin, CARC's chairman from 1955 to 1965, explained this reasoning best: "Closing a church, mosque, or synagogue, or removing the registration of a sectarian religious society, unfortunately does not at all indicate that from that moment the believer will become an atheist. Actually, the opposite is usually the case." Report, May 5, 1961, BM JT 1516/1/94/51.
52. Shkarovskii, *Russkaia pravoslavnaia tserkov'*, 360.
53. While running party affairs in Moscow and Ukraine in the 1930s, he had "devoted no small effort towards the destruction of shrines" associated with the Russian Orthodox Church. Ibid., 349.
54. The issuance of the aforementioned November 10, 1954, decree represented a defeat for Khrushchev at mid-decade.
55. Shkarovskii, *Russkaia pravoslavnaia tserkov'*, 358.
56. Ibid., 372.
57. Davis, *Long Walk to Church*, 36. Shkarovskii gives the figure of ninety-one religious societies (*Russkaia pravoslavnaia tserkov'*, 366).
58. Shkarovskii, *Russkaia pravoslavnaia tserkov'*, 364.
59. Report, December 1957, BM JT 1516/1/59/1; Report, April 6, 1963, BM JT 1516/2/25/23; Report, February 22, 1964, BM JT 1516/2/36/3.

60. Report, January 22, 1960, BM JT 1516/1/84/43.

61. Report, May 30, 1959, Russian State Archive of Contemporary History (hereafter RGANI), Moscow, 5/33/125/17.

62. Report, June 29, 1959, RGANI 5/33/125/114; Report, April 10, 1959, KR BMA 2597/1s/83/181; Report, 1962, KR BMA 2597/1s/93/11; and Report, April 25, 1963, KR BMA 2597/2s/57/19-20.

63. Report, April 10, 1959, KR BMA 2597/1s/83/181; Report, June 13, 1959, RGANI 5/33/125/98; and Report, June 3, 1959, RGANI 5/33/125/98 l. 38.

64. Report, March 10, 1965, O'zR MDA r-2456/1/443/23.

65. Brian LaPierre, "Redefining Deviance: Policing and Punishing Hooliganism in Khrushchev's Russia, 1953–1964" (PhD diss., University of Chicago, 2006); and Sheila Fitzpatrick, "Social Parasites: How Tramps, Idle Youth, and Busy Entrepreneurs Impeded the Soviet March to Communism," *Cahiers du Monde Russe* 47, nos. 1–2 (2006): 377–408.

66. Tasar, "Soviet and Muslim," 282.

67. Ibid., 287–89.

68. Ibid., 249–337. See also John Anderson, *Religion, State and Politics in the Soviet Union and Successor States* (Cambridge: Cambridge University Press, 1994), 6–67; and Ro'i, *Islam in the Soviet Union*, 205–13.

69. N. S. Khrushchev, *Imperialism—Enemy of the People, Enemy of Peace: Selected Passages, 1956–1963* (Moscow: Foreign Languages Publishing House, 1963).

70. Tareq Y. Ismael, *The Communist Movement in the Arab World* (London, 2005), 69.

71. SADUM had ties with organizations in more than fifty countries by 1970. Report, early 1971, O'zR MDA r-2456/1/515/23.

72. Although all four muftiates participated in the international exchange and propaganda, SADUM by far played the dominant role. Tasar, "Soviet and Muslim," 340n765.

73. Report, June 6, 1958, BM JT 1516/1/67/24 (June 6, 1958).

74. Take, for example, the strikingly deferential birthday wishes of a senior Soviet bureaucrat to SADUM's mufti in 1978. Report, January 18, 1978, State Archive of the Russian Federation (hereafter GA RF), Moscow, r-6991/6/1347/44-7.

75. Tasar, "Soviet and Muslim," 501–15.

76. Ibid., 498–501.

77. For example: although illegal mosques thrived in the northern Caucasus, the region's muftiate (based in Dagestan) undertook no publication activity. After a 1981 visit to the Chechen-Ingush Autonomous Soviet Socialist Republic (ASSR), a senior SADUM figure reported that "many of the region's Muslims are followers of various Sufi sects. No one has explained to them the true teachings of the Quran and Sunnah. New mosques have been built in the region. The majority of mosques are in good condition and taken care of, staffed by individuals with an ancient worldview. Qurans and other religious literature are not available in sufficient quantity in the mosques. A letter arrived from the representative [of the CRA] of the Chechen-Ingush ASSR, asking us to reserve religious literature for the republic, two or three copies of [SADUM's] sermons, and [SADUM's] journal *Muslims of the Soviet East*." Report, June 10, 1982, O'zR MDA r-2456/1/654/54-55.

78. Report, January 24, 1974, O'zR MDA r-2456/1/551/4-6.

79. Report, February 18, 1983, KR BMA 2597/2s/120/164; Report, May 12, 1988, KR BMA 2597/2s/131/57-8.

80. Report, Fall 1980, O'zR MDA r-2456/1/624/156-7.

81. Tasar, "Soviet and Muslim," 399.

82. Ibid., 400–406.

83. However, as Artemy Kalinovsky argues, the decision to invade Afghanistan in December 1979 stemmed entirely from geo-strategic considerations and political alignments in the Politburo. Fears about cross-border influences upon Central Asian Muslims did not figure as a significant consideration. See his "Decision-Making and the Soviet War in Afghanistan: From Intervention to Withdrawal," *Journal of Cold War Studies* 11, no. 4 (Fall 2009): 49–51. Indeed, concerns about the "Islamic factor" (*Islamskii faktor*), and its relevance for Central Asia in the aftermath of the Iranian Revolution of 1978 and the 1979 invasion, were not voiced within the CRA until 1981. This concern manifested itself in rhetorical statements about the reactionary tendencies of unregistered religious figures not working for the muftiates. After 1984 references to the "Islamic factor" do not appear in the CRA's Central Asian documentation. What small changes took place in the implementation of religious policy during these years had more to do with Andropov's tenure as party secretary (1982–1984) than the war in Afghanistan. That is to say, the Afghan war did not radically alter policy toward Islam at home. Tasar, "Soviet and Muslim," 465–67.

84. In early 1980, SADUM began receiving hate mail from Muslims abroad, while some of its former partners cut off ties with the organization. Report, July 1985, O'zR MDA r-2456/1/703/77.

85. Zalesskii and Kupchenia, *O religii i tserkvi*, 76.

86. Kh. Masud, A. Sakharov, M. Bar'ialai, and G. Poliakov, *Afganistan segodnia* [Afghanistan today] (Moscow: Planeta, 1983), 158.

87. Tasar, "Soviet and Muslim," 407–17.

88. Ibid., 447–69.

89. Rustambek Shamsutdinov and Shodi Karimov, *O'zbekiston tarixidan materiyallar* [Materials from Uzbekistan's history] (Andijon, Uzbekistan: Matbaa, 2004), 609.

90. B. M. Babadzhanov, A. K. Muminov, and A. fon Kiugel'gen, *Disputy musul'manskikh religioznykh avtoritetov v tsentral'noi Azii v XX veke* [Disputes of Muslim religious authorities in central Asia in the twentieth century] (Almaty, Kazakhstan: Daik, 2007), 7–31; Allen J. Frank and Jahangir Mamatov, *Uzbek Islamic Debates: Texts, Translations, and Commentary* (Springfield, VA: Dunwoody Press, 2006), 1–7; Monica Whitlock, *Land Beyond the River: The Untold Story of Central Asia* (New York: Thomas Dunne, 2003).

91. Jamal J. Elias, ed., *Key Themes for the Study of Islam* (Oxford: Oxford University Press, 2010); Roxanne L. Euben and Muhammad Qasim Zaman, eds., *Princeton Readings in Islamist Thought: Texts and Contexts from al-Banna to Bin Laden* (Princeton, NJ: Princeton University Press, 2009); Charles Kurzman, ed., *Modernist Islam, 1840–1940: A Sourcebook* (New York: Oxford University Press, 2002).

92. James Critchlow, *Nationalism in Uzbekistan: A Soviet Republic's Road to Sovereignty*

(Boulder, CO: Westview Press, 1991), 177. The details of this episode remain shrouded in mystery. Although demonstrations took place in Tashkent in 1989 calling for the mufti's removal, it is also likely that Uzbekistan's government engineered the ouster.

93. For example, SADUM's estranged *qadi* (representative) in Kyrgyzstan established an "Islamic Center of Kyrgyzstan" in the spring of 1991 without seeking permission from the muftiate or the Kyrgyz government. Report, May 23, 1991, KR BMA 2597/2s/133/158.

94. In the Soviet Union as a whole, 237 religious societies became registered during the first half of 1988, compared to 104 in all of 1987 and 67 in 1986; see Report, July 26, 1988, KR BMA 2597/2s/130/60. In the second half of 1988, 1373 religious societies received registration; see Report, April 24, 1989, KR BMA 2597/2s/133/3.

95. Report, January 29, 1990, KR BMA 2597/2s/133/63.

96. Report, January 30, 1990, KR BMA 2597/2s/132/90.

## References

ARCHIVES
Central Archive of the Republic of Tajikistan, Dushanbe
Central State Archive of the Republic of Kyrgyzstan, Bishkek
Central State Archive of the Republic of Uzbekistan, Tashkent
Russian State Archive of Contemporary History, Moscow
State Archive of the Russian Federation, Moscow

SELECTED PUBLISHED WORKS
Babadzhanov, B. M., A. K. Muminov, and A. fon Kiugel'gen. *Disputy musul'manskikh religioznykh avtoritetov v tsentral'noi Azii v XX veke* [Disputes of Muslim religious authorities in central Asia in the twentieth century]. Almaty, Kazakhstan: Daik, 2007.

Bennigsen, Alexandre, and Marie Broxup. *The Islamic Threat to the Soviet State*. New York: St. Martin's Press, 1983.

Chumachenko, Tatiana A. *Church and State in Soviet Russia: Russian Orthodoxy from World War II to the Khrushchev Years*. Trans. Edward Roslof. Armonk, NY: M. E. Sharpe, 2002.

Crews, Robert D. *For Prophet and Tsar: Islam and Empire in Russia and Central Asia*. Cambridge, MA: Harvard University Press, 2006.

Davis, Nathaniel. *A Long Walk to Church: A Contemporary History of Russian Orthodoxy*. Boulder, CO: Westview Press, 1995.

Keller, Shoshana. *To Moscow, Not Mecca: The Soviet Campaign against Islam in Central Asia, 1917–1941*. Westport, CT: Praeger, 2001.

Pethybridge, Roger. *One Step Backwards, Two Steps Forwards: Soviet Society and Politics in the New Economic Policy*. Oxford: Oxford University Press, 1990.

Pospielovsky, Dimitry. *The Russian Church under the Soviet Regime, 1917–1982*. Vol. 2. Crestwood, NY: St. Vladimir's Seminary Press, 1984.

―――. *Soviet Antireligious Campaigns and Persecutions*. New York: St. Martin's Press, 1988.

Ramet, Sabrina P., ed. *Religious Policy in the Soviet Union*. Cambridge: Cambridge University Press, 1993.

Ro'i, Yaacov. *Islam in the Soviet Union: From Gorbachev to the Second World War*. New York: Columbia University Press, 2000.

Shkarovskii, M. V. *Russkaia pravoslavnaia tserkov' pri Staline i Khrushcheve: Gosudarstvenno-tserkovnye otnosheniia v SSSR v 1939–1964 gg* [The Russian Orthodox Church under Stalin and Khrushchev: Church-state relations in the USSR, 1939–1964]. Moscow: Krutitskoe Patriarshee Podvor'e, Obshchestvo liubitelei tserkovnoi istorii, 1999.

Simon, Gerhard. *Church, State, and Opposition in the U.S.S.R*. Trans. Kathleen Matchett. London: Hurst, 1974.

Tasar, Eren Murat. "Soviet and Muslim: The Institutionalization of Islam in Central Asia, 1943–1991." PhD diss., Harvard University, 2010.

Zalesskii, A. M., and T. G. Kupcheniia, eds. *O religii i tserkvi: Sbornik vyskazyvanii klassikov marksizma-leninizma, dokumentov KPSS i Sovetskogo Pravitel'stva* [On religion and the church: A collection of quotations from the classics of Marxism-Leninism and documents of the Communist Party of the Soviet Union and the Soviet government]. Minsk, Belarus: Belarus, 1983.

# CHAPTER 9

# Bosnian Muslims during the Cold War

## *Their Identity between Domestic and Foreign Policies*

*Aydın Babuna*

Although the Bosnian War of 1992–1995 posed a real threat to the physical existence of the Bosnian Muslims, it produced some important results in terms of their national development.[1] The Bosnian Muslims entered the war as Muslims but emerged from it as *Bosnjaci* (Bosniaks).[2] In September 1993, the Bosniak Assembly—349 Bosnian Muslim politicians, intellectuals, and clerics convening in Sarajevo as a consultative body—accepted *Bošnjastvo* (Bosnianhood) as the national identity of the Bosnian Muslims. The name *Bošnjak* (Bosniak) officially became the national identification of the Bosnian Muslims for the first time in history.[3] The fact that the Bosnian Muslims were fighting against the Bosnian Serbs as well as against the Bosnian Croats strengthened their national consciousness as a distinct nation. During the war, Alija Izetbegovic continued to act as the president of Bosnia-Herzegovina, while the Muslims controlled the Bosnian army and the state bureaucracy, which had a multiethnic character. Both during and after the war, the Muslim leadership acted as an independent political agent involved in international negotiations concerning the political future of Bosnia-Herzegovina. In the Dayton Constitution, the Bosnian Muslims were referred to as Bosniaks and their language as Bosnian, and the Dayton Accords confirmed the status of the

Bosnian Muslims as a constituent nation along with the Croats in the establishment of the Federation of Bosnia-Herzegovina.[4]

Although the Bosnian Muslims were referred to as Bosniaks in the Dayton Constitution, the Bosnian media continued to use the term *Muslimani* (Muslims) alongside the term *Bosniaks*, and often both terms together, as in *Bosnjaci-Muslimani*. The leaders and the intellectuals of the Bosniak community, who consider *Bosniak* the national term to be applied to the Bosnian Muslims, nevertheless have various perceptions of the label. Some of them point to its Islamic content, while others stress the purely secular and national character of the term and its connection with Bosnian territory and history.[5] On one hand, despite the fact that *Muslim* is still in use and despite various perceptions of the term, in the Bosniak community it seems that *Bosniak* has become established as the national name of the Bosnian Muslims. On the other hand, the national distinctiveness of Bosniaks is today less controversial than ever, although some Serbian and Croatian nationalists are still disinclined to accept the Bosniaks as a nation of their own.

The national development of the Bosniaks in the post-Communist period was based on the achievements of the socialist period. In 1968, the Bosnian Muslims were recognized by the socialist regime of Yugoslavia as "Muslims in the national sense," the first time Bosnian Muslims had been recognized as a nation by any state in which they lived. However, the phrase "Muslims in the national sense" was somewhat ambiguous, and the nationalist Serbs and Croats continued to reject the idea of a distinct nationality for the Bosnian Muslims, as did some Western scholars.[6] This chapter explores the complicated process of the recognition of the Bosnian Muslims as a nation during the socialist period, together with the rationale behind it; that is, this analysis shows the crucial importance of the Cold War period in the national development of the Bosniaks.

## Economy, Decentralization, and the National Question

Socialist Yugoslavia was established in 1945 as a federation of six republics and their five constituent nations. The Slovenes, Serbs, and Croats were recognized as nations alongside the Macedonians and Montenegrins, who had not previously been recognized as separate entities.[7] Bosnia-Herzegovina was the only republic that, because of its mixed demographic structure, was not established on a national basis.[8] The Bosnian Muslims were not at that time recognized as an ethnic group but were treated as a religious or ethnically undefined community. In 1948, Yugoslavia and Bulgaria signed an agreement for the formation of a new federation. The preference that the Yugoslav leadership gave to

Bulgaria over Albania shows that the "brotherhood and unity" concept had not abandoned the South Slavic dimension.[9] Tito seems to have hesitated over leaving behind this aspect of Yugoslav cohesion, at least in the early postwar years, although in his later speeches he would claim that he had never entertained the thought of creating a Yugoslav nation.[10]

After World War II, the Yugoslav regime hoped to eliminate the traditional loyalties and conflicts among the various ethnic and regional groups through rapid economic development and the transfer of funds from the more highly developed to the less advanced regions of the country. The strategy of creating a new socialist Yugoslav citizen through rapid industrialization—what might be called "revolutionary fusion"—was to continue until the early 1950s.[11] The early 1950s witnessed efforts to create a more humane form of socialism that also brought about a change in the nationality policy of the regime. The Yugoslav leadership, in their anxiety to survive the break with the Soviet Union and to consolidate the regime, found themselves obliged to take serious note of deeply rooted group sensibilities. In this new period, education, an important instrument in state building in a multiethnic community, constituted one of the bases of the new nationality policy, although it would prove ineffective.[12] Economic development was still an important instrument of official policy, but the process was now viewed as a much longer-term enterprise.[13] It was only in the second half of the 1960s that another radical shift occurred in the nationality policy of the regime.[14]

In the early years after World War II, the Muslims were regarded by the socialist regime in Yugoslavia as potential Serbs, Croats, or Yugoslavs. Some party officials considered the Muslims a nonnational core around which a future Yugoslav nation could be created.[15] However, the Bosnian Muslims stressed their ethnic distinctiveness indirectly by refusing to declare themselves either Serbs or Croats in the censuses of 1948, 1953, and 1961.[16] In the 1948 census, the Muslims were presented with three options: "Serb Muslim," "Croat Muslim," and "undecided Muslim." The overwhelming majority of Bosnian Muslims (more than 89 percent) seem to have chosen the third alternative. In the 1953 census, a new option—"undecided Yugoslav"—was incorporated; this time, the overwhelming majority of Bosnian Muslims (over 93 percent) opted for the new category.[17] The 1961 census marked the first recognition of Muslims as a distinct group, forming an ethnic but not a national category: they now had the option of classifying themselves as "ethnic Muslims."[18] Finally, in the census of 1971, with the introduction of the category "Muslims in the national sense," Muslims were treated for the first time as constituting a nation of their own on the same level as Serbs and Croats.

Economic and political developments in Yugoslavia in the 1960s provided suitable soil for the growth of the nationalism that had been on the rise since the early 1950s.[19] The early 1950s saw the introduction of a self-management system that, in its initial stages, showed signs of success. However, factors such as the domination of the local party apparatus, the insistence on wage equalization, the growth in unemployment, and the dependence on consumer goods culminated in an economic crisis in the early 1960s.[20] In a speech in Split in May 1962, Tito voiced his concern regarding the rise of nationalism, particularly among the youth.[21] But the same speech included a renewed call for the integration of socialist culture and the economy. Tito emphasized the need for the party to take the lead in integrating the economy into a single unit. He linked economic integration to the "uniform socialist Yugoslav culture" that had been proposed at the party congress of 1958. Edvard Kardelj (a longtime Communist and political theorist who favored the decentralization of Yugoslavia) argued that a socialist division of labor would replace the prewar policy of assimilating the various ethnic groups into a single entity by a new sort of Yugoslav consciousness.[22] By the late 1950s, the party leadership was already divided over economic policy and its political implications.[23] Between 1962 and 1966, Yugoslavia witnessed an intense political debate that would shape not only the course of economic reforms but also the future of the state itself. Basically, there were two schools of thought. The first group, led by Kardelj, claimed that only self-management and the parallel decentralization of political power could solve the problems facing the Yugoslav economy, while the second group, led by Alexander Ranković, favored centralization.[24] Tito seemed to shift his support back and forth between Kardelj and Ranković several times between 1962 and 1966.[25] He finally sided with Kardelj.

"De-étatization" sounded the death knell for *jugoslovenstvo* (Yugoslavism), although the right of citizens to declare themselves Yugoslavs survived a challenge in the drafting of the new constitution.[26] In 1963, a new constitution was adopted that was intended to support the economic reform. For the first time, the powers of the federal government were reduced, as were those of the Communist Party's central hierarchy, to the benefit of the republics and the regions. The right to secede formerly enjoyed by the republics was restored (provided all agreed), and a constitutional court was set up to hear the appeals of the republics against federal laws that allegedly infringed on their rights.[27] The new constitution created a framework in which national particularities could become entrenched within the party apparatus of the republics, which had been established in 1946 on an ethnic and historical basis. One group that was to gain from this round of constitutional tinkering was Muslims.[28] The new constitution made further concessions to the thesis that Muslims formed a distinct ethnic group.[29] Muslims were recognized, at least indirectly, as a separate nation by the 1963 constitution, which referred to Bosnia-Herzegovina as a republic inhabited by Serbs, Croats, and Muslims.

However, the Muslims of Sanjak, a region divided between Serbia and Montenegro, were excluded.[30]

Nevertheless, the decisions taken at the eighth congress of the League of Communists of Yugoslavia (LCY) in 1964 were potentially more important than anything contained in the new constitution. According to a new statute adopted at this meeting, the republics were to convene their own congresses immediately before the congress of the entire party, and they were granted the right to present their respective positions at the national gathering.[31] This marked the beginning of the confederation process of the LCY.[32] Although Tito remained the supreme arbiter of the political system, these changes set in motion a shift in emphasis away from the institutions and values that had formed the basis of Yugoslav unity since that country's establishment. A result of this process was the diminishing importance of Yugoslavism as a defining identity.[33]

The root causes of the revival of the national question in the 1960s seem to have been primarily but not exclusively economic in nature. The first manifestations of national conflict took the form of an intersectoral and interregional rivalry for centrally controlled investment funds and disputes over development priorities.[34] By the 1970s, all the regions of Yugoslavia were economically better off compared to their situation in the early post–World War II years, but the differences between the richer and poorer areas had shown a marked increase. The gap between economically developed regions (such as Slovenia, Croatia, Vojvodina, and Serbia proper) and less developed regions (such as Kosovo, Macedonia, Montenegro, and Bosnia-Herzegovina) was steadily widening.[35] By the early 1960s, it had become clear that the policy of accelerating the development of the underdeveloped regions through irregular federal grants had failed. In 1961, it began to be stressed within the party that there was a need for a special federal fund for the economic development of the less developed regions, and such a fund was actually introduced in the course of time. However, the overall trend between 1953 and 1971 was for the underdeveloped regions to be outpaced by the developed areas in the north. By 1971, per capita income in the underdeveloped regions (taken as a whole), which in 1953 had equaled 65 percent of per capita income in the developed regions, fell to 50 percent of the northern level. The biggest decline was to be seen in Bosnia-Herzegovina, where by 1953 the per capita income, which had averaged 74 percent of the rate of the northern republics, had fallen to only 53 percent.[36]

In December 1966, the representatives of Bosnia-Herzegovina on the federal fund's managing board were dissatisfied with its allocation of resources for 1967–1970 and turned to governmental institutions for redress. This unprecedented move resulted in an investigation that had no concrete results but gave further impetus to the amendment of the constitution.[37] The increasing gap between the northern and southern regions was a problem for a socialist system claiming that there could be no real equality between nations without economic equality. The failure to reverse this trend produced a growing sense of inequality and economic exploitation and promoted policies of protectionism in the more advanced republics, particularly Slovenia. The workers from underdeveloped regions felt themselves more and more marginalized in the northern republics. The Bosnians felt this in Slovenia, while the Kosovo-Albanians experienced this everywhere in Yugoslavia.[38]

First, Yugoslavia had been opened up to West European markets and then, in 1965, the most ambitious set of market-oriented reforms in the Communist world had been introduced. On the other hand, by the 1960s, the socialist establishment had granted to Yugoslavs real breathing space for intellectual freedom.[39] The economic reform of 1965 removed the barriers to free movement among people and ideas as well as goods and exerted a huge influence on Yugoslav society. Unlike the citizens of the other socialist countries, the Yugoslavs were able to travel freely for both work and leisure and to exchange ideas with the residents of other nations.[40] A more open media and the relatively free expression of opinion and religious practice formed some of the characteristics of this new period. Urban culture prospered, educational standards rose, and there was an increase in the social participation of women.[41] The relaxed intellectual climate promoted political debate outside the party and also permitted a focus on noneconomic issues. Several journals sprang up that reflected the philosophical, sociological, and political debates within the universities, while the press adopted a more controversial tone. A group founded by the Yugoslav Philosophical Association was at the center of these developments. The journal *Praxis*, founded in 1964 and published in Zagreb, became a forum for Marxian critiques of the modern world.[42] This relaxation of the intellectual atmosphere had been initiated from above, but its own momentum had propelled it beyond the control of the authorities.[43] The regime would tolerate this until 1968.[44]

## After the Fall of Ranković

Until July 1966, Alexander Ranković, the vice president of Yugoslavia, had been viewed as Tito's successor. At a meeting of the central committee known as the fourth plenum, held in July 1966, he was forced to resign, and he was also expelled from the federal assembly and the LCY. The fall of Ranković, who had been the most important opponent of market reform, constituted the start of a more liberal era.[45] After 1966, nationalist tendencies were increasingly represented in public debate, particularly in Croatia and Kosovo.[46] Economically motivated dissatisfaction found cultural expression among Croatian intellectuals.[47] In 1967, all the important cultural organizations of Croatia signed a resolution repudiating the 1954 Novi Sad agreement on the Serbo-Croatian language and asked for a constitutional amendment that would recognize Serbian and Croatian as two distinct languages, both with the status of official tongues. This was the most severe setback to cultural union in Yugoslavia.[48] Serbian intellectuals responded with a resolution entitled "A Proposal for Consideration" that demanded equality for the Serbian language and the use of Cyrillic script, particularly for the Serbs living in Croatia. The revival of the language problem was to affect different parts of Yugoslavia.[49]

The national identity of the Bosnian Muslims had long been a matter of controversy between Serbian and Croatian nationalists. The former considered Bosnian Muslims to be Muslim Serbs while the latter defined them as Muslim Croats. The 1960s witnessed an increasing rivalry between Croats and Serbs over Bosnia-Herzegovina and Bosnian Muslims. After 1966, Croatian and Serbian cultural organizations started to penetrate areas of the Bosnian Republic inhabited by Croats and Serbs.[50] Matica Hrvatska (The Croatian Center), a Croatian cultural organization, was revived in the 1960s by a group that included Franjo Tudjman, who later became the president of post-Yugoslav Croatia. In 1968, Matica Hrvatska started to publish its periodical, *Kritika*, which addressed the Croatian minorities in the other republics—particularly in Bosnia—and laid stress on the Bosnian Croat issue.[51] On the other hand, the Catholic Church became very active in Bosnia, which prompted Orthodox and Islamic organizations to increase their visibility there. The local party officials started to report serious problems regarding the general upsurge in religious instruction, the establishment of religious institutions, and the social activities organized by the religious communities. The political leadership of the League of Communists of Bosnia-Herzegovina (LCBiH) was concerned about the increase of nationalism in Bosnia-Herzegovina.[52]

In 1968, the Bosnian Muslims were recognized by the regime as "Muslims in the national sense" despite the fact that it was incompatible with socialist principles to accept the existence of a nation on the basis of religion.[53] The Bosniaks had been recognized as an ethnic group (but not as a nationality) as early as 1961, but it was not until the eighteenth session of the central committee of the LCBiH in February 1968 that they were given a national status equal to that of the Serbs and Croats. In spite of some objections among the LCY elite to the recognition of the Muslims as a nation, the fifth congress of the LCBiH in 1969 confirmed the equality in status enjoyed by the Bosnian Muslims alongside the other Yugoslav nationalities.[54] The fact that in the census of 1971 the Bosnian Muslims could declare themselves "Muslims in the national sense" showed that the federal LCY also supported the decision. The Bosnian leadership could advance its own interests more vigorously than the leaderships of the other republics in a period of rising nationalism, as the case regarding aid to the underdeveloped regions had already demonstrated. The party leaderships of the other republics were not permitted to advance regional economic and political arguments, but the Bosnian leadership could put forward similar arguments because the multinational composition of the Bosnian Communists made it impossible to accuse them of nationalism.[55] Moreover, the concept of Muslim nationhood developed by the Bosnian Muslims was carefully circumscribed to include only Serbo-Croatian-speaking Slavic Muslims—primarily those in Bosnia-Herzegovina and the Sandzak of Novi Pazar—together with a small minority in Kosovo. This combination did not challenge the identities of other nations or the authority of other political units.[56]

Although the recognition of the Bosnian Muslims as a nation was facilitated by the special conditions reigning in Bosnia-Herzegovina, it can be considered primarily as the confirmation of real sentiments among Muslims. The Bosnian Muslims not only stressed their own particular ethnic distinctiveness in the censuses by not declaring themselves as Serbs or Croats but also made direct demands through their intellectuals for the recognition of their own national identity. A professor from Sarajevo, Muhammed Filipović, was the first Muslim intellectual to raise this demand publicly, in 1967. One year later, the Muslim intellectual Avdo Humo published articles on the subject of the Muslims in Yugoslavia in the journal *Komunist*.[57] Atıf Purivatra, the president of the Commission for Interethnic Relations of the Socialist Alliance of the Working People of Bosnia-Herzegovina (SAWP BiH), was one of the most important proponents of national status for the Muslims. He stressed that Bosnian Muslims were not only followers of the Islamic religion but also constituted a nation of their own.[58] On the other hand, the Muslim historian Avdo Sućeska claimed that Bosnian Muslims had already formed an ethnic group with different social classes during the Ottoman period.[59] The Muslim intellectuals and bureaucrats did not challenge the socialist system, advancing a secular national identity based on the principle of equality already embedded in the official ideology.[60] Džemal Bijedić, the prime minister of Yugoslavia from 1971 to 1977, and Hamdija Pozderac, the president of the Socialist Republic of Bosnia-Herzegovina from 1971 to 1974, were influential in affirming the Bosnian Muslims as a nation.[61]

However, the efforts of the Muslim intellectuals failed to convince the nationalist Serbs and Croats, who continued to reject the idea of a separate national identity for the Bosnian Muslims. The question of the national identity of Bosnian Muslims was also a subject of discussion among the Muslim intellectuals themselves. More particularly, controversy concerning the national status of the Muslims was triggered by the ideas put forward by Esad

Ćimić, a professor at the University of Sarajevo and a self-declared Croat. According to Ćimić, it was too early for the Muslims to form a *nacija* (nation), although he did not exclude the possibility that Bosnian Muslims might have certain characteristic features of nationality. The response to Ćimić came from Atıf Purivatra, who stressed that Ćimić's ideas were incompatible with the LCY interethnic policy and that any suggestion that the Bosnian Muslims were in some way "immature," "insufficiently developed," or "second rate" was demeaning as well as historically false.[62] Although Purivatra's comments were primarily a response to Ćimić, they triggered a polemical exchange between Bosnia-Herzegovina and Macedonia over the status of the Muslims.[63]

Religion and *Bošnjastvo* (Bosnianhood) were two rival concepts competing for the national identity of Bosnian Muslims.[64] According to the Muslim historian Enver Redzić, *Bošnjastvo* had two different meanings. The first was the territorial-political consciousness of the different nationalities, regardless of their ethnic origins, arising from the continuity of Bosnia-Herzegovina as a political entity throughout history. On the other hand, *Bošnjastvo* meant for Muslims not only a territorial-political consciousness but also an ethnic identity.[65] Redzić's perception of *Bošnjastvo* was met with criticism from some of the other Muslim intellectuals. According to Kasım Suljević, *Bošnjastvo* represented the past of the Bosnian Muslims while *Muslimanstvo* (Muslimhood) was the appropriate concept for their contemporary ethnic identity.[66] Purivatra also denounced the more recently proposed designation "Bosniak," declaring that this label was unacceptable since it implied a denial of specificity and a negation of Muslim, Serbian, and Croatian national feeling in the Bosnian republic.[67] The comments of Purivatra reflected the official position adopted by the socialist regime concerning the concept of *Bošnjastvo* as signifying the national identity of the Bosnian Muslims.

In addition to the demands of Bosnian Muslims for national status, there were also some other important political factors behind their recognition as an independent nation, which was in effect a compromise between the interests of the Yugoslav establishment and the Bosnian Muslims themselves.[68] The socialist leadership hoped to put an end to the Serbian and Croatian rivalry over Bosnia-Herzegovina by integrating Bosnian Muslims into Yugoslavia's political system as a separate nation.[69] The LCY expected the Bosnian Muslims and Bosnia-Herzegovina to form a barrier against rising Serbian and Croatian nationalism.[70] On the other hand, the recognition of Bosnian Muslims as a separate nation also served the interests of Bosnian Muslim members of the Communist Party hoping to raise their status in the party hierarchy.[71] The Bosnian Communist Party was dominated by a coalition of Serbs, Croats, and Muslims, in which certain Muslim families and clans played an important role. This secularized Muslim party elite pushed for the recognition of Bosnian Muslims as a separate nation.[72] The affirmation of the national identity of Bosnian Muslims added another element to formulas for the construction of representative institutions and decision-making bodies on the federal level in both the state and the party.[73] By advancing the cause of Muslim nationhood, the Bosnian party leadership could also claim a greater number of positions for its cadres in the central hierarchies.[74]

Demographic developments in Bosnia-Herzegovina seem to have formed another important factor that could not be ignored by the socialist regime. Because of rapid population growth and extensive Serb and Croat migrations, Bosnian Muslims were on their way to becoming the largest ethnic community in Bosnia-Herzegovina. Muslims, who constituted 30.8 percent of the population after World War II, grew to 43.7 percent in the census of 1991. In the same period, the Serbs fell from 40.5 percent to 31.3 percent and the Croats from 22.2 percent to 17.5 percent.[75] According to the 1981 census, 1,760,333 out of 23 million Yugoslavs had changed their permanent place of residence from one republic to another during their lifetime. The direction of migration shows that the Croats moved predominantly to Croatia and the Serbs to Serbia, while Bosnian Muslims remained committed to their own territories.[76] The policy of the socialist regime toward Muslims also coincided with the general trend of modernization in Bosnian society, which introduced more and more Muslims to an urban and industrialized lifestyle as well as to higher education.[77] The urban population of Bosnia rose from 14 percent in 1948 to 28 percent in 1971 while the number of agricultural workers declined from 77 percent in 1948 to 40 percent in 1971.[78] During the socialist period, Muslims began to profit from their increasingly secular education, rapidly overcoming the relative backwardness characteristic of their community.[79] As a result, some Muslim intellectuals and officials rose in the state bureaucracy while some members of the Muslim elite were to play a crucial role in the affirmation of Bosnian Muslims as a separate nation.

In April 1981, *Zëri i Popullit*, the main daily in Tirana, Albania, claimed that an artificial Muslim nationality had been established in the 1960s in Bosnia-Herzegovina, Kosovo, and other regions where Albanians resided. The paper argued that this concept of a Muslim nationality had been invented merely to reduce the statistical number of Albanians living in different republics.[80] Even though this politically motivated commentary did not reflect the truth, it pointed to the possibility that the growing ethnic tension in Kosovo, which had reached its height in 1968, might have had a certain influence on the decision-making process of the Yugoslav regime concerning the recognition of Bosnian Muslims as a separate nation. The Kosovo question had already reached acute proportions in the mid-1950s, and until the fall of Ranković in 1966, it had been suppressed only by the use of brute force. However, after

1966, the Kosovo question had again appeared on the agenda and the rise in Albanian nationalism put great pressure on the Yugoslav regime. In Yugoslavia, Bosnian Muslims were inclined to compromise with state authorities in order to make substantial gains, whereas the Albanians preferred to engage in open conflict. The Yugoslav government thus favored the Bosnian Muslims in the hierarchy of the Islamic Community and followed an increasingly liberal nationality policy toward them.[81] This not only encouraged the integration of Bosnian Muslims into the Yugoslav political system but also weakened the relations between the two Muslim communities. The political goals of the Albanians were not supported by Bosnian Muslims.[82]

Without the shifts in the official ideology and nationality policy of socialist Yugoslavia that had taken place in the 1950s and 1960s, the recognition of Bosnian Muslims as a separate nation would not have been possible. Ideology was for the LCY much more than a merely formal justification of its political existence and, since the ideology was employed to shape the socialist Yugoslav identity, it was almost impossible to abandon it. This identity was created under the pressure of accusations of revisionism, and it was incompatible not only with past concepts of Yugoslavism but also with Soviet-style Communism. The system had two important others: interwar bourgeois Yugoslavia and Soviet Communism.[83] Between 1957 and 1966, the ideas of Kardelj met with serious resistance from the proponents of unconditional Yugoslavism and South-Slavism. Ranković, vice president and the chief of the secret service, was Kardelj's most prominent critic and his main rival to succeed Tito.[84] Ranković was responsible for the policies of suppression employed against Albanians, Hungarians, and Muslims. He laid particular stress on Yugoslav unity, attempted to suppress any discussion of a separate ethnic identity, and openly denied the existence of a Muslim nation.[85] In this sense, the fall of Ranković was a victory not only for the Albanians and the reformists but also for Bosnian Muslims.

It also meant that Kardelj was now second only to Tito in authority. In the preface to the second edition of his book *The Development of the Slovene National Question*, Kardelj (writing as "Sperans") had dropped Stalin's definition of a nation and wrote that socialism itself (like any other ideology) could neither make nor deny the existence of nations.[86] In the late 1950s, Kardelj had warned his compatriots about the illusion that a new Yugoslav nation was emerging from the Yugoslav state. According to Kardelj, pan-Slavist and Yugoslav goals were products of the bourgeois past, and nationalism posed a threat to the future of Yugoslavia. In the early 1960s, he had concluded that even the idea of socialist Yugoslavism was no longer feasible, since the Yugoslav nations had become fully constituted nations in their own right. He further argued that Yugoslavia had to transform itself from a centralized, nation-making state to a federation of sovereign nation states, and that this was the only way to challenge the interwar concept of Yugoslavism and Soviet-style Communism.[87] Kardelj's support of Muslim distinctiveness was most probable, given his championing of federal devolution and his own early work recognizing the Muslims as an ethnic group.[88]

Tito agreed with Kardelj's ideas, which were in line with the Marxist concept of the "withering away of the state."[89] This same concept provided the Yugoslav leadership with an important tool in its ideological dispute with the Soviet Union. Tito believed that de-étatization would solve the national and economic problems of the country, particularly in its undeveloped republics and autonomous regions.[90] Tito considered the party the most important unifying force in the country and wanted to strengthen it.[91] As long as the party was sufficiently strong, the stability of socialism would be guaranteed.[92] Shortly after the fall of Ranković, Tito issued a declaration calling for the recognition of the national distinctiveness and national identity of Bosnian Muslims. This paved the way for the recognition in 1968 of the Muslims as a sixth Yugoslav nationality. Tito endorsed the concept of organic Yugoslavism which, in contrast to Ranković's integral Yugoslavism, saw no incompatibility between national identity and attachment to the Yugoslav federal community.[93]

## Cold War Nonalignment and Bosnian Muslims

International developments also shaped nationality policy in Yugoslavia. After World War II, the Yugoslav government granted political legitimacy to the Macedonian nationality before the Macedonians had developed a complete cultural identity. The fact that Macedonians constituted a decisive majority in Macedonia, a region where the minorities were not even Slavs, had played an important role in the creation of the policy.[94] However, the Bulgarian denial of the existence of the Macedonian nation and language was another crucial factor that had forced the Yugoslav leaders to be more sympathetic to the Macedonian demands.[95] The Bosnian Muslims were not as lucky: in contrast with the Macedonians, Muslims did not constitute an absolute majority in Bosnia-Herzegovina. The official concept of nationality, which emphasized linguistic rather than religious boundaries, was another obstacle in the way of nationhood status for Bosnian Muslims. Moreover, the Serbian and Croatian nationalists competing for control of Bosnia-Herzegovina considered the Muslims Islamized members of their communities.[96] Finally, the international environment did not encourage the affirmation of a Muslim nation until the late 1950s, another important difference between the Macedonian and the

Bosnian Muslim cases.[97] However, this would change with the Yugoslav Cold War nonalignment policy.

Tito's nonalignment policy played an important role in the treatment of Bosnian Muslims in the Yugoslav political system.[98] The conflict between Tito and Stalin in 1948 and the expulsion of Yugoslavia from the Cominform (Communist Information Bureau) forced the country to conduct a foreign policy that would break its isolation. The nonalignment policy, however, provided more than that and enabled Yugoslavia to wield an influence in the international arena quite disproportionate to its size. As one of the leaders of the Non-Aligned Movement (NAM), Tito enjoyed high prestige in Third World countries as well as in Western countries. The unique position of socialist Yugoslavia between the East and the West helped it to establish close relations with the capitalist countries and to obtain economic and military aid of great importance for its economy. On the other hand, nonalignment provided an alternative to the diplomacy of Soviet-style Communism and became, along with the self-management system, an indispensable part of Yugoslav identity. A good Yugoslav was, by definition, loyal to the principle of self-management and the policy of nonalignment.[99]

The nonalignment policy, which was perceived as promoting the creation of an autonomous region within the international system, received a high level of internal support in Yugoslavia.[100] As a result of its foreign policy, the Yugoslav government was able to retain a balanced approach to all its domestic nationalities by offering a compromise, thus giving partial satisfaction to all.[101] The nonalignment policy was also greatly popular among Bosnian Muslims. It set acceptable limits on the relations between the different republics of the Yugoslav federation and different countries or regions. Within the framework of this system, Croatia and Slovenia were able to establish certain links with the West, the southern and eastern republics with socialist Eastern Europe, and Bosnia-Herzegovina with Middle Eastern countries. The republics and provinces also participated in the formulation of the foreign policy of Yugoslavia in different ways. They not only had representatives in the decision-making process but also could send and receive delegations from foreign countries for the purpose of economic, cultural, and border cooperation.[102] Diplomatic instruments, political-organizational links, and economic relations were among the most important tools employed by Yugoslavia as it strengthened its contacts with members of the NAM.[103] Moreover, the Yugoslav model of socialism and the policy adopted toward Bosnian Muslims constituted the most important of the soft powers used by Yugoslavia in its influence-building efforts in the Third World.[104]

The NAM included a considerable number of Muslim countries, as well as certain non-Muslim countries that had close contacts with the nonaligned

Muslim countries. Tito, as one of the leaders of the movement, was obliged to maintain close contacts with Muslim countries in the Middle East. Moreover, his strong relationship with Egypt and his uncompromising support of the Palestinian cause would eventually become characteristic features of Yugoslav foreign policy. On the other hand, Tito needed the support of the Muslim countries to strengthen his leadership in the nonalignment movement and to counteract the challenge of Cuba's Fidel Castro, who wanted to bring the movement closer to the Soviet Union. The socialist leadership of Yugoslavia was aware that a Yugoslavia that failed to give due importance to its own Muslims would lack credibility in the Third World and more particularly in Muslim countries. The Yugoslav leadership therefore had to show that in Yugoslavia, Muslims were not only tolerated but also valued.[105]

The Islamic Community had remained the sole important Bosnian Muslim organization in the early years following World War II. Under political pressure, the Islamic Community started to cooperate with the socialist regime in 1947. In exchange for its loyalty, the Islamic Community enjoyed a degree of autonomy in the management of its religious affairs within the framework of its 1947 constitution. The Islamic Community offered proof that Islam and socialism were not incompatible and it adopted a negative attitude toward pan-Islamic movements; these constituted two of the expectations of the socialist establishment.[106] In its publications, the Islamic Community kept Yugoslav Muslims informed of developments in the broader Islamic world in line with the official Yugoslav position.[107] Until the early 1970s, an Islamic Community loyal to the regime dared not comment on the nationality of Bosnian Muslims and avoided any involvement in the public debates surrounding this issue.[108]

The Islamic Community made some important contributions to the nonalignment policy of Yugoslavia. Yugoslav delegations to Muslim countries usually included Muslim representatives from Bosnia, and foreign Muslim leaders often paid visits to Sarajevo.[109] Since the 1950s, Muslim religious officials in Sarajevo had welcomed the heads of state of non-aligned countries as their guests. In 1956, when important figures of the NAM (such as Egypt's Gamal Abdel Nasser and Indonesia's Sukarno) visited Sarajevo, they were introduced to the reis-ul-ulema (the chief of the Islamic Community) and taken on trips to places where the landscape was characterized by representations of Muslim culture such as Islamic architecture and minarets.[110] Many of the Muslim delegations visited Islamic institutions such as mosques and the historical madrassa (religious school) of Gazi Hüsrev Beg in Sarajevo. Some of these delegations participated in religious ceremonies. They were also given information by the reis-ul-ulema about the legal framework regulating religious activities and the structure of the Islamic Community. The primary aim of the Islamic Community during these visits was to show that the Muslims of

Yugoslavia were treated well by the socialist establishment.[111] These activities organized by the Islamic Community were of particular interest for Muslim countries with a socialist political system.

Another important aim of the Islamic Community was to point out the difference between the treatment of the Muslim minorities in Yugoslavia and that of Muslim minorities in the Soviet Union. As early as 1952 (even before Belgrade adopted a foreign policy of nonalignment), the reis-ul-ulema criticized the concerns voiced at the World Islamic Conference in Karachi regarding the situation of Muslims in Yugoslavia, and he deliberately indicated his support of the official position adopted by Yugoslavia in opposition to that of the Soviet Union by mentioning the mistreatment of the Muslim minorities in that country.[112] In addition to interactions with the foreign delegations in Sarajevo, the Yugoslav Muslim delegations also paid visits on various occasions to Muslim nonaligned countries. These visits contributed to the strengthening of relations between Yugoslavia and these countries, as well as to the image of the Yugoslav model of socialism.[113] The hadj organizations created by the Islamic Community since the 1950s also connected Yugoslavia with Muslim countries. The lengthy reports on annual hadjs in the publications of the Islamic Community show that the hadj was considered not only a religious activity but also a social gathering that demonstrated the religious freedom characteristic of the Yugoslav model of socialism.[114] Algeria and the United Arab Republic maintained an ongoing interest in the Yugoslav model, while other nonaligned countries (such as Tanzania, Ghana, Guinea, India, Indonesia, and Afghanistan) explored its various aspects.[115]

Prior to the early 1970s, the Islamic Community had not succeeded in becoming the driving force behind the national development of Bosnian Muslims, even though it played a certain role in the change of the nationality policy of the socialist regime toward the Bosnian Muslims in the late 1960s. But, as the sole organization of the Bosnian Muslims, it nonetheless exerted a strong influence on their religious, cultural, and social lives. During the period of Hadzi Süleyman ef. Kemura, who became reis-ul-ulema in 1957, the Supreme Islamic Council was reorganized. Four regional Islamic councils were established in 1958 and this change was incorporated into the new constitution of the Islamic Community in 1969. Another important development was the introduction of religious sermons in the national language, which contributed to the awakening of the religious consciousness of Bosnian Muslims. In the 1960s, the Muslim faithful began to support the Islamic Community actively, even though some mosques drew only a meager attendance. In 1977, Sarajevo's Islamic Theological Faculty was opened, while many mosques were restored and new ones built. The Islamic Community also sent students to different Muslim countries in the Middle East and Asia.[116] These initiatives were facilitated by the nonalignment policy of Yugoslavia, which had established good relations with the Arab countries.[117]

## Conclusion

One of the legacies bequeathed by Tito and Yugoslavia was the recognition of the Bosnian Muslims as a separate nation. In 1968, Bosnian Muslims were recognized for the first time in their history by a state in which they lived. The concept "Muslims in the national sense" caused a certain confusion, however, and nationalist Serbs and Croats regarded the category as purely artificial. The recognition of the national identity of Bosnian Muslims was the result of a very complicated process involving a number of different factors, and no proper analysis of this process is possible without considering the socioeconomic developments that were taking place in Yugoslavia, particularly in the 1960s. In contrast with the other republics of Yugoslavia, Bosnia-Herzegovina had a multinational structure; this facilitated the decision of the Bosnian Communist party with regard to the national status of Bosnian Muslims.

However, other factors played the decisive role in this process. First of all, the recognition of the national status of Bosnian Muslims reflected the actual feelings of the Muslim masses, who were disinclined to declare themselves as Serbs or Croats. In the words of Kardelj, socialism itself could neither make nor deny the existence of nations. The 1960s witnessed increasing activity on the part of Muslim intellectuals and bureaucrats in support of the cause of Bosnian Muslim nationhood. The socialist Muslim elite promoted a type of secular national identity that posed no challenge to the existing political system. The rapidly increasing population of the Bosnian Muslims and the improvement in their socioeconomic status provided a solid basis for the demands of the Bosnian Muslim elite for national status. On the other hand, the affirmation of the national identity of Bosnian Muslims was a compromise between the interests of the socialist regime and those of the Bosnian Muslim elite. The socialist establishment hoped that integrating Bosnian Muslims into the political system would halt a Serbian and Croatian rivalry over Bosnia-Herzegovina that had attained dangerous dimensions, while the Muslim elite hoped to strengthen their positions in the Communist Party as the representatives of a separate nation. This compromise was the deciding factor in the timing of the recognition of the Bosnian Muslims as a nation. Another factor that seems to have played a role in the timing of this decision was the growth of Albanian discontent in Kosovo, which was to culminate in demonstrations toward the end of 1968. Integration of the Muslims into the political system as a separate nation would reduce the tension in Bosnia-Herzegovina as well as the pressure on the socialist regime, which was facing a challenge in Kosovo.

The literature on Yugoslavia describes the fall of Ranković as a turning point in the treatment of the country's different nationalities. Even though the event introduced a more liberal era, the shifts in the government's nationality policy since the 1950s formed the deciding factor. The fall of Ranković was a by-product of this. The official ideology was of crucial importance to the Yugoslav political system since it was more than merely the justification of the existing socialist regime and had a direct influence on defining the identity of the country. The official ideology was to dominate economic and political developments in Yugoslavia until the mid-1980s. Yugoslavia tried to develop a political system that would form an alternative not only to its bourgeois past, but also to Soviet-style Communism. The break between Tito and Stalin in 1948 had a profound impact on the Yugoslav ideology, which tried to develop its own path to socialism. The so-called Yugoslav model was based mainly on self-management and nonalignment, and these two pillars of the Yugoslav model also constituted the core of the country's nationality policy. Economic and political decentralization, the evolution of the Yugoslav idea, and a foreign policy in close cooperation with nonaligned Muslim countries were the most important factors in creating a suitable atmosphere for the recognition of the Bosnian Muslims as a separate nation.

## Notes

1. Aydın Babuna, "National Identity, Islam, and Politics in Post-Communist Bosnia-Hercegovina," *East European Quarterly* 34, no. 4 (2006): 419. The author would like to thank the Boğaziçi University Research Fund (project 5087) for funding this project.

2. Šaćir Filandra, *Bošnjačka politika u XX Stoljeću* [The Bosniak policy in the twentieth century] (Sarajevo: Sejtarija, 1998), 384.

3. "Pravedan rat ili nepravdan mir?" [Justified war or unjustified peace?], *Oslobođenje*, October 1, 1993, 3. For the historical development of Bosniak identity, see Aydın Babuna, *Die nationale Entwicklung der bosnischen Muslime: Mit besonderer Berücksichtigung der österreichisch-ungarischen Periode* [The national development of the Bosnian Muslims: With special emphasis on the Austro-Hungarian Period] (Frankfurt: Peter Lang, 1996).

4. Aydın Babuna, "Zur Entwicklung der nationalen Identität der bosnischen Muslime" [On the development of the national identity of the Bosnian Muslims], *Osteuropa* 46, no. 4 (1996): 340.

5. Babuna, "National Identity," 419–20.

6. For example, see Pedro Ramet, "Die Muslime Bosniens als Nation," in *Die Muslime*

*in der Sowjetunion und in Jugoslawien*, ed. Andreas Kappeler, Gerhard Simon, and Georg Brunner (Cologne: Markus Verlag, 1989), 110–11.

7. Dejan Jović, *Yugoslavia: A State That Withered Away* (West Lafayette, IN: Purdue University Press, 2009), 57.

8. Džemal Bijedić, "Razvoj SR Bosne i Hercegovine" [The development of the socialist republic of Bosnia-Herzegovina], in *Istorija i praksa SKJ* [The history and practice of the League of Communists of Yugoslavia], ed. Ljubinka Bogetić and Dragoljub Đurović (Belgrade: Književne Novine, 1984), 72.

9. Jović, *Yugoslavia*, 59.

10. Josip Broz Tito, *Nacionalno pitanje i revolucija* [The national question and revolution] (Sarajevo: Svjetlost, 1979), 357.

11. Lenard Cohen, *Broken Bonds: The Disintegration of Yugoslavia* (Boulder, CO: Westview Press, 1993), 28.

12. Ann Lane, *Yugoslavia: When Ideals Collide* (New York: Palgrave Macmillan, 2004), 117.

13. Cohen, *Broken Bonds*, 28.

14. Ibid., 29.

15. Sabrina P. Ramet, *The Three Yugoslavias: State-Building and Legitimation, 1918–2005* (Washington, DC: Woodrow Wilson Center Press; Bloomington: Indiana University Press, 2006), 286.

16. Atıf Purivatra, *Nacionalni i politicki razvitak Muslimana* [The national and political development of the Muslims] (Sarajevo: Svjetlost, 1970), 32.

17. Steven L. Burg, *The Political Integration of Yugoslavia's Muslims: Determinants of Success and Failure* (Pittsburgh: University of Pittsburgh, Russian and East European Studies Program, 1983), 21–22.

18. Ibid., 38.

19. Bijedić, "Razvoj SR Bosne i Hercegovine," 64.

20. Lane, *Yugoslavia*, 126–27.

21. Paul Shoup, *Communism and the Yugoslav National Question* (New York: Columbia University Press, 1968), 190.

22. John R. Lampe, *Yugoslavia as History* (Cambridge: Cambridge University Press, 1996), 278–79.

23. Steven L. Burg, *Conflict and Cohesion in Socialist Yugoslavia: Political Decision Making since 1966* (Princeton, NJ: Princeton University Press, 1983), 27.

24. Lane, *Yugoslavia*, 130.

25. Jović, *Yugoslavia*, 65.

26. Tito preferred to stress the notion of "de-étatization" rather than decentralization.

27. Lampe, *Yugoslavia as History*, 280–81; Shoup, *Communism*, 211–12.

28. Lane, *Yugoslavia*, 131.

29. Shoup, *Communism*, 216.

30. Lane, *Yugoslavia*, 131–32.

31. Shoup, *Communism*, 213.

32. Lampe, *Yugoslavia as History*, 281.

33. Lane, *Yugoslavia*, 132.

34. Dennison Rusinow, "Reopening of the 'National Question' in the 1960s," in *State*

*Collapse in South-Eastern Europe: New Perspectives on Yugoslavia's Disintegration*, ed. Lenard Cohen and Jasna Dragović-Soso (West Lafayette, IN: Purdue University Press, 2008), 132.

35.  Cohen, *Broken Bonds*, 34.

36.  Vinod Dubey, *Yugoslavia: Development with Decentralization* (Baltimore: Johns Hopkins University Press, 1975), 193, cited in S. P. Ramet, *Three Yugoslavias*, 267.

37.  Burg, *Conflict and Cohesion*, 66–67.

38.  *Bosanci* was a term for "Southerners"—Serbian- and Croatian-speaking manual workers—in the Slovenian colloquial vocabulary. Jović, *Yugoslavia*, 145–46.

39.  Lampe, *Yugoslavia as History*, 261.

40.  Fred Singleton, *A Short History of the Yugoslav Peoples* (Cambridge: Cambridge University Press, 1985), 244–45.

41.  Lampe, *Yugoslavia as History*, 261.

42.  Lane, *Yugoslavia*, 138.

43.  Singleton, *Short History*, 245.

44.  Lane, *Yugoslavia*, 138. Tito had told the Central Committee of the LCY as early as 1962 that freedom of expression should not go so far as to allow the emergence of nationalist polemics. Singleton, *Short History*, 245.

45.  Lane, *Yugoslavia*, 134–35.

46.  Jović, *Yugoslavia*, 118.

47.  Lane, *Yugoslavia*, 140.

48.  *Borba* (Belgrade), March 21, 1967. The declaration was originally published in *Telegram* (Zagreb), March 17, 1967, cited in Shoup, *Communism*, 195.

49.  Lane, *Yugoslavia*, 137.

50.  *Republičko savetovanje o nekim obilježima* [Republican consultation on some marks], 310, cited in Burg, *Conflict and Cohesion*, 70.

51.  Lane, *Yugoslavia*, 140–41.

52.  Burg, *Conflict and Cohesion*, 70.

53.  Aydın Babuna, "The Bosnian Muslims and Albanians: Islam and Nationalism," *Nationalities Papers* 32, no. 2 (2004): 304; Purivatra, *Nacionalni i politicki razvitak*, 30.

54.  For example, the novelist Dobrica Ćosić and the historian Jovan Marjanović were opposed to the recognition of the Muslims as a separate nation. See S. P. Ramet, *Three Yugoslavias*, 287.

55.  Burg, *Political Integration*, 41–42; and Zachary Irwin, "The Islamic Revival and the Muslims of Bosnia-Hercegovina," *East European Quarterly* 17, no. 4 (1984): 444.

56.  Burg, *Political Integration*, 42.

57.  Avdo Humo, "Muslimani u Yugoslaviji," *Komunist*, July 11, 1968, 9; July 18, 1968, 19; July 25, 1968, 15; August 1, 1968, 9; and August 8, 1968, 12.

58.  Atıf Purivatra, "O nacionalnom fenomenu bosanskohercegovačkih muslimana," *Pregled* 64, no. 10 (1974): 1019.

59.  Avdo Sućeska, "Neke specifičnosti istorije Bosne pod Turcima" [Some specifics of the Bosnian history under the Turks], *Istorijske pretpostavke Republike Bosne i Hercegovine, Prilozi* 9, no. 4 (1968): 49.

60.  Burg, *Political Integration*, 42.

61. Ivo Banac, "Bosnian Muslims: From Religious Community to Socialist Nationhood and Post-Communist Statehood, 1918–1992," in *The Muslims of Bosnia-Herzegovina: Their Historic Development from the Middle Ages to the Dissolution of Yugoslavia*, ed. Mark Pinson (Cambridge, MA: Harvard University Press, 1996), 145; Mitja Velikonja, *Religious Separation and Political Intolerance in Bosnia-Herzegovina* (College Station: Texas A&M University Press, 2003), 223; and Mujo Demirović and Mulo Hadžić, *Hamdija Pozderac. Državnost i nacionalnost BiH* [Statehood and nationality of Bosnia-Herzegovina] (Bihać: Pravni fakultet, 2008).

62. Quoted in Milan Bulajić, "Problemi samoopredeljenja nacija i čovjeka i jugoslovenski federalizam" [The problems of self-determination of nation and individual and Yugoslav federalism], in *Federalizam i nacionalno pitanje* [Federalism and the national question] (Belgrade: Savez udruženja za političke nauke Jugoslavije, 1971), 267–68, cited in S. P. Ramet, *Three Yugoslavias*, 289.

63. Ramet, *Three Yugoslavias*, 290.

64. According to a poll conducted in 1988, 54.11 percent of Bosnian Muslims thought there was a strong relationship between Islam and the national identity of Bosnian Muslims. See Ibrahim Bakić, *Nacija i religija* [Nation and religion] (Sarajevo: Bosna Public, 1994), 112; and Velikonja, *Religious Separation*, 232.

65. Enver Redzić, "O posebnosti bosanskih muslimana" [On the uniqueness of the Bosnian Muslims], *Pregled* 60, no. 4 (1970): 488.

66. Kasım Suljević, "Otpori tokovima muslimanske posebnosti" [The resistance to patterns of Muslim uniqueness], *Pregled* 60, no. 9 (1970): 264.

67. Bulajić, "Problemi samoopredeljenja," 267–68, cited in S. P. Ramet, *Three Yugoslavias*, 289.

68. For the reasons behind the recognition of the national status of Bosnian Muslims, see Redzić, "O posebnosti bosanskih muslimana." See also Husnija Kamberović, *Rasprave o nacionalnom identitetu Bošnjaka* [The discussions on the national identity of the Bosniaks] (Sarajevo: Institut za istoriju, 2009).

69. After the recognition of the national status of Muslims, there was a steady increase between 1969 and 1973 from 26 percent to 30 percent in the number of Communist Party members who had declared Muslim nationality, despite a decline of almost 9 percent in the membership of the Bosnian party. The same trend continued after 1973. See Burg, *Political Integration*, 46.

70. P. Ramet, "Die Muslime Bosniens als Nation," 109.

71. Wolfgang Höpken, "Die jugoslawischen Kommunisten und die bosnischen Muslime," in *Die Muslime in der Sowjetunion und in Jugoslawien* [The Muslims in the Soviet Union and Yugoslavia], ed. Andreas Kappeler, Gerhard Simon, and Georg Brunner (Cologne: Markus Verlag, 1989), 199.

72. Kjell Magnusson, "Bosnia-Herzegovina," in *Islam outside the Arab World*, ed. David Westerlund and Ingvar Svanberg (Richmond, UK: Curzon, 1999), 302.

73. See the speech by the president of the Bosnian party, in *Borba* (Belgrade), November 21, 1969, cited in Burg, *Conflict and Cohesion*, 71.

74. Burg, *Conflict and Cohesion*, 41.

75. Magnusson, "Bosnia-Herzegovina," 303.

76. Dušan Bilandzić, *Jugoslavija poslije Tita 1980–1985* [Yugoslavia after Tito, 1980–1985] (Zagreb: Globus, 1986), 134–36, cited in Jović, *Yugoslavia*, 178.

77. Magnusson, "Bosnia-Herzegovina," 303.

78. Robert K. Furtak, *Jugoslawien* (Hamburg: Hoffman and Campe Verlag, 1975), 158, cited in S. P. Ramet, *Three Yugoslavias*, 271.

79. Burg, *Political Integration*, 23. For the change in the socioeconomic conditions of the Bosnian Muslims, see David A. Dyker, "The Ethnic Muslims of Bosnia-Some Basic Socio-Economic Data," *Slavonic and East European Review* 50, no. 119 (1972): 238–56.

80. Cited in Jović, *Yugoslavia*, 190.

81. Through 1991, the Islamic Community was dominated by Slavic Muslims, and no Albanian ever became reis-ul-ulema in spite of the fact that Albanians constituted half of the Muslims in the former Yugoslavia. See Ferhat Šeta, *Reis-ul-uleme u Bosni i Hercegovini i Yugoslaviji od 1882 do 1991 godine* [The reis-ul-ulemas in Bosnia Herzegovina and in Yugoslavia from 1882 to 1991] (Sarajevo: PGD ISKRA, Visoko, 1991).

82. Babuna, "Bosnian Muslims and Albanians," 312.

83. Jović, *Yugoslavia*, 59.

84. Ibid., 64.

85. S. P. Ramet, *Three Yugoslavias*, 286.

86. Muhamed Filipović, "Smisao i domašaj Kardeljeve ispravke i kritike Staljinove definicije nacije za teoriju i praksu socijalisticke revolucije" [The meaning and the scope of Kardelj's correction and criticism of Stalin's definition of nation for the theory and practice of the socialist revolution], in *Nacionalno Pitanje u Jugoslovenskoj teoriji i praksi-Doprinos Edvarda Kardelja* [The national question in the Yugoslav theory and practice-contribution of Edvard Kardelj], ed. Drago Ćubrilović, Nijaz Duraković, and Franc Friškovec (Banja Luka, Yugoslavia: Glas, 1979), 157.

87. Jović, *Yugoslavia*, 62–63.

88. Irwin, "Islamic Revival," 444.

89. Jović, *Yugoslavia*, 66.

90. Tito, *Nacionalno pitanje i revolucija*, 274.

91. Ibid., 418.

92. Jović, *Yugoslavia*, 66.

93. S. P. Ramet, *Three Yugoslavias*, 287.

94. Mark Baskin, "The Secular State as Ethnic Entrepreneur: Macedonians and Bosnian Muslims in Socialist Yugoslavia," *Michigan Discussions in Anthropology* 7, no. 1 (1984): 112–13.

95. Holm Sündhaussen, *Geschichte jugoslawiens 1918–1980* [History of Yugoslavia, 1918–1980] (Stuttgart: Verlag W. Kohlhammer, 1982), 179; and Pedro Ramet, *Nationalism and Federalism in Yugoslavia, 1963–1983* (Bloomington: Indiana University Press, 1984), 59.

96. Baskin, "Secular State," 114–15.

97. For the major developments in the foreign policy of Yugoslavia in the 1950s, see Bruce McFarlane, *Yugoslavia: Politics, Economics and Society* (London: Pinter Publishers, 1988), 174–80.

98. Francine Friedman, *The Bosnian Muslim: Denial of a Nation* (Boulder, CO: Westview Press, 1996), 167.

99. Jović, *Yugoslavia*, 4.

100. Zachary Irwin, "Yugoslav Nonalignment in the 1980s," in *Yugoslavia in the 1980s*, ed. Pedro Ramet (Boulder, CO: Westview Press, 1985), 254.

101. George Klein and Milan J. Reban, *The Politics of Ethnicity in Eastern Europe* (Boulder, CO: East European Monographs, 1981), 258–59.

102. Irwin, "Yugoslav Nonalignment," 254–56.

103. Alvin Rubinstein, *Yugoslavia and the Nonaligned World* (Princeton, NJ: Princeton University Press, 1970), 184–95, 209–28.

104. For the Yugoslav model of socialism, see Branko Horvat, *An Essay on Yugoslav Society* (New York: International Arts and Sciences Press, 1967).

105. Friedman, *Bosnian Muslim*, 167.

106. Irwin, "Islamic Revival," 440–41.

107. For an example, see "Iz Islamskog Svijeta" [From the world of Islam], *Glasnik* 33, nos. 1–2 (1970): 64–67.

108. Irwin, "Islamic Revival," 442.

109. Friedman, *Bosnian Muslim*, 167.

110. For Nasser's and Sukarno's visits to Sarajevo, see Irwin, "Yugoslav Nonalignment," 256. For discussion of the reis-ul-ulema's interactions with foreign Muslim delegations, see Irwin, "Yugoslav Nonalignment," 256, and Velikonja, *Religious Separation*, 226.

111. "Posjeta delegacije iz Alzira Tuzli" [The visit of the Algerian delegation to Tuzla], *Glasnik* 32, nos. 10–12 (1969): 519; see also "Posjete stranih delegacija VIS-u" [The visits of the foreign delegations to the Islamic Community], *Glasnik* 34, nos. 1–2 (1971): 109.

112. The Yugoslav delegation had declined its invitation to the conference. Irwin, "Islamic Revival," 441.

113. For the visit of the Islamic delegation to Algiers in 1968, see "U posjeti prijatelskom Alžiru" [On the visit to friendly Algeria], *Glasnik* 32, nos. 1–2 (1969): 22–28.

114. For an example, see "Put na Hadž" [The journey to hadj], *Glasnik* 13, nos. 4–7 (1950): 130–36.

115. Rubinstein, *Yugoslavia*, 197.

116. Burg, *Political Integration*, 25–33.

117. Babuna, "Bosnian Muslims and Albanians," 302–3.

## References

### PERIODICALS
*Glasnik*
*Komunist*
*Oslobođenje*
*Pregled*
*Prilozi*

## SELECTED PUBLISHED WORKS

Babuna, Aydın. "The Bosnian Muslims and Albanians: Islam and Nationalism." *Nationalities Papers* 32, no. 2 (2004): 287–321

———. *Die nationale Entwicklung der bosnischen Muslime: Mit besonderer Berücksichtigung der österreichisch-ungarischen Periode* [The national development of the Bosnian Muslims: With special emphasis on the Austro-Hungarian Period]. Frankfurt: Peter Lang, 1996.

———. "National Identity, Islam, and Politics in Post-Communist Bosnia-Hercegovina." *East European Quarterly* 34, no. 4 (2006): 405–38.

———. "Zur Entwicklung der nationalen Identität der bosnischen Muslime" [On the development of the national identity of the Bosnian Muslims]. *Osteuropa* 46, no. 4 (1996): 331–42.

Banac, Ivo. "Bosnian Muslims: From Religious Community to Socialist Nationhood and Post Communist Statehood, 1918–1992." In *The Muslims of Bosnia-Herzegovina: Their Historic Development from the Middle Ages to the Dissolution of Yugoslavia*, ed. Mark Pinson, 129–53. Cambridge, MA: Harvard University Press, 1996.

Baskin, Mark. "The Secular State as Ethnic Entrepreneur: Macedonians and Bosnian Muslims in Socialist Yugoslavia." *Michigan Discussions in Anthropology* 7, no. 1 (1984): 99–133.

Bijedić, Džemal. "Razvoj SR Bosne i Hercegovine" [The development of the Socialist Republic of Bosnia-Herzegovina] In *Istorija i praksa SKJ* [The history and practice of the League of Communists of Yugoslavia], ed. Ljubinka Bogetić and Dragoljub Đurović. Belgrade: Književne Novine, 1984.

Burg, Steven L. *Conflict and Cohesion in Socialist Yugoslavia: Political Decision Making since 1966.* Princeton, NJ: Princeton University Press, 1983.

———. *The Political Integration of Yugoslavia's Muslims: Determinants of Success and Failure.* Pittsburgh: University of Pittsburgh, Russian and East European Studies Program, 1983.

Cohen, Lenard. *Broken Bonds: The Disintegration of Yugoslavia.* Boulder, CO: Westview Press, 1993.

Friedman, Francine. *The Bosnian Muslim: Denial of a Nation.* Boulder, CO: Westview Press, 1996.

Irwin, Zachary. "The Islamic Revival and the Muslims of Bosnia-Hercegovina." *East European Quarterly* 17, no. 4 (1984): 437–58.

———. "Yugoslav Nonalignment in the 1980s." In *Yugoslavia in the 1980s*, ed. Pedro Ramet, 249–71. Boulder, CO: Westview Press, 1985.

Jović, Dejan. *Yugoslavia: A State That Withered Away.* West Lafayette, IN: Purdue University Press, 2009.

Kamberović, Husnija. *Rasprave o nacionalnom identitetu Bošnjaka* [The discussions on the national identity of the Bosniaks]. Sarajevo: Institut za istoriju, 2009.

Lampe, John R. *Yugoslavia as History.* Cambridge: Cambridge University Press, 1996.

Lane, Ann. *Yugoslavia: When Ideals Collide.* New York: Palgrave Macmillan, 2004.

Magnusson, Kjell. "Bosnia-Herzegovina." In *Islam outside the Arab World*, ed. David Westerlund and Ingvar Svanberg, 297–314. Richmond, UK: Curzon Press, 1999.

Purivatra, Atıf. *Nacionalni i politicki razvitak Muslimana* [The national and political development of the Muslims]. Sarajevo: Svjetlost, 1970.

———. "O nacionalnom fenomenu bosanskohercegovačkih muslimana" [On the national phenomenon of the Bosnian-Herzegovinian Muslims]. *Pregled* 64, no. 10 (1974): 1019–29.

Ramet, Pedro. "Die Muslime Bosniens als Nation" [The Muslims of Bosnia as a nation]. In *Die Muslime in der Sowjetunion und in Jugoslawien* [The Muslims in the Soviet Union and Yugoslavia], ed. Andreas Kappeler, Gerhard Simon, and Georg Brunner, 107–17. Cologne: Markus Verlag, 1989.

———. *Nationalism and Federalism in Yugoslavia, 1963–1983.* Bloomington: Indiana University Press, 1984.

Ramet, Sabrina P. *The Three Yugoslavias: State-Building and Legitimation, 1918–2005.* Washington, DC: Woodrow Wilson Center Press; Bloomington: Indiana University Press, 2006.

Redzić, Enver. "O posebnosti bosanskih muslimana" [On the uniqueness of the Bosnian Muslims]. *Pregled* 60, no. 4 (1970): 457–88.

Rubinstein, Alvin. *Yugoslavia and the Nonaligned World.* Princeton, NJ: Princeton University Press, 1970.

Rusinow, Dennison. "Reopening of the 'National Question' in the 1960s." In *State Collapse in South-Eastern Europe: New Perspectives on Yugoslavia's Disintegration*, ed. Lenard Cohen and Jasna Dragović-Soso, 131–47. West Lafayette, IN: Purdue University Press, 2008.

Shoup, Paul. *Communism and the Yugoslav National Question.* New York: Columbia University Press, 1968.

Singleton, Fred. *A Short History of the Yugoslav Peoples.* Cambridge: Cambridge University Press, 1985.

Sündhaussen, Holm. *Geschichte jugoslawiens, 1918–1980* [History of Yugoslavia, 1918–1980]. Stuttgart: Verlag W. Kohlhammer, 1982.

Tito, Josip Broz. *Nacionalno pitanje i revolucija* [The national question and revolution]. Sarajevo: Svjetlost, 1979.

Velikonja, Mitja. *Religious Separation and Political Intolerance in Bosnia-Herzegovina.* College Station: Texas A&M University Press, 2003.

# CHAPTER 10

# Religion, Power, and Legitimacy in Ngo Dinh Diem's Republic of Vietnam

*Jessica M. Chapman*

That Ngo Dinh Diem's South Vietnamese administration was bookended by violent conflicts with religious entities—the sect crisis in 1955 and the Buddhist crisis in 1963—suggests that religion was critical to his quest to establish power and legitimacy, and that religion may provide the key to understanding his ultimate failure. Many have claimed that Diem, a devout Catholic from one of the most powerful Catholic families in Vietnam, was out of touch with the more than 80 percent of his countrymen who considered themselves Buddhist, and perhaps even incapable of asserting a legitimate right to lead them.[1] To make matters worse, he took advantage of the massive influx of Catholic refugees who fled from the North to the South after the Geneva Agreements in 1954 to establish a base of support for his government, rooting it in a community of outsiders.

Plain as these facts may be, historians have yet to tease out fully the relationship between religion and politics in Diem's Republic of Vietnam (RVN). The government's conflicts with the politicized Hoa Hao and Cao Dai religious organizations and the nationalistic Binh Xuyen criminal group, commonly referred to as "sects" in the sect crisis and the Buddhists in the Buddhist crisis, were not primarily religious in a doctrinal sense. Yet they stemmed from Diem's heavy-handed efforts to impose a universal ethical system—perhaps best characterized as a civic religion—on the people of South Vietnam in the form of personalism. Diem's administration imbued this Catholic-based philosophy with elements of Confucianism as part of an effort to appeal more broadly to the people of South Vietnam, but then undercut that appeal by pairing personalist propaganda with a patronage system that benefited Catholics and a violent political clampdown that targeted members of Vietnam's other religious groups disproportionately.[2] Diem had flirted with joining the priesthood as a young man and resided in US seminaries as an adult. He gave political privileges and positions of power to Catholics because of their belief systems and their institutional affiliations. It was not the beliefs of this minority religious group that spurred criticism against the southern government, but the system of patronage benefiting its members. As they pertained to South Vietnam's political history and that country's role in the Cold War, religious categories served to denote a system of political inclusion and exclusion based on group identification, rather than on inherently oppositional belief systems.[3]

Long before Diem came to power, Vietnam had a history of integrating external religions and philosophies with indigenous beliefs to form a unique religious and cultural identity that largely defined Vietnamese patriotism.[4] The people of premodern Vietnam assimilated tenets of Buddhism from India and Confucianism from China seamlessly into their existing beliefs in local deities and ancestor worship. As recent scholarship shows, both Confucianism and Buddhism in Vietnam underwent constant redefinition in response to changing historical conditions, in the manner of most enduring religions.[5] Confucianism, more a system of political and social organization than a religious framework, allowed for coexistence with other religious beliefs as long as they complemented each other or refrained from imposing on each other's dominant spheres of influence in society. As one group of Vietnamese scholars wrote, perhaps a bit too simplistically, "Wherever Buddhism went, it accommodated itself easily to the customs and lifestyles as well as historical and political circumstances of the local people and states."[6] Although Vietnam's adaptation of Buddhism might not have been quite this seamless, the country certainly did have a long history of religious assimilation and tolerance of multiple faith systems living side by side, often overlapping. However, in Vietnam's particular postcolonial context, several critical factors militated against the hybridization of Catholicism and other dominant religious traditions.

Perhaps the foremost reason for Vietnam's failure to subsume Catholic elements into its national religious culture was the explicit link between the Catholic Church and France's colonizing mission. Just as France sought to civilize and transform Vietnamese culture, politics, and society, the Catholic Church in Vietnam sought to convert followers rather than to assimilate with local traditions. As a result, the Catholic Church in Vietnam came to represent for many non-Catholic Vietnamese patriots an element of the French colonial regime that needed to be eradicated. Following their seizure of power in 1945 via the August Revolution, the Communist Vietminh first aimed to win support from Catholic communities but ultimately came to view them as legitimate targets of anticolonial violence. This violent persecution, much more prevalent in the North (where the Vietnamese Catholic Church was far more populous and powerful than it was in the South), drove Vietnamese Catholics to seek physical separation from the rest of society for the sake of security, as well as for cultural and religious solidarity. This pattern of separation continued as northern Catholics moved south between 1954 and 1956.

Diem, himself a product of both Mandarin and Catholic influences, set out to impose on his people a uniform ethical system under the rubric of personalism, a philosophy adapted from liberal French Catholic thinkers.[7] The philosophy proposed a middle ground between liberal capitalist and Communist models of development and envisioned a type of communal responsibility that seemed to coincide with Confucian thought. At the heart of Diem's version of personalism was anti-Communism, which he defined as the only true manifestation of Vietnamese patriotism.[8] His Ministry of Information iteratively defined all opponents of the Saigon government as Communists and thus traitors against the nation of Vietnam. This meant that the Cao Dai, the Hoa Hao, and the Binh Xuyen in 1955 and the Buddhists in 1963 automatically fell prey to charges of Communist collaboration, regardless of their real political motivations and connections. Diem took power in 1954; renowned for his insularity and his reluctance to trust outsiders, and proceeded quickly to establish a government comprising primarily his family members, close confidants, and known Catholics—in his mind the only people he could trust not to betray Vietnam to the Communists.

South Vietnamese society under Diem was thus inevitably bifurcated along Catholic and non-Catholic lines, the former holding disproportionate power relative to its percentage of the population and the latter often targeted by the government and oppressed for failing to conform to Diem's narrow vision of the personalist "national revolution" he sought to lead. However, at the heart of both the sect crisis and the Buddhist crisis rested questions of political representation, group autonomy, and freedom of expression, rather than the religious belief systems themselves.[9] In both cases, coalitions of groups and individuals formed in opposition to Diem's rule not because of their uniform religious beliefs, but because of their mutual objections to his government's nepotism and its oppressive, authoritarian policies. The two crises took on the cast of religious clashes for a number of reasons, not least of which was Diem's overwhelming identification of his government with Catholicism. He took aid from US Catholic organizations and placed Catholics in powerful administrative and military positions to the exclusion of non-Catholics who often commanded greater respect in the local communities in question. This served only to compound many Vietnamese nationalists' association of the Catholic Church with foreign rule.

Diem's Catholicism came to represent for many not only his authoritarianism, but also his connections to the United States, in an era when most politically engaged Vietnamese were determined to secure their national independence. Meanwhile, in challenging his government, the politically active religious organizations and to a far greater degree the Buddhists emphasized issues of religious persecution. Diem's pattern of excluding from power and persecuting individuals and groups in part on the basis of their non-Catholic religious identification precipitated both conflicts. His insularity and intolerance, coupled with the violent oppression exercised by his government against anyone who dared speak against it, gave the politicized religious groups and the Buddhists a moral high ground from which they could appeal to both their countrymen and international opinion. As we will see, the Buddhists in 1963 used this moral platform far more successfully than the Hoa Hao, the Cao Dai, and the Binh Xuyen, for myriad reasons.

## Diem, the Politico-Religious Organizations, and the Consolidation of Power

During the summer of 1954, as the First Indochina War (1946–1954) drew to a close, Chief of State Bao Dai appointed Diem prime minister of the State of Vietnam (SVN). He took this step while French and Vietnamese representatives to an international conference in Geneva negotiated a ceasefire agreement that divided Vietnam in two at the seventeenth parallel, with Ho Chi Minh and the Communist Vietminh in charge of the North, and Diem's anti-Communist, US-backed government in control of the South. The signatories intended the division to last only two years, at which point an International Control Commission would oversee nationwide reunification elections to determine the country's future leadership. Diem, however, refused to sign the agreement and later stonewalled talks to prepare for the elections, insisting that it would be impossible to conduct a fair vote in the North under a Communist system. His US patrons, determined above all to prevent the spread of Communism, assisted him in attempting to build a non-Communist bastion south of the seventeenth parallel.

Washington supported Diem from the outset. Indeed, the United States played a large if not decisive role in his selection as prime minister, mainly because of the vocal influence of the American Friends of Vietnam, a group of powerful politicians, academics, and Catholic leaders that he had cultivated during his stay in the United States from 1950 to 1953.[10] According to some historians, Washington backed Diem precisely because he was Catholic—and virulently anti-Communist—which made him far more palatable to Western sensibilities than his less understood and therefore less predictable Buddhist countrymen.[11] When Diem assumed power, US officials recognized that his government was fragile and beset by challenges from South Vietnam's non-Communist organizations. They hoped for his short-term survival and long-term success, but frequently during the first year of his administration their hope turned to doubt.

When Diem arrived in Saigon in June 1954, he was greeted by a crowd of barely five hundred, most of whom were Catholic.[12] As he took his oath of office in July, he exerted little real power over the country he was supposed to govern. Nguyen Van Hinh, the son of a former SVN prime minister with close ties to France, exerted independent control over the national army, which was by no means loyal to Diem. Meanwhile, roughly one-third of the countryside rested under the dominion of the Hoa Hao, the Cao Dai, and the Binh Xuyen. Of the three, the Hoa Hao and the Cao Dai were religious, while the Binh Xuyen was a purely political organization. The Binh Xuyen, often referred to as the "mafia of Vietnam," controlled the Saigon-Cholon police and security agency, and also held a monopoly on all the capital city's major vice industries.

The Cao Dai, a syncretistic religious organization, was founded in Tay Ninh, a province on the Cambodian border, in 1926. Its fundamental premise was that a single God had revealed itself in different ways at different times to the founders of every major religion, and that it had chosen to reveal this fact to the Vietnamese at this critical moment in world history to enable them to form a hybrid religion with the potential to do away with religious, ethnic, and national strife. Although it was anticolonial in its politics, the Cao Dai adopted the organizational structure of the Catholic Church, even to the point of appointing a pope of its own. It grew quickly to be the largest, most powerful, and most idiosyncratic of South Vietnam's politicized religious groups. The more conservative Hoa Hao was founded in 1939 in An Giang Province, farther south on the Vietnamese-Cambodian border, and spread rapidly throughout the Mekong Delta. It was rooted in ancient Chinese religious traditions and drew heavily on earlier Vietnamese anticolonial religious movements, though it was much less flamboyant than the Cao Dai. The Hoa Hao held broad appeal among the peasantry, as it espoused a form of Buddhism that eschewed emphases on exterior, material manifestations of the religion, such as costly offerings to ancestors, and advocated a more pure, interior practice of faith.[13]

All three groups developed autonomous political administrations sometimes referred to as "states within a state," complete with their own taxation systems and military organizations. The military leadership of both the Hoa Hao and the Cao Dai factionalized during the First Indochina War (1946–1954), but despite their turf battles, the various factions within and between the three organizations retained a base level of cooperation rooted in shared interests. All three groups detested the Vietminh, which had turned on all non-Communist nationalist leaders as it sought to consolidate power after the 1945 August Revolution. As a result, they were left with little choice but to change tack and ally with the French in 1947 and 1948 on the terms that they would defend their zones against Vietminh advances in exchange for equipment and financial subsidization. Thus, as the French War drew to a close, the Hoa Hao, the Cao Dai, and the Binh Xuyen relied heavily on French subsidies, even as they cast themselves as anticolonial, anti-Communist nationalists in hopes of earning greater representation in the postwar SVN. Especially during the final year of fighting, they vied with Diem's brother Ngo Dinh Nhu and other nationalist leaders for influence in the Saigon government. After the ceasefire, they faced the end of French financial support, which forced a crisis over how to maintain their military forces. Once Diem was appointed prime minister, they suddenly were reliant on him not only to provide for their troops—perhaps by integrating them into the national army—but also to appoint their representatives to positions of authority in the new administration commensurate with the control they exerted on the ground.

In the months preceding the ceasefire, as Diem's name was floated about as a potential leader for South Vietnam, sect spokesmen indicated that they knew too little about him to come out for or against him. One Hoa Hao general expressed reservations about appointing a Catholic to rule over a predominantly Buddhist population. Others worried that Diem's reputation for insularity and fence-sitting might limit his effectiveness and prompt him to exclude Vietnam's diverse political and religious groups from his government.[14] However, this did not necessarily indicate a religious divide, as even the Catholic bishop of Phat Diem Province in the North advised US officials that Diem lacked popular appeal and was unsuited to leadership.[15]

Representatives of the Cao Dai, the Hoa Hao, and the Binh Xuyen initially presented a facade support for Diem when he returned to Saigon to take office. But this veneer quickly crumbled when the prime minister formally took the helm and announced his cabinet in July 1954. His initial selection of government appointees spoke volumes of the manner in which he would shore up his administration by stonewalling and eventually eradicating all political opposition over the next two years. He packed his cabinet full of individuals with close ties to himself or his family, many of whom belonged to the country's Catholic minority. Religious leaders resented their near-total exclusion from real positions of power and realized that they needed to act quickly to confront Diem before he could coordinate the all-out attack he intended to launch against them.

The first challenge to Diem's government came in August 1954 with what is known as the Hinh crisis. In early August, the Cao Dai, the Hoa Hao, and the Binh Xuyen entered into a haphazard conspiracy with General Hinh and a few token anti-Diem Catholics to overthrow the government.[16] French leaders, who had been skeptical of Diem's prospects from the outset, suggested that Washington replace him with a coalition government to include representatives from the politicized religious organizations. However, the United States remained committed to Diem. The US ambassador to Vietnam, Donald Heath, assured Cao Dai general Nguyen Thanh Phuong that "any action or agitation against [the] Diem government at this time would have a very bad reaction in the US and abroad."[17] In the negotiations that ensued, a Cao Dai colonel conveyed to Heath the depth of his dissatisfaction with Diem's administration. He insisted that the prime minister's previously reported negotiations with the Hoa Hao, the Cao Dai, and the Binh Xuyen "had not been negotiations at all as Diem's representatives had been obscure and inept and no practical political concessions or accommodations had been proffered." He claimed Hinh and the three organizations were in the advanced stages of planning to overthrow Diem, and brazenly requested US permission to do so. In the end, though, he and other leaders of the three groups proved willing to cooperate with the prime minister if he agreed to broaden his government to include them in sufficiently powerful positions.[18]

As the crisis continued, it became evident to all that the Hoa Hao, the Cao Dai, and the Binh Xuyen would not be able to obtain their demands without support from the US, which eluded them. In early September, beginning with the powerful Cao Dai, they began to back out of the anti-Diem coalition. Although their leaders gave no indication that they were any more satisfied with Diem's rule than they had been prior to the standoff, they changed tack and entered into negotiations in an effort to secure significant representation in his cabinet.[19] According to US observers, initial demands by the Hoa Hao, the Cao Dai, and the Binh Xuyen were overambitious, but the crisis convinced US officials that the prime minister should make more of an effort to accommodate them. Heath concluded on September 14 that "there is no question *but that [Diem] must broaden support for his government if he is to survive*" (emphasis in the original).[20]

Although the Cao Dai, the Hoa Hao, and the Binh Xuyen suspended their efforts to overthrow the prime minister, they made clear their disgust with his conduct during the standoff. On September 16, Cao Dai, Binh Xuyen, and Hoa Hao leaders issued a joint declaration condemning Diem's exclusive, unresponsive leadership. They claimed that the conflict between the government and the army was "basically a rivalry for personal power and that it could result in bloody internal conflict." They blamed the government for failing to resolve the crisis adequately, criticizing Diem for thwarting the "legitimate aspirations of the people" and for pursuing policies that threatened to destroy Vietnam's nationalist base.[21]

The standoff continued for some time, as Hinh appeared determined to deploy the national army in a coup against Diem. By late September, though, it had become clear that a coup was not to be. On September 24, several Hoa Hao and Cao Dai leaders agreed to take up token positions in Diem's cabinet in exchange for financial compensation.[22] Finally, in November, Hinh abandoned his plot and fled to Paris, relinquishing command of the national army on his way out. An immediate crisis was averted, but this was not the end of the struggles between Diem and the Hoa Hao, the Cao Dai, and the Binh Xuyen.

In early 1955, Diem took a number of steps intended to neutralize potential opposition and consolidate his own power. That January, he announced his intention to nationalize the police and security agency owned and operated by the Binh Xuyen, and threatened to remove Binh Xuyen police chief Lai Van Sang from his post.[23] Shortly thereafter, he further antagonized the Binh Xuyen by refusing to renew its license to operate the profitable Grande Monde Casino in Cholon. Diem's crackdowns served as a troubling warning to other opposition leaders that he was prepared to risk confrontation rather than accommodate their existing power. His moves to strip power from the Binh Xuyen provoked hostility from all three groups and bound them together in defiance against his government.

What historians refer to as the sect crisis began on March 4, 1955.[24] That afternoon, the Cao Dai pope Pham Cong Tac announced the formation of the United Front of Nationalist Forces, an organization dominated by Hoa Hao, Cao Dai, and Binh Xuyen figures. It demanded that Diem reform his government to be more inclusive, protect individual sovereignty, and guarantee the right of individual political participation. In a barely veiled reference to Diem, the front denounced "dictatorship and sectarian policy which would provoke fratricidal war and cause [the] collapse of [the] nationalist cause."[25] Using funds channeled through Edward Lansdale, a CIA officer assigned to work closely with Diem, the prime minister made limited efforts to generate internal divisions within the United Front by bribing certain politico-religious factions to join the national army while stonewalling others. These efforts accomplished little, however.

On March 21, the United Front stepped up its ultimatum, this time with open support from the formerly pro-government Hoa Hao generals Trinh Minh The and Nguyen Thanh Phuong. The Cao Dai pope charged the prime minister with obstructing unification movements to keep the public divided for his own advantage, and accused him of governing through a system of nepotism and insularity that imperiled the nation. The front claimed that his management of refugee resettlement, during which 810,000 people—over 75 percent of whom were Roman Catholics—fled from the North to the South, was tainted with odious favoritism.[26] In what was surely motivated at least in part by the need to appeal to the United States for support, the pope insisted, "After nine months in power Diem has not been able to realize any program while the Vietnamese people are confused and Communist forces continue [to] advance."[27]

Despite their anti-Communist appeals, the politico-religious groups failed to win US sympathy. After the second United Front ultimatum, an existing rift between US and French officials over the future of Saigon's government began to deepen. Since the summer of 1954, France had been looking for reasons to deem the "Diem experiment" a failure, and its low regard for his leadership clashed with Washington's determination to support him. During late March and all through the next month, the sect crisis brought more and more pressure to bear on Diem's government to the point that its collapse began to appear almost inevitable. Several of the prime minister's key cabinet members resigned, and tensions grew even more intense following a violent clash between Binh Xuyen troops and government forces on the evening of March 30. France urged the United States to consider replacing Diem's administration with a coalition government that would share power among Bao Dai, politico-religious leaders, and other non-Communist nationalists, perhaps even including Diem.

As the crisis dragged on, French general Paul Ely and US special representative to Saigon J. Lawton Collins became increasingly frustrated with Diem's growing determination to isolate himself politically. The prime minister appeared less willing than ever to broaden his cabinet and consider input from individuals outside his immediate family and an ever-shrinking pool of personal advisers. On April 7, Collins sent a request to Secretary of State John Foster Dulles to consider replacing Diem. "His lack of practical political sense," wrote Collins, "his inability to compromise, his inherent incapacity to get along with other able men, and his tendency to be suspicious of the motives of anyone who disagrees with him, make him practically incapable of holding this government together."[28] Washington resisted the idea of abandoning Diem, but came to see little alternative as the crisis appeared to tip in the United Front's favor.[29]

Soon thereafter, a military clash between the Binh Xuyen and the Vietnamese national army turned the crisis on its head. Partly because two leading Cao Dai generals, Nguyen Thanh Phuong and Trinh Minh The, had recently defected from the front to join the national army, government forces pulled out a rapid and decisive victory in the Battle of Saigon. By April 30, Binh Xuyen rebel troops fled into the jungles surrounding the capital. The United Front disbanded, but many rebel leaders joined the newly formed Revolutionary Council, which angled to exert political pressure on Diem to reform his government. In response to Diem's swift and unexpected victory against Binh Xuyen forces, Dulles changed his tune. Disregarding prior evidence that the prime minister's nepotism and political favoritism might compromise his ability to lead, the secretary asserted, "Diem rightly or wrongly is becoming a symbol of nationalism struggling against French colonialism and corrupt backward elements."[30] To both Dulles and Diem, the Cao Dai, the Hoa Hao, and the Binh Xuyen were indeed "backward elements" that stood in the way of national unity and progress.

Within Vietnam, Diem's suppression of this challenge to his government generated little public reaction against his administration. This was in part because popular identification with the United Front agenda was limited, and in part because the resolution of the crisis itself signaled a new phase in which Diem's government proved both willing and able to stifle dissent through violent and intimidating tactics. In this instance, the Saigon government minimized its vulnerability to charges of religious intolerance by taking care not to attack religious organizations on grounds of belief-based doctrinal differences for fear of turning peaceful, largely apolitical followers against Diem. Instead, the prime minister denounced politically active religious leaders for characteristics that seemed to have little to do with their religious affiliation, including their violent tendencies, their unethical practices, their feudalism, and their connections to French colonialists and Communist agents. However, his association of the Hoa Hao, the Cao Dai, and the Binh Xuyen with feudalism, though subtle, was indeed an indictment of their belief systems as a hindrance to the political progress he wanted to deliver to the country. Meanwhile, the government's victory over the Binh Xuyen led many, especially among South Vietnam's military personnel, to invest some hope in his potential to generate stability and centralized order in what had been a highly fragmented South Vietnamese society.[31]

Prior to the Battle of Saigon, Diem had had little opportunity to exercise oppression—indeed, to implement a comprehensive governing strategy of any sort—as his prime focus had been surviving the onslaught of challenges against his administration. However, after the sect crisis, his administration, with Nhu's heavy involvement, sought to establish a network of institutions in the realms of politics, security, and propaganda that would preclude future challenges. Ironically, this would create the oppressive conditions that fueled popular support for the Buddhist movement in 1963.

After driving the Binh Xuyen out of the capital, Diem's first order of business was to pursue and destroy all the remaining rebels in order to prevent them from reconstituting and attempting to overthrow his government down the line. In May 1955, by launching the Nguyen Hue operation against his retreating opponents, he defied French and US advice to eschew a costly military campaign in favor of concentrating his resources and energy on reforming and training the national army and building South Vietnam's political infrastructure. In his words, his goal was to initiate a national revolution that would "destroy the sources of demoralization, however powerful, before getting down to the problem of endowing Vietnam with a democratic government in the Western sense of the word."[32] He accomplished one aspect of this by late summer 1956, by which time his forces had decimated remaining antigovernment armies and either killed their leaders or forced them into exile.

Concomitant to the Nguyen Hue operation, his administration began to construct a harsh security apparatus throughout the countryside. In July 1955, Nhu and his Can Lao (personalist Labor) Party inaugurated the Denounce the Communists Campaign, with a mission "to condemn indifferent, reactionary and pro-Communist attitudes."[33] Ostensibly aimed at rooting out Communist agents of the Hanoi government, the Denounce the Communists Campaign targeted a broad range of individuals and groups in the South that dared criticize Diem's administration.[34] In 1956, the prime minister expanded his program with an ordinance calling for the arrest and detention of all persons deemed dangerous to the state, which provided legal justification for creating political prison camps throughout the country and suspending all habeas corpus laws. He imposed a number of antitreason laws that permitted armed agents of his administration to terrorize anyone who demonstrated the inclination to challenge or criticize his government.[35] When the Ngo brothers intensified their oppressive security apparatus with the promulgation of Law 10/59 in May 1959, which authorized the death penalty for crimes "against the security of the state," their opponents were driven to oppose him more aggressively or risk total annihilation. This helped precipitate Hanoi's 1959 decision to back the resumption of armed struggle in the South, which fostered the creation of South Vietnam's National Liberation Front (NLF) in December 1960. According to Douglas Pike, a US Foreign Service officer who arrived in Saigon just in time to witness the formation of the NLF, "Many of the original participants in the NLF had turned to it because they had been denied participation in South Vietnam's political process even in the role of loyal opposition." These participants were drawn largely from Hoa Hao, Cao Dai and Binh Xuyen ranks, but also included members of several ethnic minority groups, idealistic youths recruited from universities and technical schools, representatives of framers' organizations in parts of the Mekong Delta plagued by serious land tenure problems, military deserters, and leaders of small parties or groups, and intellectuals who had been alienated from Diem's government.[36]

Undergirding the Ngos' attempts at securing the countryside and establishing political legitimacy was a heavy reliance on the support base provided by South Vietnam's Catholics, most of whom had fled from the North to the South after Article 14(d) of the 1954 Geneva accords mandated a three-hundred-day period of free movement between the two zones of Vietnam. In late 1955, Diem began to take charge of the process of resettling refugees from the North, who were overwhelmingly but not exclusively Catholic. Refugees fled for many reasons, but chief among them for Catholics was the fear that they would be targets of violence, retribution, and land seizure at the hands of a Vietminh government that associated the Catholic Church with the remnants of French power it so fervently sought to eradicate.[37] Recent research by Peter Hansen suggests that in late 1955, once Diem had finally established his authority in the South, refugee resettlement "was more heavily shaped by the Ngô Đình Diệm government's concerted efforts to move the Bắc di cư [refugees] in ways that would fulfill certain long-term economic, security, and political goals."[38] It was then that the government began moving refuges out of crowded areas and into more thinly populated areas in the Mekong Delta and Central Highlands.

Jean Lacouture and others have suggested that Diem deliberately resettled Catholic refugees strategically to create a "ring of steel" around Saigon to protect himself from Communists and other enemies of his government.[39] Hansen, however, argues that the government's involvement with resettlement, while undoubtedly serving political and military ends, was more haphazard and circumstantial than Lacouture allows. Moreover, he maintains that the refugees themselves played a large role in determining their destinations and in making the decision to settle in distinct communities rather than dispersing themselves among the southern population. This pattern prevented assimilation and encouraged the people of South Vietnam to think of Buddhists and Catholics as separate groups with different and often conflicting interests. Despite his skillful complication of the myth of Diem as the strategic mastermind of the resettlement process, Hansen still concludes, "By the late 1950s . . . the growing popular resentment toward northern Catholics was fueled by the perception that they were receiving special treatment from their coreligionist Ngô Đình Diệm."[40] Indeed, Catholics were heavily overrepresented in the upper ranks of South Vietnam's public administration, military, judiciary, and educational system. Not all Catholics benefited from such favoritism, but the overwhelming system of partiality that did exist created a model of political inclusion and exclusion apparently predicated on religious affiliation. This fueled the resentment toward Diem's government that erupted in the 1963 Buddhist crisis.

The most vocal and potent opposition to Diem's government during that final crisis of his administration would come from students, politicians, religious figures, and other disaffected residents of South Vietnam's urban centers. Much of their frustration with the government harkened back to Diem's management—or mismanagement—of land reform and village governance in the countryside, and of the general repression that accompanied the administration's quest to consolidate power in rural areas. Such urban opposition to Diem's rural policies became abundantly evident as early as 1960, when a group of eighteen senior Saigon politicians met with US officials at the famous Caravelle Hotel in Saigon to express their grievances with the government. They primarily focused on the Ngos' policies in the countryside, which were driving the peasantry to support the Communists. They also demanded US assistance with ending Vietnam's press censorship and detentions without trial, as well as stopping the abuses committed by Nhu's secret police.[41] These concerns expressed by the Caravelle group were widespread in South Vietnamese society. Indeed, similar complaints led Diem's own military to stage an unsuccessful coup attempt within a few months. From this early stage, then, Diem's urban opponents aligned their cause against his oppressive policies in the countryside. When they witnessed the Ngos' increasingly violent suppression of Buddhist protestors and sympathizers in the summer of 1963, they viewed it as another manifestation of the system of repression and exclusion that the administration had long pursued in the villages of South Vietnam.

## The Buddhist Crisis of 1963

The clash between the Saigon government and South Vietnam's Buddhists that began in early May 1963 stemmed from the way Diem structured his administration, the favoritism he bestowed on his coreligionists, and the intolerance he displayed for modes of political and religious expression that deviated from the personalist norms he had set in place using the Ministry of Information and enforced via his brother's antisubversive security system. The fallout it produced against Diem came not only from Buddhist officials, but from a much broader range of individuals dissatisfied with his regime. The fact that public opinion both within South Vietnam and internationally sided squarely with the Buddhist plight and against Diemist oppression, callousness, and intransigence forced a rift between the United States and Diem that ultimately led US officials to withdraw their backing of the prime minister and tacitly support the military coup that ended his administration and his life.

The Buddhist crisis began on the evening of May 8, 1963, when violence broke out in the imperial capital of Hue between government officials and Buddhist followers who had gathered for a peaceful celebration of the Buddha's 2,527th birthday. The previous day, the local province chief in charge of security—himself a Catholic—had invoked Decree 10, a law on the books since 1958 that had been previously ignored. The decree prohibited the display of religious flags without special permission from local authorities. This provocation came from the top; Diem himself had sent the order to invoke the decree. Buddhists found the resulting restriction on their religious expression particularly infuriating since just one week earlier, the city's Catholics had brandished their white and gold papal streamers freely in honor of the twenty-fifth anniversary of Diem's brother Ngo Dinh Thuc as archbishop. On May 7, as soon as they learned that local officials were prohibiting them from doing the same type of display, Hue's Buddhist residents unfurled thousands of multicolored flags atop their homes and pagodas in open defiance of the law. The next morning, the bonze (highest-ranking monk) in residence gave a speech condemning Diem's government for its repression of religious freedom and its favoritism to Catholics, and proclaimed that "now is time to fight."[42] By that night, the celebration of the Buddha's birthday morphed into a demonstration of protest in front of the Hue radio station, in response to which the police fired into an assembly that US officials described as "apparently not unruly but perhaps deemed menacing by authorities." Several among the crowd were killed or wounded. US reports indicated that some, as the crowd dispersed, were heard chanting, "Down with Catholicism."[43] Religious conflict clearly prompted the outbreak of this crisis; yet, as historian Philip Catton shrewdly observes, the incident "also served as a lightning rod for all those discontented with the palace's incumbents."[44]

On the evening of May 9, the RVN-controlled National Revolutionary Movement (NRM) attempted to stage a meeting to cast the violence of the night before as a Vietcong terrorist act. This reflected the Ngo brothers' longstanding conflation of all dissent against the Saigon government with Communist conspiracy. According to the historian Howard Jones, "It seems safe to say that the Diem regime believed what it said—that the Vietcong was using the Buddhists to achieve its own ends and that the cry of religious oppression had no basis in fact."[45] However, rather than buying the administration's line that the Buddhist demonstrations and resulting violence were part of a Communist plot, the people of Hue failed to appear for the NRM meeting, and large groups—primarily youths—marched around the old citadel at the heart of the old capital denouncing Diem's government. Meanwhile, the leading bonze Thich Tri Quang angled to turn the local incident into a national rallying point for South Vietnam's citizens, asking them to unite in mourning the dead from May 8 and in opposing Diem's system of oppression.[46] In a private meeting with US officials, he insisted that Diem was the source of all discord and warned, "The United States must either make Diem reform or get rid of him. If not, the situation will degenerate, and you worthy gentlemen will suffer most."[47]

On May 10, the Buddhist bonzes and faithful at Tu Dam Pagoda in Hue issued a manifesto requesting that the government take the following five actions to ameliorate the crisis and improve Catholic-Buddhist relations in the South: to permanently retract the official cable repressing the Buddhist religious flag; to grant the Buddhists an exception to Decree 10 similar to that afforded to Catholics, Protestants, and Chinese missions; to stop arresting and terrorizing Buddhist followers; to allow Buddhist bonzes and faithful the freedom to preach and observe their religion; and to provide compensation for those killed in the May 8 melee and mete out proper punishment to the instigators of the murders.[48] On May 13, a government representative met with Buddhists in Hue to discuss the manifesto, but ultimately deemed most of their demands groundless and noted that the ultimatum-like tone of their message was a mistake. Two days later, Buddhist leaders met with Diem in Saigon for further discussion.

Violence soon spread from Hue to Saigon and other locales across South Vietnam. Buddhist monks protested what they viewed as religious discrimination and terrorism carried out by the Catholic-dominated Diem government. The vocal few leading the protests claimed to have a mandate from heaven to stage a revolution against the current administration; a revolution aimed at securing religious freedom.[49] Those who advanced this confrontational approach were politically active Mahayana monks who, in response to Diem's oppressive measures, had by mid-1963 pushed aside more low-key, apolitical Theravada monks to hold the center of Buddhist control. One of the key leaders was Thich Tri Quang, about whose political orientation policy makers and historians have long speculated. Most recently, the historian Mark Moyar has argued, as Diem did, that Thich was a Communist agent.[50] However, James McAllister has provided a much more compelling case, asserting that Thich was not a Communist subversive, but that he, like many other Vietnamese nationalists, communicated with Communist agents to coordinate methods of contesting the oppression stemming from Saigon's successive governments.[51] McAllister argues convincingly that Thich and his fellow monks were motivated by the imperative of protecting Vietnamese Buddhists from Diem's persecution, not by Communist convictions. However, while the contention that "only religions count in Vietnam" may have applied to Thich and his cohort, they attracted support from a much broader swath of southerners who sought to escape Diemist persecution of all types. Most Vietnamese people at the time embraced a patchwork of religious and political beliefs that included Buddhism, but the majority were not Buddhists in a strict sense, and thus were represented by the monks more as a result of their shared resistance to Diem's oppression in general than because of religious oppression in particular.

The Buddhist crisis reached its climax on June 11, when an elderly monk, Thich Quang Duc, sat calmly in the lotus position in the middle of a busy Saigon street and set himself on fire. This first and most shocking in the series of Buddhist self-immolations in South Vietnam that summer seared an image of martyrdom in the minds of observers at home and abroad. US support for Diem began to wane as he appeared more and more the violent persecutor of peaceful protestors who seemed to demand nothing more than the right to practice their religion freely. US-RVN relations continued to deteriorate over the summer when, rather than responding to Washington's requests that he respond peacefully and diplomatically to the Buddhists' demands, Diem and his army engaged in a brutal crackdown that turned domestic and international opinion irrevocably against the Ngo family. On July 7—"Double Seven Day," the anniversary of Diem's ascent to power—a violent clash erupted outside a Buddhist ceremony in Saigon between Diem's forces and US journalists whose reports had become increasingly critical of the president. Thereafter, the CIA speculated that the Buddhist protest "may well have transformed itself into an entirely new political force whose aims transcend the basically religious purposes for which it was originally set in motion."[52]

Diem, convinced that the Buddhist protestors were Communist agents intent on harming the war effort against the NLF, failed to recognize the movement's increasingly popular appeal. He continued to authorize violent military crackdowns on Buddhist activity. A series of brutal attacks and arrests by government forces at Buddhist pagodas throughout South Vietnam the night of August 21, accompanied by a declaration of martial law, put the final nail in the coffin of US support for his government. From then on, it was a downward slide toward tacit US support for a coup. Early in the morning of November 2, 1963, Diem and his brother Nhu died at the hands of their own military officers, not because they were Catholic, but because their administration's actions over the short and long terms had lost them the domestic and international support necessary to retain power.

Diem responded as he did to the 1963 Buddhist protests for two key reasons. First, he viewed the Buddhist opposition with reference to the politico-religious movement that had challenged his government in 1955. From the sect crisis and its aftermath, he had gleaned that the best way to respond to dissent was to crush and delegitimize its leaders while disclaiming its premises. His instincts had led him in this direction long before he assumed power, and the apparent success of this strategy reinforced his gut perceptions. Between 1955 and 1959, his administration built up an extensive security and propaganda apparatus designed to stifle opposition by conflating dissent with Communism and condemning practitioners of the latter to the harshest punishments. By the early 1960s, despite the radically altered military and political circumstances in Vietnam and on the international stage, he appeared unable to recognize how his countrymen as well as his US backers would respond differently to the Buddhist crisis. His miscalculation would cost him US support, which allowed the murderous military coup against him and his brother to succeed in October 1963. In turn, these events undermined the already imperiled US-RVN project of keeping South Vietnam out of Communist hands, a project that had consumed Diem throughout his rule.

As the historian Robert Topmiller notes, the greatest significance of the Buddhist crisis to Vietnam's political history was the extent to which it "exposed wide divisions in South Vietnamese society and close to universal opposition to Diem's dictatorial rule."[53] What started out as a limited movement by a small number of Buddhists in Hue to assert their right to free religious expression rapidly drew support from a range of individuals throughout South Vietnam who opposed Diem's government for its generally oppressive practices and for its cronyism, the latter benefiting a small cohort of mainly— though not exclusively—Catholic figures. His attempts to undermine the Buddhists' moral legitimacy by hurling at them accusations of Communist conspiracy and his efforts to stamp out peaceful Buddhist protests through brutal force rather than meaningful reforms, negotiation, or conciliation further inflamed public opinion within Vietnam and confirmed widely held beliefs among the populace that his administration served to inhibit rather than foster national political independence and individual liberties.

The United States read this writing on the wall to a woefully limited extent. By fall 1963, Washington perceived the need to withdraw support for Diem in order to retain any hope of preserving a non-Communist Vietnam south of the seventeenth parallel. However, what US policy makers failed to recognize sufficiently was that the people of Vietnam who had in recent years been tempted with promises of freedom, independence, and political inclusion—and tormented by a brutally oppressive state security apparatus and an inadequate land reform program—would not be satisfied by the mere ouster of Diem and Nhu. Nor did South Vietnam's disenfranchised majority long simply for the authoritarian reimposition of order and security that most Americans expected would shore up the RVN against Communist threats.[54] After the military coup that toppled the Ngos, many Vietnamese quite accurately viewed successive US-backed regimes as continuations of the Diemist clique that sought to preserve access to power for a select few while suppressing dissent—indeed political expression of all sorts—in the name of anti-Communism.[55] The irony, of course, was that this served only to encourage support for and participation in the NLF among significant non-Communist segments of the population, including Buddhists of many branches. Most of those who turned to the NLF did so not because of any faith-based objection to Catholic leadership, nor out of any particular zeal for Communist philosophy. They did so as a means of reclaiming agency over their own lives and asserting the stake in their country's political system of which they had so long been deprived, first under French colonialism and then under Diem.

## Notes

1. Piero Gheddo, *The Cross and the Bo-Tree: Catholics and Buddhists in Vietnam*, trans. Charles Underhill Quinn (New York: Sheed and Ward, 1970); see also Frances FitzGerald, *Fire in the Lake: The Vietnamese and the Americans in Vietnam* (New York: Vintage Books, 1972), 97.

2. Diem's melding of ideas borrowed from the West with Confucian traditions was common among Vietnamese anticolonial leaders after the turn of the twentieth century. See Mark Philip Bradley, *Vietnam at War* (New York: Oxford University Press, 2009), 9–39.

3. On religion as an identity category as opposed to a doctrinal differentiation, see Jonathan Z. Smith, *Imagining Religion: From Babylon to Jonestown* (Chicago: University of Chicago Press, 1982).

4. See, for example, Pham Quynh Phuong and Chris Eipper, "Mothering and Fathering the Vietnamese: Religion, Gender, and National Identity," *Journal of Vietnamese Studies* 4, no. 1 (2009): 49–83.

5. Liam C. Kelley, "'Confucianism' in Vietnam: A State of the Field Essay," *Journal of Vietnamese Studies* 1, no. 1–2 (February 2006): 314–70; Alexander Woodside, "Classical Primordialism and the Historical Agenda of Vietnamese Confucianism," in *Rethinking Confucianism: Past and Present in China, Japan, Korea, and Vietnam*, ed. Benjamin A. Elman, John B. Duncan, and Herman Ooms (Los Angeles: UCLA Asian Pacific Monograph Series, 2002), 116–43; and Shawn McHale, "Mapping a Vietnamese Confucian Past and Its Tradition to Modernity," in Elman, Duncan, and Ooms, *Rethinking Confucianism*, 397–430.

6. Minh Chi, Ha Van Tan, and Nguyen Tai Thu, *Buddhism in Vietnam from Its Origins to the 19th Century* (Hanoi: The Gioi, 1999), 13.

7. On French personalism, see John Hellman, *Emmanuel Mounier and the New Catholic Left, 1930–1950* (Toronto: University of Toronto Press, 1981); Eugene Weber, *The Hollow Years: France in the 1930s* (New York: Norton, 1994); and Jean-Louis Loubet del Bayle, *Les non-conformistes des années 30: Une tentative de renouvellement de la pensée politique française* [The nonconformists of the 1930s: An attempt at revitalizing French political thought] (Paris: Editions de Seuil, 1969). On personalism and the Republic of Vietnam, see John C. Donnell, "Politics in South Vietnam: Doctrines of Authority in Conflict" (PhD diss., University of California, Berkeley, 1964); Philip E. Catton, *Diem's Final Failure: Prelude to America's War*

*in Vietnam* (Lawrence: University Press of Kansas, 2002); Edward Miller, "Vision, Power, and Agency: The Ascent of Ngô Đình Diệm, 1945–1954," *Journal of Southeast Asian Studies* 35, no. 3 (October 2004): 433–58; and Matthew B. Masur, "Hearts and Minds: Cultural Nation Building in South Vietnam, 1954–1963" (PhD diss., Ohio State University, 2004).

8. See *Achievements of the Campaign of Denunciation of Communist Subversive Activities (First Phase)* ([Saigon?], Republic of Vietnam: People's Committee for the Denunciation of Communist Subversive Activity [CDCSA], 1956).

9. The term "sect," commonly used to refer to the Hoa Hao, Cao Dai, and Binh Xuyen, is inaccurate, since only the Hoa Hao and Cao Dai were religious, while the Binh Xuyen more closely resembled a mafia group. Therefore, I refer to these three organizations throughout this chapter as politico-religious organizations. However, because the clash between these organizations and the Saigon government in the spring of 1955 is widely known as the "sect crisis," I employ that term when discussing the event.

10. On Washington's role in Diem's appointment, see Joseph Morgan, *The Vietnam Lobby: The American Friends of Vietnam, 1955–1975* (Chapel Hill: University of North Carolina Press, 1997); David L. Anderson, *Trapped by Success: The Eisenhower Administration in Vietnam, 1953–1961* (New York: Columbia University Press, 1991), 53; Catton, *Diem's Final Failure*, 6–7; Denis Warner, *The Last Confucian* (New York: Macmillan, 1963), 65–66; Dennis J. Duncanson, *Government and Revolution in Vietnam* (New York: Oxford University Press, 1968), 210; Miller, "Vision, Power, and Agency," 441–47, 454–65; and Seth Jacobs, *America's Miracle Man in Vietnam: Ngo Dinh Diem, Religion, Race, and U.S. Intervention in Southeast Asia, 1950–1957* (Durham, NC: Duke University Press, 2004), 52–56. Miller and Jacobs continued this debate in "*America's Miracle Man in Vietnam* Roundtable," *H-Diplo Roundtable Review* 8, no. 6 (June 12, 2007), *www.h-net.org/~diplo*.

11. For the most recent and thoroughly developed version of this argument, see Jacobs, *America's Miracle Man*, especially 1–87.

12. Stanley Karnow, *Vietnam: A History* (New York: Penguin Books, 1984), 218.

13. Victor L. Oliver, *Caodai Spiritism: A Study of Religion in Vietnamese Society* (Leiden, Netherlands: Brill, 1976); Gabriel Gobron, *History and Philosophy of Caodaism* (Saigon: Le Van Tan Printing House, 1950); Bernard B. Fall, "The Political-Religious Sects of Viet-Nam," *Pacific Affairs* 28 (September 1955): 235–53; Hue Tam Ho Tai, *Radicalism and the Origins of the Vietnamese Revolution* (Cambridge, MA: Harvard University Press, 1992); Hue Tam Ho Tai, *Millenarianism and Peasant Politics in Vietnam* (Cambridge, MA: Harvard University Press, 1983); Jayne Susan Werner, *Peasant Politics and Religious Sectarianism: Peasant and Priest in the Cao Dai in Viet Nam* (New Haven, CT: Yale University Southeast Asian Studies, 1981); R. B. Smith, "An Introduction to Caodaism I: Origins and Early History," *Bulletin of the School of Oriental and African Studies* 33, no. 2 (1970): 335–49; R. B. Smith, "An Introduction to Caodaism II: Beliefs and Organization," *Bulletin of the School of Oriental and African Studies* 33, no. 3 (1970): 586–89; Frances R. Hill, "Millenarian Machines in South Vietnam," *Comparative Studies in Society and History* 13, no. 3 (July 1971): 335; and

Joann L. Schrock, William Stockton Jr., Elaine M. Murphy, and Marilou Fromme, eds., *Minority Groups in the Republic of Vietnam* (Washington, DC: Cultural Information Analysis Center, Ethnographic Study Series, 1966).

14. "Note au sujet du Président Tran Van Huu—Bruits concernant la formation d'un nouveau gouvernement—Départ pour la France de M. Vuong Quang Nhuong, Ngo Dinh Diem" [Note on the subject of President Tran Van Huu—Rumors concerning the formation of a new government—Departure for France of M. Vuong Quang Nhuong, Ngo Dinh Diem], July 27, 1953, Center of Overseas Archives (Centre des Archives d'Outre Mer; hereafter CAOM), Aix-en-Provence, France, HCI, SPCE 361; and "Activités politiques et gouvernementales vietnamiennes," Haute Commisariat de France en Indochine, Direction des Services de Sécurité, August 8, 1953, CAOM, HCI 267/768.

15. Cited in Jacobs, *America's Miracle Man*, 57.

16. Bishop Le Huu Tu was one of the most notable Catholic leaders in league with Nguyen Van Hinh and the sects at this time.

17. Telegram from US Embassy in Saigon to Department of State, August 13, 1954, National Archives and Records Administration II (hereafter NARA II), College Park, MD, Record Group (RG) 59, 751G.00/8-1354.

18. Telegram from US Embassy in Saigon to Department of State, August 26, 1954, NARA II, RG 59, 751G.00/8-2654.

19. Telegram from US Embassy in Saigon to Secretary of State, September 8, 1954, NARA II, RG 59, 751G.00/9-854.

20. Telegram from US Embassy in Saigon to Secretary of State, September 14, 1954, NARA II, RG 59, 751G.00/9-1454.

21. Telegram from US Embassy in Saigon to Secretary of State, September 17, 1954, NARA II, RG 59, 751G.00/9-1754.

22. Telegram from US Embassy in Saigon to Secretary of State, September 24, 1954, NARA II, RG 59, 751G.00/9-2454.

23. In 1953, the Binh Xuyen had purchased the Saigon-Cholon police concession from Bao Dai for $1.2 million.

24. Jessica M. Chapman, "The Sect Crisis of 1955 and the American Commitment to Ngô Đình Diệm," *Journal of Vietnamese Studies* 5, no. 1 (February 2010): 37–85.

25. Telegram from US Embassy in Saigon to Secretary of State, March 8, 1955, NARA II, RG 59, C0008, Reel 2, 751G.00/3-855.

26. Peter Hansen, "Bắc Đi Cư: Catholic Refugees from the North of Vietnam, and Their Role in the Southern Republic, 1954–1959," *Journal of Vietnamese Studies* 4, no. 3 (Fall 2009): 173–211.

27. Telegram from US Embassy in Saigon to Secretary of State, containing the full text of the March 21 declaration of the United Front of Nationalist Forces and the March 22 motion by politico-religious organizations transmitted to Ngo Dinh Diem, March 22, 1955, NARA II, RG 59, C0008, Reel 2, 751G.00/3-2255.

28. Telegram from US Embassy in Saigon to Secretary of State, April 7, 1955, NARA II, RG 59, C0008, Reel 2, 751G.00/4-755.

29. Telegram from Secretary of State to US Embassy in Saigon and US Embassy in Paris, April 27, 1955, NARA II, RG 59, C0008, Reel 3, 751G.00/4-2755.

30. Telegram from Secretary of State to US Embassy in Vietnam, May 1, 1955, in US Department of State, Office of the Historian, *Foreign Relations of the United States, 1955–1957*, vol. 21, *East Asian Security* (Washington, DC: US Government Printing Office, 1990), 344.
31. Rufus Phillips, *Why Vietnam Matters* (Annapolis, MD: Naval Institute Press, 2008), 82.
32. *President Ngo Dinh Diem* (Saigon: Presidency of the Republic of Vietnam Press Office, 1957), 13.
33. *Achievements*, 67.
34. Robert Scigliano, *South Vietnam: Nation under Stress* (Boston: Houghton Mifflin, 1963), 167.
35. FitzGerald, *Fire in the Lake*, 112.
36. Douglas Eugene Pike, *Viet Cong: The Organization and Techniques of the National Liberation Front of South Vietnam* (Cambridge, MA: MIT Press, 1966), 83.
37. Lan T. Chu, "Catholicism vs. Communism, Continued: The Catholic Church in Vietnam," *Journal of Vietnamese Studies* 3, no. 1 (February 2008): 157.
38. Hansen, "Bắc Đi Cư," 194.
39. Jean Lacouture, *Vietnam: Between Two Truces*, trans. Konrad Kellen and Joel Carmichael (New York: Vintage, 1966), 105.
40. Hansen, "Bắc Đi Cư," 200.
41. See FitzGerald, *Fire in the Lake*, 149–50.
42. Document 116, telegram from the consulate at Hue to the Department of State, May 10, 1963, in US Department of State, *Foreign Relations of the United States, 1961–1963*, vol. 3, *Vietnam, January–August 1963* [hereafter *FRUS* 1963] (Washington, DC: US Government Printing Office, 1991), 284–85.
43. Document 112, telegram from the consulate at Hue to the Department of State, May 9, 1963, *FRUS* 1963, 277–78.
44. Catton, *Diem's Final Failure*, 192.
45. Howard Jones, *Death of a Generation: How the Assassinations of Diem and JFK Prolonged the Vietnam War* (New York: Oxford University Press, 2003), 252.
46. Document 116, telegram from the consulate at Hue to the Department of State, May 10, 1963, *FRUS* 1963, 284–85.
47. Quoted in Jones, *Death of a Generation*, 249.
48. Document 118, manifesto of Vietnamese Buddhist clergy and faithful, May 10, 1963, *FRUS* 1963, 287–88.
49. Ellen J. Hammer, *Death in November: America in Vietnam, 1963* (New York: Dutton, 1987), 83–84; and Jones, *Death of a Generation*, 247–48. The traditional Confucian notion of a "mandate of heaven" held that a leader, as long as he remained ethical, would retain heaven's sanction to govern and legitimacy in the eyes of his constituents, but as soon as he compromised his position as a benevolent leader, he would immediately lose the will of heaven and with it the support of the people. The allegiance of both would shift to a newly anointed sovereign.
50. Mark Moyar, "Political Monks: The Militant Buddhist Movement during the Vietnam War," *Modern Asian Studies* 38, no. 4 (October 2004): 749–84.

51. James McAllister, "'Only Religions Count in Vietnam': Thich Tri Quang and the Vietnam War," *Modern Asian Studies* 42, no. 4 (July 2008): 751–82.

52. Quoted in Jones, *Death of a Generation*, 286.

53. Robert J. Topmiller, *Lotus Unleashed: The Buddhist Peace Movement in South Vietnam, 1964–1966* (Lexington: University Press of Kentucky, 2002), 2–3.

54. See Mark Moyar, *Triumph Forsaken: The Vietnam War, 1954–1965* (Cambridge: Cambridge University Press, 2006). Moyar argues that Diem was indeed succeeding as a strongman leader in South Vietnam until US leaders misguidedly advised him to undertake liberalizing reforms. Moyar's work has provoked a great deal of discussion among scholars of the Vietnam War. See, for example, Andrew Wiest and Michael Doidge, *Triumph Revisited: Historians Battle for the Vietnam War* (New York: Routledge, 2010).

55. See McAllister, "Only Religions Count." Though McAllister may overemphasize the role that religious doctrine and identification played in generating and sustaining popular opposition to Diem's government and the administrations that succeeded it, he points out quite rightly that Buddhists and other politically active South Vietnamese—many of whom were non-Communist if not anti-Communist—objected to the series of governments that followed from Diem's assassination because they represented a structural continuation of the corrupt, nepotistic Diemist clique that the country had condemned so broadly during the 1963 Buddhist crisis.

## References

### ARCHIVES

Center of Overseas Archives (Centre des Archives d'Outre Mer), Aix-en-Provence, France

General Sciences Library (Thu Vien Khoa Hoc Tong Hoc), Ho Chi Minh City, Vietnam

National Archives and Records Administration II, College Park, MD

Vietnamese National Archives II (Trung Tam Luu Tru Quoc Gia Viet Nam), Ho Chi Minh City, Vietnam

### SELECTED PUBLISHED WORKS

*Achievements of the Campaign of Denunciation of Communist Subversive Activities (First Phase).* [Saigon?], Republic of Vietnam: People's Committee for the Denunciation of Communist Subversive Activity (CDCSA), 1956.

Bradley, Mark Philip. *Vietnam at War.* New York: Oxford University Press, 2009.

Catton, Philip E. *Diem's Final Failure: Prelude to America's War in Vietnam.* Lawrence: University Press of Kansas, 2002.

Chapman, Jessica M. "The Sect Crisis of 1955 and the American Commitment to Ngô Đình Diệm." *Journal of Vietnamese Studies* 5, no. 1 (February 2010): 37–85.

FitzGerald, Frances. *Fire in the Lake: The Vietnamese and the Americans in Vietnam.* New York: Vintage Books, 1972.

Gheddo, Piero. *The Cross and the Bo-Tree: Catholics and Buddhists in Vietnam.* Trans. Charles Underhill Quinn. New York: Sheed and Ward, 1970.

Hansen, Peter. "Bắc Đi Cư: Catholic Refugees from the North of Vietnam, and Their Role in the Southern Republic, 1954–1959." *Journal of Vietnamese Studies* 4, no. 3 (Fall 2009): 173–211.

Jacobs, Seth. *America's Miracle Man in Vietnam: Ngo Dinh Diem, Religion, Race, and U.S. Intervention in Southeast Asia, 1950–1957.* Durham, NC: Duke University Press, 2004.

Jones, Howard. *Death of a Generation: How the Assassinations of Diem and JFK Prolonged the Vietnam War.* New York: Oxford University Press, 2003.

Masur, Matthew B. "Hearts and Minds: Cultural Nation Building in South Vietnam, 1954–1963." PhD diss., Ohio State University, 2004.

McAllister, James. "'Only Religions Count in Vietnam': Thich Tri Quang and the Vietnam War." *Modern Asian Studies* 42, no. 4 (July 2008): 751–82.

Miller, Edward. "Vision, Power, and Agency: The Ascent of Ngô Đình Diệm, 1945–1954." *Journal of Southeast Asian Studies* 35, no. 3 (October 2004): 433–58.

Moyar, Mark. "Political Monks: The Militant Buddhist Movement during the Vietnam War." *Modern Asian Studies* 38, no. 4 (October 2004): 749–84.

———. *Triumph Forsaken: The Vietnam War, 1954–1965.* Cambridge: Cambridge University Press, 2006.

Pham Quynh Phuong, and Chris Eipper. "Mothering and Fathering the Vietnamese: Religion, Gender, and National Identity." *Journal of Vietnamese Studies* 4, no. 1 (2009): 49–83.

*President Ngo Dinh Diem.* Saigon: Presidency of the Republic of Vietnam Press Office, 1957.

Topmiller, Robert J. *Lotus Unleashed: The Buddhist Peace Movement in South Vietnam, 1964–1966.* Lexington: University Press of Kentucky, 2002.

US Department of State, Office of the Historian. *Foreign Relations of the United States, 1955–1957.* Vol. 21, *East Asian Security.* Washington, DC: US Government Printing Office, 1990.

———. *Foreign Relations of the United States, 1961–1963.* Vol. 3, *Vietnam, January–August 1963.* Washington, DC: US Government Printing Office, 1991.

Werner, Jayne Susan. *Peasant Politics and Religious Sectarianism: Peasant and Priest in the Cao Dai in Viet Nam.* New Haven, CT: Yale University Southeast Asian Studies, 1981.

# CHAPTER 11

# Brazil

## *Nation and Churches during the Cold War*

Iain S. Maclean

**B** razil is the largest Latin American nation, with the second-largest Roman Catholic Church in the Americas. During the years of the Cold War, Catholics (as well as many Protestants and Pentecostals) came to oppose the authoritarian government that had overthrown the democratic government in 1964 and controlled the nation for the next twenty years. In this non-democratic situation, Brazil was one of the first Latin American nations to experience the traditional church (long viewed as the unquestioning supporter of the ruling elite and the state) criticizing the state publicly, both through episcopal pronouncements and the work of liberation theology.

Liberation theology was an indigenous Latin American development. Drawing on earlier Vatican declarations and their contextualization by the Conference of Latin American Bishops (Consejo Episcopal Latinoamericano, or CELAM), it merged biblical themes and Latin American social and political realities into a coherent theological system. The name "liberation" itself came from the 1971 work *Theology of Liberation*, by the Peruvian Roman Catholic priest Gustavo Gutiérrez.[1] This theology claimed that the church and the state are subject to the norms set by the historical Jesus. These include, for the state specifically, the upholding of human rights and the improving of the living and working conditions of the majority, the poor.

Brazil had already implemented political and economic developmental programs during the 1950s among the rural poor of the Northeast and the

229

urbanizing workers in the South. During the 1960s, the church extended its work among these programs and beginning in the 1970s, as the church and state relationship collapsed, the first Brazilian liberation theologians emerged. Instead of Western theology, which focused on the (Western) issues of secularism and atheism, these young theologians developed a theology focused on the dignity of the human—the actual political, social, and economic context of Brazil—and proposed a socialist and holistic alternative. This theology (admittedly in differing strains) was developed by Leonardo Boff, his brother Clodovis Boff, João Comblin, João Batista Libânio, and Frei Betto, with notable contributions from the Protestant Rubem Alves.

The second CELAM conference, in Medellín, Colombia (1968), had a critical impact on national churches' self-understanding, for it convened when Latin America was experiencing not only modernity but also the effects of the Cold War on military and authoritarian regimes, with the loss of political and personal freedoms under national security doctrines aimed primarily at perceived Communist subversions of the state. The Cold War had in the meantime also led to political and economic alliances throughout the Americas—NATO in the North and in the South, the Rio Pact, and the Organization of American States. Beyond these alliances there was military intervention, either covert (as in Guatemala, Nicaragua, Brazil, and Chile) or overt (as in Cuba, the Dominican Republic, and Panama). Of course, this is not to overlook the use of US and European economic aid in the form of development projects, an approach favored in relations with close US allies such as Brazil from the post–World War II period on.[2]

The situation had altered dramatically in the Americas when, after the successful overthrow in 1959 of the Fulgencia Batista regime in Cuba, Fidel Castro openly supported the Soviet Union, initiated socialist national reforms, and eventually permitted the Soviets to place missiles on the island, only a hundred miles from the US coastline. This action would precipitate a standoff between US president John F. Kennedy and Soviet premier Nikita Khrushchev and bring the world close to global nuclear war.

Fortunately both leaders backed away from that option, but socialist Cuba remained, close to the US mainland and actively seeking to export its socialist revolution to other Central and South American nations. Now many countries were under threat of radical change, and attempts to avoid this alternative led to a series of military or authoritarian civilian governments replacing weak democratic regimes.

The first domino to fall was Brazil. On April 1, 1964, in a bloodless coup, the Brazilian military removed President João Goulart and a government that it perceived as disorganized and leftist, and as having led the nation to the brink of economic collapse. The military justified its action by calling on its role as the protector of the fatherland and the needs of national security against Communist subversion. The Roman Catholic Church, a strong supporter of the state, accepted this coup because it preserved order and prevented a takeover by Communists, who denied human freedoms and denied God. The military actions even resulted in a complimentary message from the National Conference of Brazilian Bishops (Conferência Nacional dos Bispos do Brasil, or CNBB).[3]

Brazil would be joined by an increasing number of post–World War II Latin American nations that fell under authoritarian rule. These were to include Argentina (1966, 1973), Chile (1973), and Uruguay (1973). By the mid-1970s, only four nations (Colombia, Costa Rica, Venezuela, and the Dominican Republic) were democratic. This was in stark contrast to the situation a mere fifteen years earlier in 1960, when well over 60 percent of the Latin American nations had a democratic form of government.[4]

Brazil's authoritarian government set out to create programs of national development and modernization, in the process severely limiting democratic expression and human rights. These programs led to such rapid economic national growth by 1967 that they became known as the "Brazilian miracle." However, in this process, political parties were abolished and two controlled parties established: the official government party, the National Renovation Alliance (Aliança Renovação National, or ARENA) and the official opposition party, the Brazilian Democratic Movement (Movimento Democrático Brasileiro, or MDB).

In terms of the relationship between government and church, the period from 1964 to the restoration of civilian rule in 1984 can be divided into four periods.[5] The first period, from 1964 to 1968, was one in which the military's action was seen by many as justified and for the benefit of the nation. However, the failure of the government party, ARENA, prompted fears of disorder, and the military responded with the harsh Institutional Act 5 of December 1968. This act removed the legal barriers to arbitrary arrest and indefinite detention, closed the national congress indefinitely, imposed censorship, and canceled the scheduled 1970 elections. Numerous Roman Catholic organizations were affected, and church support for the generals wavered as most of civil society was shut down.

The second period, from 1968 to 1974, witnessed continuous state repression of dissidents and the eradication of the Communist Party and anyone suspected of subversion. This soon included bishops, priests, and Catholic lay leaders. It was not so much CELAM's 1968 decisions on implementing the reforms of the Second Vatican Council (1963–1965) that led to Brazilian ecclesiastical opposition to the military government, but the murder in May 1969 of Padre Antônio Henrique Pereira Neto, an associate of Dom Hélder Câmara of Recife.[6] It was this killing that turned the church against the military government. The continuing threats made against the church and its workers led to it becoming the "voice for the voiceless," as the regime feared the reaction from the Vatican and elsewhere if it censored the church. However, this did not stop the state and many conservatives, claiming that the church was showing Communist sympathies and supporting enemies of the state.[7]

The third period, from 1974 to 1978, was marked by President Ernesto Geisel's policy of "decompression" (in Portuguese, *distensão*), through which he sought to lessen the strictures of the national security state while maintaining that any democratization could not contain the diverging political tendencies. This period saw the official opposition beat the government party 14–10 and the creation (formally in 1979) of the independent Workers Party.

The fourth period, from 1978 to 1985, was of the opening (in Portuguese, *abertura*) to democracy and the New Republic. It began in June 1978 when President Geisel issued a schedule of gradual reform. This included the repeal of the Institutional Act and the legalization of political parties. These and other reforms would lead to Brazil's first free congressional elections in 1984.

At the time of the military overthrow of civilian government in 1964, Brazil was (and still is) the largest Latin American Roman Catholic nation, with the highest number of bishops (around three hundred) outside of Italy and the United States. The political function of the Roman Catholic Church has often been overlooked, particularly its relationship to political theory, emerging civil society, and democratic governments within specific national contexts.

This chapter will focus primarily on the ideological and theological ideas that have directed the interests of the church as an institution—that go beyond mere self-preservation, contrary to the assumptions of many political and social theorists. The history of the nation (and the church) under authoritarian or military rule, outlined above, provides the context within which the status and the roles of the Roman Catholic, Protestant, and Afro-Brazilian religions can be understood.

First, prior to the Cold War and the imposition of authoritarian rule in 1964, the Roman Catholic Church had rebuilt itself from the devastation of the 1891 disestablishment. The end of the Portuguese empire and the monarchy in 1889 and the subsequent disestablishment had left the church with only twelve dioceses (thirteen bishops and eight seminaries), few facilities, and no state funding (on which it had depended for four centuries)., in a nation that according to the 1890 census had 14.5 million inhabitants, 70 percent of whom were rural. This resulted in a sharp break between the church and the ruling elite, and a turn to the people rather than to the anticlerical elite. This turn was to bear fruit in the 1930s and later in the 1970s. To do this, the hierarchy worked to strengthen its institutions and centralize their workings.

These tasks were undertaken by the bishop of Olinda and Recife, Dom Sebastião Leme da Silveira Cintra (1882–1942). His program was laid out in his famous pastoral letter of 1916, which called for the re-Catholicization of Brazil.[8] This involved developing and reorganizing the church, regaining the elite ruling classes, and strengthening the moral and spiritual values of the nation through comprehensive educational reforms. Interestingly, it was precisely the 1891 disestablishment that enabled Dom Leme to forge closer links with the Vatican and centralize the Brazilian church hierarchy. Dom Leme aimed his message at the elite and the urban middle classes, seeking to implement the principles of Pope Leo XIII's *Rerum Novarum* (1891). In 1921, Dom Leme became archbishop of Rio de Janeiro (Brazil's capital at the time) and grasped the opportunity to implement his vision.

He strengthened the church hierarchy and by 1946 had increased the number of dioceses and bishops fivefold. Not only were Catholic organizations created but relations with the state cultivated, starting with ecclesiastical participation in the military's Easter celebrations of 1922. That year also saw the founding of the Dom Vital Center to counter the present threats of secularism, modernity, and atheism. The center promoted Catholic nationalism and anti-Communism and supported order and progress guided by Catholic moral principles.

Then in 1930, during the revolution, Dom Leme gained the confidence of the dictator Getúlio Vargas, who valued his stress on the church's role as the core bearer of the nation's unity. This was acknowledged in the 1934 constitution, which also provided state support for Catholic schools, universities, and seminaries. Thus, the alliance between church and nation was enhanced.

Dom Leme, named cardinal in 1931, continued to lead and build the church until his death in 1942. His successors focused on the issues raised by urbanization and the influence of Communism on the rural poor and the working classes, which had occurred in Europe as well as in Brazil.[9] They also decentralized the power of the church, delegating it to the bishops via to CELAM (founded in 1952) and CNBB (founded in 1955). These emphases were to continue after the military coup of 1964, which most of the bishops supported.

These changes were due not only to the desire of the ecclesiastical hierarchy to maintain church influence, but also to increased lay involvement in popular movements, many being outgrowths of Catholic Action, as well as to international legitimation for progressive stances arising out of Vatican Council II, papal pronouncements, and bishops' conferences. Such strong support for lay-led social programs and movements was not just an unintended result of the political crisis of 1964, but was rooted in the nature of the Brazilian church itself. Unlike most Latin American countries, the Brazilian church had a history of institutional weakness and a chronic shortage of indigenous clergy and religious orders. Consequently, the Brazilian church had long been influenced by lay involvement and leadership, such as that of the Dom Vital Center in the 1920s and 1930s and in the Catholic Left movements of the 1950s and the early 1960s.[10]

The 1964 crisis and its consequences focused attention on the church (and religion in general), marking a shift in traditional understandings of the church's role in society and an end to the assumption that the church would legitimate any government or minister or focus its ministry on the ruling classes. Further, these changes led to a reevaluation of scholarly approaches to the issues of church and society. The shifting role of the Roman Catholic Church in Latin America revealed the limitations of examining its relation to politics solely in terms of church-state relations, Vatican diplomacy, or the concluding of concordats. This included assessing how the leadership of the Brazilian Roman Catholic Church, during the period following Vatican II, responded to military rule, redemocratization, and appeals for democratic reforms within the church itself.[11]

Initially, theoretical reformulations were limited to institutional studies of how the church adapted to the challenges and changes of modernity as noted in the work of Ivan Vallier. This understanding of the church's role was also accepted by Brazilians such as Roberto Romano and Márcio Moreira Alves.[12] Thomas Bruneau and Scott Mainwaring provide similar institutional analyses of the transformation of the Roman Catholic Church in Brazil. However, they disagree on how this is to be explained in terms of the category of interests. Bruneau argued in his earlier works that while the church was weak in reaching the average member, it was nevertheless a powerful institution for a country weak in institutional development.[13] Using the work of Weber and Troeltsch, amplified by Avery Dulles's work on ecclesiology, Bruneau argues for a dual focus in research, on what he describes as the institutional and the charismatic elements of the church.[14] The institutional element, involves a focus on the church's role primarily in terms of the ruling elite analysis. The charismatic focus involves examining how the church's interests are shaped by theological ideas.

During the 1960s, such approaches were limited by the Marxist and neo-Marxist approaches to social scientific research that dominated academic discourse in Latin American universities. In Brazil, Luiz Alberto Gómez de Souza and Carlos Palácio argued that institutional analysis failed to account for the role of class conflict within and outside the church.[15] Gómez de Souza sharply criticizes Scott Mainwaring and other non-Brazilian scholars who fail to employ a class analysis and thus, he claims, fail to comprehend the conflictual and violent context of society.[16] According to Paulo Kriscke, this commitment to the people or the popular classes seems to originate from a prior understanding that fails to fully account for the significance of institutions in shaping society. Kriscke himself employs a Gramscian approach in mediating between North American analyses and those that are primarily class-based.[17]

Bruneau points out that such analyses assume that class or socioeconomic factors have totally permeated the church and dominate its thought and action. He notes that this is to overdetermine such details—to confuse social science facts with values or meaning commitments. The truth in such analyses is distorted by such approaches, for the church can be committed to the people and yet still be independent, following its own injunctions as well as those of Rome. In addressing theological and ethical ideas, the influence of other factors in analysis has to be kept in mind. This is taken further by analyses that correctly observe the role of linkages with international institutions. The transnational factor in analyzing the church in Latin America was first noted by Vallier, who explored the implications of understanding the church as part of an international network.[18] This has been developed further by figures such as Scott Mainwaring and Ralph Della Cava. The latter's research demonstrates how class-dominated analyses fail to deal adequately with the effects that linkage with the Vatican places on a national institution. This model helps explain how the ideas of progressive clergy and popular movements in northeast Brazil were consolidated and disseminated across the country (for example, through the CNBB). Of course, the reverse also applies: if the larger institutions do not support specific ideas or programs, these will not be encouraged or supported by the rest of the country. This linkage model thus helps explain the decline, beginning in the early 1980s, of certain progressive elements in the Brazilian Church.

As noted earlier, the military repression of civil society had led the church by 1974 to withdraw support for the state and to criticize its actions openly. In effect, the institutional church had taken the side of the people against the state, as the "voice of the voiceless."[19] This alternative stance for the church had in fact been set out in 1970 in the works of the Peruvian Dominican priest Gustavo Gutiérrez and those of the Brazilians Rubem Alves, a Presbyterian, and Leonardo Boff, a Franciscan priest.[20] Their writings expressed a different way of doing theology, one that was to be called "liberation theology."

The dominant theme of liberation theology, first articulated by Gustavo Gutiérrez, is that theology begins from praxis, the actual human situation. This emerges from his claim in his book that there is only one history, not two; spiritual history and secular history are not separate entities. This rejection of any dualism—of the spiritual and the material as separate realms—is fundamental to liberation theology in its rejection of what it understood as Western dualisms that not only devalued the human self but ended up spiritualizing material poverty. If atheism was a problem for the West, it was not one for Latin Americans, who were religious. Their problem was their status as humans who had been made in God's image but were everywhere oppressed and marginalized. Poverty, the major social problem, was not a choice (contrary to traditional Catholic thought, which assumed poverty to be a choice that religious persons made as monastic vows), but a present political social and economic reality created by humans and thus a reality humans had the ability to change.

The Brazilian theologians Leonardo Boff and Clodovis Boff both declare that given its starting point in life, liberation theology is a radical rejection of traditional theologies. It is not restricted by intellectual doctrines or ecclesiastical control. Rather, it is articulated by those already working among the people, reflecting on scripture and using the social sciences to understand the human situation more fully. They draw the term "liberation" directly from the record of Jesus's first sermon in the Gospel of Luke 4:18–21, where the text declares that he had come to liberate the oppressed. Jesus, a human figure, announces the approaching Kingdom of God, and declares that it is for the poor and needy. Jesus is human, Jesus's message encompasses all of life, and God has a "preferential option for the poor."[21] Oppression is the result of sin, interpreted not purely as personal but as social, involving structures of human life. So, sin includes national dependency, capitalism, and development policies that fail the people, resulting in oppressed and poverty-stricken classes and underdevelopment. Liberation theologians further justified their new approach by arguing that in following the reforms of the Second Vatican Council they were simply following the example of the historical Jesus, who preached to the poor, thus prioritizing the "option for the poor."[22] The basic method of this theology, adapted from Joseph Cardinal Cardijn's threefold prescription for Catholic Action, involved the three actions of "see, judge, act." These three simple verbs were transformed by Clodovis Boff into the three steps of analysis: the social-analytical, the hermeneutical or interpretive, and the praxis-pastoral.[23] The first of these steps proved to be the most controversial, as liberation theologians argued that they were only using Marxist class analysis as a tool to expose the realities of the people's situation. Conservative theologians and bishops, as well as other opponents, argued that the use of such analysis implied the reduction of the human to economic categories and in fact encouraged class conflict. This, of course, was repugnant to traditional Catholics, who held to the church social teaching that encouraged reconciliation of opponents.[24]

The term "liberation" was used to argue that God was concerned with both the spiritual and the material, the church and the state, the individual and society, and the personal and the public. Thus, liberation theologians engaged in critique not only of the church but also of the state and held up the requirement of justice before the state. They tended to be critical of what they called "liberal" (formal) democracies and European and North American developmental policies. They rejected such policies for producing effects opposite to the development intended, benefiting the elite and not the poor. Instead of failed "capitalist" or mere "formal liberal" democracy, they advocated socialism or forms of participatory democracy. It is not quite accurate to claim that liberation theology is anarchist, for though there may be parallels between anarchist thought and certain aspects of Gustavo Gutiérrez's and Leonardo Boff's early works, there are no historical connections between these traditions.[25]

The first period of the development of Brazilian liberation theology was from its inception during military repression to the year 1980, when the focus of its thought shifted to the popular ecclesial base community (*comunidade eclesial de base*, or CEB) movement.[26] This period witnessed shifts in the leadership of the Brazilian Roman Catholic Church following Vatican II, responses to military rule, calls for redemocratization, and even appeals for democratic reforms within the church itself.[27] To the extent that the teachings of the Roman Catholic Church upheld the value of democracy, the rise of liberation theologies in the early 1970s questioned both the church's position within the Latin American context and its support of the liberal democratic development assistance programs advocated by Latin American governments and funded by the United States and other international agencies.[28] Beginning in 1970, when these very development programs and the associated regimes became repressive dictatorships, liberation theology emerged in support of an alternative vision.[29] Its proponents criticized the state for its human rights abuses and, through their theology, argued for an alternative socialist society. Thus the 1970s witnessed both theological and political critics accusing Latin American liberation theologians of being Marxist.[30] This was because they used Marxist class analysis, rejected capitalism, and opted uncritically for socialism as a model, as well as (in the view of such critics) misinterpreting the teachings of Vatican II.[31] The charge of Marxism played well to fears of Communist infiltration of Latin America.

It is important to recognize here what Scott Mainwaring has well demonstrated, which is that neo-Marxist analyses of the church underestimate the role of ideas and tend to subsume everything under the rubric of class or as merely the reflection of class interests.[32] He points out that class analysis fails to note that in Brazil (unlike, for example, in Nicaragua or El Salvador), the division between conservative and progressive does not correspond to hierarchy versus laity, but rather cuts across these lines. He also criticizes approaches that assume a monolithic conception of interests and do not recognize that differing ecclesiologies will produce differing understandings of interests and different outcomes.[33] He criticizes institutional analyses that fail to deal with conflict and change within the institution. He correctly observes that such analyses confuse instrumental goals with ultimate goals and values.[34] Values and goals, within limits, are variable, and are the outcome of choices and internal struggles. He stresses understanding what the mission of the church is and should be, rather than seeing it purely in terms of interests, for the understanding of mission determines what and how interests are prioritized. Bruneau would add to this analysis that the existence of newer theologies arising from international linkages enabled progressives to argue and legitimatize their position.[35] These progressives included not only liberation theologians but parish clergy and many bishops, in Brazil and elsewhere.

The rise of the authoritarian military regimes drove many bishops to reject the assumption of church support for the state. Figures such as the Salvadorian archbishop and martyr Oscar Romero and the Brazilian archbishop Dom Hélder Câmara gained international recognition for their criticism of their governments and support of human rights. They took these stances through their recognition of liberation theology's "preferential option for the poor." They, along with others, came to represent "the progressives," who supported democratization, freedom for multiple parties, and the preservation of human rights. However, the often public stances taken by these figures and others forced individual bishops and churches to take positions that divided the church into groupings of "progressives," "conservatives" and "moderates."

Scholars such as Scott Mainwaring and Ralph della Cava highlight the role of lay movements in the late 1950s and early 1960s in the process of the church's development. In particular, the repression directed against such movements by the military regime after 1964 was instrumental in drawing the church into the political arena. The hierarchy's support both protected lay movements and their interests and contributed to internal change. In the case of Brazil, such support began long before the military coup, for the linkages with progressive elements within the Vatican to Brazil, via Dom Hélder Câmara and the then papal nuncio, Dom Armando Lombardi, existed from the 1950s, as did national episcopal support for the rural social movements.[36] Thus, church support internationally and nationally was critical for popular support against military regimes. However, this support led to the exposure of sharp differences within the church itself.

Beginning in the 1980s, there was a shift in emphasis in liberation theologians' writings. This shift attended more to theological and spiritual themes than to the Marxist or other forms of social analysis that had dominated earlier writings.[37] Liberation theologians focused on the increase of CEBs, which gathered people together for Bible study, fellowship, and political action, largely in urban areas. These groups were to give rise to much speculation, controversy over political party affiliation, and claims by theologians of their innovative potential. Leonardo Boff was to declare that God's spirit was independently creating new congregations, independent of clergy, a claim that would lead to his eventual silencing by the Vatican and his resignation from his order and the priesthood.[38]

Were CEBs simply an example of anarchic social formation, or a strengthening of popular support for open democracy? Indeed, some CEBs and their leadership distrusted political organization beyond the local. This focus on the base (*basismo*) could look anarchic, but the CEBs themselves were part of a national system of CEBs, not to mention the parochial and diocesan structures under which most of them operated.[39] Did the desire of popular movements, including the CEBs, to remain close to the base while perhaps preventing the corruption of the leadership lead to a failure to create alliances and thus to make a wider political impact in society? In the case of the CEBs, this criticism does not quite fit. First, they were not purely local, but were often connected to each other through the local parish and certainly at the national level through their biannual national assemblies.[40] Second, they defined themselves as religious groups and not as the wing of any particular political party; thus, each member was free to make his or her own decision regarding affiliation with a particular political party.[41] This was critical, because the Brazilian CNBB had rejected, as far back as the 1960s, any official church party, such as a Christian Democratic Party in Chile.[42]

What is more critical is not so much the making of alliances or connections beyond the local, but the nature of those alliances. In the case of the CEBs in the present day, the withdrawal of diocesan support as a result of conservative pressure in many areas is crippling the local movement by limiting linkage and thus access to resources beyond the individual CEB. Thus, paradoxically, the *basismo* for which the CEBs are criticized is not entirely of their own making. Nonetheless, whether inherent in the CEBs' stress on the popular and participatory elements or due to lack of ecclesiastical support, CEB political impact has been less than what liberation theologians had hoped for and expressed in the early 1980s. It was precisely the focus on the progressive and liberation theological sectors of the church in the early 1980s that obscured the strength and influence of the neoconservative reaction against liberation theology and its political agenda both within and beyond the church.[43] As noted above, the conservative criticisms gained the attention of the Vatican, and numerous instructions and limitations were placed on liberation theologians by an increasingly conservative hierarchy seeking ecclesiastical unity as a means of resisting the spread of Protestantism.

In outlining the divisions within the Brazilian Church and the impact of these differences on lay movements on the ground, it is critical to not overlook the linkage between the national and international levels. For the church, the essential linkage is with the Vatican and conservative forces there and in the international church. These extranational forces, such as the Vatican (headed by a strongly anti-Communist pope, John Paul II) and conservative Catholic movements, had a powerful limiting force on the progressive elements within the Brazilian Church. These led to numerous conservative critiques, both internal and external to Brazil, that were typically and specifically directed at themes such as the nature of theology, the use of Marxist categories, the use of class and dependency analyses, the option for the poor, and socialism.[44]

Further, the national context of a rapidly shifting religious field set challenges for the national church. In particular, since the military rule of the 1970s, the Afro-Brazilian religions had been legalized and Protestantism had grown, especially since the military had turned to the Presbyterians to gain legitimacy after being criticized by the Catholic hierarchy.[45] The Presbyterians were eager to accept this role (though it did lead to a split in the denomination) as this was their chance to show one could be both Protestant and a Brazilian patriot. This is not to forget the dramatic rise of Pentecostalism, which is often regarded by Latin American scholars with great suspicion as foreign, unpatriotic, and funded largely from North America (specifically as the religious wing of conservative North Americans).[46]

Yet such linkages are critical for any movement's survival and success. Political movements, as much as sectors within the church, rise and fall through the social pacts and alliances they form. Thus, shifting alliances within the church from the 1960s through to the 1980s led to alternative theological and thus political positions.

The fall of the Berlin Wall and the subsequent collapse of Eastern European socialist regimes (and the Soviet Union itself) effectively ended the Cold War. For progressive Catholics in Brazil and Latin America, the fall of existing socialist states also effectively removed the appeal of such as a viable political alternative. The Brazilian national hierarchy was now dominated by conservatives. Since his election in 1978, Pope John Paul II had installed more than 125 new bishops in Brazil. Support for the progressive wing and for liberation theologies waned as the church sought to reaffirm traditional interpretations of Vatican II and address the challenges posed by growing Protestantism. Nonetheless, it had changed dramatically from what it was before 1964. It had included the disenfranchised urban and rural poor, resisted and outlasted an authoritarian regime, and become a "voice for the voiceless" in advocating human rights. In addition, it had exposed the extent of state torture in the clandestinely assembled and published *Brasil: Nunca Mais* (1985). The first free election in the 1980s presented the Catholic Church, the Protestant churches, and the Afro-Brazilian religions with a more open society—one that could even be considered secular—without an official state church.

## Notes

1. Gustavo Gutiérrez, *A Theology of Liberation* (Maryknoll, NY: Orbis, 1973). Originally published as *Theologiá de la liberación* (Lima: CEP, 1971).
2. For specific national details, see Peter Smith, *Democracy in Latin America: Political Change in Comparative Perspective* (New York: Oxford University Press, 2005); and Lars Schoultz, *National Security and United States Policy toward Latin America* (Princeton, NJ: Princeton University Press, 1987).
3. Conferência Nacional dos Bispos do Brasil (CNBB), "Declaracão da CNBB sobre a situacão nacional" [Declaration of the National Conference of Bishops of Brazil on the national situation], *Revista Eclesiastica Brasileira* 24 (1964): 491–93.
4. See details in ch. 1, Smith, *Democracy in Latin America*.
5. This periodization is based on the work of Ralph Della Cava, "The Church and *Abertura* in Brazil, 1974–1985," Working Paper 114, Helen Kellogg Institute for International Studies, University of Notre Dame, November 1988.
6. Scott Mainwaring, *The Catholic Church and Politics in Brazil, 1916–1985* (Stanford, CA: Stanford University Press, 1986), 8.
7. See the interesting article by Carla Simone Rodeghero, "Religiã o epatriotismo: O anticomunismo Catolico nos Estados Unidos e no Brasilos anos da Guerra frio" [Religion and patriotism: Catholic anti-Communism in the United States and Brazil during the Cold War], *Revista Brasileira de História* 22, no. 44 (2002): 463–88.
8. Sebastião Leme, *Carta pastoral à Olinda* [Pastoral letter to Olinda] (Petrópolis, Brazil: Editora Vozes, 1916).
9. The loss of ruling class membership was halted somewhat in Europe by the formation of Catholic unions and political parties. See Michael P. Fogarty, *Christian Democracy in Western Europe, 1820–1953* (Notre Dame, IN: University of Notre Dame Press, 1957), parts 1 and 3.
10. The lay initiatives encouraged by church authorities are well documented by Madeleine Adriance in *Opting for the Poor* (Kansas City: Sheed and Ward, 1986), 33–61.
11. Leonardo Boff, *Eclesiogênese: As comunidades eclesiais de base reinventam a igreja* [Ecclesiogenesis: The ecclesial base communes reinvent the church] (Petrópolis, Brazil: Editora Vozes, 1977) and *Igreja: Carisma e poder* [Church: Charisma and power] (Petrópolis, Brazil: Editora Vozes, 1981).
12. Roberto Romano, *Brasil: Igreja contra estado* [Brazil: Church against state] (São Paulo: Kairos Livraria, 1979); and Márcio Moreira Alves, *A igreja e a política no Brasil.* [Church and politics in Brazil] (São Paulo: Editora Brasiliense, 1979).
13. Thomas Bruneau, *The Political Transformation of the Brazilian Catholic Church* (Cambridge: Cambridge University Press, 1974) and *The Church in Brazil: The Politics of Religion* (Austin: University of Texas Press, 1982).

14. Avery Dulles, *Models of the Church* (New York: Doubleday, 1974); and Thomas Bruneau, "Church and Politics in Brazil: The Genesis of Change," *Journal of Latin American Studies* 17 (1985): 292–93.

15. Luiz Alberto Gómez de Souza, *Classes populares e igreja nos caminhos da história* [Popular classes and church in the paths of history] (Petrópolis, Brazil: Editora Vozes, 1982) and *A JUC: Os estudantes católicos e a política* [JUC: Catholic students and politics] (Petrópolis, Brazil: Editora Vozes, 1984), ch. 1; and Carlos Palácio, "Uma consciência histórica irreversível, 1960–1979: Duas décadas de história da igreja no Brasil" [An irreversible historical conscience, 1960–1979: Two decades in church history in Brazil], *Síntese* 17 (1979): 19–40.

16. Gómez de Souza, *Classes populares*, 12–17. Luiz Alberto Gómez de Souza is a social scientist and theologian working out of the Centro João XXIII of the Instituto Brasileiro de Desenvolvimento Social [Brazilian Institute of Social Development] in Rio de Janeiro. His criticism of non-Brazilian scholarship is a common refrain in Brazilian works, whether by social scientists or by theologians using sociological approaches. The critique often appears as a foil to the author's preferred approach, as in Gómez de Souza, *A JUC*, ch. 1.

17. Paulo Kriscke, *A igreja e as crises políticas no Brasil* [The church and the political crisis in Brazil] (Petrópolis, Brazil: Editora Vozes, 1979); "Brasil: Problemas teóricos de las relaciones entre la iglesia y el estado en la crisis de 1964" [Brazil: Theoretical problems of the relations between church and state in the crisis of 1964], *Revista Mexicana de Sociología* E43 (1981): 2043–67; and with Scott Mainwaring, *A igreja nas bases em tempo de transição* [The church and its bases in the time of transition] (Porte Alegre, Brazil: L&PM Editores, 1986).

18. This overlooked aspect is emphasized by Scott Mainwaring in *The Catholic Church and Politics in Brazil, 1916–1985* (Stanford, CA: Stanford University Press, 1986), 17–19. See also Ivan Vallier, "The Roman Catholic Church: A Transnational Actor?," in *International Organization*, ed. Joseph S. Nye and Robert O. Keohane (Cambridge, MA: Harvard University Press, 1972), 129–51.

19. Bruneau, "Church and Politics in Brazil," 284–85.

20. Gustavo Gutiérrez and Rubem Alves, *A Theology of Human Hope* (Washington, DC: Corpus Publications, 1969) and *Tomorrow's Child* (New York: Harper and Row, 1972). Alves, a Brazilian Presbyterian minister and a colleague of Richard Shaull and Harvey Cox, wrote the earliest works on liberation theology. Disillusioned with Protestant support for the military, he resigned from the Presbyterian Church in the 1960s.

21. Gutiérrez, *A Theology of Liberation*, 36.

22. Note that in the later "Instruction on Christian Freedom and Liberation" by the Congregation for the Doctrine of the Faith, this phrase is rephrased as "a preferential love for the poor." *Origins* 15, no. 44 (April 17, 1986).

23. Clodovis Boff, *Theology and Praxis* (Maryknoll, NY: Orbis, 1987).

24. See the definitive Vatican statement issued by the Congregation for the Doctrine of the Faith, "Instruction on Certain Aspects of Liberation Theology," *Origins* 14, no. 13 (September 14, 1984): 193–217.

25. Linda H. Damico, *The Anarchist Dimension of Liberation Theology* (New York: Peter Lang, 1987).

26. Paul Sigmund, "Whither Liberation Theology," *Crisis*, January 1987, 5–14.

27. L. Boff, *Eclesiogênese*.

28. These include the International Monetary Fund, the Alliance for Progress, and the "National Security Doctrines" propounded later during the 1970s. See Alfred Stepan, *Democratizing Brazil* (New York: Oxford University Press, 1989), and José Comblin, *The Church and the National Security State* (Maryknoll, NY: Orbis, 1979). Challenges to the church's position have been most powerfully expressed in liberation theologians' calls for the church to make a "preferential option for the poor," a position endorsed by CELAM in Puebla. "CELAM III," in *Puebla and Beyond: Documentation and Commentary*, ed. John Eagleson and P. Scharper (Maryknoll, NY: Orbis, 1979), xxx.

29. By the end of the 1960s, both the reformist programs of the Christian Democratic parties in Chile and Peru as well as the development programs of populist nationalism in Brazil had collapsed as viable political strategies for national development.

30. See the surveys of the literature in Arthur F. McGovern, *Liberation Theology and Its Critics: Towards an Assessment* (Maryknoll, NY: Orbis, 1989), and Alistair Kee, *Marx and the Failure of Liberation Theology* (London: SCM Press, 1990).

31. This provides the focus for the critiques leveled by L. Trujillo, *Liberation or Revolution* (Huntingdon, IN: Our Sunday Visitor, 1975), and Roger Vekemans, *Teologia de la liberacion y Cristianos por el socialismo* [Liberation theology and Christians for socialism] (Bogota: Cedial, 1976). On the preference of Brazilian liberation theologians for socialism, see Leonardo Boff, "O Socialismo como desafio teológico" [Socialism as a theological challenge], *Vozes* 81, no. 6 (November–December 1987): 47–57; and Clodovis Boff, *Cartas teológicas sobre o socialismo* [Theological letters on socialism] (Petrópolis, Brazil: Editora Vozes, 1989). José Comblin rejects existing forms of socialism.

32. Mainwaring, *Catholic Church and Politics in Brazil*, 12–13. He sees the church as relatively autonomous with regards to the class struggle.

33. Ibid., 4.

34. Scott Mainwaring, "Grassroots Catholic Groups and Politics in Brazil, 1964–1985," in *The Progressive Church in Latin America*, ed. Scott Mainwaring and Alexander Wilde (Notre Dame, IN: University of Notre Dame Press, 1989), 153.

35. Bruneau, "Church and Politics in Brazil," 291.

36. Vatican support for the progressive elements within the Brazilian hierarchy is detailed in Bruneau, *Political Transformation*, chapters 1–3, and in Raimundo Caramuru de Barros, *Para entender a igreja no Brasil: A caminhada que culminou no Vaticano II (1930–1968)* [Understanding the Brazilian church: A journey that culminated in Vatican II (1930–1968) (Petrópolis, Brazil: Editora Vozes, 1994), chapters 1–2.

37. Paul Sigmund, *Liberation Theology at the Crossroads: Democracy or Revolution?* (New York: Oxford University Press, 1990), appendix 1.

38. See the materials discussed in Harvey Cox, *The Silencing of Leonardo Boff* (Oak Park, IL: Meyerstone Books, 1987), and Joseph Ratzinger and V. Messori, *The Ratzinger Report* (San Francisco: Ignatius Press, 1985).

39. In many regions of Brazil, the polarization between CEBs and the local parish is not as sharp as Pedro A. Ribeiro de Oliveira claims in his "Conflict and Change in the Brazilian Catholic Church," in *A Democratic Catholic Church*, ed. Eugene Bianchi and Rosemary Ruether (New York: Crossroads, 1992), 139–55. Also, see John Burdick, *Looking for God in Brazil: The Progressive Catholic Church in Brazil's Religious Arena* (Berkeley: University of California Press, 1993), chapters 3 and 7.

40. The first of the national assemblies (also known as *encontros* [encounters] and interecclesials) was held in Vitória, Espírito Santo, Brazil, in 1975; the CEBs convened again in 1976, and have met every two years since then. Reports on each national assembly are printed in the following edition of *Revista Eclesiástica Brasileira*.

41. Such decisions were clearly made at the fourth *Inter-Eclesial* of the CEBs at Itaicí (April 1981). See the report by Gómez de Souza in *Revista Eclesiástica Brasileira* 41 (December 1981): 724.

42. Iain S. Maclean, *Opting for Democracy: Liberation Theology and the Struggle for Democracy in Brazil* (New York: Peter Lang, 1999), 44.

43. See the critiques of liberation theology in Craig Nessan, *Orthopraxis or Heresy: The North American Theological Response to Latin American Liberation Theology* (Atlanta: Scholars Press, 1989), and Sigmund, *Liberation Theology at the Crossroads*.

44. Leading critics have included Dom Boaventura Kloppenburg, who wrote *A igreja popular* [The popular church] (Rio de Janeiro: Livraria AGIR Editora, 1983); Eugênio Cardinal Sales, archbishop emeritus of Rio de Janeiro; the archbishop emeritus of Olinda and Recife, Dom José Cardoso Sobrinho, who closed the seminary and institutes founded by his predecessor, Dom Hélder Câmara; and auxiliary bishop Karl Josef Romer of Rio de Janeiro. Conservative publications include the journal *Boletim da Revista do Clero* and the Portuguese language edition of *Communio*. External critique comes primarily from West Germany and the United States. In the United States, critics include Michael Novak, who wrote *Will It Liberate? Questions about Liberation Theology* (New York: Paulist Press, 1986) and *The Spirit of Democratic Capitalism* (New York: Simon and Schuster, 1982). D. P. McCann is a moderate critic who seeks to incorporate insights from Niebuhr's critical realism in *Christian Realism and Liberation Theology* (Maryknoll, NY: Orbis, 1982). The American Enterprise Institute is an important center for promulgating conservative ideas.

45. See David Stoll and Virginia Burnett, eds., *Rethinking Pentecostalism in Latin America* (Philadelphia: Temple University Press, 1994), for reevaluations of Protestantism and Pentecostalism. For Afro-Brazilian religions, *As seitas* [The sects] is used with varying degrees of inclusiveness. In its broadest sense, it would include all non-Catholic religious groups. In its narrower sense, it includes only the Afro-Brazilian religions, which often blend with spiritism originating from the nineteenth-century spiritualist leader Alan Kardec. Roger Bastide, *The African Religions of Brazil* (Baltimore: Johns Hopkins University Press, 1978); Carlos Rodrigues Brandão, *Os deuses do povo* [The gods of the people] (São Paulo: Brasiliense, 1980); and Leilah Landim, *Sinais dos tempos: Igrejas e seitas no Brasil* [Signs of the times: Churches and sects in Brazil] (Rio de Janeiro: ISER, 1989).

46. The standard work on this topic is Francisco Cartaxo Rolim's *Pentecostais no*

*Brasil: Uma interpretação sócio-religiosa* [Pentecostalism in Brazil: A socioreligious interpretation] (Petrópolis, Brazil: Editora Vozes, 1985). For a recent evaluation of classical theories on the role of Protestants and Pentecostals, see Jean-Pierre Bastián, "The Metamorphosis of Latin American Protestant Groups: A Socio-historical Perspective," *Latin American Research Review* 28, no. 2 (1993): 33–61. The suspicions of Latin American scholars were not unfounded, given the case documented in *The Rise and Fall of Project Camelot*, ed. Irving L. Horowitz (Cambridge, MA: MIT Press, 1967). For a rebuttal of such accusations, see Martin Stoll, *Is Latin America Turning Protestant? The Politics of Evangelical Growth* (Berkeley: University of California Press, 1990).

## Selected References

Alves, Márcio Moreira. *A igreja e a política no Brasil* [Church and politics in Brazil]. São Paulo: Editora Brasiliense, 1979.

Boff, Clodovis. "Bases teológicas do ideal democrático primeiras colocações" [Theological bases of the democratic ideal]. In Conferência Nacional dos Bispos do Brasil, *Sociedade, igreja e democracia: Seminário "Exigências eticas da ordem democrática"* [Society, church, and democracy: Seminar on the ethical requirements of democratic order]. São Paulo: Edições Loyola, 1989.

Boff, Leonardo. *América Latina: Da conquista à nova evangelização* [Latin America: From conquest to the new evangelization]. São Paulo: Editora Atica, 1992.

———. "CEBs: Que significa 'novo modo de toda a igreja ser'?" [CEBs: What does a new way of being church signify?]. *Revista Eclesiástica Brasileira* 49, no. 195 (September 1989): 546–62.

———. *Eclesiogênese: As comunidades eclesiais de base reinventam a igreja* [Ecclesiogenesis: Ecclesial base communes reinvent the church]. Petrópolis, Brazil: Editora Vozes, 1977.

———. "A implosão do socialismo autoritário e a teologia da libertação" [The collapse of authoritarian socialism and the theology of liberation]. *Revista Eclesiástica Brasileira* 50, no. 197 (March 1990): 76–92.

Bruneau, Thomas. *The Church in Brazil: The Politics of Religion*. Austin: University of Texas Press, 1982.

———. *The Political Transformation of the Brazilian Catholic Church*. Cambridge: Cambridge University Press, 1974.

Burdick, John. *Looking for God in Brazil: The Progressive Catholic Church in Brazil's Religious Arena*. Berkeley: University of California Press, 1993.

Comblin, José. *The Church and the National Security State*. Maryknoll, NY: Orbis, 1979.

Conferência Nacional dos Bispos do Brasil (CNBB). "Cartas e manifestações de bispos por ocasião da IX Assembléia Geral da CNBB" [Bishops' letters and statements on the occasion of the Ninth Assembly of the CNBB]. *Revista Eclesiástica Brasileira* 28, no. 3 (September 1968): 709–23.

Congregation for the Doctrine of the Faith. "Instruction on Certain Aspects of the Theology of Liberation." *Origins* 14, no. 13 (September 13, 1984): 193–217.

———. "Instruction on Christian Freedom and Liberation." *Origins* 15, no. 44 (April 17, 1986): 713–27.

Della Cava, Ralph. "Catholicism and Society in Twentieth Century Brazil." *Latin America Research Review* 11, no. 2 (1976): 7–50.

———. "The Church and *Abertura* in Brazil, 1974–1985." Working Paper 114, Helen Kellogg Institute for International Studies, University of Notre Dame, November 1988.

Gutiérrez, Gustavo. *A Theology of Liberation.* Maryknoll, NY: Orbis, 1973.

Leme, Sebastião. *Carta pastoral à Olinda* [Pastoral letter to Olinda]. Petrópolis, Brazil: Editora Vozes, 1916.

Maclean, Iain S. *Opting for Democracy: Liberation Theology and the Struggle for Democracy in Brazil.* New York: Peter Lang, 1999.

Mainwaring, Scott. *The Catholic Church and Politics in Brazil, 1916–1985.* Stanford, CA: Stanford University Press, 1986.

Mainwaring, Scott, and Alexander Wilde, eds. *The Progressive Church in Latin America.* Notre Dame, IN: University of Notre Dame Press, 1989.

Schoultz, Lars. *National Security and United States Policy toward Latin America.* Princeton, NJ: Princeton University Press, 1987.

Sigmund, Paul. *Liberation Theology at the Crossroads: Democracy or Revolution?* New York: Oxford University Press, 1990.

———. "Whither Liberation Theology." *Crisis*, January 1987, 5–14.

Smith, Peter. *Democracy in Latin America: Political Change in Comparative Perspective.* New York: Oxford University Press, 2005.

# CHAPTER 12

# Service with Body and Soul

## *The Institutionalized Atheism of the Security Service Officers in Communist Poland, 1944–1989*

*Leszek Murat*

I will be devoted to service with my body and soul.

—General Jerzy Gruba, commander
of the security office in Katowice

This chapter examines religiosity in Communist Poland and evaluates the role of institutionalized atheism as part of the code of socialist morality. I focus primarily on the purest of the purest—the functionaries of the security service, designed to be the first solely atheist segment of Polish society. I argue that the regime's materialistic, atheistic, and explicitly anticlerical doctrine, demanding undivided loyalty from its cadres, was in fact a kind of religion itself, but not attractive enough to uproot Christian beliefs even out of the security functionaries. I explore the regime's methods of extirpating religiosity from the security officers, as well as the forms of constant surveillance it employed to track its security personnel's religious activity. The regime's atheistic campaign failed because of its lack of homogeneity, its internal contradictions, and its inability to create an atheist civilization without Catholic connotations.

## The Catholic Church: Lethal Enemy of the Communist Regime

The complete annihilation of the military and political opposition to the Communist regime in the late 1940s made the Catholic Church the Communists' main target as the only meaningful independent institution still functioning in Communist Poland. The Polish Catholic Church was in a unique position: other religious institutions within the Soviet bloc either had been destroyed or were controlled by the Communist regimes. According to the historian Hanna Diskin, the Polish Church was "the main force behind the opposition movement in Poland and Eastern Europe, and despite suffering a series of serious blows and retreats, the opposition movement increased its power over the decades until its dramatic victory in 1989."[1] Ironically, the Catholic Church in Poland survived because of Stalin, who decided to spare it despite the numerous pleas of zealous Polish Communists asking for permission to attack and destroy it.[2] For Stalin, the Catholic clergy was necessary to legitimize the new Polish regime, encourage the fearful Poles to populate vast territories annexed from Germany, and maintain a neutral presence as he ferociously campaigned against non-Communist organizations.[3] Of course, Stalin's leniency was not a genuine gesture of acceptance, but rather the Bolshevik tactic of concentrating his efforts on one enemy at a time.[4] As early as 1949, the Communists' swift success in monopolizing power placed the church in the precarious position of being the only autonomous actor on the sociopolitical stage in Poland. Since the early 1950s, the regime perceived the church as its main internal enemy, but despite many assiduous campaigns to alter this state of affairs, this classification did not change for the next four decades (except during the early 1980s, when the Solidarity movement occupied the position of chief enemy). Throughout that time, the Catholic Church was continuously exposed to the brunt of the regime's vicious endeavors to eradicate the clergy by complete penetration from within and unending siege from without.[5] These tasks were, however, not easy, and therefore rested on the shoulders of the elite soldiers of the party—the most fanatic and trusted functionaries of the security apparatus, the *Bezpieka*.

The Communists' vehement hostility toward the Catholic Church resulted not only from the church's institutionalized independence, but also its unflagging teachings from the pulpit. The church's strong stance on key socioreligious matters—not always anti-Communist but simply different—provided an alternative to the propaganda of socialist morality. Regardless of how attractive or not Catholic doctrine might actually have been to the average Pole, the mere fact of its availability reduced the effectiveness of Communist social engineering. This frustrated the Stalinist regime because its inability to monopolize teaching complicated its plan for imposing the Communist way of life on the entire society. The contrasting beliefs of Marxism and Catholicism were notably the product of ontological differences between the party and the church, entities that were possible to placate temporarily but impossible to reconcile permanently.[6] Thus, only the destruction of the church would have satisfied the Communists.

Jan Widacki, the former head of the Ministerstwo Spraw Wewnętrznych (MSW; Ministry of Internal Affairs) and a vehement critic of the regime after 1989, acknowledged this grievous doctrinal polarity by noting that it existed on three levels: philosophical, ideological, and psychological.[7] In the philosophical sense, the church propagated its own values and vision of humanity, which were very different from those of Marxist ideology. Ideologically, the church managed to maintain its political independence and institutional integrity, and in spite of many Communists' efforts remained largely uncontrollable, albeit relatively predictable. Moreover, in a psychological sense, growing social respect for the clergy exasperated many ambitious security functionaries, sometimes to the point of murderous fury. In 1969, a MSW vice minister, Franciszek Szlachcic, blamed the other side for its bellicose attitude: "We need to distinguish between politics and ideology. Détente from time to time is possible, as we have now. But the ideological fight is still on and intensifies. The ideological activity of the clergy is a part of their ideological sabotage."[8] For the vice minister, the religious activity of the church was intrinsically ideological and thus unacceptable to the regime. The only acceptable modus vivendi would be total control of the church by the state. For these reasons, the regime was unwilling to tolerate a strong church in the mode of peaceful co-existence.[9] The government's attack on the church was inevitable.

The party's full-fledged crusade against the church and religiosity in general began in 1949 and employed the whole battery of state institutions—a secular school system, ferocious propaganda, derisive media coverage, and ubiquitous censorship.[10] The Bezpieka undoubtedly played a critical role in organizing and supervising relentless anticlerical campaigns. Its methods of operation varied from the clandestine harassment of village priests to the preparation of a public trial of a bishop.[11] After the Polish October (1956), which marked the end of Stalinism (the Polish Stalinists were removed from government by the nationalist-Communists led by Władysław Gomułka), the security apparatus began tackling the church mainly with administrative tools: instituting a military draft, rejecting church construction permits, and rationing fuel for winter.[12] Although they varied in spitefulness, all these methods served the same purpose—to break as many clergy as possible to the point of numbness and threaten the most stubborn of them to the point of coronary failure.[13]

## The Religious Masquerade of the Regime: Prelude to Attack

Ironically, in the late 1940s, many Communist Party dignitaries were involved in a campaign designed to show their supposedly tolerant stance toward the Catholic Church. To win the support of Catholic Poles, the regime tried to exploit the mistakes of the main opposition leader, Stanisław Mikołajczyk, who had antagonized the church through numerous polemics against the Catholic press, his support of amendments to family law (such as separation of civil and religious marriage), and the neopagan radical agrarianism of his party colleague Józef Niećko.[14] Until the destruction of its political opposition and the anti-Communist military units, which was accomplished by 1950, the regime covered its atheistic face with a religious mask, as its hunger for power was larger than its ideological anticlericalism. The most visible "convert" from atheism to ostensible Catholicism was Bolesław Bierut, the leader of the Polish Communist Party, who went far beyond tolerant phrases: on several occasions, with folded hands, he made pilgrimages to the "bastion of superstition and reaction," as the Catholic Church was called during secret briefings.[15] In the meantime, the Polish Catholic Church quickly regained its strength after being debilitated by five years of brutal Nazi rule. Nevertheless, after 1945, Poland was a unique case among all the states behind the Iron Curtain, for while religious groups of all kinds were under fierce Communist attack in Hungary, Lithuania, and Czechoslovakia, the Catholic Church in Poland enjoyed relative peace.[16] As Hanna Diskin noted in reference to the late 1940s, "Church baptism and a Catholic education of Communist Party members, including senior party members, had . . . borne witness to the extraordinary influence of the Polish Church."[17] Indeed, for the Polish Communists of the late 1940s, there was nothing incongruous about participating in religious parades, baptisms, religious funerals, or church weddings, especially if their leader did such things publicly.[18] At the same time, however, the security functionaries put the clergy and the religious Communists under strict surveillance, gathering evidence for future trials. In the eloquent words of Józef Światło, a high-ranking security officer who escaped to the West, "For the regime there was no holiness whatsoever."[19]

The church's fine liturgy and splendid ceremonials presumably did not impress Bolesław Bierut, since in 1949 he threw off the mask of mildness and showed (from the church's perspective) a particularly diabolical face. The Bezpieka's machinery began to accelerate its ferocious anticlerical campaign— spying on, arresting, misinforming, blackmailing, and bribing the clergy.[20] The attacks were so intense that on July 13, 1949, Pope Pius XII excommunicated Bierut and his Communist colleagues. This was not the first time a formerly devout ruler had met with papal damnation, and paradoxically, this might have been a good moment for Bierut to follow Henry VIII's example of creating a new, state-friendly church. The efforts to do so using the PAX and "patriotic priests" were, however, unsuccessful.[21] Ultimately, it was not the papal excommunication but Soviet premier Nikita Khrushchev's anti-Stalinist speech that scared Bolesław Bierut to death: he died of a heart attack in Moscow, days after the twentieth Soviet Communist Party Congress turbulently deposed Joseph Stalin from his exalted pedestal.[22]

## The Security Functionary as *Homo Sovieticus*

The regime's materialistic, atheistic, and explicitly anticlerical doctrine, demanding undivided loyalty, was in fact a kind of religion itself.[23] Each member of the security apparatus was expected to believe uncritically in the Communist Party. There is nothing strange in this fact since each man had to be an exemplary Communist who

> has absolute faith in the Party, which means that his faith in it is uncritical at every stage, no matter what the Party is saying. It is a person with the ability to adapt his mentality and his conscience in such a way that he can unreservedly accept the dogma that the Party is never wrong, even though it is wrong all the time—something the Party itself actually admits with every new stage it enters.... Whoever is able to reconcile that contradiction or, to put in Marxist terms, that dialectical process—the Party's infallibility and its fallibility—is a Communist.[24]

This definition of a Communist, provided by the Stalinist editor in chief of the Polish Press Agency, unabashedly reveals the essentials of the functionaries' creed. Ironically, the dogma of the party's infallibility was strikingly similar to the dogma of papal infallibility: it was supposed to be unquestioned and essential for personal *survival*, while the latter was unquestioned and essential for personal *salvation*.[25] The assertion of "an absolute faith in the party" embellished the regime with an aura of secular divinity based on "scientific historical determinism."[26] Surely faith in the party—a substitute for the old God—required a high level of devoutness, and in many cases sacrifice to the point of martyrdom. Indubitable and wholehearted service to the regime regardless of anything (and sometimes regardless of everything) must have been accompanied by a large dose of fanaticism, dexterity, or both. Functioning in constant dialectical fusions of extremes trained the security officers to the point of spiritual numbness, mental stillness, and ideological ossification.

These were, however, the essentials for becoming the "new kind of man" who fit the definition of *Homo sovieticus* provided by the Polish priest and philosopher Józef Tischner.[27] For Tischner, *Homo sovieticus* is a man who is averse to responsibility, opportunistic, aggressive toward the weakest and loyal toward the strongest, intellectually incapacitated, deprived of dignity, and totally subordinate to the party.[28] In other words, nothing more than a robot of the regime.

The party was well aware that only officers free from religious "flaws" could evolve into *Homo sovieticus*. To prevent functionaries from flirting with religiosity, the regime organized internal anticlerical campaigns, fervently ridiculed the church as bankrupt by denigrating the clergy as hypocrites, and poured scorn on religious ceremonialism as completely benighted. In this respect, the security personnel were strictly instructed to regard the materialistic worldview (*światopogląd materialistyczny*) as the only acceptable one, because it had been scientifically proven. Although the regime claimed it cared for both "material and spiritual needs over all other social problems," the materialistic approach it propagated substantially simplified human nature by neglecting eschatology, transcendence, and spirituality.[29] Widacki observed that the security functionaries were not allowed to engage in ontological disputes and told to accept the spiritless, ephemeral vision of humanity as dogma. Moreover, the Bezpieka elevated atheism to the rank of a moral virtue and condemned each act of religious activism as a serious infringement on the socialist "rule of ethics."[30]

Archival documents reveal that the regime considered the church an arrogant enemy. The institutionalized atheism among its security cadres was a preventive measure to make the Bezpieka immune to potential infiltration by the clergy: "We have to hit the enemy—the clergy. We deal with an extremely devious foe that knows very well how to use intrigue and other methods associated with the term 'Jesuits'."[31] Moreover, aware of possible influence from the functionaries' Catholic relatives, the regime demanded that their wives also be nonbelievers: "An operational functionary cannot be a believer, nor can his wife. This especially concerns employees of Department V.[32] Very often, a wife tries to exercise an influence on her husband and the clergy uses family as a means to get to us."[33] Moreover, to protect the security body from religious "infection," all candidates for "soldiers of the party" were questioned about their faith. In addition to submitting a detailed resume, each applicant had to fill out a form that asked, among other questions, about their religious attitudes. Widacki noted that although he examined hundreds of personal files, he never saw the entry "Roman Catholic" or any other religion without the note "non-practicing." Most applicants, however, claimed themselves to be either "non-believers" or "atheists"—exactly what the regime was looking for.[34] In this vein, Jerzy Gruba, the future commander of the Bezpieka in Katowice, assured the reviewers of his questionnaire in 1953 that he would serve the regime "with body and soul."[35] He got the job.

Such preventive measures were accompanied by intellectual brainwashing. Ironically, the Communist Party's internal campaigns against religiosity borrowed words with religious connotations to refer to the regime itself. In this semantic mishmash, materialistically senseless words such as "soul" received new, "rationalized" meanings: "Care for party vigilance, party attitude, for 'party soul,' and for party raising should become the continuous responsibility of us all, our everyday effort."[36] This was not the only spiritually charged statement of Stanisław Radkiewicz, the minister of public security (1944–1954), who had a general fondness for using pious expressions in his secret speeches. Once, he called the security apparatus "*devoted* and saturated with the party's *spirit*"; on a different occasion, he criticized "functionaries with *sins* of crimes"; at another time, he urged their "growing in the *spirit* of frankness."[37] The minister's ethereal vocabulary became popular, his style keenly copied by other dignitaries. For example, one of the vice directors of public security sanctified the Bezpieka's vigilance as being "the most *holy* duty," while his colleague Colonel Humer lamented over functionaries who were "*soulless* and lacking party *conscience*."[38] Edward Ochab, the first secretary of the Communist Party, called the Bezpieka a "*devilish* mill functioning without control," and Franciszek Szlachcic, the MSW minister from February to December 1971, pointed at "the security apparatus' *venial original sin*" (*ciężki grzech pierworodny*).[39] The most awkward and humorous instance of religious language in Communist discourse was Edward Gierek's reaction to Karol Wojtyła's election as pope in 1978. According to one of his aides, when Gierek was greeted with the surprising news, the first secretary of the party painfully exclaimed, "Oh, for God's sake!"[40]

The secrecy of these comments, with the exception of Szlachcic's, precludes the possibility that such religious rhetoric was used for some kind of propaganda. The semantic syncretism of the Bezpieka's newspeak can be explained in two ways. First and foremost, it may have been force of habit, since many functionaries had been raised as Catholics and were accustomed to expressing their feelings using words with religious connotations.[41] Moreover, many of them were barely educated and therefore unable to communicate with a more refined and less religious vocabulary. Second, the Marxist language itself might have been too narrow to express thoughts such as *party spirit*—terms that were understandable yet indefinable. In any event, the jargon of the Bezpieka made its atheism a farce as long as the security dignitaries were unable to free themselves from the influence of religious semantics.

## The Inquisition within the Bezpieka

Despite anticlerical campaigns in the 1950s and 1960s, the Catholic Church remained independent and hugely popular. The Communist Party was aware of its potential influence on all sections of society, including the security functionaries. Although the Bezpieka's department of human resources was flooded with assurances of religious contempt, the Bolshevik rule of limited trust called for constant monitoring of the cadres. Between 1944 and 1981, the "spiritual care" of security functionaries was in the hands of party organizations operating at every level of the Bezpieka's convoluted structure. In 1981, the internal inquisition was institutionalized in the form of the Pion Polityczno-Wychowawczy (PPW; Political-Educational Unit), a copy of a similar unit that had existed in the Ministry of National Defense since 1943.[42] Militaristic in discipline and fanatical in attitude, the PPW pedantically and scrupulously combed through the backgrounds of security personnel, looking for Catholic proselytes. The hunt for ideological infidels quickly won the PPW infamy as the government's most hated investigative unit. However, for the last chief of the PPW, it was a cause for pride: "We did not make a mistake by laying a special stress on the forming and the uninterrupted developing of the functionaries' moral and ideological values. We always cared that the superiors raised their subordinates. . . . Those functionaries who, for better results, violated the rule of law or collided, even slightly, with the ethics or law, were met with general condemnation and severity."[43]

Indeed, the six hundred employees of the PPW unrelentingly stalked their colleagues, ensuring that no one lost sight of the "pulsating beacon of Marxist-Leninism." If they caught a co-worker breaking the socialist rules of ethics (for example, by baptizing a child), they automatically reported the "ideological conflict" to their superiors, accompanied with a plea for dismissal of the culprit. It is no wonder that the PPW's zeal scared the security personnel into more cautious behavior, which the chief of the PPW proudly admitted: "Soon after, life confirmed that the decision to set up the PPW was right. The new unit immediately began to intensively influence the functionaries' actions. It encouraged the superiors to take more attentive care to the moral and political state of their subordinates and to consider the 'upbringing function' as primary."[44]

After the scandalous murder of Rev. Jerzy Popiełuszko by four functionaries from the echelons of the MSW (October 1984), the minister of internal affairs demilitarized the PPW by granting its oversight to a civilian with a rank of MSW vice minister. It was a smart move intended to increase the PPW's prestige without fundamentally changing its formula at the same time. The PPW's first civilian director placed much stress on indoctrinating the cadres through various nondisciplinary means—mainly speeches and publications. The PPW prepared periodicals such as the *Biuletyn* (Bulletin) to educate the functionaries about the clandestine activity of their enemies. However, these periodicals contained no sophisticated methods for fighting the church. The articles raised the security personnel's intellects to the mere level of a popular encyclopedia: in one issue of the *Biuletyn*, for example, readers could find out that *Vatican* is the name of a hill in Rome, and that the name derives from Latin *viticino*, which means "forecast" or "prediction."[45] The journal *Ancora*, which printed a new issue each month between 1976 and 1983, was much more sophisticated. Officially published by the Polish Center for the Second Vatican Council Renewal, it was in fact prepared by the Bezpieka, with the goal of dividing the church from within.[46] The journal was addressed to the clergy to supposedly create an impression of a strong dissident movement against Primate Stefan Wyszyński and the Polish episcopate.[47] The *Ancora* (printed in a primitive manner for better credibility) contained translations and reprints of pieces by Western theologians and Catholic dissidents such as Hans Küng, as well as articles written by professors at the Academy of Catholic Theology secretly recruited to work for the Bezpieka.[48] The journal did not break the church, but the attempt shows how the security functionaries were ingenious when it came to fighting it. Next to terror and primitive propaganda, the security apparatus employed sophisticated tactics that relied on the highest theological quality.[49]

In addition to such inquisitional and educational efforts, the PPW also specialized in ideological resurrections. The unit took special care of the "mentally weakest" functionaries, who were usually the youngest in service and often "politically unstable."[50] While these functionaries were not always considered lost, they needed "caring ideological and educational help . . . that would restore their faith in . . . socialist rules and strengthen [their] ideological attitude based on the socialist hierarchy of values."[51] This ambitious goal was carried out by breathing a new "socialist spirit" into such officers. For the PPW, the revival of faith in socialism was just a matter of competent indoctrination based on a "wise and true interpretation of facts."[52] Obviously, the goal of indoctrination in the Marxist spirit was to convince doubtful officers that the party was always right, and that all failures were temporary or necessary to reach the more advanced stages of socialist development during the long pilgrimage to the Communist paradise. Thus, to keep the socialistic pilgrimage moving at all costs, the PPW tried to restore the functionaries' sense of duty and hope in socialism, actualizing the aphorism that socialism without hope is like a church without faith.[53]

The PPW's efforts were, however, only partially successful: its chief once moaned that young officers were more receptive to ideological rather than moral transformations.[54] The party decided to try to counteract this with the Zarząd Ochrony Funkcjonariuszy (ZOF; Board for Functionaries' Security), which became yet another remedy for moral perversions and legal trans-gressions.[55] Called by Bezpieka officers "security within security," the ZOF's role—exactly as its name indicates—was to protect the security functionaries from themselves. One can see in the ZOF a desperate effort to prevent the officers from seeing hopelessly catastrophic economic reality by keeping them "mentally incapacitated." This two-hundred-headed Leviathan living parasiti-cally inside the Bezpieka's body was a pacemaker for the slacking "heart of the party," as the security apparatus was often metaphorically called.[56]

In exceptional cases, the ZOF was allowed to recruit security personnel as secret collaborators. But to avoid endangering solidarity among the offi-cers—essential for coordinated teamwork—each collaborator was traditionally dismissed after the investigation in question was closed. In any case, the scope of ZOF activity was virtually unlimited, as its curiosity was not satisfied by studying officers' potentially harmful behavior. The ZOF was also interested in the officers' attitudes, which justified intrusions into every possible sphere of a functionary's life, including the intimate. The eyes of the Bezpieka's Leviathan tended to squint convergently, into functionaries' personae, as well as diver-gently, onto functionaries' surroundings. In one such example, the ZOF main-tained complete surveillance of the families of Captain Grzegorz Piotrowski and Colonel Adam Pietruszka—the infamous murderers of Rev. Popiełuszko, the chaplain of Solidarity. The bugs were active for five years, until the ZOF's demise in 1989.[57]

## The "Degenerate" Functionaries

In spite of all these endeavors, some security functionaries were still unable to "unchain their minds" from Catholicism, participating clandestinely but more or less regularly in religious ceremonies. The idea of raising a function-ary in the spirit of duplicity—a clever tactic to deceive the regime's enemy—turned against the regime itself in numerous cases. If a functionary's duplicity accidentally reversed its polarity, the double-edged sword of slyness could become dangerous for the sheath of the security apparatus. Numerous sources indicate that the religiosity of the Bezpieka personnel did not appear only in isolated cases. Lieutenant Colonel Józef Światło, a defector, publicly admitted that "security functionaries, even if they do not participate in weekly religious activities, still try to get married in the church. Many times, they travel to dis-tant locations for the wedding. . . . I know that these cases were numerous."[58] The security minister, discussing the Bezpieka's problems with its executives during a secret conference in 1954, made a similar observation: "There are still cases of religious devoutness, petit bourgeois mentality, bossiness, drunkenness, and hooliganism."[59] The most striking discussion, however, seems to have been among the security dignitaries who met in secret during one of the most tumultuous times in the Bezpieka's history, in December 1984. During the fall, Rev. Popiełuszko's murder had been covered on the front pages of newspapers around the world, forcing the security apparatus to retreat.[60] At the meeting, the minister furtively discussed ways to uproot religious devotion out of the security cadres: "The problem of religious devotion has reached a level from which we cannot escape. So far, we have been reacting to it in various ways, but we need uniform tactics, regulations, and methodology."[61] The minister's idea of setting strict rules against religiously devout and ideologically devious functionaries was enthusiastically supported by all the conference participants as a useful step ahead—a step toward institutionalized atheism.[62]

It would be naive, however, to think that the party leaders trivialized religiosity as something that would disappear if the functionaries physically cut themselves off from the church. As early as 1953, one of the security vice ministers warned his party comrades that

> overcoming religious superstitions is not easy and simple. In many cases, we consider the employee a nonbeliever because he does not go to church and does not participate in religious ceremonies. It is an unrealistic and superfluous judgment. The reality is different. In practice, people dither for a long time, and it may last forever if they are left without political and ideological help from the party organizations and all active Communists. Often we are caught by surprise: one hid his religiosity, the other baptized his child in the village church, another secretly traveled the country to get married in church.[63]

For this apparatchik, the roots of the problem lay in the Bezpieka recruitment procedure, which favored candidates of a peasant or proletarian pedigree, which in fact worked in favor of the church, not the regime. Despite its constant filtering of applications, the Bezpieka accepted many peasants and workers who had been raised in the Catholic faith since the cradle. The vice minister warned that "it would be naïve to think that such an employee could cut off his religious ties within a year or two."[64] This strikingly pragmatic assessment of the situation called for the redefinition of a *nonbeliever*. To the vice minister, mere physical withdrawal from the church did not alone constitute an atheist: it had to be accompanied by an internal transformation in the "spirit of the materialistic outlook."[65] The regime realized this by the supplanting of the cult of Yahweh with the cult of the party. To achieve this goal, its brainwashing program focused on denigrating religiosity to the level of socially accepted pathologies such as drunkenness and hooliganism.[66] Thus, given its redefinition as morally depraved, devoutness was clearly not considered an element of socialist ethics, but rather a grievous violation.

In the 1980s, it became customary for "morally degenerate functionaries" who blemished the code of socialist ethics by dipping their fingers into holy water to be "amputated" as atrophied members of the security apparatus. Catching an officer inhaling incense was proof that he had already ingested a dangerous dose of the Catholic spirit and therefore betrayed the regime. "The militia had trust in you, and you betrayed them by having a relationship with the clergy!": these words accompanied the dismissal order of Sergeant Tadeusz Milczewski, signed by the security minister himself.[67] Sergeant Milczewski "betrayed" the party by having a religious wedding with a woman who had three priests in her family and not reporting this "outrageous" fact to his superiors.[68] These kinds of cases were numerous, many of them concerning even less grievous acts.[69]

Before dismissing a proselyte from the Bezpieka, a superior usually tried to break him mentally by giving him a glimmer of hope for institutionalized forgiveness if he showed enough remorse. The forms of this varied: while Colonel R. was asked to sign a plea for his dismissal, Sergeant Milczewski was encouraged to sign a derogatory statement denouncing his beliefs and family: "I broke with my in-laws [because of their religiosity] and moved with my wife and child to a rented room. I did not baptize the child. I am against Christianity."[70] Self-criticism, no matter how sincere, was usually in vain, because the final decisions (made in the 1980s by the MSW minister himself) were predominantly negative.[71] Presumably, the dialectics of "a functionary publicly fighting against the church and privately attending religious ceremonies with a wife" were impossible to reconcile. The party wanted both its soldiers' bodies and souls; any compromise was ruled out.[72]

If there was no evidence of other subversive activity, religious functionaries were usually expelled from service, which meant financial and social denigration but at least no criminal repercussions. Many of the dismissed officers were later accepted into the reformed post-Communist police force in 1990. The recruitment procedure revealed an interesting case: on one occasion, the police accepted a functionary previously dismissed for religious activity, but the commission later revealed that he had previously dismissed his colleagues for the same "moral violations."[73] This was a typical example of the moral schizophrenia the Communist environment had nurtured for years. The regime elevated hypocrisy to a moral virtue, hiding its inner immorality behind the facade of a peculiar phrase with a presumably positive charge: *działania pozorne* (the ostensible activities). For example, Minister Kiszczak theoretically relied on a group of people in the MSW to prepare anniversary cards for the hated clergy. "Personally, I am very happy that His Holiness, John Paul II, vested in you such an honorable dignity, you—whom I honor with deepest respect and trust"—with these lofty words, the MSW minister greeted Alojzy Orszulik as a new bishop.[74] The "card unit" must have lacked the necessary panache, however, since these warm wishes reflected the minister's corrections to the unit's draft.[75] Notably, copies of such cards were sent via administrative channels to the director of the MSW department responsible for fighting the church. This paradoxical procedure was nothing less than a microcosm of the socialist morality: the minister sent cards with grandiloquent wishes to a bishop, while his subordinates sent criminals to burn the bishop's car. In the regime's masquerade, everyone played their assigned roles: some were to be ostensibly friendly, while others were realistically ruthless.

Being involved in antichurch activities undoubtedly brought some of the functionaries into the church's sphere of influence. Spying on nuns, eavesdropping on priests, and recording sermons must have exposed security personnel to a condensed dose of theoretical and practical Catholicism. Some officers became closer to the altar than many of the most devout nonpolice Catholics could dream. Particularly interesting here is the MSW project of examining all sermons for their antiregime content. During one Sunday, the many sections of the security apparatus recorded several thousand sermons throughout Polish churches. The material was later reheard and reexamined by church specialists. The most complex exegesis of sermons in the history of the world homiletics revealed that over 90 percent of them did not have any ideological connotations whatsoever.[76] Did they bring the officers closer to Christianity? The archives do not contain an answer to this question.

## The Catholic Church on the Offensive

There is evidence that the regime's perception of the church as an arrogant enemy was partially justified. Virtually every member of the party, regardless of rank and experience, could become a target for evangelization. One striking case of conversion concerned Colonel Julia "Bloody Luna" Brystygier, one of the most fervent anticlerical Stalinists in the Communist government. Luna's fanatic pro-Soviet attitude and exceptional intelligence (Brystygier was a doctor of philosophy who had attended the Sorbonne) opened doors wide for her career in the security apparatus. Between 1950 and 1954, Colonel Brystygier was a director of Department V, which was responsible for fighting the church. Next to preparing long-term anticlerical strategies, she personally enjoyed inflicting sexual torture—her favorite was hitting the genitals of naked priests with a whip while interrogating them.[77]

On occasion, Bloody Luna was exposed to daring attempts to convert her to Catholicism. During an interrogation, for example, a nun, Maria Okońska, tried to exploit Luna's suspiciously kind attitude toward her by boldly questioning the colonel about faith.[78] This trivial conversation had an unexpected outcome. Maria Okońska promised Luna that she would pray for her by thinking of her in "the most beautiful way a man can think about another man."[79] This daring attempt at evangelization, ending with a cordial hug between the victim and the oppressor, within a week won freedom for the nun and encouraged her to pray even more intensely for the "poor Communist." A year later, Maria Okońska was on the full offensive, voluntarily visiting Colonel Brystygier with a New Testament—a gift offered to Luna by Primate Wyszyński himself.[80] For the time being, it was fruitless: a few years later, Wyszyński was arrested and the antichurch campaign intensified. In 1956, however, Bloody Luna lost her job in public security and for a long time lived in poverty.[81] Her frequent visits to a friend in the Catholic House for the Blind in Laski exposed the former colonel to the Catholic way of life and finally made her convert to Catholicism and ask for baptism (being Jewish by origin, she had not been baptized in childhood). By the end of her life, she received Communion every day, prayed a lot, gave large sums of money to the blind children and, finally, "died completely reconciled with God."[82] Some were suspicious of the authenticity of her conversion, but a new friend, Rev. Antoni Marylski, was sure that Luna had undergone a real conversion because "she realized how much evil and unhappiness was caused by her actions and now she tries to fix a lot by a new Christian life."[83]

The regime viewed Luna's conversion in Laski as an example of the church's dangerous power. Many members of the party, Communist intellectuals, and security officers—including those who fought against the church—visited the house in Laski looking for spiritual help.[84] The house was visited by atheist Jews as well as by former Catholics who had previously abandoned their faith for their careers in the state apparatus. Secret baptisms of the Communists and their children (sometimes as adults) became a norm.[85] Not surprisingly, the regime put the house under strict surveillance and infiltrated the personnel in several operations, one of them code-named "Cobra."[86] A dense network of agents spied on the repentant Communists coming from all sections of the Ministry of the Internal Affairs.[87]

## Law and Religious Freedom

One would be mistaken to think that being a Catholic functionary in Communist Poland constituted a crime *ex lege*. The Constitution of 1952 (the Stalin Constitution) explicitly guaranteed freedom of religion to *all* citizens, in Article 70.1:

> The Polish People's Republic guarantees its citizens freedom of conscience and religion. The church and other religious groups can freely conduct their religious functions. No one can force citizens not to participate in religious duties and ceremonies. Also, no one can force anybody to participate in religious duties and ceremonies.[88]

The benevolence of Article 70.1 seems suspicious, given the actual Communist attitude toward religion. If freedom of "conscience and religion" concerned all citizens, it must have included security functionaries as well. In these kinds of disputes, the main problem usually lies in legal interpretation. Although Communist Poland officially honored religious freedom, the regime abused it in practice on the pretext of state and church separation, as expressed in Point 2 of Article 70: "The church is separate from the state. The relation between the state and the church, as well as the legal and financial status of religious denominations, will be regulated in statutes."[89] Point 2 of the Stalin Constitution indirectly legalized purging the Bezpieka of religion: the security apparatus—a state institution to the core—was designed to be free from the church. The institutional separation of the Bezpieka does not mean, however, that their employees' personal beliefs had to be scrutinized as well. Article 70.1 unambiguously prohibited forcing citizens not to participate in religious duties and ceremonies. The party's instructions to penalize the security personnel for private religious activism were therefore blatantly unconstitutional. Strikingly, throughout the thirty-six years of the Stalin Constitution, the regime did not even make an effort to legitimize the PPW's and ZOF's inquisitorial hunts by means of a statutory regulation. For the Communists, Point 3 of Article 70 provided enough protection: "Abuses of freedom of conscience and religion against the interests of the Polish People's Republic are penalized."[90] Certainly, the party had the unchallenged monopoly on defining state interests, and if the prescribed penalty was to be only administrative (such as dismissal from service), it did not have to be put into statutory law. Most probably, the infringement on the ethical rules of institutionalized atheism was left undefined in the statutes on purpose, so a daring functionary's complaint against his or her dismissal order could be contained in the safe wardrobes of Bezpieka dignitaries. The documents in my archival research have not revealed cases of officers disputing with their superiors on paper—a sign that the personnel was well aware that a legal duel with the regime would be as suicidal as valorous.

Strikingly, within the scope of Communist penal law, the Bezpieka's inquisitors were more than assailants—they were criminals. The penal code of 1969 recommended up to five years in prison for anyone who "limits a citizen's rights in regards to his or her religious affiliation or the lack of such" (Article 192).[91] Moreover, Article 196 prescribed the same penalty for a person forcing anyone not to participate in a religious activity or ceremony.[92] These crimes did not have any exceptions. Ironically, while the Communists were powerful enough to legitimate the Bezpieka's internal anticlerical watch, it was severely penalized *ex lege*. The situation surely must have been confusing for the security employees, especially those legalistically inclined, given that the officers were obligated to know the provisions of all the laws applicable to their service.[93] The practice of keeping Articles 192 and 196 inactive was an ominous signal to the functionaries that they worked in a lawless environment. In this tenebrous "state within a state," the actual rules were dictated ad hoc by the Bezpieka dignitaries. To survive in the jungle of the Bezpieka, the officers had to obey the law at all costs—that is, the law of the strongest, not necessarily the law of the statutes. The internalization of this reality was broad. For instance, during his trial, Lieutenant Waldemar Chmielewski testified that his superior had assured him about their impunity: "No one will be allowed to interrogate us, take our fingerprints, or cross-examine us."[94] Chmielewski was very unlucky: called by General Wojciech Jaruzelski (the leader of the Communist Party in the 1980s) "the rotten cell in the entrails of the security body," he was "amputated with exemplary openness."[95] With a dose of reluctance, but to preserve the reputation of the security apparatus, the regime sacrificed a few of its members by turning the inactive law into a sharp scalpel suitable for amputations. If the regime had been a consistent surgeon, society would have witnessed the Bezpieka's total mutilation. As usual, the dogma of the party's infallibility took priority.

## Conclusion

Ironically, for the regime in which "every religious idea, every idea of God, even flirting with the idea of God, [was] unutterable vileness, vileness of the most dangerous kind, contagion of the most abominable kind," the security officers were compelled to become fanatical believers: unconditionally devoted to Communism and uncritically accepting of the party's infallibility.[96] They were meant to be the apostles of the new religion of Marxist-atheism, which developed many of the external trappings of religion: rites, ceremonies, language, and worship of its leaders. There was, however, one paramount difference concerning Poland. Unlike other Central-Eastern European states, where Communists deliberately destroyed religion in the course of their accession to power and then twisted atheist materialism to fill the vacuum, Poland had no religious void, as Catholicism remained dominant.[97] Here, scientific historical determinism had to compete against Catholicism. Thus, the antagonisms between these two systems of beliefs were ontological and ultimately irreconcilable; at least one of them had to eventually perish. Such a polarized view on religious reality forced the Communist regime to dramatically promote its own vision of humanity and the world, as it was a matter of survival.

To destroy the church, the regime created an entire structure out of its own morals, where institutionalized atheism was elevated to the highest virtue and religiosity was denigrated to the level of socially accepted pathologies. In this respect, the security apparatus was both an agent for the transformation of Polish society and a laboratory of atheist experiments on its own community. The party cared a lot about the "purity" of the Bezpieka's cadres since they were to be the first solely atheist segment of the Polish society, radiating to others their socialist optimism and ideological expertise. To have the Bezpieka entirely atheist, the regime established strict rules of admission, trying to filter out the candidates inclined to Catholicism. Those accepted to service were under constant surveillance as the internal inquisitorial units ceaselessly searched for degenerate functionaries—the religiously devout and ideologically devious. Tolerating Catholic officers was impossible: in the party's eyes, functionaries who participated in religious ceremonies were unwilling and unable to transform into *Homo sovieticus* and thus had to be eliminated from the security apparatus before infecting their colleagues with "intellectual depravity."

Despite full-fledged efforts to exterminate religiosity, the religion of Marxism-atheism could not compete with Polish Catholicism. Many officers rejected the spiritual and mental death deemed necessary to serve constant dialectical fusions of extremes, remaining (at least secretly) religious. In addition, the regime's policy was confusing, since Communist dignitaries officially participated in religious ceremonies and borrowed words with religious connotations to describe the secular world. Also, Communist law—the emanation of the Party's will—unambiguously honored religious freedom. These confusing signals were falsely recognized by some functionaries as institutionalized acceptance of Catholicism. Considering the actual bellicose attitude to the church, working in the Bezpieka required duplicity—another chief socialist virtue. Yet the officers who kept their intellectual and emotional distance from the party had to realize that dialectic materialism was in fact an incurable moral schizophrenia. Mainly for these reasons, the regime's goal of promoting a new, Marxist-atheist outlook on life through the security functionaries proved to be unachievable.

## Notes

1. Hanna Diskin, *The Seeds of Triumph: Church and State in Gomułka's Poland* (New York: Central European University Press, 2001), 1, 62.
2. Andrzej Paczkowski notes that the Polska Partia Robotnicza (PPR; Polish Workers' Party) followed Stalin's advice (and disregarded the wishes of some radicals) when it refrained from launching an open war against the church: *Stanisław Mikołajczyk czyli klęska realisty* [Stanisław Mikołajczyk: Failure of the realist] (Warsaw: Agencja Omnipress, 1991), 160. For example, in 1944, the Communist government of Poland pushed for an agrarian reform of real estate exceeding certain limits. Wanda Wasilewska, the deputy chief of the Polski Komitet Wyzwolenia Narodowego (PKWN; Polish Committee of National Liberation), testified in her memoirs that the decision not to include church lands in the agrarian reform was made by Stalin himself. See *Secretariat General du Gouvernement* (1959), 9, cited by Diskin, *Seeds of Triumph*, 54, 266.
3. Stalin perceived that there would be a widespread reluctance to settle in the Regained Territories (the western territories) if the government failed to organize religious services for newcomers: Diskin, *Seeds of Triumph*, 65; see also Ronald C. Monticone, *The Catholic Church in Communist Poland, 1945–1985* (Boulder, CO: East European Monographs, 1986), 18–20.
4. In a chapter devoted to the first period of Władysław Gomułka's activities versus the church, Diskin notes that "in the light of the main objectives which Stalin considered critical, and in the face of the difficulties of which he was highly aware, the Soviet Union adopted, as part of its (stage-by-stage) tactics, a policy of postponing and disguising its ideological objectives, which had exceptional significance in terms of agriculture as well as religion and the church in Poland." *Seeds of Triumph*, 32–33.
5. The Catholic Church was constantly under strict Bezpieka surveillance. The primary supervision was performed by the network of secret collaborators. For an extensive analysis of the clergy under Communist surveillance, see Tadeusz Isakowicz-Zaleski, *Księża wobec Bezpieki* [Priests toward the Bezpieka] (Kraków: Wydawnictwo Znak, 2007). For details concerning the surveillance of Karol Wojtyła, the future pope, see Marek Lasota and Marek Zając, "Donos na Wojtyłę" [Denunciation of Wojtyła], *Wydawnictwo Znak*, 2006. For a general overview of efforts to repress the church, see *Leksykon duchowieństwa represjonowanego w PRL w latach 1945–1989* [The encyclopedic dictionary of the persecuted clergy in the Polish People's Republic, 1945–1989], vol. 1–3, ed. J. Myszor (Warsaw: Verbinum, 2002). Particularly interesting is a note by Colonel Goroński about internal rifts within the church and the possibility of exploiting the animosity between Kraków archbishop Karol Wojtyła and the primate, Stefan Wyszyński: "Notatka majora katowickiej SB Zygmunta Nikla z wykładu wicedyrektora Departamentu IV MSW płk Zenona Gorońskiego na kursokonferencji dla pracowników jednostek terenowych pionu IV SB zorganizowanej na początku kwietnia 1969 r. w Wiśle" [Note made by Major Zygmunt Nikiel of the Katowice Służba Bezpieczeństwa (SB; Security Service), based on the lecture of Colonel Zenon Goroński, vice director of the Ministry of Internal

Affairs, Department IV, during the conference of the functionaries of the district units of SB, Department IV, early April 1969], Institute of National Remembrance (Archivum Instytut Pamięci Narodowej; hereafter AIPN) Ka, Wojewódzki Urząd Spraw Wewnętrznych (WUSW; District Office of Internal Affairs) w Katowicach, 056/59, t. 2.

See also these monographs in English: Diskin, *Seeds of Triumph*; Michel Patrick, *Politics and Religion in Eastern Europe: Catholicism in Hungary, Poland, and Czechoslovakia* (Oxford: Polity, 1991); Norbert Zmijewski, *The Catholic-Marxist Ideological Dialogue in Poland, 1945–1980* (Brookfield, VT: Gower, 1991); and Vladimir Gsovski, ed., *Church and State behind the Iron Curtain: Czechoslovakia, Hungary, Poland, Romania, with an Introduction on the Soviet Union* (New York: Praeger, 1955).

6. For a detailed analysis of the antagonism between the Catholic faith and Communist doctrine, see Diskin, *Seeds of Triumph*, 13–14.

7. Jan Widacki, *Czego nie powiedział generał Kiszczak* [What General Kiszczak did not reveal] (Warsaw: Polska Oficyna Wydawnicza, 1992), 82.

8. "Trzeba rozróżnić politykę od ideologii. W polityce są możliwe okresowe odprężenia, jak obecnie. Ale w ideologii walka trwa i nasila się. Ideologiczne działania kleru stanowią część dywersji ideologicznej." In "Notatka z narady w Departamencie IV MSW sporządzona przez naczelnika Wydziału IV KWMO w Katowicach 4 lutego 1969 roku" [Note from the meeting in Department IV of the Ministry of Internal Affairs made by the director of Department IV of the Komenda Wojewódzka Milicji Obywatelskiej (KWMO; District Headquarters of Citizens' Militia) in Katowice on February 4, 1969], quoted in *Metody pracy operacyjnej aparatu bezpieczeństwa wobec Kościołów i związków wyznaniowych 1945–1989* [The operating methods of the security apparatus against the church and religious groups, 1945–1989], ed. Adam Dziurok (Warsaw: Instytut Pamięci Narodowej, 2004). All translations from non-English-language sources quoted in this chapter are mine.

9. For a thorough analysis of the ideological duel between the party and the church, see Zmijewski, *Catholic-Marxist Ideological Dialogue*.

10. Many of these actions were orchestrated by Group D, an independent operation within Department IV of the Ministerstwo Spraw Wewnętrznych (MSW; Ministry of Internal Affairs). For example, it supervised the publication of harmful articles in periodicals such as *Ancora*, *Samoobrona Wiary* (Self-defense of faith), and *Nowa Droga* (The new road). Other methods included sending harassing letters, spreading false rumors, and blackmailing based on the information received from secret collaborators. For more information, see Krzysztof Persak and Łukasz Kamiński, *A Handbook of the Communist Security Apparatus in East Central Europe, 1944–1989* (Warsaw: Instytut Pamięci Narodowej, 2005), 9, 268.

11. According to the historians Antoni Dudek and Andrzej Paczkowski, the Bezpieka's activity slowly moved up the ladder of the Catholic hierarchy, beginning with propaganda assaults, then summoning priests to interrogation, up to arrests (Persak and Kamiński, *Handbook*, 267–69). The first clergyman brought to trial was the bishop of Kielce, Czesław Kaczmarek, arrested in 1951; for more details, see Persak and Kamiński, *Handbook*, 267–69.

12. For details, see Tony Kemp-Welch, "Khrushchev's 'Secret Speech' and Polish Politics: The Spring of 1956," *Europe-Asian Studies* 48, no. 2 (1996): 181–206. For a detailed list of the Bezpieka's repertoire against the church, see Bogdan Szajkowski, *Next to God . . . Poland: Politics and Religion in Contemporary Poland* (New York: St. Martin's Press, 1983), 9–24.

13. For example, the functionaries of the Bezpieka who murdered Rev. Popiełuszko employed various methods to break him psychologically: Krystyna Daszkiewicz, *Uprowadzenie i morderstwo Ks. Jerzego Popiełuszki* [The kidnapping and murder of Rev. Jerzy Popiełuszko] (Poznan, Poland: Kantor Wydawniczy SAWW, 1990), 276. During the meeting of Department IV of the SB between September 15 and 19, 1984, Colonel Adam Pietruszka stated: "That is the end of the game with Rev. Popiełuszko and Rev. Małkowski. We move to more vigorous actions. We need to shake them to the edge of a heart attack" (ibid., 303).

14. Andrzej Paczkowski notes that relations between Mikołajczyk's party, Polskie Stronnictwo Ludowe (PSL; The Polish People's Party), and the Catholic Church were never straightforward. *Stanisław Mikołajczyk*, 160–61.

15. "Ciemnogród i zabobonność." In his memoirs, Jan Widacki recollects numerous nicknames for the church used by the regime, such as "agents" (*agenci*), "imperial emissaries" (*emisariusze imperializmu*), and "warmongers" (*podżegacze wojenni*). *Czego nie powiedział generał Kiszczak*, 87–88.

16. For conflicts between the Catholic Church and Communism in Eastern Europe, see, for example: R. F. Miller and T. H. Rigby, eds., *Religion and Politics in Communist States* (Canberra: Australian National University, 1986); and Bohdan R. Bociurkiw and John W. Strong, eds., *Religion and Atheism in the U.S.S.R. and Eastern Europe* (London: Macmillan, 1975).

17. Diskin, *Seeds of Triumph*, 52.

18. Ibid.

19. Quoted by Zbigniew Błażyński in *Mówi Józef Światło* [Józef Światło speaks] (London: Polska Fundacja Kulturalna, 1988), 45.

20. For details and case studies, see *Operacja zniszczyć Kościół* [Operation Destroy the Church], ed. Filip Musiał and Jarosław Szarka (Kraków: Instytut Pamięci Narodowej, 2007); and Szajkowski, *Next to God*, 9–28.

21. According to Józef Światło, a special role in subjugating the church was played by Bolesław Piasecki and his organization, PAX. This organization was supported by the regime in order to weaken the church. Światło also reveals the role of the "patriotic priests" used by the Communists to destroy the church from within. See Błażyński, *Mówi Józef Światło*, 174–89. For the activities of "patriotic priests" in other Soviet bloc countries, see G. Gorman, ed., *Church and State in Postwar Eastern Europe: A Bibliographical Survey* (New York: Greenwood Press, 1987); and Robert Goeckel, *The Lutheran Church and the East German State: Political Conflict and Change under Ulbricht and Honecker* (Ithaca, NY: Cornell University Press, 1990). The Stowarzyszenie PAX (PAX Association) was a pro-Communist secular religious organization created to undermine grassroots support for the Polish Catholic Church: Norman Davies, *Boże igrzysko* [God's playground] (Kraków: Wydawnictwo Znak, 1998), 626–27.

22. The reasons for Bierut's death were examined by Sławomir Stępień in *Reakcje bezpieki na śmierć Tow. "Tomasza"* [The Bezpieka's reactions to the death of Comrade "Tomasz"] (Warsaw: Instytut Pamięci Narodowej, 2005).

23. Historians and philosophers debate whether Communism was a substitute for religion. Nathaniel Davis claims that Communism shared with many religions the physical attributes of worship, including ceremonies, shrines, and rites, of which Lenin's mausoleum and the Red Square parades are examples: *A Long Walk to Church* (Boulder, CO: Westview Press, 2003), xxii. This belief is shared by John C. Bennett in *Christianity and Communism* (New York: Haden House Associated Press, 1948), 33–34; and Albert Boiter in *Religion in the Soviet Union* (Beverly Hills: Sage Publications, 1980), 10. This notion is opposed by, for example, Paul Gaber, who thinks that atheism does not require an act of faith, but is rather the negation of faith: *And God Created Lenin* (Amherst, NY: Prometheus Books, 2005), 22.

24. This definition was provided by Stefan Staszewski, the first secretary of the Warsaw Communist Party Committee in the 1950s and the editor in chief of the Polish Press Agency, when he was asked the question "Who is a Communist?" For the entire interview with Staszewski and other Polish Communists of the Stalinist era, see Teresa Torańska, *"Them": Stalin's Polish Puppets* (New York: Harper and Row, 1987), especially 128.

25. The dogma of papal infallibility was declared in 1870 in the "Dogmatic Constitution on the Church" promulgated by Pope Pius IX. For more information, see Francis Sullivan, *Creative Fidelity: Weighing and Interpreting Documents of the Magisterium* (New York: Paulist Press, 1996).

26. This is the Marxist-Leninist stance that events are historically predetermined, used to justify the leadership role of the Communist parties.

27. The term *Homo sovieticus* was initially introduced by the Soviet sociologist Aleksandr Zinoviev as a pejorative commentary to the concept of the "New Soviet Man" postulated by the Soviet Communist Party. For details, see Aleksandr Zinoviev, *Homo sovieticus* (Boston: Atlantic Monthly Press, 1985).

28. For an extensive analysis of *Homo sovieticus*, see Józef Tischner, *Etyka solidarności i Homo sovieticus* [Solidarity ethics and *Homo sovieticus*] (Kraków: Społeczny Instytut Wydawniczy Znak, 1992).

29. "Wyższość systemu socjalistycznego . . . [polega na tym], że troskę o człowieka i jego potrzeby materialne i duchowe wysuwa na czoło wszystkich problemów i zadań społecznych": "Referat ministra bezpieczeństwa publicznego Stanisława Radkiewicza na krajową naradę aktywu kierowniczego aparatu bezpieczeństwa publicznego z dnia 4 marca 1954 roku" [Speech by Stanisław Radkiewicz, the minister of public security, to the National Executive Committee of the Security Apparatus, March 4, 1954] (hereafter Speech by Stanisław Radkiewicz, 1954), AIPN, Ministra Bezpieczeństwa Publicznego (MBP; Ministry of Public Security), 14, k. 1–42.

30. Widacki mentions a militia functionary who was fired for organizing a religious funeral for his wife. In an explanatory document, the functionary was accused of violating "ethical rules." *Czego nie powiedział generał Kiszczak*, 78.

31. "Trzeba bić takiego wroga jak kler. Mamy bowiem do czynienia z przeciwnikiem

najbardziej wyrafinowanym, najlepiej umiejącym posługiwać się podstępem i tym wszystkim, co łączy się z pojęciem jezuici": speech by Stanisław Radkiewicz, October 1947, quoted in Musiał and Szkarka, eds., *Operacja*, 5. In another speech, Radkiewicz warned against Catholic clergy trying to sneak into the Bezpieka: "Materiały narady aktywu MBP w dniach 23–25 marca 1949 roku" [Documents of the council of the MBP's executives, held between March 23 and 25, 1949] (hereafter "Materiały"), Archiwum Akt Nowych (Central Archives of Modern Records), Warsaw (hereafter AAN), KC Polska Zjednoczona Partia Robotnicza (PZPR; Polish United Workers' Party), Papiery B. Bieruta [B. Bierut Papers], 11/68.

32. Department V of the Ministry of Public Security was responsible for preventing hostile infiltration, as well as fighting political parties and church influence. For details on the structure of the MBP and its evolution, see Mirosław Piotrowski, *Ludzie Bezpieki w walce z Narodem i Kościołem* [The Bezpieka's men fighting against the nation and the church] (Lublin, Poland: Klub Inteligencji Katolickiej, 2000).

33. Speech by Radkiewicz, "Materiały."

34. "I had in my hands hundreds of personal files of the MO and SB functionaries. I saw hundreds of personal queries. I have never seen in any of them the entry 'Roman-Catholic' or any other without a note 'non-practicing.' Most of them, however, wrote 'nonbeliever' or 'atheist.'" Widacki, *Czego nie powiedział generał Kiszczak*, 151.

35. Ibid., 173.

36. Speech by Stanisław Radkiewicz, 1954.

37. "Growing in the *spirit* of frankness": *Sekretariatu KC PZPR w sprawie pracy organów bezpieczeństwa, przyjęta na posiedzeniu w dniu 24 lutego 1949 roku* [Resolution of the PZPR Central Committee concerning the work of the security apparatus, accepted on February 24, 1949], AAN, KC PZPR, t. 2. Speech by Stanisław Radkiewicz in "Materiały odprawy szefów WUBP z 10 czerwca 1948" [Documents concerning the briefing for the executives of the District Offices of Public Security, June 10, 1948], Centralne Archiwum MSW (Central Archive of the MSW; hereafter CA MSW), 17/x/77, t. 4. "Wychowanie w duchu szczerości": speech by Stanisław Radkiewicz, 1954.

38. "The most holy duty": speech by Henryk Chmielewski (vice director of Department V of the MBP) during the MBP council held between March 23 and 25, 1949, AAN, KC PZPR, Papiery B. Bieruta 11/68. "Bezduszność i brak sumienia partyjnego u niektórych pracowników aparatu śledczego": *Stenogram dyskusji na krajowej naradzie aktywu aparatu bezpieczeństwa publicznego 4 marca 1954 r.* [Words of Colonel Humer spoken during the briefing for the National Council of the Security Apparatus's management, March 4, 1954], AIPN, MBP, 14.

39. Edward Ochab to the Communist chiefs in Katowice, April 1956, quoted by Franciszek Szlachcic in his memoirs, *Gorzki smak władzy* [Bitter taste of power] (Warsaw: Wydawnictwo FAKT, 1990), 13. "Ciężki grzech pierworodny": ibid.

40. "O rany boskie!" (literally, "For God's wounds!"): quoted in Stanisław Kania, *Zatrzymać konfrontację* [To stop the confrontation] (Warsaw: Polska Oficyna Wydawnicza BGW, 1991), 146.

41. "Przemówienie wiceministra Ptasińskiego z dnia 3 września 1953 roku na zakończenie kursu wykładowów zawodowych" [Speech by Vice Minister Ptasiński

on September 3, 1953, at the conclusion of the workshops for professional lecturers], AIPN, MBP, 10.

42. The unit was the Oficerska Szkoła Polityczno-Wychowawcza (Political Educational School for Officers). For more details, see Dariusz Kozerawski, *Wyższe szkolnictwo wojskowe w Polsce w latach 1947–1967* [College military education in Poland between 1947 and 1967] (Warsaw: Wydawnictwo Neriton, 2005).

43. Jan Widacki claims that PPW "was a unit particularly hated by the majority of functionaries" ("była to formacja szczególnie znienawidzona przez ogół funkcjonariuszy"). *Czego nie powiedział generał Kiszczak*, 149.

44. "Referat wiceministra MSW Czesława Staszczaka wygłoszony w Akademii Spraw Wewnętrznych w Warszawie w 1987 roku" [Speech by MSW vice minister Czesław Staszczak at the Academy of Internal Affairs in Warsaw, 1987], AIPN, BU 0437/12.

45. Widacki, *Czego nie powiedział generał Kiszczak*, 148.

46. Its editor in chief was Colonel Konrad Straszewski, the chief of Department IV, which was responsible for fighting the church. He was also a member of the infamous Group D established for "special operations." For details, see Jan M. Rokita and Antoni Dudek, *Raport Rokity: Sprawozdanie sejmowej komisji nadzwyczajnej do zbadania działalności MSW* [The Rokita Report: The report of the special parliamentary commission to examine the MSW's Work].

47. "Esbeckie ministerium nieprawości" [The SB ministry of injustice], *Panorama Dolnośląska*, April 2006. The article was also published at *medeksza.blogspot.com*.

48. Rev. Father Hans Küng is a controversial Swiss Catholic theologian who rejected the doctrine of papal infallibility and criticized Pope John Paul II for his restoration of the pre–Vatican II status quo. See, for example, Hans Küng, *Infallible? An Inquiry*; *Papal Ministry in the Church* (Garden City, NY: Doubleday, 1971). For more on the Bezpieka's actions, see "Esbeckie ministerium nieprawości."

49. For more information about the *Ancora*, see M. Lasota, "O raporcie sejmowej komisji poświęconym samodzielnej grupie 'D' w MSW" [About the parliamentary commission's report on the independent group "D" in the MSW], *Biuletyn IPN* 1 (2003): 35.

50. The PPW director, Czesław Staszczak, warned in one of his secret speeches against the susceptibility of the "mentally weakest functionaries" to "political wobbling," in "Referat wiceministra MSW Czesława Staszczaka."

51. Ibid.

52. "Mądra i właściwa interpretacja zdarzeń": ibid.

53. This observation is supposedly Willy Brandt's, although this is unconfirmed.

54. "Sooner than later, our daily work revealed that it would be easier to infuse the young functionaries' consciousness with the political and ideological rules than with the ethical and moral principles." In "Referat wiceministra MSW Czesława Staszczaka."

55. Zarząd Ochrony Funkcjonariuszy (ZOF) was created by a regulation (Zarządzenie Ministra Spraw Wewnętrznych [Order of the Minister of Interior Affairs]) quickly signed by General Kiszczak in the last days of December 1984. Paweł Piotrowski claims that ZOF was disliked by the functionaries because over 90 percent of its investigations concerned financial or criminal offenses: Paweł Piotrowski,

"Przemiany MSW w latach 1989–1990" [Changes in the Ministry of Interior Affairs between 1989 and 1990], *Biuletyn IPN*, no. 4 (2004): 47.

56. Thirty officers worked in the MSW headquarters. There were two hundred MSW functionaries in total. Andrzej Zybertowicz, *Służby Specjalne i samolikwidacja komunizmu* [Secret services and the self-termination of Communism] (Warsaw: Wydawnictwo ANTYK, 1993), part 1, 36. See also Andrzej K. Kunert, ed., *Bijące serce partii* [Beating heart of the party] (Warsaw: Oficyna Wydawnicza ADIUTOR, 2001).

57. The surveillance of Pietruszka's family by the Bezpieka (Operation Teresa) was aimed at solving all the circumstances of Rev. Popiełuszko's death. See Paweł Tomaski, "Adam Pietruszka [ur. 1938], zastępca dyrektora Departamentu IV MSW" ["Adam Pietruszka (born in 1938), the vice director of MSW Department IV], in *Aparat represji w Polsce Ludowej 1944–1989* [The apparatus of oppression in the People's Poland, 1944–1989], ed. Bogdan Strycharz, 528.

58. Błażyński, *Mówi Józef Światło*, 184.

59. "Występują jeszcze przejawy religianctwo, obyczajowości drobnomieszczańskiej, dygnitarstwo, pijaństwo i chuligaństwo": speech of Stanisław Radkiewicz, 1954, 14.

60. See, for example: "Priest Seized by Vigilantes, Poles Suspect," *Los Angeles Times*, October 26, 1984; Roger Boyes, "Poland: Alert for Kidnapped Priest," *Times* (London), October 29, 1984; "Kidnapped Priest Found Murdered," *Times* (London), October 31, 1984; and Matthew C. Vita, "Priest Is Mourned in Warsaw," *Boston Globe*, November 1, 1984.

61. "Narósł u nas problem religianctwa od którego nie możemy uciec. Różnie podchodzimy do przypadków religianctwa i konieczne są w tym zakresie jednolita polityka, zasady i praktyka." General Kiszczak's speech during the MSW executives' conference held on December 5, 1984, AIPN, BU 0859/733.

62. The other participants were Generals Jedynak, Pożoga, Beim, Czubiński, and Zaczkowski.

63. "Przemówienie wiceministra Ptasińskiego z dnia 3 września 1953 roku na zakończenie kursu wykładowców zawodowych" [Speech by MBP vice minister Ptasiński at the end of the Workshop of the Professional Lecturers, September 3, 1953], AIPN, MBP, 10.

64. Ibid.

65. "Therefore, the cadres of teachers and all the educational workers are to fight the religiousness in the spirit of the materialistic outlook on the Word." Ibid.

66. "Występują jeszcze przejawy religianctwo, obyczajowości drobnomieszczańskiej, dygnitarstwo, pijaństwo i chuligaństwo": speech of Stanisław Radkiewicz, 1954.

67. Order 1294 of the minister of internal affairs, Czesław Kiszczak, AIPN, BU 0859/733. The details of Milczewski's case were explored by the press. See, for example, "Rozkaz Kiszczaka: Zwolnić za ślub" [Kiszczak's order: To fire for having a wedding], *Gazeta Wyborcza*, September 16, 2008.

68. This information was revealed during Kiszczak's trial, which was launched in September 2008. Kiszczak was accused by Milczewski of violating the law; for details, see "Rozkaz Kiszczaka."

69. Ibid.

70. Milczewski's statement was read by Judge Ewa Kopacz at the trial. Quoted in "Rozkaz Kiszczaka."

71. "Rozkaz Kiszczaka."

72. Colonel Jerzy Siedlecki, the director of the functionaries' personnel bureau, used the phrase "its soldiers' bodies and souls" when discussing the influence of the church on the Bezpieka. *Odprawa z dnia 21 listopada 1949 roku* [The briefing on November 21, 1949], CA MSW 17/IX/77, t. 5.

73. Widacki, *Czego nie powiedział generał Kiszczak*, 151.

74. Quoted in ibid., 91.

75. Widacki, *Czego nie powiedział generał Kiszczak*, 91.

76. Ibid.

77. A former Armia Krajowa (AK; Home Army) prisoner wrote in his memoirs that Luna Brystygier was not only a sadist but also sexually deviant. See A. Rószkiewicz-Litwinowiczowa, *Trudne decyzje: Kontrwywiad Okręgu Warszawa AK 1943–1944, więzienie 1949–1954* [Hard decisions: Counterintelligence in the Warsaw District of the AK 1943–1944, and in the prison, 1949–1954] (Warsaw: Państwowy Instytut Wydawniczy, 1991), 106.

78. Maria Okońska was the most important figure of the Primate's Institute (Instytut Prymasowski) and a close assistant of Primate Stefan Wyszyński; for more details, see her memoirs: *Przez Maryję wszystko dla Boga: Wspomnienia 1920–1948)* [Through Mary, everything to God: Memoirs, 1920–1948] (Warsaw: Wydawnictwo im. Stefana Kardynała Wyszyńskiego Soli Deo, 2008).

79. Jan Grzegorczyk, "Wielki Piątek Anno Domini 1949" [Good Friday, Anno Domini 1949], *W Drodze* 9, no. 337 (2001).

80. Grzegorczyk, "Wielki Piątek." See also J. Góra and J. Grzegorczyk, *Skrawek nieba albo o Ojcu i Królu* [Piece of heaven; or, About the Father and the King].

81. "Sprawa Operacyjna 'Kobra'" [Files related to Operation "Kobra"], AIPN, 01178/591, k. 281.

82. Stefan Budzyński, *Między wiarą a zwątpieniem* [Between faith and despondency] (Warsaw: Adam, 2001).

83. Rev. Marylski's words were recorded in a report by the secret collaborator "Rawski" in 1969: AIPN, 01178/591, k. 190.

84. Jan Żaryn, "Córka marnotrawna, czyli Luna w Laskach" [Prodigal daughter, Luna in Laski], *Biuletyn IPN* 11, no. 58 (November 2005): 46.

85. Archival documents pertaining to the House in Laski surveillance of the Catholic House for the Blind in Laski, AIPN, 01178/591.

86. For a detailed analysis of Operation Kobra, see Żaryn, "Córka marnotrawna."

87. Some of the secret collaborators' codenames were "Rawski," "Jasiński," "Mariusz," "Alfa," and "Stefan."AIPN, 01178/591, k.67. See also Żaryn, "Córka marnotrawna," 46.

88. *Konstytucja Polskiej Rzeczypospolitej Ludowej uchwalona w dniu 22 lipca 1952 roku* [The constitution of Poland, enacted on July 22, 1952]: Dz.U. 1952, nr 33, poz. 232.

89. Ibid.

90. Ibid.

91. Dz.U. 1969, nr 13, poz. 94.

92. "Whoever forces another person to participate in a religious activity or to participate in a religious ceremony, as well as not to participate in the religious activity or ceremony, is subject to the penalty of up to five years in prison." Ibid.

93. Orders, rules, instructions, guidelines, and ministerial regulations were scrupulously recorded by the Bezpieka units. According to Instruction Og P-3, every functionary was to read the new laws and acknowledge this by signing a special roster. See also *Instrukcja nr 01/60 z 20 kwietnia 1960 roku w sprawie trybu wydawania i prowadzenia ewidencji przepisów służby bezpieczeństwa* [Instruction no. 01/60 concerning publication and recording of the security service's rules from April 20, 1960], AIPN, A2 935/60, IPN Ld pf. 13/387, k. 137.

94. Quoted in Daszkiewicz, *Uprowadzenie i morderstwo*, 147–48.

95. Jaruzelski's words are from a press conference in Jabłonna concerning the Popiełuszko murder. Quoted in Daszkiewicz, *Uprowadzenie i morderstwo*, 423.

96. "Every religious idea . . ." is attributed to Lenin; quoted by David Powell in *Antireligious Propaganda in the Soviet Union: A Study of Mass Persuasion* (Cambridge, MA: MIT Press, 1978), 15.

97. Gaber, *And God Created Lenin*, 22.

## References

### ARCHIVES
Central Archives of Modern Records, Warsaw, Poland
Institute of National Remembrance, Bydgoszcz, Poland
Institute of National Remembrance, Krakow, Poland
Institute of National Remembrance, Lodz, Poland
Institute of National Remembrance, Warsaw, Poland

### PERIODICALS
*Boston Globe*
*Gazeta Wyborcza*
*Los Angeles Times*
*Times* (London)

### SELECTED PUBLISHED WORKS
Błażyński, Zbigniew. *Mówi Józef Światło: Za kulisami bezpieki i partii 1940–1955* [Jozef Światło speaks: Inside the security apparatus and the party, 1940–1955]. London: Polska Fundacja Kulturalna, 1988.

Bociurkiw, Bohdan R., and John W. Strong, eds. *Religion and Atheism in the U.S.S.R. and Eastern Europe*. London: Macmillan, 1975.

Daszkiewicz, Krystyna. *Uprowadzenie i morderstwo Ks. Jerzego Popiełuszki* [The kidnapping and murder of Rev. Jerzy Popiełuszko]. Poznan, Poland: Kantor Wydawniczy SAWW, 1990.

Diskin, Hanna. *The Seeds of Triumph: Church and State in Gomułka's Poland*. New York: Central European University Press, 2001.

Dziurok, Adam, ed. *Metody pracy operacyjnej aparatu bezpieczeństwa wobec Kościołów i związków wyznaniowych 1945–1989* [The operating methods of the security apparatus against the church and religious groups, 1945–1989]. Warsaw: Instytut Pamięci Narodowej, 2004.

Gaber, Paul. *And God Created Lenin.* Amherst, NY: Prometheus Books, 2005.

Gsovski, Vladimir, ed. *Church and State behind the Iron Curtain: Czechoslovakia, Hungary, Poland, Romania, with an Introduction on the Soviet Union.* New York: Praeger, 1955.

Isakowicz-Zaleski, Tadeusz. *Księża wobec Bezpieki* [Priests toward the Bezpieka]. Kraków: Wydawnictwo Znak, 2007.

Kemp-Welch, Tony. "Khrushchev's 'Secret Speech' and Polish Politics: The Spring of 1956." *Europe-Asian Studies* 48, no. 2 (1996): 181–206.

Kersten, Krystyna, and Michael H. Bernhard, eds. *The Establishment of Communist Rule in Poland, 1943–1948.* Berkeley: University of California Press, 1991.

Miller, R. F., and T. H. Rigby, eds. *Religion and Politics in Communist States.* Canberra: Australian National University, 1986.

Monticone, C. Ronald. *The Catholic Church in Communist Poland, 1945–1985.* New York: East European Monographs, 1986.

Musiał, Filip, and Jarosław Szarka, eds. *Operacja zniszczyć Kościół* [Operation Destroy the Church]. Kraków: Instytut Pamięci Narodowej, 2007.

Myszor, J., ed. *Leksykon duchowieństwa represjonowanego w PRL w latach, 1945–1989* [The encyclopedic dictionary of the persecuted clergy in the Polish People's Republic, 1945–1989]. Warsaw: Instytut Pamięci Narodowej, 2006.

Okońska, Maria. *Przez Maryję wszystko dla Boga: Wspomnienia 1920–1948* [Through Mary, everything to God: Memoir, 1920–1948]. Warsaw: Wydawnictwo im. Stefana Kardynała Wyszyńskiego Soli Deo, 2008.

Paczkowski, Andrzej. *Aparat bezpieczeństwa w Polsce w latach 1944–1949: Taktyka, strategia, metody* [The security apparatus in Poland between 1944 and 1949: Tactics, strategy, methods]. Warsaw: Instytut Studiów Politycznych PAN, 1996.

———. *Aparat bezpieczeństwa w Polsce w latach 1950–1952: Taktyka, strategia, metody* [The security apparatus in Poland between 1950 and 1952: Tactics, strategy, methods]. Warsaw: Instytut Pamięci Narodowej, 2000.

———. *Aparat bezpieczeństwa w Polsce w latach 1953–1954: Taktyka, strategia, metody* [The security apparatus in Poland between 1953 and 1954: Tactics, strategy, methods]. Warsaw: Instytut Pamięci Narodowej, 2004.

———. *Stanisław Mikołajczyk czyli klęska realisty* [Stanisław Mikołajczyk: Failure of the realist]. Warsaw: Agencja Omnipress, 1991.

———. *Zdobycie Władzy* [Seizing of power]. Warsaw: Wydawnictwa Szkolne i Pedagogiczne, 1993.

Patrick, Michel. *Politics and Religion in Eastern Europe: Catholicism in Hungary, Poland, and Czechoslovakia.* Oxford: Polity, 1991.

Persak, Krzysztof, and Łukasz Kamiński. *A Handbook of the Communist Security Apparatus in East Central Europe, 1944–1989.* Warsaw: Instytut Pamięci Narodowej, 2005.

Piotrowski, Mirosław. *Ludzie Bezpieki w walce z Narodem i Kościołem* [The Bezpieka's men fighting against the nation and the church]. Lublin, Poland: Klub Inteligencji Katolickiej, 2000.

Rokita, Jan M., and Antoni Dudek. *Raport Rokity: Sprawozdanie Sejmowej Komisji Nadzwyczajnej do Zbadania Działalności MSW* [The Rokita Report: The report of the Special Parliamentary Commission to Examine the MSW's Work]. Kraków: Wydawnictwo Arcana, 2005.

Rószkiewicz-Litwinowiczowa, A. *Trudne decyzje: Kontrwywiad Okręgu Warszawa AK 1943–1944, więzienie 1949–1954* [Hard decisions: Counterintelligence in the Warsaw District of the AK, 1943–1944, and in the prison, 1949–1954. Warsaw: Państwowy Instytut Wydawniczy, 1991.

Stępień, Sławomir. *Reakcje bezpieki na śmierć Tow. "Tomasza"* [The Bezpieka's reactions to the death of Comrade "Tomasz"]. Warsaw: Instytut Pamięci Narodowej, 2005.

Szajkowski, Bogdan. *Next to God . . . Poland: Politics and Religion in Contemporary Poland.* New York: St. Martin's Press, 1983.

Tischner, Józef. *Etyka solidarności i Homo sovieticus* [Solidarity ethics and *Homo sovieticus*]. Kraków: Społeczny Instytut Wydawniczy Znak, 1992.

Widacki, Jan. *Czego nie powiedział generał Kiszczak* [What General Kiszczak did not reveal]. Warsaw: Polska Oficyna Wydawnicza, 1992.

Żaryn, Jan. "Córka marnotrawna, czyli Luna w Laskach" [Prodigal daughter in Laski]. *Biuletyn IPN*, no. 11 (November 2005): 58.

*Zasady etyki i obyczajów funkcjonariuszy służby bezpieczeństwa i milicji obywatelskiej PRL* [Principles of ethics and customs of the security apparatus and militia functionaries in the Polish People's Republic]. Warsaw: Ministry of International Affairs, 1985.

Zmijewski, Norbert. *The Catholic-Marxist Ideological Dialogue in Poland, 1945–1980.* Brookfield, VT: Gower, 1991.

# CHAPTER 13

# Political Islam, the Jamaat-e-Islami, and Pakistan's Role in the Afghan-Soviet War, 1979–1988

*Zahid Shahab Ahmed*

As the decade of the 1970s neared its close, relations between the United States and Pakistan were seemingly at a historic low. The close strategic relationship between Washington and Islamabad had first been frayed by what Pakistan viewed as insufficient support from the United States during its wars with India in 1965 and 1971. Relations further soured after General Zia-ul-Haq took power in a military coup in July 1977. In response to Zia's coup, the administration of Jimmy Carter, which had entered the White House five months earlier, was determined to place a renewed focus on human rights as a guiding factor of US foreign relations. Pursuant to that strategy, the administration put economic sanctions on Pakistan and cut off its military aid. But Washington's ostracization of Islamabad would not last long. Events throughout the region inclined the United States to conclude that strategic Cold War concerns outweighed adherence to its newly established emphasis on human rights and led the Carter administration to rekindle its relationship with Pakistan.

1979 was a tumultuous year in the Middle East, especially in the Persian Gulf region. The year began with the Islamic Revolution in Iran and ended with the Soviet invasion of Afghanistan. The Iranian Revolution generated a lot of concern in the West. The founder of the Islamic Revolution, Ayatollah Khomeini, anointed the United States the "Great Satan" and the religion of pro-US Muslim countries as "American Islam," causing Washington to fear that Khomeini might seek to export his revolution into pro-US states in the region such as Saudi Arabia or Jordan.[1] That November, the US embassy in Tehran was attacked, and fifty-three US citizens working there were taken hostage. Later in the month, antigovernment rebels in Saudi Arabia occupied the *Kaaba*, the central courtyard of the *Masjid al-Haram* (Grand Mosque) in Mecca, the most sacred site in Islam. In Pakistan, rumors spread that the assault on the Masjid al-Haram was part of a US conspiracy against the Muslim world; in response, Pakistani students, egged on by Jamaat-e-Islami supporters, set fire to the US embassy in Islamabad, burning it to the ground.[2] At this point, US-Pakistani relations were at their lowest ebb.

Strategists in Moscow closely observed these developments in the Muslim world and soon came to the conclusion that the time was right for a military operation in Afghanistan. On Christmas Eve 1979, the Soviets went into Afghanistan, having realized that US influence in the Middle East and Southwest Asia had perished. The Soviets also wanted to prevent the spill-over effects of the Islamic Revolution from reaching Soviet central Asia. Washington, for its part, wanted to prevent the spread of Soviet influence in the oil rich Gulf region. In the end, Afghanistan became a US-USSR proxy war and the battleground for the concluding episode of the Cold War.

US policy made a drastic shift to establish close ties with Islamic countries in order to isolate Iran. It was a two-pronged strategy: (1) to unite a billion Muslims worldwide to wage jihad (holy war) against the Soviets, and (2) to turn an ideological difference between Sunni and Shia Muslims into a political divide.[3] In this context, it is imperative to look into the understanding of "jihad," as defined in the teachings of Islam. The simple translation of the word "jihad" means "struggle"; however, in the Islamic tradition, it is subclassified into *jihad akbar* (the greater jihad) and *jihad asghar* (the lesser jihad). *Jihad akbar* is a struggle against weaknesses of self and is an effort to lead a pure life as per the codes of conduct defined in Islam. In comparison, *jihad asghar* is about self-defense; a Muslim is allowed to practice it only when his or her survival is at stake.[4] The later struggle became the modus operandi for the *mujahideen* (holy warriors; the ones participating in jihad) and the architects of the Afghan-Soviet War from 1979 to 1988. As far as Pakistan's involvement in the war was concerned, certain domestic factors and actors greatly influenced Islamabad's support of the Afghan Jihad. Among these, the most salient was the rise of political Islam. Support from the United States—restored after the Soviet invasion of Afghanistan—was a crucial factor in Zia's ability to use Islam to strengthen his rule.

Political Islam has challenged governments and policy makers over issues of ideology, governance, modernization, development, pluralism, democracy, women's empowerment, and relations with the West. Since the late 1960s, Islamic groups in different parts of the world have chanted slogans such as

"Islam is the solution" and "Islam is the complete code of life" to fight against challenges of all sorts—mainly poverty, hunger, and natural disasters. Governments in Afghanistan, Egypt, Iran, Libya, Malaysia, Morocco, Saudi Arabia, Pakistan, and Sudan have used Islamic rhetoric to obtain support for their policies. The Jamaat-e-Islami (Jamaat) has been identified as the most prominent Islamic movement in South Asia, with incomparable influence on the socioreligious and political fabrics of Pakistan. John L. Esposito has identified the liberation war in East Pakistan (1971–1972) as a key catalyst for political Islam in the region, in addition to the Iran Revolution of 1978–1979.[5]

In this chapter, I present a case study of the Jamaat to understand the rise of political Islam in Pakistan and to examine the party's role in the phenomenon addressed herein, which is the role of political Islam in the Afghan-Soviet War. It is true that another group in the country, the Jamiat-ul-Ulama-i-Islam (JUI), was also at the forefront during the 1980s; through its close ties with the Zia administration, the JUI recruited and supplied thousands of jihadis to the Afghan Jihad. But the case of the Jamaat is exceptional because it was not only the most prominent party since 1947 in relation to the Islamization of the Pakistani state, but also because it had opportunities to gain power through partnerships with dictators in the past (e.g., during the war of liberation in East Pakistan, 1970–1971). In comparison to the JUI or any other Islamic group involved in the Afghan-Soviet War, the Jamaat was the most organized, with offices stretched across the country and many more followers than the JUI. During the Zia era, Jamaat members were given high positions in the government, which allowed the party to play a key role in policy making through reforms in the religious and education sectors. Since its establishment in 1941 by Maulana Maududi, the Jamaat had been growing in terms of its foreign relations, and its extra-regional ties suddenly increased during the era of jihad in Afghanistan because the party was virtually formulating the Zia government's Afghan policy.

For the above-mentioned reasons, this chapter is limited to the role of the Jamaat vis-à-vis the rise of political Islam in Pakistan and the country's role in the Afghan-Soviet War. I explore the way religious rhetoric shaped the course of the Afghan-Soviet War, with an emphasis on examining the jihadi factor in this particular episode of the Cold War. The Jamaat and its leadership of that time played a crucial role in labeling the Afghan resistance against the Soviet occupation as "jihad," and the party was also aggressively and directly engaged in the war, recruiting, training, and sending thousands of jihadis to Afghanistan. The Jamaat was not the only party giving a religious look to the war, as there were external factors doing the same, and I study all these aspects in this comprehensive look at the role of religion during the decade-long war in Afghanistan.

## Political Islam in Pakistan: The Case of the Jamaat

Islam plays a key role in shaping Pakistan's domestic and international politics. It is through Islamic ideology that the policy makers in the country define national interests so as to guide foreign policy in regional and global affairs.[6] In Pakistan, irrespective of the type of regime, Islam is a guiding force in both domestic and international affairs. This was not the vision of the founder of Pakistan, Muhammad Ali Jinnah, but he could not play a pivotal role in the development of the state and its constitution, as he died in 1948. Since 1952, Pakistan has been an Islamic state.

For almost three decades after the independence of Pakistan, the Jamaat had numerous ups and downs in its relations with the government. In 1948, the founder of the Jamaat, Maulana Maududi, was arrested for opposing the government's support of insurgents in the Indian-administered Kashmir. In the early 1950s, because of the party's anti-Ahmadiya protests, the Jamaat was perceived as "public enemy no. 1." It was an era of hardship for the Jamaat, because the government fired hundreds of party members from public jobs. Anxiously waiting for any opportunity to establish friendly ties with the state, and the Jamaat found its opening through the liberation movement in East Pakistan. General Yahya Khan, the head of state at that time, asked Maududi to help crush the insurgency in East Pakistan.[7] Maududi wholeheartedly accepted this request and ordered Jamaat devotees to fight alongside the armed forces in an attempt to preserve a united Pakistan. The Jamaat even declared the war against Bengali insurgents a "jihad." The Jamaat was side by side with the Pakistani army to the extent that the party's militia groups, the al-Badr and the al-Shams, were trained by the army to curtail secessionism in East Pakistan.[8]

After an embarrassing defeat in the 1971 war against India, which followed the loss of East Pakistan, the government of Zulfiqar Ali Bhutto badly needed the support of all the country's factions to sustain itself. In the mid-1970s, Bhutto initiated a policy of Islamizing Pakistani society by prohibiting alcohol and by declaring Friday the weekly public day off in respect of Islamic traditions. He even used the slogan of Islamic socialism in an attempt to win votes and popular support in the country, but he was ultimately unsuccessful. Bhutto was removed from power by General Zia-ul-Haq in 1977. Zia stepped up the process of Islamization started by Bhutto and used all the means at his disposal to stay in power. His rule (1977–1988) is consequently known as an era of harsh dictatorship in the country. The interim constitution of March 1981 empowered Zia to dissolve any political party whose operations contradicted Islamic ideology.[9] This forced the major political parties out of the scene, providing Islamic parties with an opening. Stepping into the vacuum, they created a mullah-military alliance. It was a give-and-take relationship: Zia wished to stay in power and found refuge in Islamization. In return, mullahs climbed up Pakistan's political ladder, obtaining prominent leadership positions for the first time in the history of the nation-state. According to Mohammed Ayoob, "An integral part of the strategy was the bestowing of state patronage on fundamentalist religious groups and institutions in order to build a support structure among them."[10]

Zia affirmed his commitment to the ideological stance of the Jamaat not only because he and the party's leader of that time, Mian Tufayl Muhammad, both belonged to the Aryan clan.[11] It was a campaign to achieve a variety of domestic and international policy goals, which led Zia to shower members of Islamic parties, in particular the Jamaat, with choice positions within his regime. Appointments were made within the Ministry of Education as well as within the military, police, and government bureaucracy. The beginning of Zia's era therefore offered the Jamaat a prominent role in the policy making of the country. In return, the party defended Zia on all fronts, from religious and educational reforms in the country to jihad against the Soviets.

To please his mullah friends further, Zia made religious reforms in the economic, educational, social, and legal spheres. These reforms included abolishing bank interest for Muslims through the establishment of Islamic financial institutions, placing a greater emphasis on inculcating Islamic values by increasing Islamic content in textbooks, strictly enforcing the Islamic code of conduct by prohibiting gambling and alcohol, and launching the controversial Hudood Ordinance, which was a clear violation of women's rights.[12]

The Jamaat not only cooperated with Islamabad toward achieving Pakistan's foreign policy objectives, but also on occasion collaborated with foreign governments, including Iran and Saudi Arabia. Since the 1960s, Riyadh in particular has found in the Jamaat an important international nonstate assistant for implementing its policies in relation to Iran, Afghanistan, and central Asia—and also to some extent within the Arab world. Luckily, for the Jamaat, the kingdom also involved the party in its international agencies, such as the Rabitah al-Alam al-Islami (World Muslim League); in this way, Saudi Arabia lavished funds on the party.[13]

The Jamaat was consulted by Zia on a range of issues, earning the party the sobriquet of the "Martial Law's B team."[14] Pakistan's human rights record, particularly concerning women and minority rights, was dismal during Zia's era, and somehow it was all defended by the Jamaat. At that time, the Women's Action Forum (WAF) opposed aspects of Islamization that violated women rights. In response, the Jamaat criticized the WAF and emphasized the notion that Muslims have their own ideals of human rights, which are different from Western conceptions. Moreover, in reaction to international concerns about violations of the rights of Christians and *muhajirs* (migrants) in the country, the Jamaat defended the Zia regime by saying that it is the right of the state and the majority Muslims to guard their particular interests.[15]

In addition to the above mentioned reforms, Zia issued Martial Law Order 5, which for the first time in Pakistani history authorized the Islamic punishment of amputation of the right hand for theft, robbery, and murder.[16] The Islamization program led to the growth of sectarianism in the country in the form of Shia-Sunni conflict. Simultaneously, Pakistan's participation in the Afghan Jihad (along with that of certain radical Islamic parties at home) initiated Islamic militancy.[17] It was because of Zia's Islamization program that Islamic fundamentalism became integrated into the Pakistani armed forces, mainly in the officer corps, as their loyalty to the regime was tested on the basis of their observance of Islamic rituals.[18]

Zia brought Islamic parties into the mainstream, but it was the Afghan-Soviet War that brought them into a militant mode. The parties, such as the Jamaat and the JUI, with thousands of bases in the tribal areas of Pakistan, were at the forefront of the Afghan Jihad. Therefore, they were able to obtain immense financial resources, connections in the diplomatic world, and links with the Pakistani military and the CIA in order to acquire lethal weapons for their own military offshoots.[19]

## The Cold War in South Asia

Afghanistan was not a US ally during the first three decades of the Cold War era and Washington continued to ignore the significance of forging an alliance with Kabul up until the late 1970s. This happened partially because Pakistan was at the center stage of international security cooperation with the United States during the first two decades of the Cold War. Pakistan became a US ally for many reasons, including its opposition to atheistic Communism, but the major impetus was its ongoing conflict with India over Kashmir. Islamabad saw a Cold War alliance with Washington primarily as a means to acquire Western military and diplomatic support vis-à-vis India.

Soon after coming into existence in 1947, Pakistan became a member of the British Commonwealth. At that time, Pakistan's military greatly depended on British military training and equipment. Pakistan also became a member of the Middle East Defense Organization (later renamed the Central Treaty Organization, or CENTO, and commonly referred to as the Baghdad Pact) in 1955. Although the United States was never a full member of the defense pact, it did allow both the United States and Great Britain to use Pakistani military facilities. For example, an Air Force airbase outside Peshawar was made accessible for US military operations and used as the departure point for intelligence flights over the Soviet Union. In 1954, Pakistan and the United States signed formal defense agreements that resulted in Pakistan joining the US-sponsored anti-Communist military alliance, the Southeast Asia Treaty Organization (SEATO), the following year. SEATO was meant to block Soviet access to Southeast Asia.

In Pakistan, high hopes dwindled into frustration as these security arrangements failed to provide Islamabad with tangible benefits during its two wars with India in 1965 and 1971. Washington discontinued its military aid to Pakistan after the Indo-Pakistani War of 1965. In the 1971 war, Pakistan lost its province of East Bengal (modern-day Bangladesh), in part because of Indian intervention, which resulted in Pakistani prime minister Zulfiqar Ali Bhutto claiming that his country had been betrayed by its Cold War allies, in particular the United States. As a result, Bhutto drastically reoriented Pakistani foreign policy toward greater links with the Muslim world. In 1969, Pakistan joined the Organization of the Islamic Conference (OIC) and almost a decade later withdrew from SEATO. Bhutto kept Pakistan's membership in CENTO because it needed to maintain strategic relations with both Iran and Turkey, but this organization was itself disbanded following the Islamic Revolution in Iran in 1979. With these actions, Pakistan joined the Non-Aligned Movement in an effort to maintain neutrality in the Cold War rivalry between the United States and the Soviet Union.[20]

The stage was set for superpower rivalry in Afghanistan in 1973, when an Afghan prince, Muhammad Daud Khan, ousted the Afghan king, Mohammad Zahir Shah, with support from Moscow. With Afghanistan's location on the Soviet Union's southern border, sandwiched between two potentially hostile neighbors (Pakistan and Iran), both recipients of considerable US military aid, the advantages of a Soviet-Afghan relationship became clear to both Moscow and Kabul. Washington viewed Daud's revolution through the prism of the Cold War and thus regarded the coup as a challenge to the US position in the greater Persian Gulf region. The CIA soon commenced its endeavors to fund an Islamic resistance movement to counter Daud's pro-Soviet regime, mainly via the Hizb-e-Islami, led by Gulbuddin Hekmatyar.[21] It was at this point that the United States started to actively engage its regional allies—Iran and Pakistan. The CIA began covertly coordinating its activities with the intelligence agencies of Iran (Sazeman-e-Ettelaat va Amniyat-e-Keshvar, or SAVAK) and Pakistan (Inter-Services Intelligence, or ISI) to enlist their support in building an Islamic resistance inside Afghanistan.

In Pakistan, the Bhutto government, weary of Daud's Pashtun-nationalist rhetoric and eager to break the alliance between New Delhi and Kabul, which threatened to encircle Pakistan with hostile neighbors, began assisting the Afghani Islamic resistance. They engaged Qazi Hussain Ahmad, then a Jamaat leader in Khyber Pakhtunkhwa (formerly known as the North-West Frontier Province of Pakistan), to assist the government in formulating its Afghan policy. Following Nur Muhammad Taraki's coup in 1977 (discussed below), General Zia-ul-Haq and Lieutenant General Fazl-i-Haq met with the Jamaat leadership to explore ways in which the Jamaat could promote Pakistan's policy on Afghanistan.[22]

In April 1978, Daud was killed in a pro-Communist coup known as the Saur Revolution, and Afghanistan moved ever closer to Moscow. Nur Muhammad Taraki and the People's Democratic Party of Afghanistan (PDPA) emerged as the new leaders of the country and declared Afghanistan a Communist state. Soon afterward, a civil war developed between the new Communist government and local Islamic mujahideen. With multiple foreign actors with diverse interests operating in Afghanistan, the country quickly descended into turmoil by 1979. In March, the PDPA turned to Moscow for help in putting down an uprising against the central government in Herat Province. At that time, the Kremlin leadership was unwilling to take the step of armed intervention to support its Afghan allies.[23] By the end of the year, however, Soviet willingness to intervene had increased as a result of Taraki's death at the hands of his rival Hafizullah Amin (whom the Soviets suspected of wanting to shift Kabul's foreign policy toward Washington); the general decline in détente between the Soviet Union and United States; the fear that the "loss" of Afghanistan would be a blow to the Soviets' international reputation; and concern for the effect that the Islamization of the conflict in Afghanistan and Ayatollah Khomeini's revolution in Iran would have on the Soviet republics of central Asia (which were predominantly populated by Muslims).[24] Another request came from Kabul for Soviet assistance in propping up the PDPA regime against the mujahideen insurrection. This time, Moscow responded, sending thousands of its troops into Afghanistan on Christmas Day, 1979. In the invasion, Soviet troops stormed into the presidential palace, killing Amin so that he could be replaced with Babrak Karmal (leader of the PDPA-Parcham faction), the Kremlin's handpicked choice to head the country its army now occupied.

## The Jihad Factor in the Afghan-Soviet War

It should be made clear that religion was not a uniting factor between Pakistan and Afghanistan prior to the Soviet occupation of the latter. In 1947, Afghanistan was the only country in the United Nations to reject Pakistan's existence as an independent state. Afterward, Afghanistan's support for Pashtunistan, an independent state for cross-border Pashtuns (an ethnic group residing along the border between Afghanistan and Pakistan), further aggravated Pakistan.

Thus, prior to the Afghan-Soviet War in 1979, Pakistan had always considered Afghanistan a political irritant. In 1980, however, the Soviet Union invaded Afghanistan, and Pakistan began taking an active interest in the affairs of its neighbor. The Soviet occupation of Afghanistan posed a geostrategic threat to Pakistan in light of the Soviet dream of acquiring a warm-water port on the Indian Ocean.

It was their mutual interest in frustrating Soviet objectives in Afghanistan that mended the frayed relationship between Pakistan and the United States and turned the Afghan-Soviet War into a religious war. According to Hussain H. Zaidi, after the United States reforged its alliance with Pakistan, "the Afghan war became a Jihad and the Afghanis on the US side [became] Mujahideen. The people of Pakistan were made to believe that the Communist USSR invasion of Afghanistan had endangered Islam and therefore it was the religious duty of the government and the people to fight in the war on the side of America, which was said to be fighting for Islam."[25] The United States, of course, was not really concerned about either jihad or the protection of Islam—its only motive was to fulfill its anti-Communist agenda by defeating the Soviets in Afghanistan—and portraying the Soviet occupation in terms of Islam versus atheism proved to be an effective way for Washington to accomplish this goal.

With Washington promoting the conflict as a holy war in order to rally international support within the Muslim world to its cause, and Islamabad and the Afghani mujahideen doing the same for both domestic and international reasons, the war quickly devolved into an international jihad against the Soviet "infidels."[26] Soon after the Soviets began their occupation of Afghanistan, young mujahideen from across the Muslim world, in particular from Saudi Arabia, Egypt, Algeria, and Pakistan, arrived in Peshawar and Afghanistan to wage jihad against the Soviets. The mujahideen's organizational hierarchy was based on social standing, education, leadership abilities, and commitment to Islam. Ex-soldiers accounted for only 15 percent of their membership, and most of them were sidelined by religious fundamentalists in an effort to seize control of the Afghan Jihad.

The mujahideen who came to fight in Afghanistan were Muslim volunteers whose goal was to protect their religion and *ummah* (Muslim brotherhood). The response would not have been nearly as significant if the war had been portrayed simply as a fight for Afghan sovereignty. Turning the Afghan-Soviet War into a jihad also facilitated the growth of Arab influence in this part of the world. Even though there were mujahideen fighters from all parts of the world, the Arabs were greater in number and possessed more financial resources, and thus enjoyed greater decision-making power. Well-known al-Qaeda members, such as Osama bin Laden, Abdullah Azzam, Omar Abdur Rahman, Taseer

Abdullah, and Ayman al-Zawahiri (all of whom are Arab), had frontline roles in the Afghan-Soviet jihad.[27] Ironically, Osama bin Laden was recruited by the CIA to support the United States' clandestine war against the Soviets, through a high-level deal between the United States and Prince Turki al-Faisal, then head of Saudi intelligence.[28] In addition to thousands of Arabs, a large number of mujahideen came from Algeria. One estimate put the number of Pakistani visas issued to Algerians in the mid-1980s at roughly 2,800.[29]

Overall, approximately 100,000 Muslims took part in the Afghan Jihad, including at least 35,000 foreigners from more than forty countries and tens of thousands of Pakistani madrassa students.[30] For this purpose, madrassas (Islamic schools) were set up closer to the Afghan border in Khyber Pakhtunkhwa. There, the mujahideen received military training along with religious indoctrination.[31] Peshawar, the provincial capital of Khyber Pakhtunkhwa, was the central headquarters of the mujahideen. From there, a well-trained force was groomed to fight against the Soviets.[32] The jihad against the Soviets and their Afghan allies was organized by Afghan and Pakistani militant groups based in Khyber Pakhtunkhwa and received massive logistical support from the Pakistani government, military support from the United States, and financial support from Saudi Arabia. It was under the stewardship of the CIA and the US Pacific Command that the mujahideen were equipped with guerrilla training to wage their jihad in Afghanistan.[33] The United States tactfully persuaded its oil-rich ally, Saudi Arabia, to finance the Afghan Jihad. Funding for the war in Afghanistan also came from the United States, China, Iran, the United Kingdom, Western Europe, Arab states, Japan, and Israel. In total, billions of dollars of aid were channeled through Pakistan to the mujahideen in Afghanistan.[34] Except for the top leadership, there was no direct contact between the mujahideen and Washington, as most of the communication was done through the Pakistani ISI, further magnifying Islamabad's role in the insurgency.[35] The Pakistani army and military intelligence virtually took over control of the Afghan Jihad, albeit with no intention to engage directly in a war with the Soviets. Therefore it was with massive US, Saudi, and Pakistani assistance and encouragement that the tradition of jihad as a just war was revived after a period of over four hundred years of nonexistence in South Asia.[36]

## The Afghan-Soviet War and the Jaamat-e-Islami

It is important to highlight that following the partition of the Indian subcontinent and the subsequent birth of India and Pakistan in 1947, a number of *ulema* (scholars) from Deoband migrated to Pakistan and established seminaries in the western parts of the country. Today, there are five distinct types of madrassas in Pakistan, divided along sectarian and political lines. The two main subsects of Sunni Islam, Deobandi and Barelvi, dominate this sector. There are ideological differences when it comes to sectarian disparity in the madrassa sector, mainly because of ideological and financial support from the outside. For example, the Wahhabi doctrine as propagated by Saudi Arabia is preached through Deobandi madrassas, whereas Shia madrassas are supported by Iran. The amount of external aid to madrassas in Pakistan not only increased during the Afghan-Soviet War, but a culture of violence became entrenched at some of them.[37]

At the domestic level, General Zia took every possible measure to encourage the spread of madrassas, in particular Deobandi madrassas, in Pakistan. In the late 1970s, Zia relaxed *zakat* (tithing) restrictions by allowing direct public contributions to local mosques and madrassas. As a result, the Deobandi madrassas grew fivefold between 1979 and 1984.[38] Many madrassas hosted Afghan refugees; thus, they became the raison d'être of promoting jihad through madrassas. In the view of Kalim Bahadur, this strategy was adopted in Islamabad "to create a group of religion-oriented students, who would assist Mujahideen to drive out the Soviet army from Afghanistan."[39] There are several other explanations for the rapid growth of Pakistani madrassas and the number of students studying in Islamic institutions, but the major reason was the country's failure to provide an affordable or free education to the poor segments of society.

There was also a growing relationship between the mujahideen and Pakistan's Islamic political parties. Islamabad chose four of the country's most religiously fundamentalist organizations to help coordinate the Afghan Jihad, which allowed the leaders of these organizations to expand their domestic political strength.[40] It was mainly on account of sympathy toward Afghanis that Pakistan hosted more than 3.2 million refugees during and long after the war. This posed a threat to Pakistani national security, as there was always a possibility that Afghan refugees could create a movement with local Pashtuns in Pakistan for an independent Pashtunistan.[41] Thousands of Afghan mujahideen came to Pakistan to take refuge during the war and were admitted into madrassas run by the JUI in Quetta, Peshawar, Akora Khattak, Chaman, Pishin, and Karachi.[42] These madrassas educated many mujahideen who later pioneered the Taliban movement in Afghanistan. The Harkat-ul-Jihad-i-Islami (Movement for Islamic Holy War) was set up with Pakistan's support to cater to the needs of the Afghan Jihad. The group came into being as a collaboration between two Pakistani Islamic organizations, namely the JUI and the Tablighi Jamaat. During the Afghan Jihad, it managed to establish links with prominent Afghan groups, such as the Harkat-ul-Mujahideen and the Jamait-ul-Mujahideen.

It was also during this period that the Pakistani government allowed an extremist version of Wahhabi'ism to grow. Heavy funding was coming from Saudi Arabia and the United Arab Emirates, and Wahhabi'ism suited the government's policy of promoting the Afghan Jihad.[43] As Kamran Arif states, "The dominance of the Wahhabi group meant that the tradition of religious tolerance that had become the hallmark of the Barelvis was considerably diluted."[44] This created a completely new genre of madrassas—"ones who were equally if not more concerned with Jihad than with religious scholarship," according to S. V. R. Nasr.[45]

It was the Jamaat that was at the forefront in promoting the Islamists' agenda under Zia's government, and the party confidently grabbed the opportunity to support Pakistan's involvement in the anti-Soviet war. It was easier for the Jamaat to remain affiliated with Zia, who explicitly talked of the religious policy of Nizam-e-Mustafa (Order of the Prophet), and between them there was ideological conformity. Subsequently, the Jamaat devotedly cooperated in the jihad against the Soviets in solidarity with the Muslims in Afghanistan.[46] In the decade from 1980 to 1990, approximately seventy-two pro-Jamaat students lost their lives while fighting in Afghanistan, some of whom were sons of high-ranking party officials.[47]

The Islamic Revolution in Afghanistan was instigated by Gulbeddin Hekmatyar, Ahmed Shah Masoud, and their teacher at the University of Kabul, Burhanuddin Rabbani. All three actively took part in the movement to oust the monarchy of King Zahir Shah and to revive an Islamic revolution. These radical leaders were influenced by the Muslim Brotherhood of Egypt and the writings of the Jamaat's founder, Syed Abul A'la Maududi. Hekmatyar kept strong ties with the Jamaat even after he moved to Iran in the late 1980s.[48] The Jamaat was also openly involved in supporting the Afghan mujahideen and maintained close friendships with Hekmatyar's Hizb-e-Islami (Islamic Party) and Burhanuddin's Jamiat-e-Islami (Islamic Society). As the leaders of both parties in Afghanistan were strongly influenced by Mawdudi, they consequently adopted the ideological principles of the Jamaat.[49]

During the Afghan-Soviet War, many Afghan insurgents operated out of Pakistan, allowing them to establish close ties with Pakistani political elites, especially those from the Islamic parties. In this way, the Jamaat helped give birth to political Islam in Afghanistan. It is said that the founder of the Jamaat, the renowned Islamic scholar Maulana Maududi, had contributed to the strengthening of relations between Islamists in Afghanistan. During the Afghan-Soviet War, a frontline Jamaat leader, Qazi Hussain Ahmed (a Pashtun by ethnicity) was the main contact person between Zia's administration and the mujahideen both in Afghanistan and Pakistan. According to Vali Nasr, Pakistan looked to Qazi Hussain Ahmed and Gulbedin Hikmatyar "to serve as Pashtun nationalism leaders."[50] Basically, the Jamaat was running Pakistan's Afghan policy and making it "jihad oriented."[51] Through the 1980s, the Jamaat also served as a conduit for donors like Saudi Arabia to channel funds to the Afghan refugees and the mujahideen.[52]

The Jamaat had the power to approach people from all walks of life through sermons in mosques, its organized offices across the country, its members, and regular publications in local languages. The party used all the means available to it to promote the Afghan Jihad. The Soviet occupation of Afghanistan was labeled as an act of aggression by infidels as well as a war against Islam; therefore, the Jamaat called for jihad in the name of Islam to crush the rise of Communism in Afghanistan.

Prior to the Afghan Jihad, the Jamaat had criticized Zia on many counts relating to democracy; nevertheless, the party strongly supported his Afghan policy. It was in large part the activism of the Jamaat that allowed Zia to obtain the necessary public support at home in support of the jihad. The major portion of the Jamaat's contribution to the Afghan War was to give credibility to the notion of jihad among Pakistanis.[53] In return, Zia not only involved the Jamaat in the religious education of the Afghan refugees, but also in the organization of the mujahideen and the planning and execution of the jihad next door in Afghanistan. The Jamaat had strong support among the prominent mujahideen groups operating out of Peshawar, and they became involved in the Afghan Jihad as equal partners with the Pakistani army. In this way, the Zia administration converted the Jamaat from a mere domestic party to an actor at the regional level.

## US Aid to Pakistan

Because of Pakistan's diplomatic and military endeavors against the Soviet occupation of Afghanistan, Washington showered Islamabad with both military and economic assistance. Reversing the previous economic sanctions against Islamabad, President Carter now offered a total of $400 million in aid to Pakistan. This was refused by General Zia, who was apparently holding out for a better offer of compensation for the services his country was lending to the United States. It proved a wise gamble: in 1981, the Reagan administration launched a six-year aid package worth $3.2 billion for Pakistan. The aid package, which was increased to $4.02 billion in 1987, was a mix of $1.74 billion in military aid and $2.28 billion in economic aid.[54] The United States also promised to supply forty F-16 fighter planes to Pakistan.[55] As a faithful and valuable Cold War ally, Pakistan became the world's third-largest recipient of US aid after Israel and Egypt.[56]

This aid also allowed Pakistan to nourish its nuclear program, despite the fact that the Pressler Amendment of 1985 required the US president to certify to Congress on an annual basis that Islamabad was not using US aid to develop nuclear weapons. However, at the time, defeating the Soviets in Afghanistan was deemed more important than curbing Pakistan's nuclear program, so the Reagan administration disingenuously provided Congress with factitious certifications declaring the nonexistence of nuclear activity in Pakistan.[57]

For Pakistan, there was a downside to Washington's largesse. As Ayesha Siddiqa rightly put it, "US financial and military assistance to Pakistan has always come with strings attached—and it will be used to tweak the Pakistani establishment whenever the need arises."[58] For instance, a huge chunk of the aid given to Pakistan was diverted to educational reforms in the country. The culture of violence introduced through the Pakistani public and madrassa education systems was fostered in part by such assistance. Syed Nadir El-Edroos explores the history of this process and the crucial role played by the United States. He writes that at the start of the 1980s, textbooks for Pakistani schools printed at the University of Nebraska at Omaha made a pointed effort to justify the use of jihad against the Soviet nonbelievers. These books were published by the United States Agency for International Development (USAID) and distributed throughout Pakistan.[59] During this period, roughly ten thousand madrassas opened in Pakistan, many of them with extremist ideology. Since the United States needed the Pakistani people—especially the youth—to wage jihad against the Soviets, it provided substantial aid to Islamabad and encouraged the spread of religiously oriented jihadist thinking.[60]

Such aid, including the religious dimensions of it, was welcomed by the Zia administration, which continued to lobby at international forums for support in relation to the Afghan Jihad. Islamabad was successful in persuading Islamic countries at the forum of the OIC to support the Afghani mujahideen. The OIC leaders at the Third Islamic Summit Conference in Mecca in January 1981 expressed deep concerns about the Soviet invasion of Afghanistan. In addition, the OIC assured to the Muslim world its support for the withdrawal of all foreign troops from Afghanistan, calling on its secretary general and the foreign ministers of Guinea, Iran, Pakistan, and Tunisia to cooperate with the secretary general of the United Nations to resolve the situation in Afghanistan.

Throughout the 1980s, Pakistan successfully built an international consensus in the United Nations to condemn the Soviet occupation of Afghanistan. Islamabad also defeated the attempts of the pro-Soviet government in Kabul to gain sympathy within the OIC and the Non-Aligned Movement. The OIC morally supported the Afghan resistance at the First Islamic Conference of Information Ministers in Jeddah. In October 1988, the delegates of forty-three OIC member states applauded the heroic achievements of the Afghan mujahideen in the form of the Geneva Accord and pledged the OIC's assistance with alleviating the suffering of the Afghani people in the postwar era. The OIC maintained the same stance on Afghanistan at its fourth summit, in Casablanca (January 1984), and its fifth summit, which was held in Kuwait (January 1987).

It was in this context that Ronald Reagan, in 1983, labeled the Soviet Union the "evil empire." Spoken at a crucial stage in the Afghan-Soviet War, the comment found resonance in the Islamic world and helped rally Muslim opposition toward the Soviet Union. At this point, Washington was continuing its mission to convince the Muslim world about the evil motives of the Soviets. Muslims were made to believe that the "infidels" from the Soviet Union had invaded Afghanistan to remove an Islamic state and replace it with a Communist government. The mujahideen were not only financially supported and trained as holy warriors with directions from the United States and its frontline ally Pakistan, but their struggle was formally appreciated on several occasions in Washington. For example, in 1985, Reagan hosted a group of Afghan mujahideen in the White House, calling them "the moral equivalents of America's founding fathers."[61]

## Conclusion

In 1985, the new leader of the Soviet Union, Mikhail Gorbachev, realized that Moscow would need to withdraw its troops from Afghanistan. It had become evident that Soviet troops were losing the battle at the hands of the mujahideen. Later, in 1986, Babrak Karmal was replaced by Mohammad Najibullah as the head of the Soviet-backed government in Kabul, in the hope that a change in the leadership of Afghanistan would stabilize the situation enough for Soviet troops to begin their withdrawal.[62]

The year 1986 is seen as one of great achievement by the mujahideen resistance. With strong US backing (in the form of millions of dollars and weaponry) and Pakistani logistical support, they managed to cause serious damage to the Soviet war machine. The introduction of sophisticated US-supplied surface-to-air missiles, rockets, mortars, and state of the art communications equipment helped the mujahideen launch a number of successful attacks on Soviet convoys. The Soviets were optimistic to the very end about the eventual success of their military operations in Afghanistan, largely because they underestimated the US-Pakistani-Saudi-armed mujahideen in much the same way that the United States had underestimated the Soviet-Chinese-armed Vietminh and Vietcong in the jungles of South Vietnam. It is no surprise then that Afghanistan became "the Soviet Vietnam." It took the Kremlin ten years, tens of billions of dollars, and thirteen thousand deaths before it accepted defeat in 1989.[63] For Afghanistan, the toll was even greater: 1.5 million Afghans died in the war, and millions more suffered from starvation, disease, displacement, and trauma.[64] Moreover, the war ushered in a period of societal instability, which after Washington's disengagement following the end of the Cold War, culminated in remnants of the mujahideen forming the Taliban and taking over the country, instituting an Islamic fundamentalist government in the process and offering Osama bin Laden and al-Qaeda a safe haven.

The transformation of the Afghan-Soviet War into a holy war expanded its scope to involve not only many states but also tens of thousands of non-state actors from across the Muslim world who answered the call to fight a jihad against the Soviet occupation of Afghanistan. In the short run, the religious card played by Washington and Islamabad paid off well; the jihadi rhetoric lifted the spirits of the anti-Soviet forces and ensured that Moscow would become embroiled in an unwinnable quagmire. The war also provided the context for General Zia to launch his Islamization program in Pakistan, which was greatly influenced by Islamic political parties who themselves subsequently became the primary beneficiaries of such policies. The Islamization at home also provided justification for Zia to support the US-led proxy war with the Soviet Union in Afghanistan because he was strongly backed by mullah parties, his closest allies within Pakistan.

Even if the Jamaat had to compromise on its democratic values by wholeheartedly supporting Zia's military dictatorship, the party achieved what it wished for, a greater role in Pakistani policy making. Even after the Afghan-Soviet War and the era of Zia, the Jamaat remained among the government elite, because Nawaz Sharif, Pakistan's prime minister from 1990 to 1993, had formed friendly ties with the party during the Afghan-Soviet War. He was closely associated with Qazi Hussain Ahmad of the Jamaat during his time leading the country, honoring Qazi with the status of prime ministerial adviser. In addition, as the Jamaat's contact person with the Zia administration on the Afghan Jihad, Qazi was given almost a free hand to formulate the Afghan and Kashmir policies of the Sharif government. These opportunities greatly benefited the Jamaat in becoming a mainstream political actor in the country.

## Notes

1.  Mahmood Mamdani, "Good Muslim, Bad Muslim: A Political Perspective on Culture and Terrorism," *American Anthropologist, New Series* 104, no. 3 (2002): 770.
2.  Hiroki Fukamachi, "Trilateral Relations among Afghanistan, Pakistan, and the

United States," in *Crisis of Statehood? Afghanistan and Pakistan*, ed. H. Fukamachi and H. Oda (Chiba, Japan: Institute of Developing Economies, Japan External Trade Organization, 2002), 7.

3. Mamdani, "Good Muslim, Bad Muslim," 770.

4. Ibid., 768.

5. John L. Esposito, "Political Islam and the West," *JFQ Forum*, Spring 2000, 49–55.

6. Vali Nasr, "Islamic Extremism and Regional Conflict in South Asia," in *Prospects for Peace in South Asia*, ed. R. Dossani and H. S. Rowen (Hyderabad: Orient Longman Private, 2006).

7. Jere Van Dyk, *Islamic Fundamentalism in South Asia* (Carlisle, PA: Strategic Studies Institute, 2007), 3.

8. Husain Haqqani, "The Ideologies of South Asian Jihadi Groups," in *Current Trends in Islamist Ideology*, ed. H. Frandkin, H. Haqqani, and E. Brown (Washington, DC: Hudson Institute, 2005), 1:12–26.

9. Ibrahim A. Karawan, "Monarchs, Mullas, and Marshals: Islamic Regimes?," *Annals of the American Academy of Political and Social Science* 524 (November 1992): 117.

10. Mohammed Ayoob, "South-West Asia after the Taliban," in *South Asia in the World: Problem Solving Perspectives on Security, Sustainable Development, and Good Governance*, ed. R. Thakur and O. Wiggen (Tokyo: United Nations University Press, 2004), 379.

11. S. V. R. Nasr, "Islamic Opposition to the Islamic State: The Jamaat-I Islami, 1977–88," *International Journal of Middle East Studies* 25, no. 2 (1993): 263.

12. Karawan, "Monarchs," 116. The Hudood Ordinance was a law in Pakistan put into force in 1979 as part of General Zia's Islamization plan. The law was intended to implement Islamic law (Shari'a) by enforcing punishments mentioned in the Quran and the Sunnah (practices of the prophet Muhammad) for *zina* (extramarital sex), false accusation of *zina*, theft, and the drinking of alcohol.

13. Vali Nasr, *International Relations of an Islamist Movement: The Case of Jama'at-I Islami of Pakistan* (New York: Council of Foreign Relations, 2000).

14. Mohammad Waseem, "Origins and Growth Patterns of Islamic Organizations in Pakistan," in *Religious Radicalism and Security in South Asia*, ed. S. P. Limaye, R. G. Wirsing, and M. Malik (Honolulu: Asia-Pacific Center for Security Studies, 2004), 22.

15. V. Nasr, *International Relations*, 21.

16. Kalim Bahadur, "Regional Implications of the Rise of Islamic Fundamentalism in Pakistan," *Strategic Analysis* 30, no. 1 (2006): 21.

17. Ibid.

18. Ayoob, "South-West Asia."

19. Waseem, "Origins," 23; and Shibil Siddiqi, *Afghanistan-Pakistan Relations: History and Geopolitics in a Regional and International Context* (Toronto: Walter and Duncan Gordon Foundation, 2009), 23.

20. Stephen Cohen, "Pakistan and the Cold War," in *Superpower Rivalry and Conflict: The Long Shadow of the Cold War on the Twenty-First Century*, ed. C. Chari (London: Routledge, 2010); and Siddiqi, *Afghanistan-Pakistan Relations*, 19.

21. Gulbuddin Hekmatyar was the prime minister of Afghanistan from June 17, 1993, to June 28, 1994.

22. V. Nasr, *International Relations*, 32.

23. Artemy Kalinovsky, "Decision-Making and the Soviet War in Afghanistan," *Journal of Cold War Studies* 11, no. 4 (Fall 2009): 49.

24. For a discussion of Soviet motivations for invading Afghanistan, see Kalinovsky, "Decision-Making," 48–51; M. Hassan Kakar, *Afghanistan: The Soviet Invasion and the Afghan Response, 1979–1982* (Berkeley: University of California Press, 1995); and Odd Arne Westad, *The Global Cold War: Third World Interventions and the Making of Our Times* (New York: Cambridge University Press, 2007), 316–26. Both Kalinovsky and Eren Tasar (see Chapter 8 of this volume) discount the role the fear of the region's growing Islamization played in Soviet decision making.

25. Hussain H. Zaidi, "Whose War Are We Fighting on Our Soil?," *Dawn*, January 17, 2010.

26. V. Nasr, "Islamic Extremism," 25.

27. Rahimullah Yusufzai, "The Taliban Primer," *Himal Southasian* 22, no. 4 (2009): 28.

28. Mamdani, "Good Muslim, Bad Muslim," 770.

29. Ibid., 771.

30. Saira Yamin, *Peace Building in Afghanistan: Revisiting the Global War on Terrorism* (Colombo: Regional Centre for Strategic Studies, 2008), 16.

31. Bahadur, "Regional Implications," 15.

32. Eamon Murphy and Ahmad Rashid Malik, "Pakistan Jihad: The Making of Religious Terrorism," *IPRI Journal* 9, no. 2 (2009): 26.

33. C. K. Lal, "The Mid-Summer Ferment," *Himal Southasian* 22, no. 7 (2009): 23–25, and Mamdani, "Good Muslim, Bad Muslim".

34. Rasul Bakhsh Rais, "Afghanistan: A Forgotten Cold War Tragedy," *Ethnic Studies Report* 18, no. 2 (2000): 137; Siddiqi, *Afghanistan-Pakistan Relations*, 23; and Murphy and Malik, "Pakistan Jihad," 26.

35. Mamdani, "Good Muslim, Bad Muslim," 771.

36. Ibid., 770.

37. Zahid Shahab Ahmed, "Madrasa Education in the Pakistani Context: Challenges, Reforms and Future Directions," *Peace Prints: South Asian Journal of Peacebuilding* 2, no. 1 (2009): 53–65.

38. Robert G. Wirsing, "Political Islam, Pakistan, and the Geo-Politics of Religious Identity," in *Growth and Governance in Asia*, ed. Y. Sato (Honolulu: Asia-Pacific Center for Security Studies, 2004), 172.

39. Bahadur, "Regional Implications," 15.

40. The four organizations were the Jamaat-e-Islami, the Jamiat-ul-Ulama-i-Islam, the Tablighi Jamaat, and the Harkat-ul-Jihad-i-Islami.

41. Marvin G. Weinbaum, "Pakistan and Afghanistan: The Strategic Relationship," *Asian Survey* 31, no. 6 (1991): 498; and Fukamachi, "Trilateral Relations," 497.

42. Ahmad Ejaz, *United States Policy on Terrorism* (Lahore: Centre for South Asian Studies, University of the Punjab, 2007), 82.

43. Wahhabi is a strictly orthodox Sunni sect. It is predominant in the Kingdom of Saudi Arabia.

44. Kamran Arif, "The Establishment of a Taliban Emirate," *Himal Southasian* 22, no. 4 (2009): 31. Barelvis are followers of a movement of Sunni Islam. The Barelvi movement was initiated in 1880 on the Indian subcontinent to defend contemporary

traditional Islamic values and practices, including Sufism, from the criticism of Deobandi and Ahl-e-Hadith.

45. S. V. R. Nasr, "The Rise of Sunni Militancy in Pakistan: The Changing Role of Islam and the Ulama in Society and Politics," *Modern Asian Studies* 34, no. 1 (2000): 145.
46. Graham E. Fuller, *Islamic Fundamentalism in Pakistan: Its Character and Prospects* (Santa Monica, CA: Rand, 1991), 18.
47. S. V. R. Nasr, "Rise of Sunni Militancy," 33.
48. Syed Saleem Shahzad, "Mujahideen Take Up the Taliban Fight," *Asia Times*, November 16, 2001.
49. Haqqani, "Ideologies."
50. V. Nasr, "Islamic Extremism," 26.
51. S. V. R. Nasr, "Rise of Sunni Militancy," 18.
52. Bahadur, "Regional Implications."
53. S. V. R. Nasr, "Rise of Sunni Militancy," 32.
54. Weinbaum, "Pakistan and Afghanistan," 7.
55. Fukamachi, "Trilateral Relations," 7.
56. James Raymond Vreeland, "Between the Lines: Pakistan's Debt of Gratitude," *Foreign Policy* 129 (March–April, 2002): 72.
57. Cohen, "Pakistan and the Cold War," 79. For a good account of Pakistan's nuclear program and the Reagan administration's tolerance of it, see Adrian Levy and Catherine Scott-Clark, *Deception: Pakistan, the United States, and the Secret Trade in Nuclear Weapons* (New York: Walker and Company, 2007).
58. Ayesha Siddiqa, "The Politics of US Aid," *Newsline*, December 11, 2007, *www.newslinemagazine.com*.
59. Syed Nadir El-Edroos, "Do We Need Madrasas?," *News*, May 4, 2008.
60. Ahmed, "Madrasa Education," 55.
61. Quoted in Eqbal Ahmad, "Why Practise Double Standards? Genesis of International Terrorism-11," *Dawn*, October 6, 2001, *archives.dawn.com/2001/10/06/op.htm#4*.
62. Mohammad Najibullah was the last president of the Democratic Republic of Afghanistan.
63. Rais, "Afghanistan," 137.
64. Yamin, *Peace Building*, 17.

## Selected References

Ahmed, Zahid Shahab. "Madrasa Education in the Pakistani Context: Challenges, Reforms and Future Directions." *Peace Prints: South Asian Journal of Peacebuilding* 2, no. 1 (2009): 53–65.
Ayoob, Mohammed. "South-West Asia after the Taliban." In *South Asia in the World: Problem Solving Perspectives on Security, Sustainable Development, and Good Governance*, ed. R. Thakur and O. Wiggen, 373–96. Tokyo: United Nations University Press, 2004.
Bahadur, Kalim. "Regional Implications of the Rise of Islamic Fundamentalism in Pakistan." *Strategic Analysis* 30, no. 1 (2006): 7–29.

Cohen, Stephen. "Pakistan and the Cold War." In *Superpower Rivalry and Conflict: The Long Shadow of the Cold War on the Twenty-First Century*, ed. C. Chari, 74–87. London: Routledge, 2010.

Esposito, John L. "Political Islam and the West." *JFQ Forum*, Spring 2000, 49–55.

Fukamachi, Hiroki. "Trilateral Relations among Afghanistan, Pakistan, and the United States." In *Crisis of Statehood? Afghanistan and Pakistan*, ed. H. Fukamachi and H. Oda, 7–8. Chiba, Japan: Institute of Developing Economies, Japan External Trade Organization, 2002.

Fuller, Graham E. *Islamic Fundamentalism in Pakistan: Its Character and Prospects.* Santa Monica, CA: Rand, 1991.

Haqqani, Husain. "The Ideologies of South Asian Jihadi Groups." In *Current Trends in Islamist Ideology*, ed. H. Frandkin, H. Haqqani, and E. Brown, 1:12–26. Washington, DC: Hudson Institute, 2005.

Jamaat-e-Islami. "Pak Rulers on US Side against Muslims: Qazi" (in Urdu) *Jamaat-e-Islami Pakistan*, December 12, 2008, *jamaat.org/news* (accessed February 4, 2009).

Kakar, M. Hassan. *Afghanistan: The Soviet Invasion and the Afghan Response, 1979–1982.* Berkeley: University of California Press, 1995.

Kalinovsky, Artemy. "Decision-Making and the Soviet War in Afghanistan." *Journal of Cold War Studies* 11, no. 4 (Fall 2009): 46–73.

Karawan, Ibrahim A. "Monarchs, Mullas, and Marshals: Islamic Regimes?" *Annals of the American Academy of Political and Social Science* 524 (November 1992): 103–19.

Mamdani, Mahmood. "Good Muslim, Bad Muslim: A Political Perspective on Culture and Terrorism." *American Anthropologist, New Series* 104, no. 3 (2002): 766–75.

Murphy, Eamon, and Ahmad Rashid Malik. "Pakistan Jihad: The Making of Religious Terrorism." *IPRI Journal* 9, no. 2 (2009): 17–31.

Nasr, S. V. R. "Islamic Opposition to the Islamic State: The Jamaat-I Islami, 1977–88." *International Journal of Middle East Studies* 25, no. 2 (1993): 261–83.

Nasr, Vali. *International Relations of an Islamist Movement: The Case of Jama'at-I Islami of Pakistan.* New York: Council of Foreign Relations, 2000.

———. "Islamic Extremism and Regional Conflict in South Asia." In *Prospects for Peace in South Asia*, ed. R. Dossani and H. S. Rowen, 19–36. Hyderabad, India: Orient Longman Private, 2006.

Rais, Rasul Bakhsh. "Afghanistan: A Forgotten Cold War Tragedy." *Ethnic Studies Report* 18, no. 2 (2000): 137–49.

Siddiqi, Shibil. *Afghanistan-Pakistan Relations: History and Geopolitics in a Regional and International Context.* Toronto: Walter and Duncan Gordon Foundation, 2009.

Waseem, Mohammad. "Origins and Growth Patterns of Islamic Organizations in Pakistan." In *Religious Radicalism and Security in South Asia*, ed. S. P. Limaye, R. G. Wirsing, and M. Malik, 17–33. Honolulu: Asia-Pacific Center for Security Studies, 2004.

Weinbaum, Marvin G. "Pakistan and Afghanistan: The Strategic Relationship." *Asian Survey* 31, no. 6 (1991): 496–511.

Westad, Odd Arne. *The Global Cold War: Third World Interventions and the Making of Our Times.* New York: Cambridge University Press, 2007.

Wirsing, Robert G. "Political Islam, Pakistan, and the Geo-Politics of Religious Identity." In *Growth and Governance in Asia*, ed. Y. Sato, 165–78. Honolulu: Asia-Pacific Center for Security Studies, 2004.

Yamin, Saira. *Peace Building in Afghanistan: Revisiting the Global War on Terrorism.* Colombo: Regional Centre for Strategic Studies, 2008.

# Contributors

**Zahid Shahab Ahmed** is a PhD candidate at the University of New England in Australia. His major publications include (with R. Balasubramanian) *Extremism in Pakistan and India: The Case of the Jamaat-e-Islami and Shiv Sena* (Regional Centre for Strategic Studies [RCSS], 2010) and (with M. A. Baxter) *Attitudes of Teachers in India and Pakistan: Texts and Contexts* (Women in Security, Conflict Management and Peace [WISCOMP], 2007).

**David Ayers** is professor of modernism and critical theory at the University of Kent, England. He is the author of *Wyndham Lewis and Western Man* (Palgrave Macmillan, 1992), *English Literature of the 1920s* (Edinburgh University Press, 1999), *Modernism* (Wiley-Blackwell, 2004), *Literary Theory: A Reintroduction* (Wiley-Blackwell, 2008), and *Modernism, Internationalism, and the Russian Revolution* (forthcoming).

**Aydın Babuna** is professor of diplomatic history at Boğaziçi University in Istanbul. He specializes in Balkan history and politics. His publications include *Die Nationale Entwicklung der bosnischen Muslime: Mit besonderer Berücksichtigung der österreichisch-ungarischen Periode* [The national development of the Bosnian Muslims: With special reference to the Austro-Hungarian period] (Peter Lang, 1996).

**Jessica M. Chapman** is assistant professor of history at Williams College. Her publications include "The Sect Crisis of 1955 and the American Commitment to Ngô Đình Diệm," *Journal of Vietnamese Studies* (February 2010), and "Staging Democracy: South Vietnam's 1955 Referendum to Depose Bao Dai," *Diplomatic History* (September 2006).

**Kai Yin Allison Haga** is adjunct professor at National Sun Yat-sen University. She contributed nine encyclopedia articles to *The Encyclopedia of the Korean*

*War: A Political, Social, and Military History*, 2nd ed., ed. Spence C. Tucker (ABC-CLIO, 2010).

**Jonathan P. Herzog** is the author of *The Spiritual-Industrial Complex: America's Religious Battle against Communism in the Early Cold War* (Oxford University Press, 2011).

**Wudu Tafete Kassu** is assistant professor of history at Addis Ababa University, Ethiopia. He has published several articles on Ethiopian history, specifically on the relationships between religion, state, and nationalism.

**Iain S. Maclean** is professor of Western religious thought at James Madison University. His research and publications are in the fields of religion and politics. He has coedited the *Encyclopedia of Religion and American Politics* (Greenwood, 1999) as well as the *Encyclopedia of Religion and War* (2003). He has written *Opting for Democracy: Liberation Theology and the Struggle for Democracy in Brazil* (Peter Lang, 1999) and edited *Reconciliation: Nations and Churches in Latin America* (Ashgate, 2006). His work includes comparative studies between Europe, North and South America, and sub-Saharan Africa.

**Argyris Mamarelis** is a research fellow at the Hellenic Observatory of the London School of Economics and Political Science. His research interests include modern Greek history, World War II history, and Balkan history and politics. His most recent publication is *The Last Ottomans: The Muslim Minority of Greece, 1940–1949* (with Kevin Featherstone, Dimitris Papadimitriou, and Georgios Niarchos; Palgrave Macmillan, 2011).

**Philip E. Muehlenbeck** is professorial lecturer at George Washington University. His publications include *Betting on the Africans: John F. Kennedy's Courting of African Nationalist Leaders* (Oxford University Press, 2012) and, as editor, *Race, Ethnicity, and the Cold War: A Global Perspective* (Vanderbilt University Press, 2012).

**Leszek Murat** is a graduate of the State University of New York in Albany (PhD in history) and of the Adam Mickiewicz University in Poznan, Poland (JD). His publications include books on traffic lawmaking in Poland and on legislative intent in New York State law.

**Andrew Preston** is senior lecturer in American history and a fellow of Clare College at Cambridge University. He is the author of *The War Council: McGeorge Bundy, the NSC, and Vietnam* (Harvard University Press, 2006) and coeditor, with Fredrik Logevall, of *Nixon in the World: American Foreign Relations, 1969–1977* (Oxford University Press, 2008). He has also written extensively on religion and US foreign policy.

**Ahmed Khalid al-Rawi** is a postdoctoral researcher at Sohar University. His books include *Media Practice in Iraq* (Palgrave Macmillan, forthcoming) and *Omani Women's Folktales* (Cambria Press, forthcoming). His papers have been published in journals such as *Arab Studies Quarterly, International Journal of Contemporary Iraqi Studies, Journal of Colonialism and Colonial History,* and *Journal of Arab and Muslim Media Research.*

**Eren Murat Tasar** is lecturer in central Asian history in the History Department at Harvard University.

**JonDavid K. Wyneken** is associate professor of history at Grove City College in Pennsylvania. His publications include "Memory as Diplomatic Leverage: Evangelical Bishop Theophil Wurm and War Crimes Trials, 1948–1952" (*Kirchliche Zeitgeschichte* 19, no. 2 [2006]).

# Index

www.ingramcontent.com/pod-product-compliance
Lightning Source LLC
Chambersburg PA
CBHW080412270326
41929CB00018B/2996